SF ACCESS

W9-AUX-015

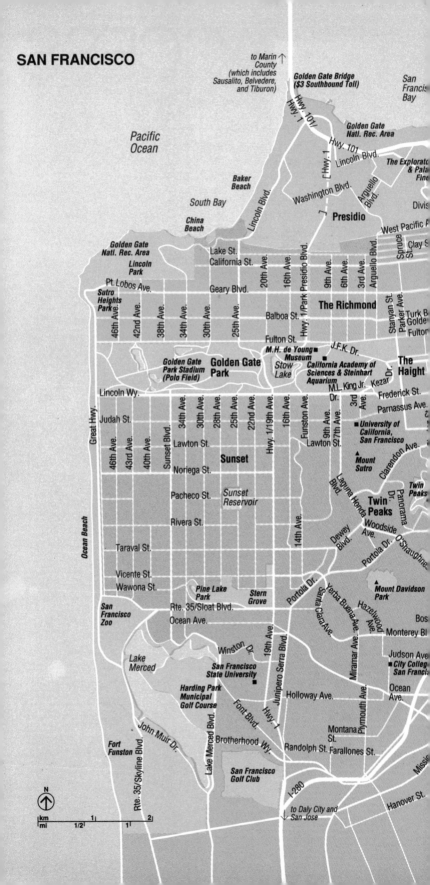

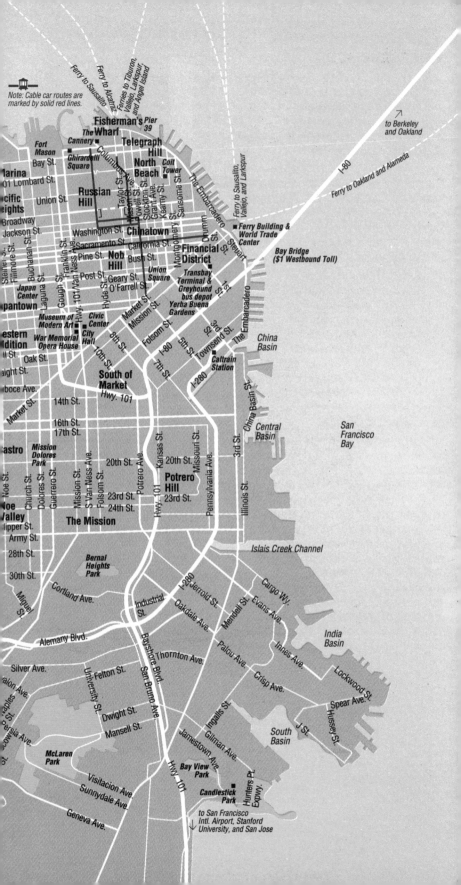

Orientation

The City by the Bay's stature as one of the US's most attractive, welcoming destinations is well deserved. Honeymooners continue to be lured by San Francisco's romantic charm, seasoned travelers like the civilized pace and dramatic views, families appreciate the many attractions for children, and executive types *love* to have their conventions here year after year. And in 1993, even the sophisticated readers of *Condé Nast Traveler* magazine picked San Francisco as their number one city in the world, adding to an international reputation that belies its modest size.

San Francisco covers only 47 square miles; it is situated on a peninsula, with the **Pacific Ocean** to the west, the **Golden Gate Strait** to the north, and the **San Francisco Bay** stretching north to east. Its 724,959 inhabitants make it the second-largest city in the nine-county **Bay Area,** aced out by the more than one million residents of sprawling **San Jose,** 50 miles to the south. All in all, the Bay Area is home to more than 6.2 million people and is the fourth-largest metropolitan center in the nation.

Originally inhabited by the Ohlone Indians and reputedly visited by British admiral Sir Francis Drake in 1579, the region saw five flags fly overhead—representing England, Spain, Mexico, the Republic of California, and the United States—from 1579 through 1850. This part of the West Coast has been the subject of world curiosity ever since gold was discovered at Sutter's Mill in 1848. San Francisco became known as a place to get rich quick—and a place to spend it all, as the miners and other high rollers flooded to the pleasure palaces of the Barbary Coast. When the city was largely demolished by the 1906 earthquake and fire, attention was again riveted on the region. But San Francisco was quickly rebuilt, sowing the seeds of the indomitable image that persists today.

Since then, San Francisco has cultivated its original freewheeling reputation and made news on different fronts, from the kitchens of its famous restaurants to the violent scenes of labor unrest on the docks and the assassination of the mayor and a member of the board of supervisors in the 1970s. The city has been in the forefront of social movements since the arrival of the flower children and the "summer of love" in the late 1960s; and today the large gay and lesbian community presses for change as it continues to lobby hard for homosexual rights. San Francisco ranks in the front lines of culture, with a world-class opera house, symphony, and ballet company, as well as one of the best Asian art museums in the country. Europeans love San Francisco because, in many respects, it is the most European of American cities. Hispanics gravitate to the Spanish-speaking community that exists here, and Asians also feel at home since the city

RIK OLSON

Golden Gate Bridge

as one of the largest Chinese populations in the country, a substantial panese community, and increasing numbers of Vietnamese, Cambodian, aotian, and Filipino immigrants. Even New Yorkers are comfortable in San ancisco, frequently comparing it the Big Apple. Locals have been accused of :ing smug about their city, and the charge is probably valid. San Franciscans how and love the Bay Area, and enjoy sharing its attractions. And, as the isitor soon discovers, the city they take such pride in is no three-day town, ut one that unfolds its many treasures over the course of time.

How To Read This Guide

AN FRANCISCO ACCESS® is arranged by eighborhood so you can see at a glance where ou are and what is around you. The numbers next o the entries in the following chapters correspond o the numbers on the maps. The type is color-oded according to the kind of place described:

Restaurants/Clubs: Red   Hotels: Blue

Shops/ Outdoors: Green **Sights/Culture:** Black

lating the Restaurants and Hotels

he restaurant ratings take into account the quality, ervice, atmosphere, and uniqueness of the estaurant. An expensive restaurant doesn't ecessarily ensure an enjoyable evening; however, small, relatively unknown spot could have good ood, professional service, and a lovely tmosphere. Therefore, on a purely subjective asis, stars are used to judge the overall dining alue (see the star ratings at right). Keep in mind hat chefs and owners often change, which ometimes drastically affects the quality of a estaurant. The ratings in this guidebook are based n information available at press time.

he price ratings, as categorized at right, apply to estaurants and hotels. These figures describe eneral price-range relationships among other res-aurants and hotels in the area. The restaurant price atings are based on the average cost of an entrée or one person, excluding tax and tip. Hotel price atings reflect the base price of a standard room for wo people for one night during the peak season.

Restaurants

★	Good	
★★	Very Good	
★★★	Excellent	
★★★★	An Extraordinary Experience	
$	The Price Is Right	(less than $10)
$$	Reasonable	($10-$15)
$$$	Expensive	($15-$25)
$$$$	Big Bucks	($25 and up)

Hotels

$	The Price Is Right	(less than $80)
$$	Reasonable	($80-$120)
$$$	Expensive	($120-$180)
$$$$	Big Bucks	($180 and up)

Map Key

1 Entry Number   Freeway
City/Town ●   Tunnel
    Highway
Point of Interest ■   Tertiary Road
    Cable Car Route   ▲ Mountain

rea code 415 unless otherwise noted.

ietting to San Francisco
iirports

an Francisco International Airport (SFO)

FO is 14 miles south of San Francisco on the ninsula, and is reached from well-marked exits off ghway 101 (also called the Bayshore Freeway). You in also get to the airport from Interstate 280, exiting Highway 380, which then connects with Highway 1 and the exit to the airport. For long-term airport rking, take Highway 101, exiting at San Bruno enue East. There is free shuttle-bus service from e parking lots to and from all the airlines, 24 hours day.

rport Police 876.2424

ir Rental
Avis 877.6777
Budget..877.4415
Dollar 244.4130

Hertz	877.1600
National	877.4745
Customs	876.2816
Immigration	876.2876
Information and Paging	761.0800
Lost and Found (M-F only)	876.2261
Medical Clinic (24 hrs)	877.0444
Parking	877.0227
Traveler's Aid	877.0118

Transportation between terminals is provided by airport shuttles located on the upper level. There is service every five to seven minutes from 6AM to midnight, and every 10 to 15 minutes, midnight to 6AM.

The San Francisco airport is the fifth-busiest in the nation and the seventh-busiest in the world.

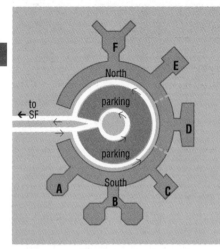

San Francisco International Airport

Gate Locations for Major Airlines

A Air Canada
Southwest Airlines
USAir
B Alaska Airlines
Continental Airlines
TWA
C America West
Delta Air Lines
Northwest Airlines

D International Flights
E American Airlines
American Eagle
Canadian Air
Midwest Express
F American Trans Air
United Airlines
United Express

Car-rental agencies and baggage-claim areas are located on the lower level.

Transportation to and from San Francisco International Airport
SamTrans buses take you north to the bus terminal at First and Mission Streets. Buses leave from the airport's upper level every 30 minutes between 6AM and 12:30AM. The *7B* bus, which travels along Mission Street and stops at First, Third, Fifth, Seventh, and Ninth Streets, allows you to carry luggage. The *7F* bus restricts luggage to what will fit on your lap. It follows the same route, stopping at every block on Mission Street. **SamTrans** also operates bus *3B* between the airport and the **Daly City BART** station. For information, call 508.6200 or 800/660.4287 elsewhere in California.

Door-to-door shuttle services in small vans are generally reasonably priced. Shuttle operators include the **Bay Area Super Shuttle** (558.8500) and the **Yellow Airport Shuttle** (282.7433). Catch them on the upper level.

Lorrie's Airport Service offers door-to-door service from the upper level of **SFO** and has group rates. For more information, call 334.9000.

The **SFO Airporter** offers service to all major hotels on **Union Square,** with departures every 20 minutes from the lower level. For information, call 673.2433.

Taxis are located on the lower level of the terminal.

Oakland International Airport (OAK)
Located five miles south of downtown **Oakland** on Highway 17 (the Nimitz Freeway), off the Hegenberger Drive exit, this airport is smaller than **SFO,** making it less confusing to navigate. Plus, parking is easier here—and less expensive.

Airport Police......................510/569.0740

Car Rental
Avis......................510/577.6370
Budget......................510/568.4770
Dollar......................510/638.2750
Hertz......................510/568.6777
National......................510/632.2225

Information......................510/577.401
Lost and Found (M-F only)......................510/577.409
Paging and Information......................510/577.400
Parking......................510/633.257

Transportation to and from Oakland International Airport
Air-BART is a shuttle bus that carries passengers from the airport to the **Coliseum/Oakland BART** station, where you can catch a train to San Francisco or other regions of the Bay Area. It stops every 15 minutes in front of Terminals 1 and 2. For schedule information, call 510/832.1464 or 800/545.2700.

AC Transit *Bus 58* runs approximately every 15 minutes and also stops at the **Coliseum/Oakland BART** station. At the airport, the bus picks up passengers at Terminals 1 and 2 and at Airport Drive and Armstrong Street. For information, call 510/839.2882.

Other transportation companies serving San Francisco from **Oakland International Airport** include **Paramount Limousine** (510/569.5466) and the **Bayporter Express** (467.1800).

Some of the major taxi companies are **Associated Cab** (510/893.4991), **Goodwill Cab** (510/836.1234) and **Yellow Cab** (510/444.1234).

San Jose International Airport (SJC)
This airport is located about two miles from downtown San Jose and approximately 50 miles south of San Francisco via Highway 101. Although farther from the city than either **SFO** or **OAK,** it often offers less expensive flights to some destinations.

Airport Administration......................408/277.536

Car Rental
Alamo......................408/453.818
Avis......................408/993.222
Budget......................408/286.785
Dollar......................408/280.220
Hertz......................408/437.572

formation 408/287.9849, 408/277.4500

ost and Found (M-F only) 408/277.5419

aging..408/277.4759

arking 408/293.6788

ransportation to and from San Jose nternational Airport

everal shuttle companies provide transportation to owntown San Jose and San Francisco, including **outh and East Bay Airport Shuttle** (800/548.4664) nd **VIP Shuttle** (800/235.8847).

IV Transportation provides light-rail and van ervice to downtown San Jose. For more formation, call 408/248.4810.

axi companies include **San Jose Taxi** 408/437.8700) and **Yellow Cab** (408/293.1234).

Destination	Miles from SF	Drive Time
Berkeley	12	25-30 mins
Los Angeles	390	7-8 hrs
Napa/Sonoma	44	1-1½ hrs
Oakland	10	20-30 mins
Palo Alto	33	45-60 mins
Sacramento	88	1½-2 hrs
San Jose	50	1¼ hrs
SF International Airport	14	25-45 mins
Sausalito	8	20-30 mins
Yosemite	200	4 hrs

Getting around San Francisco

Bay Area Rapid Transit (BART) is a clean, reliable, easy-to-use underground transportation system serving parts of San Francisco, **Daly City,** and the **East Bay.** The system operates Monday through Friday from 4AM to 1:30AM, Saturday from 6AM to 1:30AM, and Sunday from 8AM to 1:30AM. On weekdays, trains run on all four routes approximately every 15 minutes, and extra service is offered during rush hours. After 7PM on Sunday, trains run on only two routes every 20 minutes, and you may have to transfer to another train to get to your final destination. On Saturday, they run on four routes every 20 minutes until 6PM; after 6PM they run on two routes every 20 minutes. Brochures about using the system and train schedules are available at all **BART** stations. All stations have facilities for people with disabilities.

To buy a ticket, check the prominently displayed information chart to determine your destination and the ticket value required for a one-way trip. Ticket machines sell tickets for any amount between 80¢ and $40. One ticket, therefore, can be good for many rides.

Save the ticket to exit the station.

Discount tickets are available for senior citizens (age 65 and older), people with disabilities, and children ages 5 to 12. You can also buy discounted high-value tickets. All discounted tickets are sold *only* at participating institutions (for information about where, call 464.7133), and *not* at **BART** stations. An excursion-ride ticket allows you to tour the entire system, visiting any of the 34 stations for up to three hours as long as you enter and exit at the same station. If you get out anywhere en route, the fare gate will compute the normal fare (obviously, this is a good deal for hard-core train buffs only).

Cyclists *with permits* are allowed to take their bikes on trains during non-commute hours only (weekdays from 4AM to 6:30AM and 6:30PM to 1:30AM and all day on weekends and holidays). For permit and locker-rental information, call 464.7133.

For information about **BART** and connecting bus service, call 788.2278.

Driving in San Francisco's **Downtown** and **Financial** districts is suitable only for extremely patient people who can handle the frustration of slow-moving traffic. **North Beach, Chinatown,** and **Telegraph Hill** are also congested areas, and parking is very difficult. Many parking meters are maddeningly timed to provide only a half hour of parking, and traffic cops patrol frequently. Unless otherwise posted, meters operate Monday through Saturday, generally from 7AM to 6PM (but check to be absolutely sure).

Some curbs are painted various colors, all of which have specific meanings, and those who violate the color code will incur costly fines. A **white curb** indicates a drop-off zone for passengers. This code is in effect only when the facility it fronts (a restaurant, theater, or other enterprise) is in operation. If nothing is going on, it's OK to park. A **green curb** signifies parking for 10 minutes only—just long enough to pop into a shop to quickly pick something up. **Yellow curbs** are for loading and unloading commercial vehicles, and **blue curbs** are reserved for drivers or passengers with disabilities who have an official placard prominently displayed in their car window. Unless information is otherwise posted, it's generally legal to park in green or yellow zones after 6PM.

There are some relatively inexpensive parking garages, particularly for short-term parking, owned by the city, but parking in congested areas tends to be costly. Prices per hour escalate sharply, usually after a few hours.

Here are some low-cost parking facilities, all open 24 hours daily, unless otherwise indicated:

Downtown:

Union Square Garage 333 Post St (enter on Geary Street between Stockton and Powell Streets), 397.0631

Sutter-Stockton Garage 444 Stockton St (between Sutter and Bush Sts), 982.8370

Ellis-O'Farrell Garage 123 O'Farrell St (between Powell and Stockton Sts), 986.4800

Fifth & Mission Garage 833 Mission St (between Fourth and Fifth Sts), 982.8522

North Beach/Chinatown:

Vallejo Street Garage 766 Vallejo St (between Stockton and Powell Sts), 761.0270

Portsmouth Square Garage 733 Kearny St (between Clay and Washington Sts), 982.6353

Municipal Railway (MUNI) was first called the "Muniserable Railway" by *San Francisco Chronicle* columnist Herb Caen, and he definitely had a point. Drivers working for this citywide transportation system can be gloriously courteous or sadistically unpleasant. The nicest drivers seem to find their way onto the cable-car lines, where they often delight in entertaining the tourists. The **MUNI** system consists of all cable cars, trains (**MUNI Metro**), conventional buses, and electric buses that run within the San Francisco city limits; all operate daily until 1AM. (**BART,** the regional system, connects San Francisco proper to the East Bay and south of the city; you can, however, transfer between the two systems at a few points.) From 1AM to 5AM, nine **Owl** lines operate throughout the city. The fare on all conveyances except cable cars is $1 for adults and 35¢ for senior citizens (age 65 and older), disabled passengers with a valid Regional Transit Connection Discount Card, and youths ages 5 to 17 (children under 5 ride free). On cable cars the fare is $2 (kids under 5 are free). One-dollar bills are accepted on most buses; however, drivers do not give change. Be sure to request a transfer as soon as you board the bus; it's free and is valid for one and a half to two hours and a maximum of two rides in any direction. One-day, three-day, weekly, and monthly "passes" offer unlimited rides on buses only, while one-day, three-day, and weekly "passports" provide unlimited rides on the buses *and* cable cars. Both passes and passports are sold at the **City Hall** information booth in the **Civic Center;** at **MUNI** headquarters (949 Presidio Ave, at Geary Blvd); and at other locations around the city. You may also buy discounted passes for children, seniors, and people with disabilities, and tokens are sold in rolls of 10, 20, or 40 (tokens are good on all of the buses, but you must pay a surcharge when you use a token on the cable cars).

Maps of the **MUNI** system can be purchased at bookstores and magazine stands (a partial **MUNI** map is featured on the inside back cover of this book). Routes are also prominently displayed on bus-stop kiosks, and the "Public Transportation" section of the telephone directory's yellow pages features a **MUNI** map. For information on schedules, passes, and fares, call 673.MUNI (and expect to be put on hold for a very long time) or write to **MUNI Community Affairs** (949 Presidio Ave, Room 238, San Francisco, CA 94115).

Taxis in San Francisco tend to be expensive and are often scarce. In the downtown area, it's sometimes possible to hail a moving cab, but in general it's best to call and make arrangements for a pickup. It's also relatively easy to get a cab at any of the major hotels; however, plan on waiting a long time for one during the rush hours and when the weather is foul. Taxi companies include **Yellow Cab** (626.2345), **Luxor** (282.4141), **City Cab** (468.7200), **DeSoto Cab** (673.1414), and **Veteran's Cab** (552.1300).

FYI

Drinking The legal drinking age is 21. Bars stay open until 2AM. Wine and liquor are widely available and can be purchased in most grocery stores and supermarkets.

Money Deak International, Foreign Exchange, Associated Foreign Exchange, and many major banks handle currency exchanges. Traveler's checks are available at banks and at **American Express** and **Thomas Cook Travel** offices. Banks are open Monday through Friday, generally until 3PM, and often on Saturday morning as well (usually until 1PM).

Personal Safety Drugs and crime are unfortunate components of urban living, and San Francisco is no exception. Common sense makes the most sense. In general, neighborhoods that could be troublesome look it (of course, there are exclusions). In **Golden Gate Park,** stay on well-populated paths and avoid walking there after dark. Surrounding the downtown side of the **Civic Center** is a high-crime neighborhood called the **Tenderloin** that's often a way station for undesirable types. Toward the west side, the neighborhood is gradually improving, but caution is still advised. Once you're past the busy downtown area (from about Fifth Street and going west to Gough Street), **Market Street,** San Francisco's main thoroughfare, is distressingly seedy. At night there's a virtual parade of vagrants.

The **South of Market** area is in a state of transition; although there are many upscale shops, restaurants, and businesses, at night it helps to be cautious. The **Mission** district is another part of town that calls for extra caution, particularly after dark. And the **Haight-Ashbury** neighborhood, still filled with its share of panhandlers and lost youth, can be somewhat intimidating.

Publications The city's morning newspaper is the *San Francisco Chronicle,* and while its news coverage has been criticized for being shallow, its columnists are among the best. The afternoon paper, the *San Francisco Examiner,* tends to offer more in-depth investigative reports than its competitor, but lags behind in circulation. *San Francisco Focus,* a monthly magazine published by public television station **KQED,** covers everything from politics and personalities to fashion and food. *S.F. Weekly* and the *Bay Guardian* are both liberal, free, alternative newspapers that provide good listings of entertainment events. *BAM* (Bay Area Music), a free tabloid published twice a month, covers the local music scene. The *San Francisco Independent* is a community newspaper published three days a week (Tuesday, Friday, and Sunday), and the *Nob Hill Gazette* is a monthly that covers the society scene. These free publications can generally be found on the street, in vending machines next to those that dispense the *Chronicle* and *Examiner,* and in shops, cafes, and coffee shops around town (the *Nob Hill Gazette* is available only in that neighborhood). The weekly *Sun Reporter* serves the black community, *Hokubei Mainichi* is the Japanese-English publication that comes out every day, and the daily *Chinese Times* is the largest of several Chinese newspapers. The *Jewish Bulletin* is published every Friday. Gay and lesbian newspapers include the weekly *Bay Area Reporter,* the *San Francisco Sentinel,* and *Bay Times.* The weekly *San Francisco Business Times* is the region's largest business-oriented publication. All are available on newsstands.

Smoking San Francisco has stiff antismoking regulations. It's illegal to light up in offices, public buildings, banks, lobbies, stores, sports arenas, stadiums, and theaters, in all of the city's restaurants that don't have bars, and on public transportation.

Street Plan With the exception of certain residential neighborhoods, most of San Francisco is laid out on a grid plan, with Market Street dividing the north and south segments of the city. Each block increases its numbering by 100, so buildings on the first block of a street might start with number 1, the second block with 100, and the third with 200. Newcomers may be confused by the numerical streets and avenues, which are in two different neighborhoods. When San Franciscans speak of "the avenues," they are referring to the numerically named avenues (Second Avenue, Third Avenue, etc.) that extend through the **Richmond** and **Sunset** districts. But other numerical streets, First Street to 30th Street, span the South of Market area.

Most pronunciations are straightforward, though some retain the Spanish accent. Vallejo Street, for example, is pronounced Va-*lay*-ho. Gough Street usually perplexes newcomers; it's pronounced *Goff.* Lyon Street, however, does not follow the French pronunciation of the town by the same name; it's simply pronounced *Lion.*

Telephones Calls from pay phones to the 415 area code cost 20¢.

Tipping A 15 percent tip is standard for taxi fares and restaurants (although a 20 percent tip for a waiter or waitress providing good service is becoming more common). Hotel porters and station porters expect $1 per bag. Concierges expect tips based on the quality of their service and the generosity of the guest. If you've used the concierge's advice a lot and he or she has recommended places that made your stay more pleasurable, tip at least $5.

Tours Brochures for most tour companies can be found at the **Visitor's Information Center** (Hallidie Plaza, near the cable-car turntable at the foot of Powell St at Market St; 391.2000). It's open Monday through Friday from 9AM to 5:30PM, Saturday from 9AM to 3PM, and Sunday from 10AM to 2PM. One of the largest operators of sight-seeing tours, the **Gray Line,** runs from two locations: at Union Square, opposite the **St. Francis Hotel** (Powell St, between Geary and Post Sts); and from the bus terminal (First and Mission Sts). Call 558.9400 to make reservations.

Phone Book

Emergencies

Ambulance/Fire/Police 911

AAA Emergency Road Service 800/400.4222

Child Crisis Service (Calif. Pacific Medical Center) 387.8700

Children's Emergency Services (to report child abuse)..665-0757

Handicapped Crisis Line .....800/426.4263 (CA only)

Poison Control Center.. ....800/523.2222 (northwest CA only)

Suicide Prevention 221.1423

Women Against Rape Crisis Line 647.7273

Youth Crisis Hotline...........................800/448.4663

Visitor Information

AC Transit Bus Lines (East Bay area) ..510/839.2882

Amtrak 800/872.7245

BART 788.2278

Better Business Bureau 243.9999

Caltrain Peninsula Commuter Rail Service............ ....495.4546, 800/660.4287 (Bay Area only)

Chamber of Commerce Visitor Information Center 392.4511

Dental Society Referral Service 421.1435

Gay Medical and Dental Referral Service 565.4400

Greyhound/Trailways Bus Lines........800/231.2222

MUNI Bus Lines (San Francisco)................673.6864

Passport Information 744.4444

SamTrans Bus Lines (South Bay area) 800/660.4287

Time............POP.CORN (or 767 and any four digits)

Traveler's Aid 255.2252

24-hour events recordings:

   In English 391.2001

   In French 391.2003

   In German 391.2004

   In Japanese 391.2101

   In Spanish 391.2122

Visitor's Information Center 391.2000

Weather 936.1212

Youth Hostels ....771.7277 (San Francisco) ....331.2777 (Marin County)

About half of San Francisco's workers live in the city; the other half commute.

Civic Center

San Francisco's **Civic Center** is acclaimed by critics everywhere as the complex with the finest collection of Beaux Arts buildings in America. **Daniel Burnham**, the architect commissioned to design the city's master plan, combined a highly developed aesthetic sense with the know-how of a skilled politician. He was invited to the city for consultation by millionaire and former mayor James Phelan, who, along with other prominent citizens, had become concerned about the ugliness of the building construction that was blighting the city. **Burnham** came with his young assistant, **Willis Polk** (himself a westerner), and was immensely impressed with the potential of the natural setting. In 1904 he set up a cottage office on Twin Peaks so he could look down on the terrain as he worked out his vision of the city's future. He was generations ahead of his time in suggesting such ideas as one-way streets, downtown subways, and residential areas where backyards would be merged

into a common park. **Polk** wished to preserve the crest of the hills with access roads that curved to follow the contours of the land rather than conventional gridiron patterns. He designed a huge park for Twin Peaks with landscaped slopes and a special watercourse that would carry the city's water supply from reservoirs. But before any real action could be taken, much of San Francisco, including the old City Hall, collapsed in the 1906 earthquake and fire, literally burying **Burnham**'s plans. However, he was not ready to give up. With his enthusiastic supporters (John McLaren, first superintendent of Golden Gate Park; Phelan; sugar czar Claus Spreckels, and others), he set a campaign in motion to rebuild the city. Political scandal delayed their plans, but **Burnham** finally salvaged part of his project and convinced the supervisors to finance the monumental **Civic Center**. Alas, it was not until after his death that his recommendations were acted upon.

The man largely responsible for actually getting **City Hall** built was "Sunny" Jim Rolph. He was the mayor for two decades, and he considered the hall his proudest achievement. (Other projects launched by Rolph were the **San Francisco Public Library**, **Civic Auditorium**, **Hetch Hetchy Aqueduct**, the yacht harbor, and the campaign to build the Bay Bridge.) **City Hall**'s architect was **Arthur Brown Jr.**, a designer who had what colleague **Bernard Maybeck** admiringly called "perfect taste." **Brown** attended the Ecole des Beaux Arts in Paris along with his fraternity brother **John Bakewell Jr.** At school **Brown** garnered more prizes than had ever been received by an American. Upon their return, the two young men set up the architectural firm of **Bakewell** and **Brown**. They soon won a contest for designing the City Hall in Berkeley, and though they felt they had no chance of winning, they competed for the greater prize: the key building in San Francisco's **Civic Center** master plan, **City Hall**. Ignoring sensible restrictions, they produced a plan for a spectacular structure that even by today's standards was exorbitant in design and expense. The new team won out over established stars in the field, and their victory catapulted **Brown** to the front ranks of American architects. By 1936, when the **War Memorial Opera House** and **Veteran's Building** were in place, a unified square of stately and ornate Beaux Arts architecture had been built. And it was in this opera house that the charter creating the United Nations was signed 9 years later.

One of the more recent additions to the complex—which breaks completely with this design tradition—is the modern **Louise M. Davies Symphony Hall**, inaugurated in 1981 and renovated in 1992. Surrounding the **Civic Center** is a diverse area that includes many fine restaurants, galleries, and antiques shops. It also contains a portion of the **Tenderloin**, a rough crime- and poverty-ridden area that's approximately to the east and north of the library. Lately, the Tenderloin is showing signs of renewal as Asian immigrants, many from Vietnam and Cambodia, have settled in and opened small businesses, giving the neighborhood a stability and respectability it hasn't enjoyed for years.

Area code 415 unless otherwise noted.

1 Cathedral Hill Hotel $$$ This 400-room hotel is still known to many as the **Jack Tar Hotel**, a building reviled for its architectural tastelessness and vulgar multicolored facade. The name change was accompanied by removal of most of the tacky colored panels. There is indoor parking for guests (for a fee) and a small outdoor swimming pool on a terrace. The restaurant serves breakfast, lunch, and dinner daily. ♦ 1101 Van Ness Ave (at Geary St). 776.8200, 800/622.0855 in CA, 800/227.4730; fax 441.2841

2 Richelieu $$ A 1900s ambience pervades this 150-room hotel, where children under 12 stay free when sharing a room with a parent. The coffee bar serves continental breakfast and is open daily. ♦ 1050 Van Ness Ave (at Geary St). 673.4711, 800/227.3608; fax 673.9362

3 Lombard Hotel $$ Modern conveniences are combined with 1920s charm in this attractive hotel, which is close to Fisherman's Wharf and other activities, but located on the fringes of a questionable neighborhood. The 101 rooms have the feel of a European hostelry—there are canopied beds, shuttered windows, an open courtyard, and a rooftop deck. The lower lobby has facilities for meetings. Complimentary services include tea and sherry in the lobby, a Thursday wine reception, pay-per-view cable, and limo service from the hotel to downtown and Union Square. There is a breakfast room. ♦ 1015 Geary St (between Van Ness Ave and Polk St). 673.5232, 800/777.3210; fax 885.2802

4 Great American Music Hall Top talent appears at this premier music club, which showcases rock, pop, jazz, and comedy. It's a large place with a balcony, but the sights and sounds are excellent from almost any table. A dinner menu offering "hip bar food" such as french fries, California-style quesadillas, spareribs, pizza, and salads is available, as are drinks. ♦ Cover. Box office: M-Sa (Su if there is a show). 859 O'Farrell St (between Polk and Larkin Sts). 885.0750

5 Mitchell Brothers O'Farrell Theatre This infamous sex palace was rendered even more infamous a few years back by the slaying of one Mitchell brother by the other. As the sign warns, "Admission is limited to adults who will not be offended should they observe any type of sexual activity." The innocent mural outside belies the steamy action within. ♦ Cover. Daily. 895 O'Farrell St (at Polk St). 441.1930

6 Acorn Books Used books are bought, sold, and exchanged here. The roughly 30,000 volumes range from rare first editions to paperback mystery thrillers. ♦ Daily. 740 Polk St (at Ellis St). 563.1736

7 The Phoenix $ This 44-room urban inn is a one-acre oasis of respectability in a downscale neighborhood. It has a resortlike feel, with a pool, outdoor cafe, garden, and massage and other bodywork services on site. Popular with the artistic and celebrity sets, the hotel has hosted such exalted personages as Linda Ronstadt, Faye Dunaway, Ziggy Marley, and JFK Jr. The bedrooms and grounds feature original art from Bay Area artists, and the hotel has its own video channel featuring movies made in San Francisco. On-site parking and continental breakfast are

included. ♦ 601 Eddy St (at Larkin St). 776.1380, 800/CITY.INN; fax 885.3109

Within the Phoenix:

Miss Pearl's Jam House ★★$$ Enormously and deservedly popular with the young set, this noisy, lively, invariably crowded restaurant specializes in tongue-tingling Caribbean cuisine served in an art-filled dining room with walls cleverly painted to look aged. Jerk chicken or pork (both marinated and highly seasoned), fiery Rasta pasta, and deep-fried coo coo with salsa criolla (a cornmeal concoction) are among the many intriguing choices (though the quality of some dishes may vary from day to day). Most portions are large and easy to share; many of the appetizers will do in lieu of an entrée. Live reggae music is featured Thursday through Saturday night starting at 9:30PM, and a DJ cranks out the tunes on Wednesday night. ♦ Caribbean ♦ Tu-F lunch and dinner; Sa dinner; Su brunch and dinner. 775.JAMS

8 California Culinary Academy ★★$$ The students at San Francisco's best-known cooking school may change, but standards remain uncompromisingly high. You have a choice of two restaurants: The **Academy Grill** offers a lunch menu of sandwiches, salads, and other straightforward fare, as well as a buffet dinner; the more formal **Careme Room** serves a prix-fixe three-course lunch and dinner on most weekdays and a classic European buffet dinner on Friday (the menu reflects what students are learning to make that week). Be forewarned: Prices are not as low as many diners think they ought to be for student labor. ♦ Continental ♦ M-F lunch and dinner. Reservations recommended for the Academy Grill, required for the Careme Room. 625 Polk St (at Turk St). 771.3500

9 Federal Office Building This building was constructed in 1959 by **Albert F. Roller**, Stone/Marraccini/Patterson, and **John Carl Warnecke.** The bland face of federal government—a Miesian slab block set back from the street—offers a somber contrast to the ornate designs of the **Civic Center.** ♦ 450 Golden Gate Ave (between Polk and Larkin Sts)

10 A Clean Well-Lighted Place for Books This shop is popular with bibliophiles looking for the latest good read. Signings and readings by authors are often held. ♦ Daily; F-Sa until midnight. Opera Plaza, 601 Van Ness Ave (at Golden Gate Ave). 441.6670

10 Modesto Lanzone's ★★★$$$ Regional Italian food—ranging from sautéed rabbit with thyme, pine nuts, and olives on a bed of potatoes to turkey-stuffed pasta topped with a lime and grappa sauce—is served against a backdrop of original art from the owner's collection. (Note the Robert Arneson sculpture of Modesto as you walk into the restaurant.) This handsome restaurant-cum-art-gallery includes olive oil and vinegar displays and a bar that specializes in grappa, wine, and *spumante classico* (sparkling wine). ♦ Italian ♦ M-F lunch and dinner; Sa dinner. Opera Plaza, 601 Van Ness Ave (at Golden Gate Ave). 928.0400

10 Max's Opera Cafe ★$$ Jeans and evening gowns mix in this upscale New York–style deli and bar, a popular pre- and post-performance haunt for those attending events at the nearby **Performing Arts Center**. Waiters and waitresses sing arias and cabaret tunes nightly from 7PM to midnight. Takeout is available. ♦ American ♦ Daily lunch and dinner. Opera Plaza, 601 Van Ness Ave (at Golden Gate Ave). 771.7300

11 Stars ★★★$$$ This is the tallest feather in the cap of celebrity chef Jeremiah Tower, the owner of several restaurants. It attracts movers and shakers, socialites, and visiting glitterati, who enjoy the spirited, noisy, see-and-be-seen setting so much that they tend to convince themselves the food is equally wonderful. But while Tower maintains his high profile, things have been known to be uneven in the open kitchen. In general, however, the chef works with first-class ingredients and aims to turn out the trendiest dishes in town—and often succeeds. ♦ California ♦ Daily dinner. Reservations recommended. 150 Redwood St (entrances on Redwood St or Golden Gate Ave between Polk St and Van Ness Ave). 861.7827

12 Spuntino ★$ This high-tech Italian cafeteria features good salads and pizzas; the rest of the fare is unexciting. ♦ Italian ♦ Daily breakfast, lunch, and dinner. 524 Van Ness Ave (between McAllister and Redwood Sts). 861.7772

13 Stars Cafe ★$$ A junior version of **Stars**, this cafe, recently relocated to a larger space around the corner from its parent, has a menu that changes daily and features homier and heartier, but no less trendy, fare—meat loaf and short ribs, lots of Italian-inspired dishes, and breakfasts with homemade pastries and huge cups of café au lait. The mood is considerably more informal here, and the prices are lower. ♦ California ♦ Daily lunch and dinner. 500 Van Ness Ave (at McAllister St). 861.4344

Restaurants/Clubs: Red   **Hotels:** Blue
Shops/ ♥ Outdoors: Green   **Sights/Culture:** Black

14 Society of California Pioneers Members of this organization are descendants of those who arrived in California prior to 1850. The society maintains several public facilities, including a major library on California history and a gallery of 19th-century California artists. At press time, the organization was planning to move to an undetermined San Francisco location. ♦ Free. M-F by appointment only. 456 McAllister St (between Van Ness Ave and Polk St). Tour information 861.5278

DRAWING COURTESY OF CARLOS DINIZ

15 Edmund G. Brown State Office Building **Skidmore, Owings & Merrill** were the architects for this complex (pictured above), built in 1986. Their design complements the **Louise M. Davies Symphony Hall** down the street by facing diagonally toward **City Hall** and completing the Beaux Arts composition of civic buildings along this stretch of Van Ness Avenue. Clad in white precast concrete, it has a large seal of the State of California above the entry to the courtyard, which is disappointingly institutional in scale. ♦ Van Ness Ave (at McAllister St)

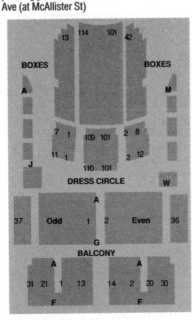

16 Herbst Theater Built in 1932, this minor component of the **Performing Arts Center** (see the plan shown above) was refurbished in 1978. But the orchestra seats are raked, and the balconies sit too far back in this

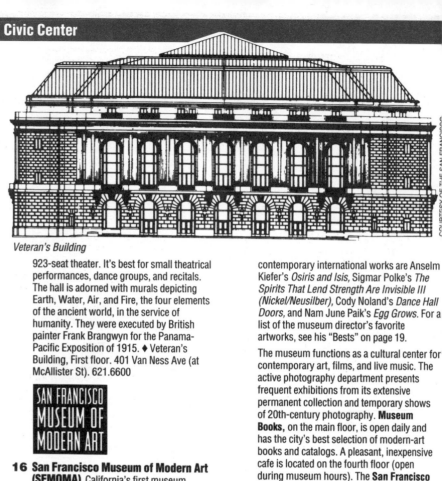

Veteran's Building

923-seat theater. It's best for small theatrical performances, dance groups, and recitals. The hall is adorned with murals depicting Earth, Water, Air, and Fire, the four elements of the ancient world, in the service of humanity. They were executed by British painter Frank Brangwyn for the Panama-Pacific Exposition of 1915. ♦ Veteran's Building, First floor. 401 Van Ness Ave (at McAllister St). 621.6600

SAN FRANCISCO
MUSEUM OF
MODERN ART

16 San Francisco Museum of Modern Art (SFMOMA) California's first museum devoted to 20th-century art is located on the third and fourth floors of the **Veteran's Building** (pictured above). At press time, the museum was moving to its new, larger quarters in **Yerba Buena Gardens** on Third Street between Mission and Howard Streets. Its handsome new home was designed by internationally acclaimed architect **Mario Botta.** The permanent collection contains works by Pablo Picasso, Henri Matisse, and Wassily Kandinsky, the Abstract Expressionists (including large holdings of Clyfford Still), Josef Albers, Isamu Noguchi, Alexander Calder, and distinguished California artists. Among the

City Hall

contemporary international works are Anselm Kiefer's *Osiris and Isis,* Sigmar Polke's *The Spirits That Lend Strength Are Invisible III (Nickel/Neusilber),* Cody Noland's *Dance Hall Doors,* and Nam June Paik's *Egg Grows.* For a list of the museum director's favorite artworks, see his "Bests" on page 19.

The museum functions as a cultural center for contemporary art, films, and live music. The active photography department presents frequent exhibitions from its extensive permanent collection and temporary shows of 20th-century photography. **Museum Books,** on the main floor, is open daily and has the city's best selection of modern-art books and catalogs. A pleasant, inexpensive cafe is located on the fourth floor (open during museum hours). The **San Francisco Museum of Modern Art Rental Gallery** (see page 102) is located at Fort Mason, Building A. ♦ Admission; free first Tuesday of the month. Tu-Su. Tours daily. 401 Van Ness Ave (at McAllister St). 252.4000

17 City Hall The focal point of the **Civic Center** complex (pictured below) was designed in 1915 by **Bakewell and Brown.** This magnificent symbol of government has a huge dome (modeled after St. Peter's in Rome), Baroque stairs, and echoing marble-clad corridors. The plaza in front of the building is disappointing by comparison; it's at its best when used for civic functions. ♦ Van Ness Ave (at McAllister St). 554.4000

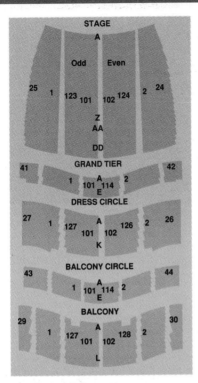

companies. The opera season opens in September with a gala—replete with splendidly gowned and bejeweled patrons—and runs through December. The ballet season follows. ♦ 301 Van Ness Ave (at Grove St). 861.4008

19 Arts Commission Gallery Indoor and outdoor exhibitions of work by both emerging and established Bay Area artists are presented here. ♦ Th-Sa. 155 Grove St (between Van Ness Ave and Polk St). 554.9682

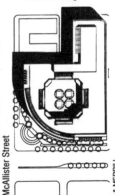

18 War Memorial Opera House This splendid and ornate house is the crown jewel of San Francisco's **Performing Arts Center.** With seating for 3,176 (see the plan shown above), it opened on 15 October 1932 and is the home of the city's renowned opera and ballet

20 Louise M. Davies Symphony Hall Designed by **Skidmore, Owings & Merrill,** this hall—named after arts patron Louise M. Davies, who contributed $5 million toward its construction—opened in 1980 after more than a decade of squabbling. It cost $33 million to build (all but $5 million of it was raised privately), and in 1992 the hall underwent a $10.25-million acoustical and architectural face-lift (see the plan shown above). The renovations included a new

Louise M. Davies Symphony Hall   **War Memorial Opera House**   **Veteran's Building**   **Edmund G. Brown State Office Building**

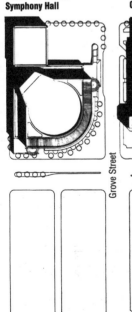

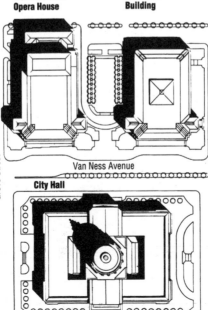

sound and video system as well as a computer-assisted resculpturing of the walls to improve acoustics. The hall is the official home of the **San Francisco Symphony,** whose season runs from September through May. Besides the symphony, the 2,743-seat **Davies** regularly books other musical and touring groups. ♦ Tours: M, W, and Sa. Van Ness Ave (at Grove St). Tours 552.8338, box office 431.5400

21 San Francisco Ballet Association Building Architect **Beverly Willis** designed this modest addition to the **Civic Center** composition in 1984. It contains administrative offices, a ballet school, and state-of-the-art rehearsal studios. The facilities are not open to the public. ♦ 455 Franklin St (at Grove St). 861.5600

22 Inn at the Opera $$$ This 46-room hotel was built in 1927 to house visiting opera stars. Elegantly restored, its luxuries include queen-size beds, large bathrooms, wet bars, small refrigerators, microwaves, 24-hour room service, concierge services, and parking. The rooms also have spectacular floral arrangements. Just a few steps away are the **Opera House** and **Davies Symphony Hall.** ♦ 333 Fulton St (between Gough and Franklin Sts). 863.8400, 800/423.9610 in CA, 800/325.2708; fax 861.0821

Within the Inn at the Opera:

Act IV ★★$$$ A popular place to gather before or after a performance, this handsome restaurant and lounge provides one of the most luxurious settings in San Francisco. A cozy fireplace, oil paintings, richly upholstered furniture, and warm woodwork all contribute to the fine ambience. Chef Kenneth Fredsted offers a varied menu featuring fresh fish, pasta, duck, rabbit, and many other very good dishes. ♦ Mediterranean ♦ Daily breakfast and dinner; M-F lunch; Su brunch. Reservations recommended. 553.8100

23 San Francisco Performing Arts Library and Museum Exhibitions related to the performing arts of the Bay Area are featured here. ♦ Free. Tu-Sa. 399 Grove St (at Gough St). 255.4800

24 Ivy's ★$$ Popular with a diverse clientele, this attractive restaurant has an interesting menu that changes weekly. The swordfish and the ravioli filled with roast chicken are two of the specials. ♦ California ♦ Daily dinner; M-F lunch; Su brunch. Reservations recommended. 398 Hayes St (at Gough St). 626.3930

24 F. Dorian, Inc. Interesting ethnic folk art and jewelry are sold here. ♦ Daily. 388 Hayes St (between Franklin and Gough Sts). 861.3191

24 de Vera This shop specializes in functional and decorative glassware, mainly from the Bay Area, as well as European designs from the 1950s and 1960s. Contemporary black-and-white photography and prints by Bay Area artists are also shown here. ♦ Tu-Sa. 384 Hayes St (between Franklin and Gough Sts). 861.8480

24 City Picnic ★$ For a fast and inexpensive salad or sandwich, this cafeteria, with a charming rear garden, is one of the choice spots around the **Civic Center.** ♦ American ♦ M-F breakfast and lunch. 384 Hayes St (between Franklin and Gough Sts). 431.8814

24 San Francisco Women Artists Gallery The work of Bay Area women artists is showcased in this nonprofit, volunteer-run sales and rental gallery. ♦ Tu-Sa. 370 Hayes St (between Franklin and Gough Sts). 552.7392

25 Hayes Street Grill ★★$$$ Seafood is the specialty here, and when the kitchen is on target, no place prepares fish with more expertise. If you want your fish well done, be sure to say so, as the cooks prefer a pink-around-the-bone style of cooking. Also worth the indulgence are the excellent french fries and sourdough bread. If you're not in the mood for fish, other delicious options are available. ♦ American ♦ M-F lunch and dinner; Sa-Su dinner. 320 Hayes St (at Franklin St). 863.5545

25 Vicolo Pizzeria ★★$ Consistently good cornmeal-crusted, California-style pizzas with unusual toppings, as well as tasty salads, are produced at this pleasant little side-street restaurant with a galvanized metal-and-glass exterior. It's a good spot for pre- and post-opera or -symphony snacking. ♦ California/Italian ♦ Daily lunch and dinner. 201 Ivy St (at Franklin St). 863.2382

26 Nuts About You All kinds of nuts, teas, baskets, coffees, and confections tempt irrepressible snackers. The store will also pack and ship orders. ♦ Daily. 325 Hayes St (between Franklin and Gough Sts). 864.6887

26 Coulars Boutique Whimsical clothing—shoes, ties; earrings, dresses—for women and children is hand-painted by owner Maryke Coulars. ♦ M-Sa; daily during December. 327 Hayes St (between Franklin and Gough Sts). 255.2925

26 Richard Hildert, Bookseller, Ltd. This cozy shop filled with old and new books specializes in interior design, but anything you want to read will happily be ordered. Call ahead to make sure it's open, as hours tend to be erratic. ♦ M-Sa; Su at owner's discretion. 333 Hayes St (between Franklin and Gough Sts). 863.3339

Restaurants/Clubs: Red	**Hotels:** Blue
Shops/ ♥ Outdoors: Green	**Sights/Culture:** Black

26 EC Studio Store Paper products never looked so pretty as they do here, all gussied up in colorful packages trimmed with big bows. Owners Caryl and Hal Brandes design and manufacture everything they sell: journals, sketch pads, stationery, cards, photo albums, and much more. Perfect for gifts. ♦ Tu-Sa. 347 Hayes St (between Franklin and Gough Sts). 621.1355

27 Evelyn's Antique Chinese Furniture For a good selection of Chinese pieces, this is the place. ♦ M-Sa. 381 Hayes St (at Gough St). 255.1815

28 Grand Central Station Antiques Two floors are filled with French, English, and Dutch furniture and collectibles from the 18th to 20th centuries. ♦ Tu-Su. 1676 Market St (between Gough and Franklin Sts). 864.2611. Also at: 595 Castro St (at 19th St). 863.3604

28 Pensione San Francisco $ This pleasant European-style hotel has 36 small, cheerful rooms with shared bathrooms (there are nine rooms and four bathrooms on each floor). ♦ 1668 Market St (between Gough and Franklin Sts). 864.1271; fax 861.8116

28 Zuni Cafe ★★$$$ Quite apart from serving one of the best hamburgers around, this outrageously popular, high-energy spot focuses on inventive adaptations of southwestern cooking. The kitchen creates masterly grilled dishes most of the time. ♦ Southwestern ♦ Tu-Su breakfast, lunch, and dinner. Reservations recommended (one-third of the dining room is reserved for walk-ins). 1658 Market St (at Rose St, between Franklin and Gough Sts). 552.2522

29 Beaver Bros. Antiques This is the largest prop-rental shop in San Francisco, so, theoretically, you can try the merchandise before buying. Victoriana, bric-a-brac, and an

Red Light, Green Light: The Heydays of the Elegant Bay Area Bordellos

Although San Franciscans didn't invent the concept of the parlor house (the term was first applied to the opulent brothels that catered to the upper class in New York), many a satisfied patron would assert that they perfected it. From the mid-1800s to the early 1900s, a wave of elegant bordellos, or parlor houses, flourished by the bay, far removed and far different from the tawdry sex dens found in San Francisco's **Barbary Coast** and **Chinatown**. The madams of these houses were so adept at ministering to their patrons' creature comforts that one visitor was moved to declare that it was his "unbiased opinion that California can and does furnish the best bad things obtainable in America."

Located in what were then respectable residential neighborhoods, mainly **Downtown** or in the upper **Tenderloin**, the parlor houses discreetly blended in with their surroundings. Lace curtains, footmen, and wrought iron masked the lascivious nature of the establishments. Even when a man entered one of these bordellos, the illusion of decorum was rigorously maintained—the houses were outfitted with grand furnishings, both the customers and the courtesans were expected to dress well, and lewd talk or any other display of vulgarity was strictly forbidden (at least in the public rooms).

The houses vied with each other to secure the most attractive and cultured ladies of the evening, training and dressing them to the hilt. One madam, for instance, "Diamond" Jessie Hayman, spent about $6,000 outfitting a new employee; in fact, each member of her staff had an ensemble that included two dozen nightgowns, more than a hundred hankies, two fur-trimmed capes, and six pairs of long kidskin evening gloves. Since San Francisco was the point of entry for all sorts of exotic imported goods, including Parisian frocks and silks from the Orient,

the madams had no trouble obtaining gorgeous wardrobes for their ladies.

Like warring couturiers, the parlor houses flaunted their finery during weekly promenades down Market Street and at theater outings, allowing the good women of San Francisco to get a glimpse of the latest fashions and permitting the men to ogle over a different type of merchandise.

In 1913 the parlor-house era came to an end, hastened by the passage of the national Red Light Abatement Act. Many prominent citizens fought against its observance in San Francisco, but the law was ultimately enforced in 1917, and most of the parlor houses were closed down. Although they enjoyed a brief renaissance after the repeal of Prohibition (when the law chose to look the other way), the bordellos never quite achieved their former stature—except, perhaps, for Sally Stanford's notable establishments.

Stanford started out in the Tenderloin but moved to **Nob Hill** in 1941, turning a mansion at **1144 Pine Street** into what she called "the most beautiful, elegant, grand temple of love." Nicknamed "the Fortress," Stanford's mansion was a parlor house in the old tradition: beautifully furnished with European and Asian antiques and staffed by decorous courtesans. Boorish behavior was not tolerated—Humphrey Bogart supposedly was once ejected after acting up—and the financial credentials of each customer were screened carefully. Stanford closed her famous "School of Advanced Social Studies" (as San Francisco Chronicle columnist Herb Caen dubbed it) in 1949. She went on to become a restaurateur and, in 1976, mayor of Sausalito. Clearly she was a favorite Bay Area resident, for when her mayoral term ended she was appointed vice-mayor for life.

eclectic assortment of other stuff from bygone eras are presented on two jam-packed floors. ♦ Daily. 1637 Market St (between Franklin and Gough Sts). 863.4344

30 Red Desert A fine collection of succulents and cacti is attractively displayed in a sandy habitat. ♦ Daily. 1632 Market St (at Rose St, between Franklin and Gough Sts). 552.2800

30 Decorum This shop has one of the largest gatherings of Art Deco and Moderne furnishings of the 1920s to 1940s housed under one roof, including a remarkable collection of lighting fixtures from those stylish eras. ♦ M-Sa. 1632 Market St (at Rose St, between Franklin and Gough Sts). 864.DECO

30 20th Century Furnishings It may be depressing to find that the furniture of one's youth is now being sold as antiques-in-the-making, but that's what this store offers. You'll find American designs from 1925 to 1960. ♦ Tu-Su. 1612 Market St (between Rose and Franklin Sts). 626.0542

30 Bahia Tropical A live Brazilian dance band at this hot spot for revelers pounds out the rhythm every night, and sexy, befeathered samba dancers gyrate Friday and Saturday (at about 11:30PM). The cover charge and two-drink minimum can make this a fairly costly experience, but when ya gotta dance, ya gotta dance. ♦ Cover. Daily until 2AM. 1600 Market St (at Franklin St). 861.8657

31 Bistro Clovis ★$ This bistro is so thoroughly French you can't even get an American-size cup of coffee, and, as in France, the staff here can be somewhat standoffish. However, the onion soup is a winner, and it's a dandy place for a fast, interesting snack before or after an opera or symphony per-formance. The bar also offers wine tastings for oenophiles who want to keep their palates in practice. ♦ French ♦ M-Sa lunch and dinner. 1596 Market St (at Franklin St). 864.0231

32 Bahia ★★$$ The owners have taken a successful stab at creating tropical ambience with rush-seat chairs, hanging stuffed parrots, and South American fare. This place packs in the customers, although service may be unreliable. The *feijoada* (a mixture of sausage and black beans) and the *muqueca de peixe* (fish marinated in lime and coconut milk) are among the most popular dishes. ♦ Brazilian ♦ Daily dinner; M-F lunch; Sa brunch. Reser-vations recommended. 41 Franklin St (at Lily St). 626.3306

Stroll, jog, or ride your bike on the terrific three-and-a-half-mile-long Golden Gate Promenade for an up-close and beautiful view of the bay, the boats, the birds, and, of course, the bridge. The trail hugs the water from Aquatic Park all the way to the Golden Gate.

33 Orpheum B. Marcus Priteca designed this 2,503-seat theater in 1926. In bygone days, it was an important part of the vaudeville scene. Today, the huge space is used for large-scale theatrical productions. The sight lines are dreadful, with an inadequately raked orchestra. When leaving, don't tarry too long; this isn't the friendliest part of town. ♦ 1192 Market St (at Hyde and Eighth Sts). 474.3800

34 United Nations Plaza This plaza memorializes the fact that the UN Charter was written and signed in this city in 1945. The plaza has become a hangout for panhandlers. ♦ Market St (at Fulton St)

34 Heart of the City Farmers' Market Fresh fruits and vegetables, direct from the growers, are sold at low prices. ♦ W, Su. UN Plaza, Market St (between Grove and Fulton Sts). 558.9455

35 Hibernia Bank At the time of its construction in 1892, **Willis Polk** described **Albert Pissis's** design as "the most beautiful building in the city." He'd take back his claim if he could see it today. Now in use as a police administration center, the tightly sealed building has certainly lost its luster. Notice how it turns the corner of Jones and McAllister Streets at Market Street with a domed vestibule. ♦ Jones St (at McAllister St)

36 La Savane West African Restaurant & Bar ★$$ Tired of that oh-so-trendy California cuisine? This pleasant, spacious spot offers a welcome alternative. Sweet-potato fries or tropical fruit soup, anyone? Or how about a heartier meal of peanut stew, seafood gumbo, or West African couscous with bell peppers, eggplant, and zucchini? Live African and Caribbean music shakes up the place on some nights. ♦ West African ♦ M-F lunch and dinner; Sa dinner. Reservations recommended. 96 McAllister St (at Leavenworth St). 861.0100

37 San Francisco Public Library The lobby of this landmark building was remodeled by **Daniel Solomon and Associates** in 1986. Within the existing entrance lobby (designed in 1916 by **George Kelham**), the checkout and return desks are in the shape of classical temples. The remodeled bathrooms contain the only real granite in the whole building.

Elsewhere, what looks like granite is either terra-cotta or plaster. The library was damaged in the October 1989 earthquake and remained closed for several months. Some 900,000 books had to be reshelved. At press time, a new library building, two and a half times the size of this structure, was under construction next door on Larkin Street at Fulton Street; it's expected to open by 1996. The architects for the new building are **Pei Cobb Freed and Partners** with **Simon Martin-Vegue Winkelstein Morris Associated Architects.** The **Asian Art Museum,** now in **Golden Gate Park,** will move into this building in 1998. ♦ M-Sa. 200 Larkin St (at McAllister St). 557.4400

Within the San Francisco Public Library:

San Francisco History Room and Special Collections Department In this combination document-and-photograph museum and research library you'll find glass cases filled with memorabilia, including photos of some of the city's classic buildings that no longer exist and of historic events such as the opening of the Golden Gate Bridge. ♦ Free. Tu, W, F afternoon; Th, Sa morning and afternoon. Third floor. 557.4567

37 Dashiell Hammett Tours Take a four-hour walk through the San Francisco of detective writer Dashiell Hammett. Tours, scheduled from May through August, start at noon on Saturday and leave from the library steps. ♦ Fee. 200 Larkin St (at McAllister St). 707/939.1214

38 Abigail Hotel $ Built in 1926 to house members of visiting theater groups, this hotel was remodeled in 1990 in an arty European style. Gone are the smiling moose head and family of stuffed elk; now there's a cozy, British feeling, complete with antiques, down comforters, and turn-of-the-century English art. While still not exactly luxurious, the 60-room hotel is a good value and conveniently located. ♦ 246 McAllister St (between Hyde and Larkin Sts). 861.9728, 800/243.6510; fax 861.5848

Within the Abigail Hotel:

MAMA JUSTICE CITY KITCHEN

Mama Justice City Kitchen ★$ Tucked off to the side of the lobby, this tiny kitchen turns out a small assortment of quick snacks—from spiced gingerbread and homemade granola with fruit and yogurt to a few selections of traditional sandwiches, pizza, and salads. ♦ American ♦ Daily breakfast; M-Sa lunch; F-Sa dinner. Reservations recommended. 861.2939

Bests

Milton Marks
California State Senator

There is no better San Francisco best, and no better value, than the Sunday concert and performance series at **Stern Grove.**

Almost pastoral, **Stern Grove** offers a rapturous outdoor environment in the middle of the city filled with the scent of eucalyptus, warmed by the sun, and serenaded by the likes of our symphony, opera, and the greats of jazz. The festival also features dance, including San Francisco's renowned ballet and companies from around the world.

John Lane
Director, San Francisco Museum of Modern Art

The best artwork at the San Francisco Museum of Modern Art:

Classic European Modernism: Henry Matisse, *Woman with the Hat,* 1905, and *The Girl with Green Eyes,* 1908; Georges Braque, *The Gueridon,* 1935; Wassily Kandinsky, *Brownish,* 1931; and Joan Miró, *Painting,* 1926

Early American Modernism: Georgia O'Keeffe, *Black Place,* 1944; Arthur Dove, *Silver Ball No. 2,* 1930; and Stuart Davis, *Deuce,* 1954

Latin American Modernism: Joaquin Torres-Garcia, *Constructivist Painting No. 8,* 1938; Frida Kahlo, *Frida and Diego Rivera,* 1931; and Diego Rivera, *The Flower Carrier,* 1935

American Abstract Expressionism and later: Arshile Gorky, *Enigmatic Combat,* 1936-37; Jackson Pollock, *Guardians of the Secret,* 1943; Clyfford Still (35 works spanning the artist's entire career); Philip Guston, *Red Sea,* 1975, *The Swell,* 1975, and *Blue Light,* 1975; Jasper Johns, *Land's End,* 1963; Robert Rauschenberg, *Collection,* 1953-54; Frank Stella, *Adelante,* 1964; Andy Warhol, *Self Portrait,* 1967; and Roy Lichtenstein, *Rouen Cathedral Set V,* 1969

California and San Francisco Bay Area artists: Richard Diebenkorn (seven works spanning the artist's career to date); Elmer Bischoff, *Orange Sweater,* 1955; David Park, *Man in a T-Shirt,* 1958; Sam Francis, *Red and Pink,* 1951; and William T. Wiley, *Ship's Log,* 1969

Kirk Webber
Chef/Owner, Cafe Kati

Watching the fog roll onto the bay and envelop the city. The top of **Twin Peaks** is one of the best places to watch, but even better would be from the Jacuzzi next to the window at the **Mandarin Oriental Hotel.**

The wind, rain, and fog are a great turn-on to me. I love the different climates even going from one part of the city to the other (**Marina, Noe Valley, Cliff House,** etc.). We San Franciscans cherish our Indian summer.

Lincoln Park Golf Course may not be the most challenging or the best kept course, but nowhere else in the city will you find nicer views of the Marin Headlands and the Golden Gate.

South of Market

Popularly known as **SOMA**, but familiar to an earlier generation as "South of the Slot," the South of Market area has evolved into one of San Francisco's most eclectic, artsy frontiers. It incorporates gay bars, trendy restaurants, a wholesale flower market, outlet shops, bus terminals, a convention center, warehouses, and rock, comedy, and jazz clubs. Artists, dancers, and musicians like the relatively modest rents for huge spaces they can convert into studios and living quarters, although rising real-estate prices have made the true bargains a thing of the past.

Close to **The Embarcadero** and the bay, SOMA has always been home to industry. Several foundries were located here in the 1850s, along with row after row of tiny houses, many prefabricated in the East, occupied by the city's first industrial population. Author Jack London, who was born on **Third Street** in 1876, reflected the rough-and-ready nature of the neighborhood in

his work. But when it became apparent that the climate was warmest on this side of town, **Rincon Hill**, long since blasted away and buried under the approach to the **Bay Bridge**, became a very prestigious address. Small, elegant shops filled **Second Street**. Adjacent **South Park** was a pioneer real-estate development promoted by George Gordan, an Englishman who set out to model an exclusive community for 64 families on the plan of terraces in London—stately Georgian houses that were built around an enclosed park to which only the residents had a gate key. Here, among others, lived cattle king Henry Miller, Senator William McKendree Gwin, and Hall McAllister, until he lost his mansion in a poker game. But before the park was half built, the decline of Rincon Hill set in because of the persistent industrialization of the neighborhood. Its residents fled to Nob Hill, abandoning their homes to Japanese immigrants. Rooming houses and machine shops took over, although remnants of grandeur can still be seen here and there, especially on

Third Street between **Bryant** and **Brannan Streets**. Signs of rebirth continue to appear throughout the neighborhood, as creative types buy, move into, and gentrify structures that have suffered decades of neglect.

In October 1993, **Yerba Buena Gardens**—the spectacular $87-million arts and cultural center—opened its doors, making the South of Market area San Francisco's new artistic hot spot. The center's striking visual-arts building, designed by renowned Japanese architect **Fumihiko Maki**, its theater created by highly acclaimed New York architect **James Stewart Polshek**, and its five and a half acres of gardens join with the **Moscone Convention Center**—northern California's largest meeting facility—in transforming what was once an area lined with skid-row flophouses into an impressive new complex with numerous satellite restaurants, shops, and hotels that have forever changed the face of SOMA.

Battery St.
The Embarcadero
Justin Herman Plaza
Ferry Building
Ferries to Sausalito, Tiburon, Vallejo, Larkspur, Oakland, and Alameda
Front St.
Davis St.
Drumm St.
6
5
4 3
7
8
to Oakland, Berkeley, and Alameda
Mission St.
Transbay Terminal
10
11
Howard St.
Stewart St.
1 Bay Bridge
Natoma St.
13 12
1st St.
Fremont St.
Beale St.
Main St.
Spear St.
9
2
2nd St.
Folsom St.
29
30
31
32
33
Harrison St.
South Park 34
Ave. South
35 Park 37
36
38
40
39
Stanford St.
The Embarcadero
Brannan St. 41
42 43
44
48
45
47
Berry St.
46
I-280
South Beach Yacht Harbor
China Basin
N
Mission Rock St.
3rd St.
Illinois St.
China Basin St.
6th St.
Central Basin
km
mi
1/4
1/2
1/2
1

In 1985 a confused whale that the public named Humphrey hogged the headlines. The great humpback mammal swam beneath the Golden Gate Bridge and then got lost in the Sacramento–San Joaquin River Delta, where he remained until underwater loudspeakers coaxed him back to the open sea by emitting the sounds of prey. Humphrey, who must have enjoyed all the attention, has returned several times since.

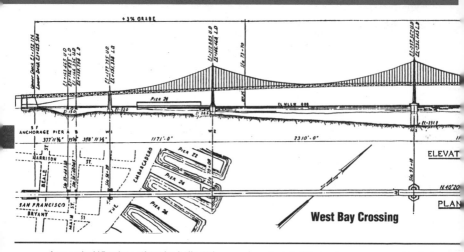

West Bay Crossing

Area code 415 unless otherwise indicated.

1 Bay Bridge **Charles H. Purcell** was chief engineer of this bridge, which eliminated the isolation between the cities of San Francisco and Oakland. The longest steel high-level bridge in the world, and one of the most costly structures ever built, it took three years to construct. The eight-mile span from approach to approach is, in fact, two bridges separated by a tunnel through Yerba Buena Island. The foundations of one of the piers extend 242 feet below water, deeper than those of any other bridge ever built. The pier is bigger than the largest of the world's pyramids and required more concrete than the Empire State Building in New York. The San Francisco side consists of a double-suspension bridge; the Oakland side is a cantilever bridge. The bridge has two levels, with five lanes in each direction. Originally, electric trains and trucks ran on the lower deck and cars on the upper deck, but the tracks were removed in the late 1950s when the trains were replaced by buses. In November 1986, a monthlong celebration of its golden anniversary included parades and fireworks. During the October 1989 quake, an upper section of the bridge collapsed onto the lower one, sending motorists fleeing from their cars and killing one person. The bridge's closure forced car-addicted commuters onto emergency ferries and other alternative forms of transportation. Through heroic construction efforts, the damage was repaired in just one month, and the reopening was celebrated with a trans-bridge walk and ceremony, including a song by vocalist Tony Bennett. Today it's the busiest thoroughfare in the area. Tolls have raised enough revenue to pay for other means of public transportation, including the **BART** tube, the San Mateo/Hayward Bridge, and most of the Dumbarton Bridge. The best

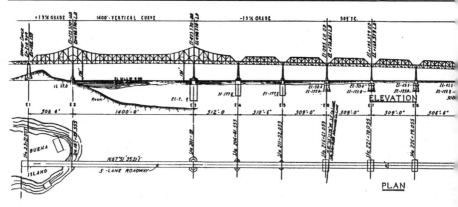

East Bay Crossing

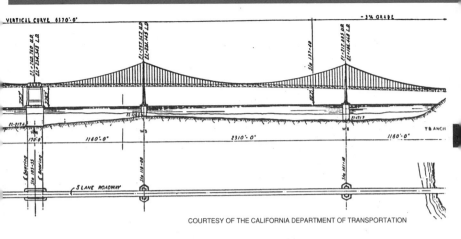

COURTESY OF THE CALIFORNIA DEPARTMENT OF TRANSPORTATION

views of the bridge are from Yerba Buena Island and from below on The Embarcadero in San Francisco. ◆ Toll westbound

2 Gordon Biersch ★★$$ This branch of the popular Palo Alto–based brewery-restaurant was a word-of-mouth success even before it opened. Beer, brick, and business suits dominate the ground floor, while diners herd upstairs to sample the sparse but tempting menu. Visually stimulating but acoustically devastating, this place—located in the old Hills Brothers coffee factory—seems to reach rock-concert decibel levels even at lunch. ◆ California ◆ Daily lunch and dinner. Reservations recommended. 2 Harrison St (at Steuart St and The Embarcadero). 243-8246

3 Harbor Court Hotel $$ When the much-hated Embarcadero Freeway was torn down due to damage caused by the 1989 quake, this hotel gained some great bay views. Housed in a 1907 building, it has 131 smallish guest rooms (30 have the views) and a magnificent lobby with a stone fireplace. Patrons are entitled to half-price entry into **Harry Denton**'s nightclub (and don't have to wait in line), plus gym privileges at the adjacent **YMCA,** complimentary wine every evening from 5PM to 7PM, and daily limousine service to the Financial District. ◆ 165 Steuart St (between Mission and Howard Sts). 882.1300, 800/346.0555

Within the Harbor Court Hotel:

Harry Denton's

Harry Denton's ★★$$ This popular saloon/supper club serves trendy comfort food in a very lively (read: noisy) atmosphere. The dishes, best described perhaps as chichi

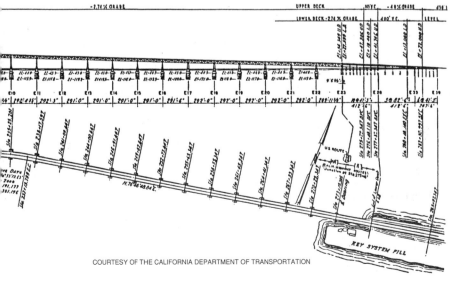

COURTESY OF THE CALIFORNIA DEPARTMENT OF TRANSPORTATION

Americana, range from light entrées like pasta with chicken-apple sausage to stick-to-your-ribs pot roast with buttermilk mashed potatoes. Don't get too carried away by the party atmosphere; as the menu warns, "Dancing on the bar prohibited unless accompanied by Harry." A rhythm-and-blues band performs in the bar, and the tables are whisked away in the back of the restaurant for dancing to DJ-spun tunes. ◆ Cover charge for bar Th-Sa after 9PM. ◆ M-F breakfast, lunch, and dinner; Sa-Su dinner. Reservations recommended. 882.1333

3 Hotel Griffon $$$ Originally built in 1907, making it the oldest hotel on the waterfront, the 63-room **Griffon** is part of the expanding Financial District, which has moved south of Market Street. It is a block from the **Ferry Terminal** and a scant two blocks from the **California Street Cable-car Line.** The rooms have minibars, and complimentary services include morning coffee and daily newspaper delivery. ◆ 155 Steuart St (between Mission and Howard Sts). 495.2100, reservations only 800/321.2201; fax 495.3522

Within the Hotel Griffon:

Bistro Rôti ★★★$$ This European-style bistro was launched by celebrity chef Cindy Pawlcyn, whose culinary stamp is on **Mustards** (in the Napa Valley) and the **Fog City Diner.** The kitchen specializes in spit-roasted poultry, lots of inventive dishes that show French inspiration, and desserts too good to pass up. A few of the especially desirable tables have views of the bay. ◆ California/French ◆ M-F lunch and dinner; Sa-Su brunch and dinner. Reservations recommended. 495.6500

4 The Jewish Community Museum Exhibitions, special programs, and classes relating to Judaism are offered in this museum, founded in 1984. Some exhibitions are free, while others carry an admission fee. ◆ Admission. M-Th, Su. 121 Steuart St (between Mission and Howard Sts). 543.8880

5 Audiffred Building Built in 1889 by **Hippolyte d'Audiffred,** this brick building was the only one south of Market to survive the fire after the 1906 earthquake. Ironically, it burned down in 1981, but has since been restored. ◆ Mission St (at Steuart St)

Within the Audiffred Building:

Boulevard ★★★$$$ Chef and restaurateur Nancy Oakes, who has been called one of the 10 best new chefs by *Food & Wine* magazine and chef of the year by *San Francisco Focus* magazine, joined forces with acclaimed restaurant designer **Pat Kuleto** in creating this handsome restaurant, which opened in late 1993. After you pass through the revolving doors, note the inlaid brick ceiling, the tile work lining the windows, and the large wood-burning oven next to the bar. Peer at the menu and you'll find such intriguing appetizers as pheasant, barley, and fresh porcini-mushroom soup or corn skillet cakes layered with fresh Maine crab salad and lemon-chive sauce topped with golden caviar. The entrées are so varied and so tantalizing you may have to flip a coin to decide from among such dishes as the spit-roasted veal chop served with a parmesan risotto cake and balsamic vinegar sauce, or the wood oven–roasted boneless rabbit stuffed with portobello mushrooms on a bed of soft polenta with artichoke hearts, a porcini-mushroom sauce, and sun-dried-tomato relish. Whatever you choose, your taste buds won't leave disappointed. ◆ Italian ◆ M-F lunch and dinner; Sa-Su dinner. Reservations recommended. Entrance on Steuart St. 543.6084

6 One Market Restaurant ★★★$$$ Celebrity chef Bradley Ogden has once again created a hit restaurant that, despite its grand size, gets so packed you often have to make reservations weeks in advance. The view and the sounds set the mood: The airy dining room lined with huge windows overlooks the side of Justin Herman Plaza and the end of bustling Market Street, and jazz piano music dominates the attractive bar in the evenings. But the food is the main attraction here, and Ogden's ever-changing menu may feature appetizers like fried-quail salad with sweet potatoes and cranberry vinaigrette or oak-baked onion flatbread with roasted garlic, tomatoes, wild mushrooms, and fontina. Main courses vary from grilled center-cut pork chop with butternut squash gratin, braised cabbage, and apple butter to Dungeness crab and shellfish stew with roasted tomato rouille served with garlic toast. You may also want to consider ordering a side dish of Ogden's delicious garlic mashed potatoes with chives and crème fraîche. Be sure to top it all off with one of the many divine desserts. ◆ California ◆ M-F lunch and dinner; Sa-Su dinner; Su jazz brunch. Reservations recommended. 1 Market St (at Steuart St). 777.5577

| Restaurants/Clubs: Red | Hotels: Blue |
| Shops/ 🌱 Outdoors: Green | Sights/Culture: Black |

7 Rincon Center The old **Rincon Annex Post Office Building,** built here in 1940 by **Gilbert Stanley Underwood,** is one of the city's masterpieces, and was incorporated into a massive complex of offices, shops, restaurants, and apartment towers in 1989 by **Johnson, Fain, and Pereira Associates.** The historic murals that were in the annex lobby are the centerpiece of the 85-foot-high skylighted atrium from which falls a magnificent cascade of water. The post office has moved to 2 Rincon Center.
♦ Spear St (at Mission St)

8 Pacific Wine Company A high-class Wines 'R' Us, this place stocks 6,000 square feet of wine, cognac, single-malt scotch, and other fine spirits. You can sample the wares at the tasting bar, and after you sip, you can have your purchases shipped around the globe. ♦ M-Sa. 124 Spear St (between Mission and Howard Sts). 896.5200

9 Mailways—Trains Are Us A terrific place for train buffs, this has model trains for everyone, from beginner to connoisseur.
♦ M-Sa. 200 Folsom St (at Main St). 982.2523

10 Beale St. Grill ★$ Formerly **Rockin' Robins,** this genial sandwich-and-burger shop retained its hot-rod facade when it switched gears. The draft beer selection is great. ♦ American ♦ M-F lunch and dinner. 133 Beale St (between Mission and Howard Sts). 543.1961

11 Transbay Terminal When the Bay Bridge was opened, this austere, functional 1939 building by **Timothy Pflueger** (with consulting architects **Arthur Brown Jr.** and **John L. Donovan**) replaced the **Ferry Terminal** as the gateway to the city. Buses to the **Amtrak** station in Oakland and bus tours to Lake Tahoe and Reno leave from here. ♦ Mission St (at First St)

Within the Transbay Terminal:

Gray Line Tours Day tours to **Muir Woods,** Sausalito, Yosemite, the Wine Country, Carmel, and Monterey—as well as city tours of San Francisco—depart from this bus terminal. ♦ Reservations required for some tours. Scheduling information 558.9400

Greyhound Bus Lines These buses continue to do the job when it comes to cheap, long-distance transportation.
♦ Scheduling information 800/231.2222

12 The Caribbean Zone ★$$ The ambience is heaped on with a trowel at this fanciful restaurant, owned and operated by Dr. Winkie, the creative force behind the popular nightspot **Club DV8.** The splashy dining hideaway was built with corrugated-metal walls around an airplane that once belonged to the Doobie Brothers. The fuselage is now suspended above the restaurant's bar, where it functions as a lounge, complete with aerial videos of land at the windows. Patrons can order such stimulating drinks as "Sex in the Jungle," and the restaurant below offers hearty portions of subtly spiced island food, served amid two waterfalls, rocky walls, and hundreds of real and fake tropical plants.
♦ Caribbean ♦ Daily lunch and dinner. Reservations recommended for lunch. 55 Natoma St (between First and Second Sts). 541.9465

13 Club DV8 Five dance floors are action-filled with young bodies wearing the trendiest of duds at this place, the largest of SOMA's dance clubs. One dance floor is in **Club Privé,** a membership club-within-the-club favored by young movers and shakers. ♦ Cover. W-Su. 540 Howard St (between First and Second Sts). 777.1419

14 Pacific Telephone Building One of the most beautiful skyscrapers in San Francisco, this 1925 building (pictured at right), by **Miller and Pflueger** and **A.A. Cantin Architects,** owes much to **Eliel Saarinen**'s celebrated design proposed for the Chicago Tribune Tower, particularly in the building's profile, detailing, and vertical emphasis. Notice the modern entrance lobby with its Chinese decorated ceilings. ♦ 130-140 New Montgomery St (between Mission and Howard Sts)

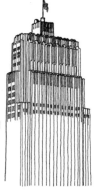

15 Crown Point Press Gallery This gallery prints and publishes etchings and woodblock editions by artists who work here by invitation. It is known internationally for its high quality and standards. ♦ Tu-Sa. 657 Howard St (between Second and Third Sts). 974.6273

16 Moscone Convention Center This 1.2-million-square-foot facility anchors the vast **Yerba Buena Gardens** complex. It's named after assassinated mayor George Moscone and was designed by **Hellmuth, Obata, and Kassabaum.** The city's premier meeting and exhibition facility was recently expanded by **Gensler & Associates** and **DMJM** to the tune of $200 million. Although largely underground, the center's imaginative use of skylights and other light-maximizing features keeps conventioneers from feeling like troglodytes. ♦ Howard St (between Third and Fourth Sts). 974.4000

17 Yerba Buena Gardens This new $87-million arts and cultural center is the result of 30 years of public planning and debate and is intended to feature the work and talents of San Francisco's diverse ethnic and artistic communities. Many of the major structures were designed by internationally acclaimed architects, including the 55,000-square-foot **Center for the Arts Galleries and Forum** by Japanese architect **Fumihiko Maki; James Stewart Polshek and Partners'** 755-seat **Center for the Arts Theater;** and the new home of the **San Francisco Museum of Modern Art,** designed by Swiss architect **Mario Botta,** which opens in January 1995 to commemorate the museum's 60th anniversary. The five-and-a-half-acre **Esplanade,** bordered by Mission, Howard, Third, and Fourth Streets, features a memorial to Martin Luther King Jr., a 20-foot-high, 50-foot-wide waterfall made of Sierra granite; the **Sister City Garden,** which is planted with flowers and plants from San Francisco's 13 sister cities from around the world; and a number of public artworks. More buildings are expected to be completed by mid-1995, including a 285,000-square-foot entertainment and retail complex, which will feature a large cinema and numerous shops and restaurants; a four-acre, $48-million **Children's Center** atop **Moscone Convention Center South;** and the new home of the **Mexican Museum.** ♦ Bounded by Third and Fourth Sts, and Mission and Folsom Sts. Program information 978.ARTS

18 ANA Hotel $$$$ Formerly the **Hotel Meridien,** this hostelry was built in 1983 by **Air France.** The sleek hotel contains 676 rooms and suites, many with sweeping city views, and is within walking distance of Union Square, the Financial District, and the **Moscone Convention Center.** Valet parking, a health club, room service, and a business center are among its amenities. ♦ 50 Third St (between Market and Mission Sts). 974.6400, 800/ANA.HOTEL; fax 543.8268

Within the ANA Hotel:

Cafe Justin ★★$$ Steak and french fries (as only the French can do them) plus other light meals and salads are featured at this brasserie. There's a different and delectable dessert buffet every day. ♦ French ♦ Daily breakfast, lunch, and dinner. 974.6400

19 Pacific Gas and Electric Substation Another of **Willis Polk**'s masterpieces, this 1907 substation is due to be restored as part of the Yerba Buena Redevelopment Project. The space behind the brick-and-stone facade, with its elaborately detailed portal and carefully proportioned windows, will probably be used for exhibitions one day. ♦ 222 Jessie St (bounded by Mission and Market Sts and Third and Fourth Sts)

20 Aston Pickwick Hotel $ This 189-room hotel is well located—across from the **Old Mint Museum,** mere footsteps from Market Street shopping, and just a block away from the **Moscone Convention Center.** It's a terrific value and has already been discovered by many European visitors. ♦ 85 Fifth St (at Mission St). 421.7500, 800/227.3282; fax 243.8066

Within the Aston Pickwick Hotel:

Raza's Cafe ★$ A San Francisco establishment for more than 15 years, this restaurant is known for its hefty half-pound, foot-long hamburgers served on a baguette with onions, tomatoes, and melted Monterey Jack cheese. Pasta, salads, and chicken and seafood specials by owner/chef Raza Mostatabi round out the menu. ♦ American/Continental ♦ Daily breakfast, lunch, and dinner. 495.4849

21 Old Mint Museum This 19th-century brick-and-stone building by **A.B. Mullett** is one of the few important monuments to survive both the 1906 earthquake and fire intact. It symbolizes the Jeffersonian ideals of the young republic. Tours of the classical-style building include viewing a million dollars in gold, a million-dollar coin collection, and restored Victorian rooms. There's also a 30-minute movie, *The Granite Lady.* Tours are offered hourly on the hour (reservations required for 10 or more only). ♦ Free. M-F. Fifth St (at Mission St). 744.6830

22 Cadillac Bar and Grill ★$$ Traditional and regional Mexican food is offered here in this lively, noisy, authentic-looking place, where the specialty is seafood. ♦ Mexican ♦ Daily lunch and dinner. 325 Minna St (between Fourth and Fifth Sts). 543.8226

23 Chevys ★$$ This popular restaurant has found a formula for success and repeated it many times throughout the Bay Area. Tortillas are made on the premises, along with terrific fajitas and other Mexican fare. They're offered in substantial portions in a deliberately funky setting, where beer cases serve as room dividers. It's a casual dining experience that's especially enjoyable when everything is washed down with a pitcher of the slushy (although not too potent) margaritas. ♦ Mexican/Takeout ♦ Daily lunch and dinner. Reservations required for eight or more. 150 Fourth St (at Howard St). 543.8060. Also at: 2 Embarcadero Center, Promenade level (between Clay and Sacramento Sts and Battery and Front Sts). 391.2323; and Stonestown Galleria (at 19th Ave and Winston Dr). 665.8705

24 Yerba Buena Square With lots of discount and outlet shopping for men, women, and children under one roof, this is a bargain hunter's heaven. The largest store in the complex is the **Burlington Coat Factory Warehouse** (495.7234), which carries a huge supply of coats and just about everything else. **The Shoe Pavilion** (974.1821), with last season's styles from well-known manufacturers at 30 to 70 percent off, is also worth checking out. ♦ Daily. 899 Howard St (at Fifth St). 543.1275

25 Martini This is *the* place to go on weekend nights if you're young and hip and love to dance. The three dance floors each have their own theme (1970s disco, modern, live music). Underclad, libidinal dancers hover in wrought-iron cages above the dance floors. It is straight on Fridays, gay on Saturdays. ♦ Cover. F-Sa to 6AM. 1015 Folsom St (between Fifth and Sixth Sts). 431.1200

26 LuLu ★★★$$ One of San Francisco's best restaurants and, given the quality of the fare, one of the most reasonably priced places in town. It's located in an immense, attractively remodeled 1910 warehouse, and features a bustling bar lining one side of the vast room, a huge wood-burning oven that dominates the back of the restaurant, and an impressive vaulted ceiling that arches over the main dining room. The service here is thoroughly professional, which makes indulging in chef Reed Hearon's French/Italian treats a particularly pleasant experience. Don't miss the roasted mussel appetizer, which is served sizzling at your table in an iron skillet, or the grilled chevre wrapped in grape leaves with *herbes de Provence* and croutons. Entrées include thin-crust pizza from the wood-burning oven, the popular moist pork loin from the wood-fired rotisserie served with garlic-and-olive-oil mashed potatoes, the trademark spit-roasted chicken, and superb fish dishes such as crispy halibut with fennel *brandade* (a creamy spread made with dried salt cod) and *tapenade* (a spread made with olives, anchovies, and capers). The warm chocolate cake with praline ice cream must be ordered with your meal to allow enough time to bake it, and it's so sinfully delicious you'll remember it long after you've left the restaurant. ♦ French/Italian ♦ M-Sa lunch and dinner; Su dinner. Reservations recommended. 816 Folsom St (between Fourth and Fifth Sts). 495.5775

Within LuLu:

LuLu Bis ★★★$$ Tucked away behind the bar of **LuLu** is a separate dining area, with a separate name. The food served in this small, narrow room is just as wonderful as what you'd get in the main dining room; however, the meals here are four-course, prix-fixe affairs (there's a choice of two main courses), served family style on long tables shared by eight to 14 diners. So if you're a party of two,

you'll order your own food but share your table with others. It's an unusual setup that confounds many diners at first, but San Franciscans love it. If you want to eat here, be sure to specify this dining room when you make your reservation. ♦ Tu-Sa dinner. Reservations recommended. 495.5775

LuLu Cafe ★★$ To further confuse first-time visitors to **LuLu**, on the side of the dining room opposite **LuLu Bis** is this tiny cafe, offering eggs and hot cereals for breakfast, a variety of salads and sandwiches for lunch, and selections from the main menu for dinner. During the day, the thick-crusted bread (baked on the premises) and tasty toppings (including *tapenade* and other sauces) are sold here. ♦ M-Sa breakfast, lunch, and dinner; Su dinner. 495.5775

27 The Friends of Photography Ansel Adams Gallery Works by the gallery's namesake, one of California's greatest photographers, are always on display. Other exhibitions focus on vintage to contemporary photography. ♦ Admission; children 12 and under free. Tu-Su. 250 Fourth St (between Folsom and Howard Sts). 495.7000

28 Max's Diner ★$$ One of many restaurants owned by Dennis Berkowitz, this serves generous portions of everything you always wanted to eat but never dared to if you cared about your weight. The decor is modern/vintage at its best—comfy booths, a long counter, and a cocktail lounge with full-time rock 'n' roll. Hearty deli sandwiches and burgers, baked meat loaf, roast turkey, cheese steak, pan-fried pork chops, baked goods, and a soda fountain are here to tempt those willing to toss dietary caution to the winds. ♦ American/Deli ♦ Daily lunch and dinner. 311 Third St (at Folsom St). 546.6297

29 The Fly Trap ★★$$ Named after a long-closed, but once popular Financial District restaurant, this is one of the area's more upscale spots, with a mirrored, casually elegant interior and a menu that borrows some culinary inspiration from its namesake. The see-and-be-seen dining room attracts both movers and shakers and SOMA habitués. The pastas are handmade, and the sautéed chicken Raphael Weill is a fine dish, sometimes offered as a special, that owes its heritage to an earlier era. The predominant culinary style is contemporary and California, but the accent is Italian. ♦ California ♦ M-F lunch and dinner; Sa-Su dinner. Reservations recommended. 606 Folsom St (at Second St). 243.0580

30 Sailors' Union of the Pacific Building **William S. Merchant**'s 1950 building symbolizes the power that unions gained after the bitter struggles and strikes of 1934. It is reminiscent of European Constructivist buildings of the 1930s. ♦ 450 Harrison St (at First St)

31 76 Tower Union Oil Company Building A landmark on top of Rincon Hill, the triangular-shaped tower designed in 1941 by **Lewis P. Hobart** is directed toward the approach ramp to the Bay Bridge. It is clad in white porcelain enamel—a material that architects have rediscovered. ◆ 425 First St (at Harrison St)

32 Embarko ★★$$ You name it, they probably have it at this eclectic, madly trendy, wildly whimsical restaurant. Marvelous salads freshen palates tempted by such well-prepared specialties as jambalaya with shrimp, Cajun chicken, and *andouille* sausage; lobster tamales; paella; and spicy, all-American meat loaf with garlic mashed potatoes and gravy. Desserts include Tennessee black-bottom pie, Ovaltine devil's food cake, and a good old American hot-fudge sundae. The great variety, however, may have something to do with the inconsistency of the kitchen, which has been known to miss by a mile. The decor is also a mixture of ethnic styles, working together to create a fun-filled melting pot. ◆ American ◆ M-F lunch and dinner; Sa-Su dinner. Reservations recommended. 100 Brannan St (at The Embarcadero). 495.2021

33 Delancey Street Restaurant ★★$$ This handsome restaurant with a great view of the bay bills itself as "an ethnic American bistro," which is a fair enough description of its eclectic fare. *Baba ganooj* (eggplant dip) shares the menu with matzo-ball soup, and quesadillas peacefully coexist with cold Szechuan noodles with peanut sauce. There's traditional heartland fare as well—barbecued chicken, meat loaf, and leg of lamb. Run by the residents of the well-regarded Delancey Street Project, a self-supporting residential community for people who were once down and out, the restaurant has been packing in customers with its terrific food and friendly service. ◆ American ◆ Tu-F lunch and dinner; Sa-Su brunch and dinner. Reservations recommended. 600 Embarcadero (at Brannan St). 512.5179

34 Cava 555 ★$$ Especially well known for its sophisticated nibbles, such as fresh oysters with champagne vinaigrette and caviar, this spot also features 70 different champagnes and sparkling wines as an accompaniment. Classical jazz is performed live during the evenings. ◆ California ◆ Tu-F lunch and dinner; Sa dinner. 555 Second St (between Bryant and Brannan Sts). 543.2282

35 South Park Cafe ★★$$ This intimate, popular, and noisy neighborhood spot bordering the park is a surprisingly faithful interpretation of the French cafe experience. The menu offers a pleasing variety of thoughtfully prepared dishes, such as roast chicken and french fries, mussels in cream, duck confit, and lovely salads. The small but choice dessert selection includes a heavenly crème brûlée, and the espresso drinks rank among the best in the city. Continental breakfasts are served here, and there is a small bar and a few tables where you can sip an aperitif and nibble on tapas at cocktail hour. ◆ French ◆ M-F breakfast, lunch, and dinner; Sa dinner. 108 South Park Ave (between Second and Third Sts, and Bryant and Brannan Sts). 495.7275

36 Ristorante Ecco ★★$$ This sophisticated parkside restaurant specializes in Northern Italian fare. Particularly *buono* is the *osso buco d'agnello* (braised lamb shanks served with white beans and *salsa verde*), which is often offered as a special. Make a selection from the outstanding list of Italian wines and ask for a window seat. ◆ Italian ◆ M-F lunch and dinner; Sa dinner. Reservations recommended. 101 South Park Ave (between Second and Third Sts). 495.3291

37 New York Cosmetics & Fragrances Stop here if you need to buy gifts or stock up on beauty aids. The prices on cosmetics and fragrances are deeply discounted. ◆ M-Sa. 318 Brannan St (at Second St). 543.3880

38 AHC Apparel Men's and women's washable silk separates with the high-status Go Silk label are carried exclusively at this outlet. Yes, the prices are still high, but they're 50 to 75 percent off regular retail prices. ◆ M-Sa. 625 Second St (at Brannan St). 957.1983

39 S.F. Fire Department Pumping Station This stripped-down classical building houses pumps for the elaborate water system designed after the 1906 earthquake and fire. It was built in 1920 by **Frederick Meyer** to ensure that the city would never again be left without adequate means of fighting a massive fire, even if the water mains from outside were ruptured. ◆ 698 Second St (at Townsend St)

40 Gunne Sax Factory Outlet You'll find great buys here on clothes for children, juniors, and women, with the Jessica McClintock, Scott McClintock, and Gunne Sax labels so popular with young romantics. There are often lots of prom, brides', and bridesmaids' dresses; a fabric and trim department is here as well. ◆ Daily. 35 Stanford St (between Second and Third Sts, and Brannan and Townsend Sts). 495.3326

41 Jack London's Birthplace A plaque on the Wells Fargo Bank marks the birthplace of this legendary writer. ♦ Brannan St (at Third St)

42 Simply Cotton The young, casual crowd loves these easy-to-wear cotton separates, especially at these low prices. ♦ M-Sa. 610 Third St (at Brannan St). 543.2058

43 The Cartoon Art Museum This fifth-floor exhibition space is devoted to art that tickles the funny bone. Classes and tours are available. ♦ Admission; reduced for children 12 and under. W-Sa. 665 Third St (at Townsend St). 546.3922

44 Six Sixty Factory Outlet Center A variety of shops selling good stuff and not-so-good stuff for men, women, and children are gathered together under one roof for the convenience of bargain hunters. ♦ M-Sa. 660 Third St (at Townsend St). 227.0464

45 San Francisco RV Park Located near the train depot and in the middle of an industrial area, this may not be the most scenic of recreational-vehicle parks, but it's the only one in the heart of the city. The good news is that it's relatively close to the area's entertainment attractions. Daily, weekly, and monthly rates are available. ♦ 250 King St (between Third and Fourth Sts). 986.8730

46 China Basin Building If this 1922 warehouse/office building by **Bliss and Faville** were put on end, it would be 850 feet high and one of the city's tallest structures. It was repainted in blue with white stripes to resemble an ocean liner. ♦ 185 Berry St (between Third and Fourth Sts)

47 Train Depot The terminal for the former **Southern Pacific Railroad** line now houses the commuter trains to San Jose. Originally it was the starting point for the famous *Coast Starlight* and *Daylight Express* trains to Los Angeles. The old mission-style station was demolished in 1979 to make way for the current utilitarian structure. ♦ At Fourth and Townsend Sts

48 Fringale Restaurant ★★$$ Loosely translated, *fringale* means "I'm starving" in French. Well, anyone who's feeling a mite peckish is in for a treat at this intimate, soothing restaurant. The Basque owners describe their food as "Gallic exotic," and although it's far removed from nouvelle cuisine, the kitchen has an equally light hand with sauces, turning out intriguing dishes such as sautéed sweetbreads and split Basque sausages. ♦ French ♦ M-F lunch and dinner; Sa dinner. Reservations recommended. 570 Fourth St (between Bryant and Brannan Sts). 543.0573

49 The Flower Market This area is fragrant with blossoms and abloom with activity when most of the city sleeps. It's the wholesale center for the floral trade, but many shops will also sell retail at very attractive prices. ♦ M-F mornings. Fifth St (between Brannan and Bryant Sts). 392.7944, 781.8410

50 Antonio's Antiques Very fine 17th- to 19th-century French, English, and continental antiques, including furnishings and accessories, fill three floors here. ♦ M-Sa. 701 Bryant St (at Fifth St). 781.1737

51 Gift Center Formerly a warehouse, this 1917 **Maurice Couchot** building was renovated in 1984 by **Kaplan/McLaughlin/Diaz** with the construction of a large atrium in place of the original light well. Designed in Art Deco style, its shops are open to wholesalers only (although the restaurants are open to the public), and it's often used for large parties. ♦ 888 Brannan St (at Eighth St). 861.7733

Within the Gift Center:

The Pavilion Cafe ★$$ Open to the public for lunch, this agreeable, light-washed space with seating on several levels offers piano music and a small but pleasant menu. Operated by caterer Dan McCall, whose client list includes some of the city's social elite, it's one of the few worthwhile places to eat around the wholesale markets. ♦ California ♦ M-F lunch. Reservations required for large parties. 552.8555

The Deli ★$ Dan McCall's catering kitchen offers great value in fast food. Prices are right, and customers get to sit in the same pleasant space as those eating in the more expensive **Pavilion Cafe**. ♦ Deli ♦ M-F breakfast and lunch. 552.8555

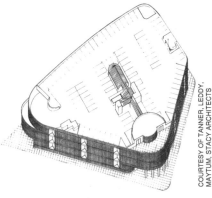

52 Diamond and Jewelry Mart This glass-block building (pictured above) was designed in 1985 by **Tanner, Leddy, Maytum, Stacy Architects** to house showrooms for the computer industry, but Silicon Valley went into an economic decline by the time it was completed. Never used for its intended purpose, it now houses wholesalers catering to the jewelry trade, and it's not open to the public. The building often appears in TV commercials. ♦ 999 Brannan St (at Division St). 255.2718

COURTESY OF TANNER, LEDDY, MAYTUM, STACY ARCHITECTS

53 Showplace Square In these restored brick warehouses are wholesale furniture and design showrooms, open to the trade. The **Design Center** consists of two warehouses linked by a modern, glass-faced atrium building used for exhibitions and conferences. A restaurant on the ground floor serves mediocre food in a very chic setting. ♦ M-F. 2 Henry Adams St (at Alameda St). 864.1500

Within Showplace Square:

Club Mirage Video screens flash computerized images ranging from birthday messages to Fellini-like film clips at this club popular with young, working-class Asians and Latinos. The lively music has an ethnic flavor, and the patrons favor flashy sportswear. ♦ Cover. F to 2AM; Sa to 3AM. First floor. 431.9046

54 San Francisco Herb Company Spice up your life; buy herbs by the pound, wholesale. ♦ M-F. 250 14th St (at Folsom St). 861.7174

55 Manora's Thai Cuisine ★★★$$ Many cognoscenti think this is one of the best Thai restaurants in the city. Try the Pooket Skewer—vegetables, scallops, prawns, calamari, mussels, and other seafood served with spicy lemon-garlic and sweet chili sauces. ♦ Thai ♦ M-F lunch and dinner; Sa-Su dinner. 1600 Folsom St (at 12th St). 861.6224. Also at: 3226 Mission St (at Valencia St). 550.0856

56 Hamburger Mary's ★$ Bikers, artists, socialites—in fact, just about every facet of San Francisco's varied population eventually makes it to this noisy, funky, well-entrenched restaurant where ear-splitting music makes conversation almost impossible. The crowd seems to like it that way, and the hamburgers are an undeniable hit. ♦ American ♦ Tu-Su lunch and dinner. 1582 Folsom St (at 12th St). 626.5767

56 Club Oasis There's live rock, R&B, New Wave, and avant-garde music here, with dancing outdoors by the pool or indoors near the bar. An outside terrace overlooks the dance floor. ♦ Tu-Sa; call for nightly hours. 11th St (at Folsom St). 621.8119

57 Paradise Lounge There's live music seven nights a week and two performance spaces in this countercultural hot spot. Downstairs, the "lounge stage" fits audiences of 200, while a larger performance area on the same floor holds up to 450 moving bodies. In **Above Paradise,** the acoustic lounge upstairs, activities include everything from poetry readings to musical performances. The dress code is relaxed. ♦ Cover F-Sa. Daily to 2AM. 1501 Folsom St (at 11th St). 861.6906

57 Holy Cow The postcollegiate set is willing to wait a long time to gain entrance to this dance bar and "meet market," marked by the presence of a large plastic cow above the front doorway and bartenders who tend to join in the fun. It's a beer-drinking, casual crowd, with a taste in clothing that runs toward anything black. ♦ Tu-Su to 2AM. 1535 Folsom St (between 11th and 12th Sts). 621.6087

57 Ace Cafe ★★$$ This popular, dress-down meeting place for the SOMA set serves an eclectic assortment of California dishes. The seared *ahi* tuna sandwich is a great crowd pleaser. ♦ California ♦ Daily dinner. 1539 Folsom St (between 11th and 12th Sts). 621.4752

58 20 Tank Brewery ★$ One of only three brew pubs in San Francisco, this warehouse-style watering hole offers up to six house-brewed ales daily. Wash down some nachos or a sandwich with a pint of Mello Glo ale, or while away an hour at the shuffleboard table. ♦ American ♦ Daily lunch and dinner. No credit cards. 316 11th St (between Harrison and Folsom Sts). 255.9455

59 Slim's Rocker Boz Scaggs is a part owner of this live music-and-dance club, which bills itself as the "home of roots music." Country, jazz, and blues musicians, some well known, some up-and-coming hopefuls, have played here, as has Scaggs himself. ♦ Cover. Daily to 2AM. 333 11th St (between Folsom and Harrison Sts). 621.3330

60 DNA Lounge Expect alternative music, pool, pinball, poetry readings, fashion shows, crazy parties, and lots of nose rings and purple hair. The dancing can get pretty frenzied, and behavior is not always up to Emily Post's standards. "IQ and ID required," says the doorman. ♦ Cover. Daily until 4AM. 375 11th St (at Harrison St). 626.1409

61 The Stud Rock, funk, oldies, New Wave, and world-beat music draw a crowd your mother might not approve of. There are some women, but the crowd is mostly male, mostly gay. ♦ Cover on some nights. M-Sa to 2AM. 399 Ninth St (at Harrison St). 863.6623

62 New Langton Arts This nonprofit gallery specializes in experimental and sometimes controversial works by American and international artists. ♦ W-Sa. 1246 Folsom St (between Eighth and Ninth Sts). 626.5416

62 Acorn Tea and Griddle ★★$$ The emphasis in this small, pleasant restaurant is on fresh, organically grown ingredients and artistic presentations. The basically California cuisine has definite French and Italian influences, and every menu includes a number of vegetarian offerings. Portions are generous, and the bread is out of this world. ♦ California ♦ Tu-F lunch, afternoon tea, and dinner; Sa brunch and dinner; Su brunch. Reservations recommended. 1256 Folsom St (between Eighth and Ninth Sts). 863.2469

Post Office and U.S. Court of Appeals Building

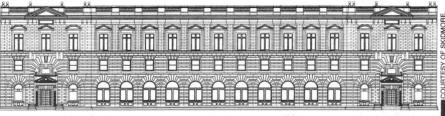

COURTESY OF SKIDMORE, OWINGS & MERRILL

THE HALF SHELL

63 **The Half Shell Restaurant and Oyster Bar** ★★$$ Hidden away in a narrow alley between warehouses and art studios, this handsome, very California dining space was created with lots of redwood, clay-tile flooring, and glass. The fare is almost exclusively seafood. There are specials served almost every night here: Monday and Saturday are Maine lobster nights; Tuesday it's oysters and ale; Wednesday it's "steamer" night (Anchor Steam beer and clams or mussels); and Thursday is crab night. Happy hour is from 5PM to 7PM. ◆ Seafood ◆ M-F lunch and dinner; Sa dinner. 64 Rausch St (between Seventh and Eighth Sts). 552.7677

64 **Julie's Supper Club** ★$$ Deliberately funky retro decor, heavy on 1950s icons that might have come from a pine-paneled rec room of that era, attracts an upwardly mobile crowd of singles to this noisy restaurant and bar with a courtyard. The food aims to be interesting, but isn't. ◆ American ◆ M-Sa dinner. Reservations recommended. 1123 Folsom St (at Seventh St). 861.0707

65 **Brain Wash** ★$ This combination laundromat and cafe makes great sense for busy singles who want to accomplish something while they socialize. The 49-seat cafe, separated from the washers and dryers, offers simple foods such as sandwiches, pasta, and chili. The last call for dryers is 9:30PM, but the merriment continues for another hour and a half in the cafe. ◆ California ◆ Daily. 1122 Folsom St (at Seventh St). Cafe 861.3663; laundromat 431.WASH

66 **Post Office and U.S. Court of Appeals Building** This Neo-Classical federal building (pictured above) boasts a stone-clad facade and a fine marble-faced postal lobby. The 1905 structure by **James Knox Taylor** sustained serious damage in the 1989 earthquake and is undergoing major rehabilitation to restore its courtrooms and corridors to their original splendor and to strengthen the foundation. The architectural firm **Skidmore, Owings & Merrill** is currently rehabilitating the building. ◆ Seventh St (at Mission St)

67 **Woodwind & Brass Workshop** They buy, sell, and repair woodwind and brass musical instruments here. ◆ M-Sa. 127 10th St (at Mission St). 864.2440

68 **Camerawork** This nonprofit gallery is devoted to photography and related visual media such as video, film, and books by artists. ◆ Tu-Sa. 70 12th St (between Mission and Market Sts). 621.1001

68 **La Mamelle** On the third floor of the same building, this alternative space is active in video distribution, maintains video archives, and distributes a monthly magazine—*Art Com*—by computer network. The video-viewing room is open by appointment. ◆ M-F. 70 12th St (between Mission and Market Sts). 431.7524

69 **Bell'occhio** All kinds of things you never knew you needed but suddenly can't live without, such as imported ribbons, nosegay frills, sachets, quills, inks, candles, and antique jewelry—mostly European—are here to tempt you. ◆ Tu-Su. 8 Brady St (off Market St, between 12th and Gough Sts). 864.4048

70 **It's Tops Coffee Shop** ★$ Breakfast or lunch at this family-run enterprise is like a trip down memory lane. The 1940s influence is everywhere. ◆ American ◆ Daily breakfast and lunch. 1801 Market St (at McCoppin St). 431.6395

70 **Limelight** This bookstore specializes in film and theater books. ◆ M-Su. 1803 Market St (at McCoppin St). 864.2265

In the 1970s Patty Hearst was held prisoner by the Symbionese Liberation Army in the building that now houses Julie's Supper Club.

Restaurants/Clubs: Red   **Hotels:** Blue
Shops/ 🌳 Outdoors: Green   **Sights/Culture:** Black

Union Square

San Francisco's most famous shopping district is the nearest thing to a crossroads you'll find in the city. Union Square, the park for which the area is named, is filled with chess players, trysting lovers, panhandlers, brown-baggers tanning when the sun is out, soapbox orators of every political and religious persuasion, many beautiful flowers, and flocks of greedy pigeons. On bordering streets are most of the legendary chic shops, including **Tiffany**, **Hermès**, and **Cartier**, that lure browsers and buyers. It's all here, from the sublime to the sleazy—whether you want high-fashion clothing, an inexpensive souvenir, jewelry, perfume, books, household items, antiques, Oriental rugs, or art.

Musicians, some of outstanding caliber, enliven the area. Many, in fact, play professionally in the evening and use their street time for practice and pocket money. There are street artists with a wide range of talents as well. Adding to the local color, both literally and figuratively, are the curbside flower stands selling whatever blooms are in season for a bit less than the florists. The

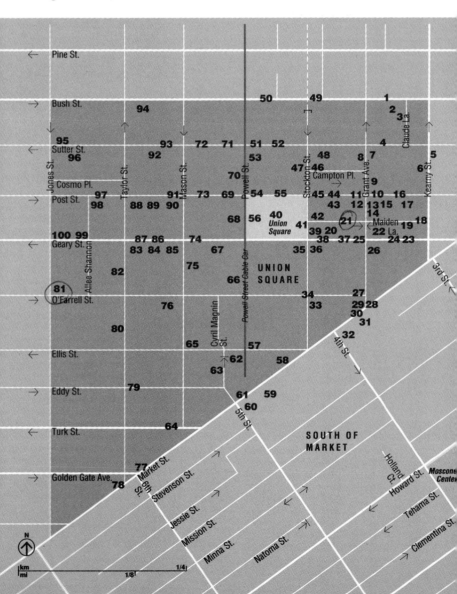

flower stands owe their beginning to civic leader and publisher Michael de Young, who in the late 1800s allowed the vendors—usually youngsters of Italian, Belgian, Irish, or Armenian descent—to sell their flowers in front of the de Young building and protected them from the police. They were licensed in 1904, and, as with the cable cars, any attempt to suppress the stands has been halted by a sympathetic public.

Maiden Lane is an elegant, tree-lined alley that extends two blocks east of Union Square from **Stockton** to **Kearny Streets.** Once known as **Morton Street** and considered a disreputable area, it now features exclusive shops and restaurants.

Area code 415 unless otherwise noted.

1 Harcourt's Modern and Contemporary Art This gallery is housed in a handsome old firehouse that's been completely remodeled. ♦ Tu-Sa. 460 Bush St (between Grant Ave and Claude La). 421.3428

2 Le Central ★$$$ Regularly patronized by Speaker of the House Willie Brown and *San Francisco Chronicle* columnist Herb Caen, this place turns out hearty, tasty fare. There are, however, more exciting French restaurants nearby. ♦ French ♦ M-Sa lunch and dinner. 453 Bush St (between Grant Ave and Claude La). 391.2233

3 Café Claude ★★$ Tucked away in an alley, this small cafe will warm the heart of any Francophile. Utterly unpretentious, authentically French, and very popular, it features furnishings rescued from a Parisian bar and a small menu of soups and light entrées. ♦ French ♦ M-Sa breakfast, lunch, and dinner. 7 Claude La (between Grant Ave and Kearny St). 392.3505

4 Jeanne Marc Women who don't like to blend into the crowd will like the unique clothing carried here. A local husband-and-wife design team (she's Jeanne, he's Marc) is the creator of the colorful line. Their signature pieces are vibrantly patterned quilted jackets. ♦ M-Sa. 262 Sutter St (between Grant Ave and Kearny St). 362.1121

4 Braunstein/Quay Gallery This third-floor gallery shows contemporary sculpture, paintings, and works on paper. ♦ Tu-Sa. 250 Sutter St (between Grant Ave and Kearny St). 392.5532

4 871 Fine Arts Contemporary California artists are represented here. The fourth-floor gallery was at 871 Howard Street until earthquake damage in 1989 forced a move but not a change of name. ♦ Tu-Sa. 250 Sutter St (between Grant Ave and Kearny St). 543.5155

4 Cable Car Clothiers This is the home of the venerable clothing store specializing in traditional men's clothing. Some women's suits and sportswear are also sold here. ♦ M-F. 246 Sutter St (between Grant Ave and Kearny St). 397.4740

5 Brasserie Chambord ★★$$ This consistently good, fairly priced French restaurant has more zest in its cuisine than most. The service is attentive and the decor attractive. Imaginative specials feature fish, and fine wines are available by the glass. Adjoining is a small dining area called **Crêpe Escape,** which serves coffee, croissants, and modest lunches from 9:30AM to 3PM. ♦ M-Sa breakfast, lunch, and dinner; Su breakfast. Reservations required. 152 Kearny St (at Sutter St). 434.3688

6 Sherman Clay After spending years here repairing music boxes, Leander S. Sherman bought out his employer in 1870 and founded this piano store. ♦ M-Sa. 141 Kearny St (between Sutter and Post Sts). 781.6000

7 Banana Republic This specialty chain of shops offers safari-style clothing in a fantasy atmosphere that's a lot more comfortable than any jungle. ♦ Daily. 256 Grant Ave (at Sutter St). 788.3087

8 Teuscher of Switzerland Expensive and delectable Swiss chocolates will tempt the most discriminating sweet tooth. ♦ M-Sa. 255 Grant Ave (between Sutter St and Campton Pl). 398.2700

8 Jasmin Although some find the attitude too snooty, others swear by this boutique, which sells costly European designer fashions. ♦ By appointment only. 253 Grant Ave (between Sutter St and Campton Pl). 433.5550

8 Erika Meyerovich Gallery The biggest names in the art world—including Pablo Picasso, Henri Matisse, Marc Chagall, David Hockney, Frank Stella, and Andy Warhol—are shown by this sleek gallery owned by Russian émigrés. The work is showcased on two floors plus a mezzanine. ♦ Daily. 231 Grant Ave (between Sutter St and Campton Pl). 421.9997

9 228 Grant Avenue Prominent galleries of contemporary art are housed in this nondescript building. The prestigious **John Berggruen Gallery** occupies three floors and handles some of the most celebrated names in American art. ♦ M-Sa. Between Post and Sutter Sts. 781-4629

Malm

9 Malm Established by a leather craftsman who arrived in San Francisco in 1856, this is one of the city's oldest businesses. It's still operated by the same family, which caters to the carriage trade with fine luggage and travel accessories. ♦ Daily. 222 Grant Ave (between Post and Sutter Sts). 392.0417. Also at: The Galleria at Crocker Center (Montgomery St at Kearny St). 391.5222; Strawberry Village, Mill Valley. 383.8060

10 The Candy Jar Chocoholics will find an instant fix here. ♦ M-Sa. 210 Grant Ave (between Post and Sutter Sts). 391.5508

10 Tom Wing & Sons Jade and pearls are the specialty at this fine jewelry shop. ♦ M-Sa. 208 Grant Ave (at Post St). 391.2500

10 Coach Leather This chain store offers a wide variety of sturdy leather bags and accessories. ♦ M-Sa. 190 Post St (at Grant Ave). 392.1772

11 Shreve & Co. Established in 1862, this is the oldest retailer in San Francisco. It moved to this elegant location just before the 1906 earthquake and obviously survived the jolt. Fine jewelry, crystal, and silver are showcased in a setting suffused with grand architectural touches from a bygone era, such as the impressive green-marble columns. ♦ M-Sa. 200 Post St (at Grant Ave). 421.2600

12 Brooks Brothers Classic clothes for men and women are purveyed at this refined haberdashery. ♦ Daily. 201 Post St (at Grant Ave). 397.4500

13 Light Opera Gallery This leading source of Russian lacquerware is patronized by serious collectors from around the world. ♦ M-Sa. 174 Grant Ave (between Maiden La and Post St). 956.9866

14 Christofle Merchandise from the Paris-based silversmiths (purveyors to the courts of Louis Philippe and Napoléon III) is offered for those with a taste for fine things. ♦ M-Sa. 140 Grant Ave (at Maiden La). 399.1931

In deference to the ladies of an earlier age who wore white gloves, the Westin St. Francis Hotel used to polish all of its change daily.

15 Max Mara Prices are steep here at the first US retail store opened by this Italian manufacturer of high-quality women's clothing. But fashionables swear the values are terrific when compared with other big names in the garment business. ♦ M-Sa. 177 Post St (between Grant Ave and Kearny St). 981.0900

16 Williams-Sonoma Epicures flock to the fabulous flagship store of this purveyor of top-quality cookware, domestic giftware, and gourmet foods. ♦ Daily. 150 Post St (between Grant Ave and Kearny St). 362.6904. Also at: 2 Embarcadero Center (at Clay and Sacramento Sts). 421.2033

17 Gump's S. G. Gump & Company was founded in 1865 by German immigrants and former linen merchants, and is now world-famous for jade and pearls, Asian treasures, and the largest collection in the country of fine china and crystal, including such prestigious names as Baccarat, Steuben, and Lalique. Many brides and grooms register here. The window displays are always worth a look. ♦ M-Sa. 135 Post St (between Grant Ave and Kearny St). 982.1616

18 Brooks Cameras In business for more than 50 years, this firm housed in a multistory building deals in new and used cameras and does video transfers and camera repairs. A visitor information desk is on the mezzanine level. The third floor includes a small photography museum and usually displays works by local photographic talents. ♦ M-Sa. 45 Kearny St (at Maiden La). 392.1900

18 Orientations Lovely Oriental furniture and interior design pieces are available at this gallery. ♦ M-Sa. 34 Maiden La (at Kearny St). 981.3972

19 Maiden Lane When this exclusive lane was known as Morton Street, it enjoyed a less-than-chic reputation. Until the 1906 fire cleaned out the cribs, prostitutes sat at open windows and solicited passersby, and there was an average of two murders a week. Gradually, shops took the place of bordellos, and as entrepreneurs struggled to change their street's image, Morton was changed to Maiden in the hopes of sparking a new era—and it has. Except for the occasional delivery truck, today it is a pedestrian-only way lined with fashionable boutiques. On nice days, tables are set out in front of the **Nosheria** (page 35) and other luncheonettes for alfresco dining. ♦ Between Stockton and Kearny Sts

20 Chanel One of Maiden Lane's most elegant and exquisite boutiques has three floors of women's clothing and cosmetics by the famous French design house. Some men's accessories are sold here as well. ♦ Daily. 155 Maiden La (between Stockton St and Grant Ave). 981.1550

20 Yosh Those who cannot do without the latest *do* come here to be coiffed. ◆ Tu-Sa. 173 Maiden La (between Stockton St and Grant Ave). 989.7704

20 Mocca ★★$$$ Tasty, albeit overpriced, fare is served at this charcuterie and cafe offering alfresco dining. ◆ California ◆ M-Sa breakfast and lunch. 175 Maiden La (between Stockton St and Grant Ave). 956.1188

21 Conacher Galleries Realism by contemporary American artists is the specialty here. ◆ M-Sa. 134 Maiden La (between Stockton St and Grant Ave). 392.5447

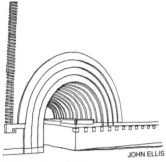

JOHN ELLIS

21 Circle Gallery Building This exquisite building (illustrated above) designed by **Frank Lloyd Wright** in 1948 contains a spiral ramp leading to the upper floor and was one of the prototypes for the architect's Guggenheim Museum in New York City. The exterior is faced with brickwork and has a superbly detailed archway at the opening. The gallery features contemporary artworks. ◆ M-Sa. 140 Maiden La (between Stockton St and Grant Ave). 989.2100

22 77 Maiden Lane Seventeen hairstylists at this chic, well-patronized salon can provide virtually any kind of look their customers want. ◆ M-Sa. Near Grant Ave. 391.7777

22 Nosheria ★$$ Oversize sandwiches, salads, and espresso draw regulars to this unpretentious cafeteria with alfresco dining. ◆ M-Sa breakfast and lunch. 69 Maiden La (near Grant Ave). 398.3557

23 Gallery Paule Anglim Celebrated contemporary American artists as well as emerging artists are showcased. ◆ Tu-Sa. 14 Geary St (between Grant Ave and Kearny St). 433.2710

Restaurants/Clubs: Red   **Hotels:** Blue
Shops/ 🌳 Outdoors: Green   **Sights/Culture:** Black

24 Anthony Shoe Service Established in 1904, this is the most comprehensive shoe-repair service to be found in San Francisco. ◆ M-Sa. 30 Geary St (between Grant Ave and Kearny St). 781.1338

25 Crate & Barrel You'll find great values in well-designed contemporary glassware, dishes, and gifts for the home. ◆ Daily. 125 Grant Ave (at Geary St). 986.4000

26 Fraenkel Gallery This gallery exhibits 19th- and 20th-century fine photography exclusively, including the work of Diane Arbus, Garry Winogrand, Carleton E. Watkins, and Edward Weston. ◆ Tu-Sa. 49 Geary St (at Grant Ave), Fourth floor. 981.2661

27 Eileen West Gifts, linens, sleepwear, and a line of beautiful dresses by this San Francisco designer with national distribution are sold here. ◆ M-Sa. 33 Grant Ave (between O'Farrell and Geary Sts). 982.2275

27 Contemporary Realist Gallery This sixth-floor gallery displays modern American paintings and sculpture. ◆ Tu-Sa. 23 Grant Ave (at O'Farrell St). 362.7152

27 Overland Sheepskin Fleece-lined sheepskin and leather clothing for men and women is stocked in a shop made to look like a set from a Western movie. ◆ Daily. 21 Grant Ave (at O'Farrell St). 296.9180

28 Wells Fargo Bank Building **Clinton Day**'s Beaux Arts design presents a gently curved facade on Market Street. The building complements its classical neighbor, the former Security Pacific Bank across the street (now the **Emporio Armani Boutique**). ◆ 744 Market St (at Grant Ave)

29 Emporio Armani Boutique This opulent mini-emporium is the product of a multimillion-dollar renovation of the former Security Pacific Bank, built in 1911 and designed by **Bliss & Faville.** The result is breathtaking—racks of beautiful clothes surrounding a beautiful cafe staffed by an army of beautiful people. Browse among the formal and informal men's and women's wear, children's clothes, luggage, shoes, and gifts. Then, if you're hungry (and if you have any money left), ask for a table on the terrace overlooking the boutique and order the pasta *puttanesca* (spicy tomato-and-olive sauce). ◆ 1 Grant Ave (between Market and O'Farrell Sts). 677.9400

30 Phelan Building One of San Francisco's best flatiron buildings, designed by **William**

Curlett and built in 1908, this cream-colored, terra-cotta-clad building may have been the inspiration for more recent flatirons, such as the one at **388 Market Street.** ◆ 760 Market St (at Grant Ave)

31 Marriott Hotel $$$$ This controversial hotel close to the **Moscone Convention Center** went up in 1989 amid considerable architectural acrimony. Critics lambasted **Anthony J. Lumsden**'s design, comparing its 40 stories to a jukebox. The hotel opened unexpectedly early when the October 1989 earthquake struck. It sprang into use as an emergency shelter, thereby muting some critical voices. The imposing structure has 1,500 rooms and suites, an indoor swimming pool, a spa and health club, a 40,000-square-foot ballroom, and more than 85,000 square feet of meeting and exhibition space. Food and beverage facilities include the **Kinoko Japanese Restaurant,** the **Garden Terrace,** the **Fourth Street Oyster Bar and Deli,** the **Atrium Lobby Lounge,** and the **View Lounge** on the 40th floor. ◆ 777 Market St (at Grant Ave). 896.1600, 800/228.9290; fax 896.6176

32 Humbolt Savings Bank Building This 1906 Beaux-Arts-style skyscraper with baroque ornament, designed by **Meyer & O'Brien Architects,** was under construction at the time of the massive 1906 earthquake. Although the building suffered relatively little damage, the architects took a second look at the design and decided to rebuild the narrow-fronted tower entirely. The current building replaced a Victorian structure on the same site; thus, the date 1869 is prominently displayed on the front of the bank as a tribute to the year the first structure was erected. ◆ 783 Market St (at Fourth St)

33 F.A.O. Schwarz This three-story branch of the world-famous toy emporium has a live red-coated soldier on duty at the front door to enchant pedestrians of all ages. Don't miss touring the store during the holiday season in November and December—the place puts on quite a display for kids of all ages. ◆ Daily. 48 Stockton St (at O'Farrell St). 394.8700

34 Macy's A wide variety of merchandise, mostly in the middle-to-high price range, can be found in two buildings across the street from each other. The store that extends to Union Square includes mini-boutiques of designer fashions for women, cosmetics, and home furnishings. The other structure focuses on menswear, children's clothing, and electronics, and includes both the **Plum Express,** a cafeteria for fast meals, and the **Plum Restaurant,** a handsome Art Deco expression in glass, chrome, and gray-flannel walls, favored for more leisurely dining. ◆ Daily. 170 O'Farrell St (at Stockton St). 397.3333

35 I.Magnin & Co. This white-marble building on the south side of Union Square is the city's finest department store for expensive—if a little staid—fashions and accessories. It has probably the poshest ladies' powder room in town, all mirrors, gilt, and green marble. ◆ Daily. 135 Stockton St (at Geary St). 362.2100

Within I. Magnin & Co.:

Narsai's at I. Magnin ★★$$ Narsai David, the well-known culinary authority, opened this basement take-out charcuterie and small restaurant to give San Franciscans a chance to sample his pâtés, croissants, and other delicacies. While not cheap, they're very good. ◆ French ◆ Daily lunch. 362.2100

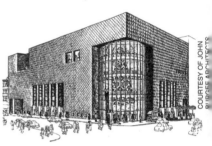

COURTESY OF JOHN BURGEE ARCHITECTS

36 Neiman Marcus Philip Johnson and **John Burgee's** architecturally underwhelming design—both inside and out—has provoked heated debate among San Franciscans since it was built in 1982. Many opposed the destruction of the **City of Paris,** a popular store occupying the site since 1896. A compromise stipulated that the building (pictured above) should incorporate the enormous glass dome that surmounted the old store. At Yuletide, the store erects the most dramatic Christmas tree in the city. ◆ Daily. 150 Stockton St (at Geary St). 362.3900

Within Neiman Marcus:

The Rotunda ★$$ This comfortable luncheon restaurant beneath the store's historic stained-glass dome has lots of cushioned booths that make it easy to have truly private conversations. Customers can't seem to get enough of the popovers and fruit-flavored whipped butter that come with every meal. ◆ California ◆ Daily lunch. Reservations recommended. 362.4777

37 Bottega Veneta Handmade and pricey leather bags and shoes, scarves, ties, and luggage are available from this famed Italian manufacturer. ◆ M-Sa. 108 Geary St (between Stockton St and Grant Ave). 981.1700

Frank Lloyd Wright designed the Circle Gallery Building at 140 Maiden Lane in Union Square. It served as one of the prototypes for his design of the grand Guggenheim Museum in New York.

N·Peal

37 N. Peal Cashmere This shop is cashmere heaven for men and women and includes one of the largest selections of cashmere socks in the world. ♦ M-Sa. 110 Geary St (between Stockton St and Grant Ave). 421.2713

38 Britex Fabrics Everything for the seamstress and tailor is offered at this huge store, from exquisite designer fabrics and notions to a whole floor filled with drastically reduced remnants. ♦ M-Sa. 146 Geary St (between Stockton St and Grant Ave). 392.2910

38 Paul Bauer Fine china and crystal, mostly from Germany (including Meissen, KPM Royal Berlin, and Rosenthal), are sold in this elegantly appointed shop. ♦ M-Sa. 156 Geary St (between Stockton St and Grant Ave). 421.6862

38 Joan & David Fine footwear for men and women, handbags, and accessories are sold in a dramatic chrome-and-black environment. ♦ Daily. 172 Geary St (between Stockton St and Grant Ave). 397.1958

38 Kris Kelly Giftware and romantic linens with lots of lace and cutwork are sold on all three levels of this lovely shop, fragrant with potpourri. ♦ M-Sa. 174 Geary St (between Stockton St and Grant Ave). 986.8822

38 North Beach Leather The trendy, costly leather clothing for men and women sold here is designed by Michael Hoban, one of the firm's partners. ♦ Daily. 190 Geary St (between Stockton St and Grant Ave). 362.8300. Also at: Fisherman's Wharf (at Beach St and Columbus Ave). 441.3208

39 Gucci The expanse of brass, marble, and fine woodwork at this world-renowned retailer creates a luxurious environment for those with lots of money to spend on clothes, leather goods, and accessories. Unlike the personnel at other **Gucci** boutiques in this country, the staff here is cordial, even friendly. ♦ Daily. 200 Stockton St (across from Union Sq). 392.2808

The Four Seasons Clift Hotel, one of San Francisco's deluxe hostelries, charged only $2 per night when it opened its doors in 1915. When the rates went up to $6 a few years later, it was considered outrageous. After Prohibition ended in 1933, the hotel added the beautiful Redwood Room, one of the most handsome drinking lounges in town.

39 Hermès of Paris The prices are heart-stopping at this internationally based boutique, where finesse and quality reign supreme in leather goods, scarves, gloves, ties, and clothing for men and women. It is also one of the few places in town where equestrians can purchase a saddle. ♦ Daily. 1 Union Sq (at Stockton St). 391.7200

39 Town & Country Club A discreet plaque identifies this exclusive women's club (open to members only), whose members are drawn from the city's Old Guard. ♦ 218 Stockton St (across from Union Sq)

40 Union Square Since 1850, this plaza (pictured on page 39) has been the heart of downtown San Francisco. The 2.6-acre park, filled with flowers, trees, box hedges, benches, and crisscrossing paths, is in the midst of the city's most bustling shopping area. Its name commemorates a Civil War rally during which demonstrators pledged their loyalty to the Union. A granite shaft celebrating the victory of Admiral Dewey's fleet at Manila Bay during the Spanish-American War marks the center of the square. The face of the bronze statue of *Victory* atop the monument was modeled after a well-known San Francisco benefactor, Mrs. Adolph de Bretteville Spreckels. ♦ Bounded by Stockton and Powell Sts, and Geary and Post Sts

41 San Francisco Ticket Box Office Service Nicknamed STBS (which is pronounced "stubs" by the locals), this nonprofit facility offers half-price tickets (plus a nominal service charge) on the day of the performance to selected cultural events. Also offered are full-price advance tickets, BASS (Bay Area Seating Service) tickets to events throughout the region, and **MUNI** bus passes. ♦ Tu-Sa. Stockton St (at Union Sq, between Post and Geary Sts). 433.STBS

42 Bally of Switzerland This upscale manufacturer sells footwear, leather goods, and clothing for men and women. ♦ Daily. 238 Stockton St (across from Union Sq). 398.7463

43 Allrich Gallery Contemporary paintings, tapestries, works on paper, museum-quality crafts, and sculpture, predominantly by California artists, are sold at this fourth-floor gallery. ♦ Tu-Sa. 251 Post St (between Stockton St and Grant Ave). 398.8896

43 Cartier The jewelry, watches, and other trinkets from this renowned French firm are for those who don't have to look at price tags. ♦ M-Sa. 231 Post St (between Stockton St and Grant Ave). 397.3180

44 Jaeger Fine woolen sportswear imported from England is stocked in this store. ♦ M-Sa. 272 Post St (between Stockton St and Grant Ave). 421.3714

45 Alfred Dunhill of London Famous for its pipes, cigars, humidors, and lighters, this firm sells leather goods as well. ♦ Daily. 290 Post St (at Stockton St). 781.3368

45 Waterford/Wedgwood The most complete collection of the namesake Irish and British imports in the US may be found here. ♦ Daily. 304 Stockton St (at Post St). 391.5610

45 Scheuer Linens Established in 1949 and run by three generations of the Scheuer family, this carriage-trade shop specializes in monogramming and traditional bed, bath, and table linens. The European collection is perhaps the largest in the West. ♦ M-Sa. 318 Stockton St (at Post St). 392.2813

46 Campton Place $$$$ This small and luxurious hotel a half block from Union Square used to be the **Old Drake Wilshire.** Although the ambience and decor are stunning, it is the service and extra touches usually found only in Europe's top hotels that the staff likes to emphasize. Professional valets pack and unpack for you, a French laundry and dry-cleaning service is available in-house, secretarial assistance is immediate, shoes are shined every night, and each of the 136 rooms contains a desk and fresh flowers. Corner suites are cozy. Tea is served daily from 2:30PM to 4:30PM in the bar. ♦ 340 Stockton St (at Campton Pl). 781.5555, 800/647.4007 in CA, 800/426.3135; fax 955.8536

Within Campton Place:

Campton Place Dining Room ★★★$$$$ The hotel's dining room is the epitome of conservative elegance: quiet, understated, and comfortable. Head chef Todd Humphries presents familiar dishes in interesting new ways. The result is gourmet California cuisine. Recommended are the roasted rack of lamb with chanterelle mushrooms, Walla Walla onions, and cranberry beans, and the pan-roasted salmon with couscous and pink lentils. Breakfasts are extra special. ♦ California ♦ Daily breakfast, lunch, and dinner. Reservations recommended. 955.5555

COURTESY OF CHARLES DINIZ

47 Grand Hyatt Hotel $$$$ Rising 36 stories above Union Square, this 693-room hotel (pictured above) is in the heart of the city and offers extensive services for business travelers, including language translation, business-equipment rental, and shipping and mailing, plus all the latest news on business and investor services. Within the hotel are the elegant **Plaza Restaurant,** crowned with a stained-glass dome, which operates as a California-style cafe on a grand scale; **Nappers,** a popular plaza-level deli; the **Grand Plaza Lounge;** a health club; and **Club 36,** a rooftop jazz club with a breathtaking view. The **Regency Club** comprises floors set aside for guests who pay a surcharge. These smartly decorated rooms include honor bars, concierge services, and complimentary breakfasts. There are also six penthouse suites serviced by trained butlers. ♦ 345 Stockton St (between Sutter St and Union Sq). 398.1234, 800/233.1234; fax 392.2536

On the Grand Hyatt Hotel Plaza:

Ruth Asawa Fountain Created by and named for the noted San Francisco artist, a bronze-relief frieze made up of 41 plaques covers the circular wall of the fountain bowl. Thousands of sculptured figures on the plaques charmingly depict different aspects of the city, from the swaying palms of **Mission Dolores** to Victorian houses with gingerbread trim. The plaques were modeled from bread dough before being cast in metal, expressing the artist's philosophy that art and everyday life are interrelated.

48 Jessica McClintock Romantic and fanciful garments by the San Francisco designer are set off perfectly in the boutique's exquisite postmodern ambience. ♦ Daily. 353 Sutter St (between Stockton St and Grant Ave). 397.0987

48 Wilkes Bashford Beautiful and expensive designer clothes for men and women are sold with disarming nonchalance. Music and wine are part of the seduction. The witty and surreal window displays are in a class by themselves. ♦ M-Sa. 375 Sutter St (between Stockton St and Grant Ave). 986.4380

Restaurants/Clubs: Red	**Hotels:** Blue
Shops/ ♣ Outdoors: Green	**Sights/Culture:** Black

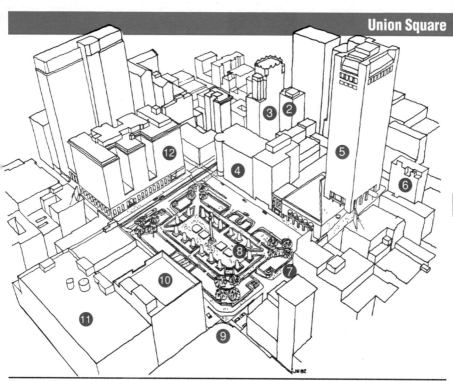

Union Square

1 Holiday Inn at Union Square
2 450 Sutter
3 Sir Francis Drake Hotel

4 Saks Fifith Avenue
5 Grand Hyatt Hotel
6 Campton Place

7 Maiden Lane
8 Union Square
9 Neiman Marcus

10 I. Magnin
11 Macy's
12 St. Francis Hotel

49 Hotel Juliana $$ This 89-year-old, 107-room hotel is perched at a convenient location on the borders of downtown, the Financial District, and Nob Hill. The decor is clever and colorful, making the building's modest proportions interesting. Rooms are appointed with comfortable and sophisticated touches. The full range of services includes continental breakfast, honor bars, room service, and limousine service, but not a restaurant. ♦ 590 Bush St (at Stockton St). 392.2540, 800/328.3880; fax 391.8447

50 Hotel Vintage Court $$ This charming European-style hotel is known mainly as the home of the popular restaurant **Masa's**. There is a refrigerator in each of the 106 rooms, complimentary wine every afternoon in the cozy lobby, and limousine service to the Financial District on weekday mornings. The location is convenient for shopping or gallery hopping. ♦ 650 Bush St (between Powell and Stockton Sts). 392.4666, 800/654.1100; fax 392.4666

Within the Hotel Vintage Court:

Masa's ★★★★$$$$ Stately and impeccable, this establishment is world-renowned as San Francisco's finest French restaurant. Chef Julian Serrano follows in the footsteps of founder Masa Kobayashi, presenting innovative gourmet fare with organically grown vegetables, all exquisitely arranged. The desserts are as delicious as they are beautiful. Book a table well in advance. ♦ French ♦ Tu-Sa dinner. Reservations recommended. 989.7154

51 Holiday Inn at Union Square $$$ One block from the square, this 400-room hotel, which recently underwent a $9-million renovation, offers an ideal location as well as fabulous views of the city. The unique **S. Holmes Esq. Public House and Drinking Salon** features a Victorian atmosphere and a 30th-floor lookout over San Francisco. ♦ 480 Sutter St (at Powell St). 398.8900, 800/465.4329; fax 989.8823

52 450 Sutter Street Office Building This medical/dental office building clad in undulating terra-cotta was designed by **Timothy Pflueger** and built in 1930. It is a good example of Art Deco architecture. Notice the elaborately designed entrance lobby with its pre-Columbian styling. ♦ Between Stockton and Powell Sts

A magazine editor who was a frequent guest at the Four Seasons Clift Hotel always stayed in the same room with his Irish setter, Tuscarora Red. The dog learned how to use the elevator, and every morning would go down to the lobby to fetch a newspaper for his master.

53 Sir Francis Drake Hotel $$$ To preserve some of the flair of its namesake, this newly renovated hotel keeps its doorman in full yeoman-of-the-guard attire. The lobby, with its murals, crystal chandeliers, mirrors, sweeping marble staircase with bronze balustrade, and vaulted gold-leaf ceiling, reflects the splendor and romance of the 1930s. Because it is small by the standard of many of its neighbors (435 rooms and suites), it is able to integrate the luxurious advantages of a larger hotel with a more personal approach to hospitality. For the business traveler, there are special rooms available with a desk and seating area for interviews or briefings. **Scala's** restaurant offers Italian fare. ♦ 450 Powell St (at Sutter St). 392.7755, 800/227.5480; fax 391.8719

54 Saks Fifth Avenue **Hellmuth, Obata, and Kassabaum** designed this building in 1981. This upscale store has escalators that can drive shoppers to distraction, forcing them to walk halfway around the store on each floor to ascend or descend. Take the elevator if you're in a hurry. On the fifth floor is a pleasant, sunny restaurant with sometimes good, sometimes so-so food, popular with ladies-who-lunch. ♦ Daily. 384 Post St (at Union Sq). 986.4300

55 Tiffany & Co. Bluebloods come here for their blue-ribbon baubles. ♦ M-Sa. 350 Post St (at Union Sq). 781.7000

56 Gray Line Tours Tickets are sold here for local and out-of-city bus tours. Night tours of the city depart from this location, while day tours depart from 425 Mission Street. ♦ Tickets sold daily 8AM-7PM. Powell St side of Union Sq, across from the St. Francis Hotel front entrance. Look for the red double-decker bus. Schedule information 558.9400

57 Hotel Union Square $$ A haunt of Dashiell Hammett in the 1930s, this 131-room hotel has been remodeled into a modern hostelry with Art Deco influences. It includes a nonsmoking floor and a seafood bar and lounge called **The Mermaid.** ♦ 114 Powell St (between Ellis and O'Farrell Sts). 397.3000, 800/553.1900; fax 339.1874

58 John's Grill ★$$ Established in 1908 and much favored by businessmen, this place was immortalized by author Dashiell Hammett, who made it a hangout for his best-known fictional character, detective Sam Spade. The restaurant is a repository for Spade/Hammett lore. The dark-wood and brass decor is pure men's-club, and meals, such as Sam Spade's favorite pork chops with a baked potato, are hearty. Steak and seafood are the specialties. Many dishes display an Italian accent, though strictly speaking, the menu covers a broad range of culinary tastes. ♦ American/Italian ♦ M-Sa lunch and dinner; Su dinner. 63 Ellis St (between Powell and Stockton Sts). 986.0069

59 Emporium The largest general department store in San Francisco has everything from gourmet cookware and wine to a shoe-repair shop and a post office. The lower level offers a variety of fast-food and take-out counters. ♦ Daily. 835 Market St (between Fourth and Fifth Sts). 764.2222

60 San Francisco Shopping Centre Located across from the **Powell Street cable-car** turntable, this $140-million construction is one of the nation's few vertical shopping malls. It is anchored by **Nordstrom,** the beloved retailing giant that carries medium- to high-priced merchandise for men, women, and children, and is known for spoiling its customers with the best service in town. In-store facilities include four restaurants: **The Pub,** for light lunches in a British-inn atmosphere; the **Champagne Exchange,** which offers a nouvelle menu of caviar, wines, and champagne; the **Cafe Express,** a cafeteria; and the **City Centre Grill,** which serves California cuisine at cloth-topped tables and a counter. The wonderful, upscale **Nordstrom** beauty spa offers all kinds of glamorizing and relaxing services, from massage and facials to makeup redesign and leg waxing. (It does not, however, include hairdressing services.) Express elevators will take you directly to **Nordstrom.**

The **Centre** is a shopping paradise that offers a mix of 90 upscale trend-setting retailers, including **J. Crew, Ann Taylor,** and **Adrienne Vittadini.** It is also unique in its use of six Mitsubishi-made spiral and stacked escalators, which carry shoppers through a central oval-shaped atrium covered by a retractable skylight. There is direct access through the **MUNI** and **BART Powell Street** station, which opens onto the concourse level. In addition, valet parking is available daily. Less expensive parking can be found nearby at the block-long garage at Fifth and Mission Streets. In addition to **Nordstrom**'s restaurants, various food services are offered on the concourse level. ♦ Daily. 865 Market St (at Fifth St). 495.5656

61 Hallidie Plaza As part of the **BART**/Market Street Renewal Program, this downtown plaza was created in 1973 by **Mario Ciampi, Lawrence Halprin and Associates,** and **Carl-Warnecke and Associates.** The subway entrance allowed the design to take the form of a terraced amphitheater. Within is a busy office of the **Convention & Visitor's Bureau,** with a wealth of material for tourists provided free or for a nominal charge. Avoid the plaza after dark, as it's often overrun by unsavory characters. ♦ Daily. Between Powell and Market Sts. 391.2000; recordings about weekly events: English, 391.2001; French, 391.2003; German, 391.2004; Japanese, 391.2101; Spanish, 391.2122

62 Monticello Inn $$ Thomas Jefferson never slept here, but he might have felt at home in this country-colonial inn with 55 rooms and 36 suites. Complimentary breakfast and evening wine are included, as is morning limousine service to the Financial District. ♦ 127 Ellis St (between Powell and Cyril Magnin Sts). 392.8800, 800/669.7777; fax 398.2650

Within the Monticello Inn:

Abiquiu ★★$$ Formerly the Corona Bar & Grill, this recently remodeled restaurant draws a lively crowd for trendy, well-prepared southwestern fare. The menu changes daily but invariably includes fresh seafood and paella. Save room for the wonderful desserts. ♦ Southwestern ♦ M-Sa lunch and dinner; Su dinner. Reservations recommended. Entrance at 88 Cyril Magnin St (at Ellis St). 392.5500

63 Parc Fifty Five $$$ Part of the Park Lane group, this imposing 1,005-room hotel is the third-largest in town, and is mere footsteps from the **San Francisco Shopping Centre** and the **Powell Street cable-car** turntable. Facilities include a fitness center, two lounges, a business communications center, a **Concierge Club** level, and two restaurants. The intimate **Piazza Lounge** offers grand piano music and cocktail service. The hotel boasts a million-dollar art collection, including vases, custom-made mirrors, sculpture, weavings, and paintings that recall an elegant Italian Renaissance theme. A handsome pair of Italianate lions stand guard in the travertine-marble lobby. At the carriage entrance is a seven-panel bas-relief sculpture by San Francisco artist Ruth Asawa, chronicling San Francisco's past, present, and future. ♦ 55 Cyril Magnin St (between Eddy and Ellis Sts). 392.8000, 800/338.1338; fax 392.4734

Within the Parc Fifty Five:

The Veranda ★$$ Although the inspired garden setting, with its lovely pastel hues, thriving plants, urns, and fountain, delights the eye, the food isn't quite up to the environs. Still, this is an exceptionally pleasant place to

have lunch. Keeping things simple—ordering the very good hamburger, for example—will avoid disappointment. ♦ California ♦ Daily breakfast, lunch, and dinner. 392.8000

64 McDonald's Bookstore More than one million used and out-of-print books, magazines, and records in good and questionable taste are heaped throughout this overstuffed store, in business since 1926. Management correctly describes the place as "a dirty, poorly lit place for books" (spoofing the name of a popular bookstore on Opera Plaza in the Civic Center area). ♦ M-Sa. 48 Turk St (near Mason St). 673.2235

65 Hotel Nikko San Francisco $$$$ The luxurious expanse of white marble in the vast two-story lobby, punctuated by the lulling sound of water falling from a fountain, may remind some visitors of a mausoleum, but the management believes it calls forth a sense of serenity. Accommodations include 522 guest rooms, including 22 suites, and two authentic Japanese tatami suites. A fitness center, which the public may patronize, has the city's only glass-enclosed indoor pool. Other amenities are Japanese soaking tubs, the **Fountain Lobby Lounge,** and the **Nikko Lounge,** which is reserved for guests on floors 23 to 25. There are two restaurants: **Benkay,** which serves excellent and expensive Japanese food, and **Cafe 222,** for regional American fare. ♦ 222 Mason St (near Ellis St). 394.1111, 800/645.5687; fax 421.0455

66 Villa Florence $$ This is a princess of a hotel. Don't be put off by the grunginess of the block; it's still only a few yards away from Union Square. The lobby is pretty, with wood-burning fireplaces, murals of Florentine scenes, and fresh flowers abloom everywhere. The 180 bedrooms are gracious, with high ceilings and country-house chintz. Amenities include complimentary limousine service to the Financial District and coffeemakers and refrigerators in every room. ♦ 225 Powell St (between Geary and O'Farrell Sts). 397.7700, 800/553.4411; fax 397.1006

Within the Villa Florence:

Kuleto's ★★★$$ The owners were so grateful to **Pat Kuleto,** the architect who designed the exciting interior, that they named their restaurant after him. If you're alone for dinner, go to the rear, where you can sit at a counter and watch the chefs work in the huge open kitchen. Adjoining is another room with ficus trees illuminated by stained-glass windows overhead. Wonderful original pastas, spit-roasted meats and fowl, and daily fish selections make this place a favorite. ◆ Italian ◆ Daily breakfast, lunch, and dinner. Reservations recommended. 397.7720

67 Handlery Union Square $$ Some poetic license has gone into the naming of this 375-room hotel, which, strictly speaking, is near but not on Union Square. There is a heated outdoor pool and a multilingual staff. Traditional Italian-style food, as interpreted in San Francisco, is served in **New Joe's Restaurant.** There is also a cocktail lounge. ◆ 351 Geary St (between Powell and Mason Sts). 781.7800, 800/843.4343; fax 781.0269

Caen and Coffee

For more than half a century, the *San Francisco Chronicle*'s Herb Caen has been the city's premier columnist, something between court jester, conscience, and camp counselor to a town where the only fad that never changes is a love of fads. Caen is the expert on the city's finest offerings and most titillating gossip. Some feel that to be a true San Franciscan, you need a morning dose of Caen to open your eyes as badly as you need that first cup of coffee.

His columns are an upbeat blend of news, gossip, vignettes, and thought-provoking dramas, spiced with random schmaltz and an occasional thorn in the side of those in power—proof that if a picture is worth a thousand words, the opposite can also be true. He is a wit and a wordsmith, and is one of the most quoted columnists in *Reader's Digest.*

Caen started writing for his high-school newspaper in Sacramento before landing a piece in the *Sacramento Union.* He served as a radio columnist for the *Chronicle* before radio and newspaper parted ways. On 5 July 1938 he wrote his first column on San Francisco—and was heartily adopted as a native son. The prolific reporter has written a number of books as well, mostly wry reflections on life in the City by the Bay.

Early film star Al Jolson died at the Westin St. Francis Hotel while playing poker.

Restaurants/Clubs: Red
Shops/ 🌳 **Outdoors:** Green

Hotels: Blue
Sights/Culture: Black

68 Westin St. Francis Hotel $$$$ The second-oldest hotel in the city, this has been a focal point for the social conditions and events in San Francisco's history for many years. Royalty, political leaders, literati, and theatrical stars have all made it their headquarters. The hotel was built in 1904 by Charles T. Crocker and his friends to cope with what they felt were inadequate accommodations for the new class of bonanza kings and their entourages. Much effort was made to initiate new ideas for better service: electric grills that cooked a steak in five minutes, perambulators that brought food to the tables, a pneumatic tube that sent service orders to the dining room instantly, and pipes that dumped ocean water into the Turkish baths. After severe earthquake damage in 1906, the reconstructed hotel was so successful that an addition brought the room total to 750, making it the largest hotel on the Pacific coast. Presently, the hotel has 1,200 rooms and a **Grand Ballroom** that can handle 1,500 revelers, plus seven restaurants. Outdoor glass elevators have been added; they offer a stunning view of the city at a spritely 1,000 feet per minute. ◆ 335 Powell St (at Union Sq). 397.7000, 800/228.3000; fax 774.0200

Within the Westin St. Francis Hotel:

Hastings This clothing store caters to the conservative businessperson. ◆ Daily. 393.8912

MCM The hand-crafted, non-leather luggage, handbags, and accessories offered here are imported from Munich. ◆ M-Sa. 989.0626

Victor's ★★$$$ This restaurant takes its name from the hotel's famous chef, who cooked for two decades after the 1906 earthquake. It's at the top of the tower, where you get a glorious view as you eat. The most famous dish is the legendary Celery Victor (braised celery hearts marinated in a vinaigrette dressing, and served with bay shrimp). ◆ California ◆ M-Sa dinner; Su brunch and dinner. Reservations and jacket required. 956.7777

Oz An adult fantasyland with a 32nd-floor view, this sumptuously decorated dance lounge rocks nightly. ◆ Cover. Daily until 2AM. 397.7000

Compass Rose ★★$$ Adjoining the lobby is this luxurious room with wonderfully eclectic decor, including many splashy-looking antiques. Lunch and high tea are served Monday through Saturday, but the real thrill for sensualists is the caviar and champagne provided against a background of live music in the evening. Legend has it that Ernest Hemingway persuaded Ingrid Bergman to star in the film version of *For Whom the Bell Tolls* over lunch here in 1943. ◆ M-Sa lunch, tea, and dinner; Su dinner. Reservations recommended. 774.0167

St. Francis Grill ★★$$$ Fresh seafood and grilled meats are served in a handsome oak-paneled dining room. ♦ Tu-Sa dinner. Reservations recommended. 774.0233

69 The Inn at Union Square $$ This European-style hotel with excellent personal service offers complimentary afternoon tea, wine, and hors d'oeuvres (but no restaurant). There are 30 rooms and suites, all individually decorated with an emphasis on a cozy English-country look, and all equipped with minibars. The concierges have a good inside track on the city. ♦ 440 Post St (between Mason and Powell Sts). 397.3510, 800/AT.THE.INN

70 Chancellor Hotel $$ A fixture on Union Square since 1914, this hotel has an intact Edwardian exterior, which is both solid and soundproofed. Its 140 rooms are fresh and contemporary. The Art Deco **Clipper Ship** lounge—once a popular meeting place for World War II servicemen—has been carefully restored to serve as a party and meeting room. It still contains an 85-foot aerial-photo mural of San Francisco from 1935. Rates, always a bargain for those in the know, have not changed much and are definitely moderate for this prime location. The members of the staff treat their longtime guests with personal interest, even sending birthday cards to some of those who have stayed here. No wonder they are now entertaining the grandchildren of some of the original guests. There's a restaurant, and room service is also available. ♦ 433 Powell St (between Post and Sutter Sts). 362.2004, 800/428.4748; fax 362.1403

71 Pasquale Iannetti, Inc. An extensive collection of prints by old masters up through the 20th century, including Goya, Daumier, Picasso, Miró, and Klee, is housed in this gallery. It also presents changing exhibitions of graphic art. ♦ M-Sa. 522 Sutter St (between Powell and Mason Sts). 433.2771

71 Cartwright Hotel $$ This is yet another downtown hotel that has been redone and prides itself on personal touches. The lobby incorporates large arched windows, giant plants, Oriental rugs, and comfortable seating and reading areas. The rooms are homey, each decorated with antiques and vases of fresh flowers. A continental breakfast is available for a modest price. Complimentary afternoon tea and cakes are served. **Teddy's** restaurant serves a full breakfast. ♦ 524 Sutter St (between Powell and Mason Sts). 421.2865, 800/227.3844; fax 421.2865

The Orchard
SAN FRANCISCO

72 The Orchard $$ A full-service European-style hotel in a gracious building dating back to 1907, this hostelry offers a high standard of personalized service. The 96 elegant rooms are equipped with private baths, direct-dial telephones, and minibars. Room service and special secretarial assistance are available around the clock. And it's located just one block from Union Square. ♦ 562 Sutter St (between Powell and Mason Sts). 433.4434, 800/433.4434; fax 433.3695

73 La Parisienne Chic and fanciful Parisian costume jewelry and posters from the turn of the century are sold while French music plays in the background. Modeled after shops in exclusive Parisian neighborhoods, this charming store delights the eye with its sign from a Paris boutique, antique vitrines and showcases, and a painted ceiling from an 1860 French pastry shop. ♦ M-Sa. 460 Post St (between Mason and Powell Sts). 788.2255

73 Theatre on the Square Just a half block from Union Square, this 800-seat house has enlivened San Francisco theater by bringing in quality Off-Broadway shows. ♦ 450 Post St (between Mason and Powell Sts). 433.9600

73 Kensington Park Hotel $$ This former Elks Lodge has 81 spacious rooms and two elegant suites with traditional English furniture, damask fabrics of rose and blue, Chippendale-style armoires, and bathrooms in marble and brass. Amenities include terry robes, complimentary breakfast, and tea and sherry served among the palms every afternoon in the beautifully restored lobby with its hand-painted Gothic ceiling. The views of the city and bay are especially good from the upper corner rooms. ♦ 450 Post St (between Mason and Powell Sts). 788.6400, 800/553.1900; fax 399.9484

43

73 Bazaar Cada Dia A wonderful selection of South American crafts, including jewelry and handwoven textiles, can be found here. ♦ Daily. 448 Post St (between Mason and Powell Sts). 391.3941

74 The Raphael $$ Europe's smaller hostelries were the inspiration for this 151-room hotel with a multilingual international staff. The charming Old World decor includes doors and woodwork hand-painted with flowers and leafy vines. The restaurant serves breakfast, lunch, and dinner. ♦ 386 Geary St (at Mason St). 986.2000, 800/821.5343; fax 397.2447

75 King George Hotel $$ This quaint hotel lives up to its billing as a unique antique in the center of the city. Its location is superb—in the theater district and within walking distance of the many restaurants and shops on Union Square. The hotel, built in 1914 for the Panama-Pacific Exposition, is tall and narrow, much like an Amsterdam canal house. Its nine floors house 143 rooms, all with private baths and in-room safes. Continental breakfast is available daily, as is an English high tea, complete with scones, crumpets, and finger sandwiches (but there's no restaurant). The hotel also has vacation packages that include whale-watching excursions, theater tickets, and meals at Fisherman's Wharf and Pier 39. ♦ 334 Mason St (between Geary and O'Farrell Sts). 781.5050, 800/288.6005; fax 391.6976

76 San Francisco Hilton and Towers $$$$ Popular with conventioneers, this block-square hotel is the largest on the West Coast (1,891 rooms total, of which 156 are suites). The marble lobby has a front desk with 14 reservation bays. Forty-four guest rooms are equipped for guests with disabilities, and 110 nonsmoking rooms are available. Some rooms are located poolside. The **Towers** form a hotel within a hotel, with seven floors of exclusive services, including a private lounge with complimentary continental breakfast and a cocktail hour. A health club, four ballrooms, and several restaurants are among the facilities. Don't miss the **Cityscape** restaurant and bar, which offers a stunning 360-degree view of the city. ♦ 333 O'Farrell St (between Mason and Taylor Sts). 771.1400, 800/HILTONS; fax 771.6807

Restaurants/Clubs: Red   **Hotels:** Blue
Shops/ 🌳 Outdoors: Green   **Sights/Culture:** Black

77 Warfield Originally built in 1922 by Marcus Loew to showcase the latest vaudeville and silent-screen productions, this theater now houses a full-service nightclub, restaurant, and bar. **G. Albert Lansburgh**'s conservative facade design belies its flamboyant interior. The ceiling fans out like a peacock tail, and murals can be found downstairs, where a speakeasy was reportedly operated. You can catch modern musical acts in an intimate setting that appears much as it has for over 70 years. ♦ 982 Market St (at Golden Gate Ave and Sixth St). 775.7722

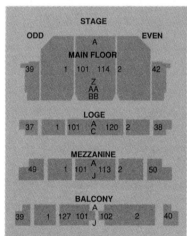

78 Golden Gate Theatre This 1922 **G. Albert Lansburgh**–designed theater (see the seating plan above) is part of the Shorenstein Nederlander empire. The management put a lot of money into refurbishing the house, and it shows in the gleaming interior. Unfortunately, sight lines in the orchestra remain poor, so try the mezzanine. The 2,400-seat theater books popular musical attractions such as the *Rockettes, The Will Rogers Follies,* and a revival of *Hair.* ♦ 25 Taylor St (between Market St and Golden Gate Ave). 474.3800

79 Club 181 ★★$$ If you're young and fashionable and love to dance, this is the place to be. This spot is not just "in" these days, it's *very* in, and for good reason. For starters, it serves wonderful California cuisine—pasta, fresh fish, fowl, steak—on outrageous table settings with mismatched retro dinnerware and elaborate candleholders. As the last desserts are served, the first of two jazz bands starts in. Around 11PM things really start swinging, as the DJ pumps out the nonstop dance tunes. Can't dance? No sweat; there are pool tables in the back. Dress nicely (no jeans) and use the valet parking—this isn't exactly the safest part of town. ♦ California ♦ Cover. W-Su until 2AM. Reservations recommended. 181 Eddy St (at Taylor St). 673.8181

80 Hotel Mark Twain $ Located in the shadow of more expensive hostelries, this hotel has a pleasant lobby and 119 comfortably furnished rooms, all appointed with refrigerators and coffeemakers (there is no restaurant). Its historical distinction is that it was the place in which the late jazz singer Billie Holiday was arrested for drug possession in 1949. A suite has been named in her honor. ◆ 345 Taylor St (between O'Farrell and Ellis Sts). 673.2332, 800/28.TWAIN; fax 398.0733

81 Pacific Bay Inn $ Simple, unpretentious, and very inexpensive, this family-owned, European-style inn with 84 rooms is located a few blocks from Union Square. Amenities include 24-hour desk and concierge service, and free in-room videos. For the price, location, and quality of the accommodations, this is one of the best deals in the city. ◆ 520 Jones St (at O'Farrell St). 673.0234, 800/343.0880 in CA, 800/445.2531; fax 673.4781

Adjoining the Pacific Bay Inn:

ℳ *Dottie's*

Dottie's True Blue Cafe ★★★$ Serving heartland cuisine with a twist, this 1950s-style coffee shop declares, "If you serve 'em crap, they won't come back," which explains the homemade bread, great French toast, and top-notch sausages. San Francisco's best breakfast (for the price) is served all day. And yes, there really is a Dottie—one of the previous owners used to work for her in a Queens, New York, luncheonette. ◆ Coffee Shop ◆ Daily breakfast; M-F lunch. 522 Jones St (at O'Farrell St). 885.2767

82 Napa Valley Winery Exchange This retail wine boutique features hard-to-find wines, mostly from (surprise!) the Napa Valley. It specializes in shipping them, too. ◆ M-Sa. 415 Taylor St (between Geary and O'Farrell Sts). 771.2887

83 Four Seasons Clift Hotel $$$$ It's been a San Francisco landmark for almost 80 years. As always, its high standards and individualized attention bring its loyal following back time and time again. Guests call their own shots here. If celebrities wish to come and go so no one knows they are in town, the hotel protects them. If they want a press conference, the hotel can arrange that, too. There are 329 guest rooms furnished simply and elegantly, with many suite combinations. The amenities include extraordinary service and a fine afternoon tea served in the lobby. Another plus is the location—two blocks from Union Square, two blocks from the airport bus terminal, and adjoining the theater district. ◆ 495 Geary St (at Taylor St). 775.4700, 800/332.3442; fax 441.4621

Within the Four Seasons Clift Hotel:

French Room ★★★$$$$ It's hard to imagine a prettier place to eat. The Caesar salad is superb, as are the veal and fish, particularly the Norwegian salmon, grilled to order and framed with vegetables. This is also the place to splurge on dessert—the chocolate-mousse cake with raspberry sauce is impossible to resist. ◆ California/French ◆ Daily lunch; Tu-Sa dinner; Su brunch. Reservations recommended. 775.4700

Redwood Room This classic Art Deco room boasts carved redwood panels and light fixtures from 1933, spectacular Gustav Klimt prints, and the soft background of an expertly played grand piano. It's a delightful place for a light lunch (when there are no banquets scheduled), and one of the nicest spots in the city for a cocktail or an after-dinner drink. ◆ California/French ◆ Daily lunch and dinner (unless closed for a private party). Reservations required. 775.4700

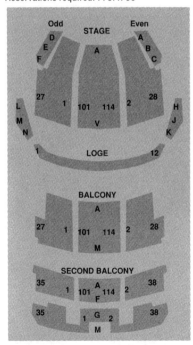

84 Curran Theatre Coproducers Carole Shorenstein Hayes and James M. Nederlander advertise this 1,678-seat theater (see the seating plan above) as the chief pit stop for their *Best of Broadway* series. The live and sometimes lively productions can be worth the hefty price of admission. Avoid the rear balconies unless you're a lip reader—the acoustics are impossible. ◆ 445 Geary St (between Taylor and Mason Sts). 474.3800

Honey, I Packed the Kids

A trip with your children in tow doesn't usually provide much in the way of rest and relaxation...but if you come to San Francisco, your vacation doesn't have to be as comically disastrous as *National Lampoon's Vacation* implies (remember Chevy Chase and his pack on their way to Wally World?). This city bends over backward to please everyone, even the most inquisitive toddlers and easily bored teenagers, so here's a guide to San Francisco's most amusing (and even educational) family-oriented sights, shops, and attractions.

Alcatraz Both the ferry ride and the spooky atmosphere at the "Rock" (Alcatraz's nickname) make this excursion a favorite with youngsters. Rent the excellent audio-tour headset on the island; it will help your kids imagine what this former federal prison was like back in the days when Al Capone and the Birdman roamed its halls. The steep walk up to the prison and the somber nature of the tour make this an activity best suited to older children. Call 546.2805 and see page 98 for more information.

Baker Beach This small, sheltered beach lies at the mouth of the **Golden Gate Bridge.** Alas, as with most of the city's beaches, swimming is dangerous because of the undertow, but there's good fishing, lovely scenery, picnic facilities, and—perhaps most important—bathrooms. Take 25th Avenue to the end, bear right, then look for signs to Baker Beach. See page 166 for more information.

Cable Cars These quaint conveyances never fail to delight the kiddies, especially if you sit in the open-air section of the car on a hilly route. The wait to climb aboard can be long, but street performers are usually around to keep children amused. For more information, see "Streetcars of Desire" on page 77 and a map of the cable-car routes on page 70.

California Academy of Sciences This well-appointed facility in **Golden Gate Park** includes the **Steinhart Aquarium,** the **Morrison Planetarium,** and the **Natural History Museum.** For information, call 750.7145 and see page 155.

Candlestick Park Stadium You can usually get tickets on short notice to see the **San Francisco Giants,** but it's just about impossible to snag any for the **San Francisco 49ers** games. Take the Candlestick Park exit off Highway 101 South. For **Giants** tickets, call 467.8000; for the **49ers,** 468.2249. For more about **Candlestick Park,** see page 135.

The Cannery, Ghirardelli Square, and Pier 39 All three of these lively tourist meccas at Fisherman's Wharf are replete with interesting shops, informal restaurants, and free performances by jugglers, mimes, musicians, and dancers. See pages 84-88 for more information.

Cliff House Walk on the beach, watch marine mammals cavort on Seal Rocks, and visit the funky **Musée Mécanique**'s antique mechanical amusements (Great Hwy, at the end of Geary Blvd). Also see page 167.

Exploratorium This dynamic, hands-on science museum will keep school-age kids (and their parents) busy for hours. The museum store has a great selection of educational and science-related toys. It is within the **Palace of Fine Arts** (3601 Lyon St, 563.7337). The grounds include a lovely duck pond. For more information, see page 101.

Golden Gate Bridge On a clear day, the vistas from this world-famous stretch of steel delight the eye and stir the imagination. Walking the 1.2-mile span takes about an hour; don't forget a warm jacket. You may also ride bicycles over the west side of the bridge on weekends (pedestrians and bicyclists share the east side on weekdays), but make sure the kids can handle their bikes—the path gets congested and very windy. See page 164 for more information.

Golden Gate Park The **Children's Playground,** with its carousel, is great fun for toddlers on up. There are all kinds of boats for rent on **Stow Lake,** and remote-control craft to watch at **Spreckels Lake.** Bicycles, in-line skates, and roller skates are available to rent, too. Other kid-pleasing attractions include the **Buffalo Paddock,** the **Japanese Tea Garden,** and the **Strybing Arboretum.** See the Golden Gate Park chapter starting on page 152 for more information.

National Maritime Museum Give little landlubbers a taste of life at sea. This museum employs photographs, memorabilia, and models to evoke the nautical history of the region, while the nearby **Hyde Street Pier** boasts three wonderful old sailing ships open to the public. For information, call 556.3002 and see page 84.

Parks When the kids need to burn off a little excess energy, nothing but a park will do. Here are some of the nicest and safest: in **North Beach, Michelangelo Park** has a great playground, basketball courts, and beautifully landscaped lawns and gardens (Greenwich St, between Leavenworth and Jones Sts). In the **Richmond,** there's **Mountain Lake Park** (north of Lake St, between Eighth and 12th Aves), with a duck pond, climbing structures, tennis courts, and a playground. **Presidio Heights** offers the lovely **Julius Kahn Playground** (off W Pacific Ave at Spruce St), **Glen Park's** recreation area has an enclosed playground for toddlers and a canyon for older kids to explore (Bosworth St and O'Shaughnessy Blvd), and the spectacular **Marina Green** (Marina Blvd, between Fort Mason Center and the Golden Gate Bridge) is the ideal spot to fly kites—or just watch the dazzling display of kites flying high on the weekends.

The Randall Museum Young nature fanciers will enjoy the animals at the Petting Corral, the gigantic whale skull, and other exhibits at this wildlife and California-history museum (199 Museum Way, 554.9600). For more information, see page 138.

San Francisco Zoo There's a lot more to this zoo than lions and tigers and bears, oh my! Highlights include the **Primate Discovery Center** (with a family of seven gorillas), the **Children's Zoo,** a gorgeous old carousel, **Koala Crossing,** the **Zebra Zephyr Train** tour, an energy-expending playground, and feeding time at the **Lion House** (Sloat Blvd at 45th Ave; for hours and special exhibits, call 753.7083). Also see page 150.

Sigmund Stern Memorial Grove Bring a picnic lunch and take in one of the free Sunday-afternoon concerts offered throughout the summer (Sloat Blvd at 19th Ave, 252.6252). For more details, see page 149.

San Francisco Shops

ESPRIT Outlet Teens love these comfortable, trendy clothes, and you'll love some of the prices at this slick outlet. There are some children's clothes, too (499 Illinois St, at 16th St, 957.2500). See page 135 for more details.

F.A.O. Schwarz Classic toys are offered in a storybook setting (48 Stockton St, at O'Farrell St, 394.8700). See page 36 for more information.

GapKids This younger version of **The Gap** specializes in sporty and well-made children's clothing, mostly in cotton (Stonestown Galleria, 3251 20th Ave, at Winston Dr, 564.7137; 100 Post St, at Kearny St, 421.4906; Laurel Village, 3491 California St, between Locust and Laurel Sts, 386.7517).

Gunne Sax Factory Outlet Preteen and teenage girls—if they're into romantic, lace-trimmed frocks—will love this outlet. Lines include Jessica McClintock, Scott McClintock, and, of course, Gunne Sax (35 Stanford St, between Second and Third Sts, 495.3326). See page 28 for more details.

Peek-a-boutique This impressive shop carries new and used children's clothing, toys, and equipment (1306 Castro St, between 24th and 25th Sts, 641.6192). See page 142 for more information.

85 Geary Theater Home to the renowned **American Conservatory Theater (ACT),** this structure was severely damaged in the October 1989 earthquake. At press time, its reopening date—originally scheduled for 1993—was still up in the air. The company continues to perform at various theaters around the city. ♦ 415 Geary St (at Mason St). ACT box office 749.2228

86 Hotel Diva $$ Awarded "Best Hotel Design" in 1994 by *Interiors* magazine, this hotel's leather, marble, glass, and chrome Euro-tech look often lures the style-conscious business traveler, but there are also classic creature comforts like down comforters and VCRs in all of the 110 rooms and suites. Each minifridge is stocked with refreshments, and original art adorns the walls. Limo service, valet parking, and a continental breakfast are also provided. The choice location, opposite the **Curran** and **Geary Theaters** and two blocks from Union Square, and the accommodating staff make it a most rewarding stay. There's no restaurant. ♦ 440 Geary St (between Mason and Taylor Sts). 885.0200, 800/553.1900; fax 346.6613

87 The Warwick Regis Hotel $$ This hotel offers 80 rooms and suites in the heart of the theater district, and within strolling distance of Union Square. The decor is a mix of French and English antiques, including canopied beds and armoires. Some suites include fireplaces. There are facilities for business travelers, 24-hour room service, and a concierge. ♦ 490 Geary St (between Mason and Taylor Sts). 928.7000, 800/82REGIS; fax 441.8788

Within the Warwick Regis Hotel:

Lobby Bar Popular with the after-theater crowd, this bar offers a menu of light food and refreshments. ♦ Tu-Su. 928.7900

88 Harold's Hometown News Magazines and newspapers from abroad and out-of-state are sold to those who want to keep in touch with hometown happenings. ♦ Daily. 599 Post St (at Taylor St). 441.2665

89 The Prescott Hotel $$$ This 166-room hotel is close to Union Square. The Edwardian-era decor features deep jewel tones; amenities include minibars, dryers, and terry-cloth robes. Complimentary evening wine, hors d'oeuvres, coffee, and tea are served. The hottest attraction, however, is that guests have an easier time than ordinary mortals getting a table at **Postrio,** the exciting dining spot in the hotel. There is also room service (provided by the restaurant) and free limousine transportation to the Financial District. ♦ 545 Post St (between Taylor and Mason Sts). 563.0303, 800/283.7322; fax 563.6831

Within the Prescott Hotel:

Postrio ★★★★$$$ Celebrity chef Wolfgang Puck's first restaurant venture outside of Los Angeles was a hit the minute the doors opened in 1989. You'll need to book a table weeks in advance, but a good excuse, such as "I'll only be in San Francisco for two days," may soften the heart of the maître d'. Sometimes just dropping in without reservations works as well. The food is inventive and the pizzas scrumptious—this is California cuisine at its most satisfying. Some typical dishes might include grilled sea scallops with shiitake risotto cake and a julienne of vegetables in coconut-milk sauce, or sun-dried tomato and parmesan sausage with herb fettuccine in a wild mushroom sauce at lunch; dinner choices could include grilled lamb chops with saffron couscous, cucumber salad, and spicy curry sauce or Chinese-style duck with spicy mango sauce and crispy fried scallions (there are one or two new dishes on the menu each night). ♦ California ♦ M-F breakfast, lunch, and dinner; Sa-Su brunch, lunch, and dinner. Reservations recommended. 776.7825

90 Donatello Hotel $$$ This is indeed a polished jewel. Throughout the hotel there is a tasteful blend of Italian marble, Murano glass, European antiques, and contemporary art. The 95 rooms and nine suites are larger here than in any other hotel in the city, although some of them could do with new furnishings. Especially appealing are the fifth-floor rooms, which open onto a private terrace. The hotel is the creation of A. Cal Rossi Jr., the hotelier who masterminded the **Stanford Court Hotel,** but here, in the absence of a Nob Hill view, the staff compensates with extraordinary service. ♦ 501 Post St (at Mason St). 441.7100, 800/792.9837 in CA, 800/227.3184; fax 885.8842

Within the Donatello Hotel:

Donatello ★★$$$ If you want good (but expensive) Italian food in a dining room pretty enough for the most important of occasions, this is the place. Try any of the pasta dishes for a superb first course. Then move on to the beautifully prepared fish. The veal here, as in so many San Francisco restaurants, is a notch below everything else. ♦ Italian ♦ Daily dinner. Reservations recommended. Jacket and tie required. 441.7182

91 The Pan Pacific Hotel San Francisco $$$ Formerly the **Portman,** this 338-room hotel was designed and built in 1987 by well-known architect **John C. Portman Jr.** The bathrooms are marble with large dressing areas, built-in cabinetry, and telephones. One personal valet is provided for every seven rooms, and room service is available 24 hours a day. Exemplary personal service, such as having a private car waiting at the airport to drive you into town, is stressed here, but the hotel staff doesn't always live up to this reputation. Business facilities include four conference suites and a boardroom with a private dining facility that provides continuous buffet service for all meetings. Secretarial, translation, and audiovisual services are offered, and personal computers are available. In addition, there is a solarium, a ballroom, and a rooftop club with breathtaking views for breakfast, tea, or cocktails. ♦ 500 Post St (at Mason St). 771.8600, 800/327.8585; fax 398.0267

Within the Pan Pacific Hotel San Francisco:

The Pacific Grill ★★★$$$ Located in the hotel lobby, this restaurant features an imaginative selection of the best of each season's produce. Chef Peter Harvey offers such eclectic fare as rack of lamb over Mediterranean couscous, pan-roasted sea bass in a saffron, fennel, and pomegranate *jus,* and grilled *ahi* tuna with a crispy wonton. One of the restaurant's enticements, aside from the food, is its all-evening valet parking service—something every San Franciscan takes into consideration when dining at Union Square. Because of its proximity to the theater district, the restaurant does a brisk pretheater dinner business. ♦ California/Asian ♦ Daily breakfast, lunch, and dinner. Reservations recommended for dinner. 929.2087

92 Hotel Beresford $ This modest, European-style hotel is located downtown near the theater district. The 114 rooms are small but pristine and comfortable. It's a good value, and family rates are also available. ♦ 635 Sutter St (between Taylor and Mason Sts). 673.9900, 800/533.6533

Within the Hotel Beresford:

The White Horse Taverne ★★$$ Uncommonly good value and great atmosphere can be savored in this cozy tavern and restaurant, a replica of an Edinburgh pub. The grilled meats are excellent and appealingly priced. ♦ Daily breakfast and lunch; Tu-Sa dinner. Reservations recommended for dinner. 673.9900

93 Hotel Sheehan $ A good location and a decent price here are combined with such amenities as an Olympic-size swimming pool, a reading room, and a large lobby (but no restaurant). It was formerly a **YWCA;** the 60 rooms have been pleasantly refurbished. ♦ 620 Sutter St (between Taylor and Mason Sts). 775.6500, 800/848.1529; fax 775.3271

94 White Swan Inn $$$ In this era of bustling hotels, this is an exciting and romantic find. The Four Sisters Inns group has managed to turn a 1900 hotel on downtown Bush Street into an English garden retreat that epitomizes charm and quiet good taste. There are 26 rooms, each with a bath, a fireplace, and a refrigerator, all furnished in handsome antiques and lovely fabrics. There's a stunning common room adjacent to a tiny garden, where a bountiful breakfast and tea, including home-baked breads and pastries, are served. You may also have sherry and wine by the fireplace and browse through the latest periodicals. Most important of all, the feeling of a real family welcome surrounds every service. ♦ 845 Bush St (between Taylor and Mason Sts). 775.1755; fax 775.5717

94 Petite Auberge $$ Just a few doors up Bush Street from the **White Swan Inn** is another offspring of the Four Sisters. This one has a French country theme and is more understated, a bit less spacious, and slightly less expensive. But if you can get past the vast collection of teddy bears inhabiting the 26 rooms and the lobby, you'll find the same kind of warmth and family hospitality that characterize its neighbor. A full breakfast is served, but there is no restaurant. Evening turndown service includes a chocolate and a rose on your pillow. ◆ 863 Bush St (between Taylor and Mason Sts). 928.6000; fax 775.5717

95 Obiko One-of-a-kind high fashion, most of it created by Bay Area designers, is offered at this cutting-edge shop. ◆ M-Sa. 794 Sutter St (at Jones St). 775.2882

96 Fleur de Lys ★★★★$$$$ This beautiful and expensive French restaurant was catapulted into the front ranks in 1986, when talented chef Hubert Keller took over the kitchen. His light and creative touch has resulted in contemporary cuisine that suits the elegant red-and-gold paisley dining room. Norwegian salmon in a light saffron sauce, mussel soup, and scallop mousse are just a few of his special dishes. ◆ French ◆ M-Sa dinner. Reservations and jacket required. 777 Sutter St (between Jones and Taylor Sts). 673.7779

97 The Andrews Hotel $ In a city rife with the posh and chic, the principal charm of this small, 48-room hotel lies in its atmosphere of civilized informality. For example, the complimentary breakfast can be carried back to bed on trays from hallway buffets. It's perfect for families, although there's no restaurant. The staff is knowledgeable about the city and happily recommends many places known only to locals. ◆ 624 Post St (between Taylor and Jones Sts). 563.6877, 800/622.0557 in CA, 800/9.ANDREWS; fax 928.6919

98 China Moon Cafe ★★★$$$ Chef/owner Barbara Tropp, long fascinated by China, where she once studied, has melded California and Asian culinary styles in her popular, albeit cramped, Art Deco restaurant. Such innovative dishes as spring rolls filled with seasonal vegetables and chicken or pork, "Buddha buns" filled with vegetables, a pot-browned noodle pillow featuring stir-fried vegetables and pork on sautéed egg noodles, followed by ginger ice cream with bitter-sweet chocolate sauce, are the keys to her considerable success, but many feel the prices are steep and the portions small. ◆ Chinese/California ◆ M-Sa lunch and dinner; Su dinner. Reservations recommended. 639 Post St (between Taylor and Jones Sts). 775.4789

99 Shannon Court Hotel $$ This landmark Spanish-style building has 169 large rooms and five suites, many with views. The hotel often offers special rates that make the already reasonably priced rooms an extraordinarily good value. The hotel's **City of Paris** restaurant offers an eclectic menu at affordable prices. ◆ 550 Geary St (between Jones and Taylor Sts). 775.5000; fax 928.6813

100 Savoy Hotel $$ Renovated by the same couple who revamped the **Sherman House** in Pacific Heights, this 83-room hotel in a 1915 building now has the feel of a country inn in Provence, with down comforters, old-fashioned etchings, and other homey touches. A continental breakfast is served every morning, and the hotel prides itself on excellent service. ◆ 580 Geary St (at Jones St). 441.2700, 800/227.4223; fax 441.2700 ext 297

Within the Savoy Hotel:

Brasserie Savoy ★★★$$ This Gallic-flavored restaurant looks very French, with a kind of throwaway elegance, and the food is also deliciously faithful to its brasserie roots. Entrées include roasted chicken with garlic mashed potatoes, and a shellfish cassoulet of mussels, Manila clams, crayfish, and house-made shrimp-and-scallop sausages. ◆ French ◆ Daily dinner. Reservations recommended. 474.8686

Bests

Holly Stiel
President, Holly Speaks, hospitality consulting and concierge training

Truth be told, I love alternative shopping at consignment shops and flea markets. The best consignment shops are on **Fillmore Street** and **Charlene's on 2** at 41 Sutter Street.

I love to ride the ferry to **Sausalito,** when I get a lazy 30 minutes to watch the seagulls and take in all the sights and sounds of San Francisco Bay.

If I'm downtown I have breakfast at **Postrio** or **Campton Place Restaurant;** on a nice day, I have lunch at **Cafe Tiramisù** on Belden Place, or eat the warm chicken salad at the **Plaza Restaurant** in the **Grand Hyatt Hotel.**

For dinner I'd choose **Embarko** or **MacArthur Park** for yummy American food.

In the evening it's back to the **Grand Hyatt Hotel** for jazz at **Club 36.**

Financial District

Often called the "Wall Street of the West," the Financial District, with its Pacific Coast Stock Exchange, several corporate headquarters, and elaborate commercial architecture, comprises an area bordered by **The Embarcadero** and **Market, Third, Kearny,** and **Washington Streets.**

When thousands of gold diggers were brought to the muddy shores of a shallow indentation known as Yerba Buena Cove, they began to grade the sand dunes along present-day Market Street, dumping sand into the mud flats of the cove. Before that was completed, they also started to build a seawall so ships could unload their cargo directly upon the wharves. For its time, this was a stupendous project, taking decades to complete. Meanwhile, the reclamation of the mud flats continued, with some of the city's smaller hills sacrificed to fill the area between the old waterfront and the new wall until, finally, the Financial District that's here today—everything east of **Montgomery Street**—arose from the sea. Within five years of the first news of the gold strike, Montgomery Street was lined with several bankers' offices. As the gold dust filtered down from the city of Sacramento, some means of handling it had to be found, and since the shopkeepers had scales for weighing the gold and safes for storing it, they were the first to become bankers.

Paradoxically, though rich in gold, San Francisco was poor in money. A pinch of gold subbed for one dollar, and a dollar's length of gold wire was divided into eight parts to serve as smaller coins, referred to as "two bits," "four bits," etc. Coins from around the world were pressed into service at a rate of exchange based on their size. The Gold Rush boom overreached itself in 1854, ending in Black Friday's panic, which forced many banks to close. Not until the colossal riches began to flow from the Nevada silver mines was San Francisco firmly established as the financial center of the West. The Great Fire in 1906 precipitated the rise of another financial giant, A.P. Giannini, a food

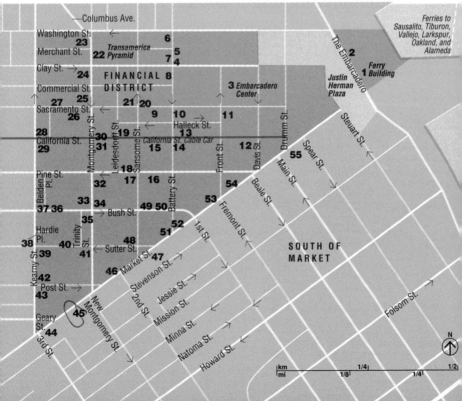

broker who had retired at age 32 to try out his banking theories with the Bank of Italy, founded by Giannini and his stepfather. Before the advancing flames reached his bank, he removed the assets and records and hauled them home in wagons from his warehouse, well camouflaged with heaps of fruit and vegetables. Consequently, the Bank of Italy was the first in the city to reopen. Later renamed Bank of America, it eventually became the biggest bank in the US (a distinction it now shares with Citibank).

Envision Montgomery Street at the water's edge or a time when Kearny Street was paved with sticks, stones, bits of tin, and old hatch coverings. Today Montgomery Street is both sleek and imposing, with walls of stone, glass, and marble lining its sides. It awakens before daybreak, when trading begins on the "Big Board" in New York. By 9AM, the skyscrapers are filled with thousands of brokers, bankers, insurance executives, and clerical workers. By dark, its canyons are largely deserted, except for cleaning crews, security guards, and a smattering of restaurant-goers and barhoppers.

"Monkey Block" was the nickname for Montgomery Block, a four-story building that for a century stood on the present site of the **Transamerica Pyramid.** It was the first office building of any significance in San Francisco, and the first to be fireproof. Much of the city's important business was carried on here. When business moved out, an amazing group moved in that included some of the most important names in American literary circles: Mark Twain, Bret Harte, Robert Louis Stevenson, Rudyard Kipling, Jack London, Ambrose Bierce, and William Randolph Hearst. All either had office space in the building or regularly hung out at the Bank Exchange, the building's legendary bar. In a second-floor office, a young doctor named Sun Yat-sen plotted the successful overthrow of the Manchu dynasty and later wrote the Chinese constitution. Although they would have mourned the destruction of Monkey Block, these legendary characters probably would be somewhat cheered to know that the site is now graced by the pyramid, one of the city's most prominent landmarks.

1 Ferry Building Modeled after the Cathedral Tower in Seville, Spain, this building (pictured above) was designed by architect **Arthur Page Brown** in 1894. For many years it was the tallest building in San Francisco. Today it serves as the headquarters of the San Francisco Port Authority and the World Trade Center. Before the bridges were built, it was the gateway to the city, with ferries transporting as many as 50 million passengers a year from all over the bay. Sadly, its fine arcades and internal galleria are filled with rather undistinguished-looking offices.
♦ The Embarcadero (at Market St)

2 Ferry Plaza Farmers' Market This festive outdoor Saturday market offers the cream of the crop of several farmers—everything from apples and almonds to radicchio and rhubarb. You'll also find a variety of decorative wreaths, fresh flowers, and gourmet products from such popular vendors as Acme (bakers of the Bay Area's best bread) and The Apple Farm from the wine country (makers of various apple products). All this fresh food sells at prices lower than any supermarket's—plus you get to shop to the beat of the live band of the week. At 10AM, a free "Shop with the Chef" tour begins when a chef from a popular Bay Area restaurant (a different one each week) leads a group around the market and shows participants how to assemble a family basket of the best produce available with a budget of $40. At about 11:30AM, the chef demonstrates how to cook some of the foods, followed by tastings. On the second Saturday of each month from April through November, the market hosts such events as a fruit festival, a chili celebration, and a family pumpkin party. There are also other cooking demonstrations and tastings, and about a half-dozen local restaurants assemble booths that sell snacks and meals. ♦ Free. Sa 9AM-2PM. The Embarcadero (in front of the Ferry Building). 981.3004

3 Embarcadero Center This flashy eight-block complex of retail and office space stretches from Clay, Battery, and Sansome Streets to Justin Herman Plaza and the **Hyatt Regency** at the foot of Market Street. Four slender, interconnected high-rise towers by **John Portman and Associates** are staggered to allow sunlight to penetrate and to break up what might easily have been a wall-like appearance; each has a triple-level shopping area that houses a total of 125 shops and restaurants. You'll find everything here from **The Gap, Banana Republic,** and **Ann Taylor** to beauty shops, bookstores, and **Boudin** sourdough bread—enough to keep the most avid shopper busy for at least a full day. Since the four original towers went up in 1982, three

buildings have been added to the center: the Embarcadero Center West and the restored Old Federal Reserve Bank at Sansome and Sacramento Streets, and the **Park Hyatt Hotel** at Clay and Battery Streets (see the illustrations below). Public areas include sculpture courts, bridges, and walkways within garden settings. The abstract *Vaillancourt Fountain* in the plaza is the center's most controversial sculpture (many think its convoluted metal shapes make it look as if it has weathered an earthquake). Parking at the center is free with validation Monday through Friday 5PM to 3AM and all day Saturday, Sunday, and major holidays; it's discounted with validation Monday through Friday 7AM to 5PM. ♦ Between The Embarcadero and Sansome St, and Clay and Sacramento Sts. 772.0550

Within the Embarcadero Center:

Chevys ★$$ As in all the other fresh-Mex members of the chain, the fajitas here are favorites and the tortillas are slapped out on the premises. Although the blended margaritas tend to taste more like virgin Slurpees, if you follow some patrons' remedy of ordering a shot of tequila on the side, you'll wind up with a mighty fine drink indeed. Sun worshipers may dine on the patio except when it's reserved for "Happy Hour" imbibing on Friday evenings. The **Chevy's Take-Out** stand is open for the lunchtime crowds on weekdays only. ♦ Mexican ♦ Daily lunch and dinner. 2 Embarcadero Center, Promenade level. 391.2323; fax (for to-go orders) 391.4404. Also at: 150 Fourth St (at Howard St). 543.8060; and 3251 20th Ave (at Stonestown Galleria). 665.8705

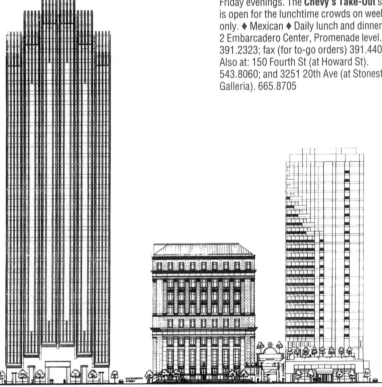

Embarcadero Center
(from left to right) 3 Embarcadero Center West, Old Federal Reserve Bank, Park Hyatt Hotel

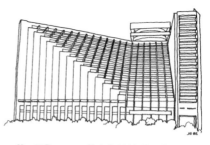

Splendido ★★$$$ Evoking the look of a centuries-old Mediterranean village, this exciting restaurant unites the talents of design genius **Pat Kuleto** and successful hotelier/restaurateur Bill Kimpton. Sophisticated, innovative cuisine beguiles diners amid a dizzying potpourri of pan-Mediterranean architectural styles and textures that range from aged brick and stone to pewter and tile. All dishes are made to order and may vary from seared peppered tuna with chive potatoes to grilled mustard-glazed veal chop with roasted garlic spaetzle. Chef Christopher Majer opts for food presentations that look "architectural" and don't just lie flat on a plate. Those who don't want full meals can opt for the good pizza, made in a handsome wood-fired oven. Award-winning desserts and breads are baked on the premises. Patio dining is available. ◆ Mediterranean ◆ Daily lunch and dinner. Reservations recommended. 4 Embarcadero Center, Promenade level. 986.3222

Harbor Village Restaurant ★★★$$$ Crystal chandeliers, etched glass, and lacquered chairs accent an interior that's more upscale than many Asian restaurants. Though more traditional entrées are offered, the dim-sum selection here is extensive and especially good. There's a patio area for those who prefer the outdoor take-out dim-sum kiosk. Executive chef Andy Wai of Hong Kong also prepares grand-style Chinese banquets. ◆ Chinese ◆ Daily lunch and dinnner. Reservations recommended. 4 Embarcadero Center, Lobby level. 781.8833

Cafe Latté II Restaurant & Catering ★$$ One of the best-looking cafeterias around, this offshoot of the highly successful **Cafe Latté I** (★$$) a few blocks away (100 Bush St. 989.2233) has pink cloths on the tables and a patio area overlooking Embarcadero Plaza. The food is trendy and tasty, and the congenial ambience draws an enthusiastic young crowd. ◆ California ◆ Daily lunch. 4 Embarcadero Center, Street level. 982.2233

San Francisco's tallest structure is the Transamerica Pyramid, 853 feet tall.

Restaurants/Clubs: Red   **Hotels:** Blue
Shops/ ♥ Outdoors: Green   **Sights/Culture:** Black

Hyatt Regency Hotel $$$$ The silhouette of this quite impressive 803-room hotel (pictured above) is an unmistakable part of the San Francisco skyline. **John Portman and Associates'** 1973 design has received national recognition for outstanding and innovative architecture. The 17-story atrium lobby is filled with plants, trees, and birds; greenery spills from the balconies; and the four-ton *Eclipse* sculpture by Charles Perry soars from a reflecting pool. The **Eclipse Cafe** serves California cuisine for breakfast, lunch, and dinner in a parklike setting, and the sweeping 60-foot-long **13 Views** watering hole is a full bar offering salads and sandwiches in the afternoon and hot appetizers in the evening. **The Equinox,** the very popular and romantic revolving-rooftop restaurant and bar, provides an incredible view of the Bay Area and serves continental cuisine for lunch and dinner daily and a Sunday brunch. The **Regency Club** offers a business center, bar, and lounge for the luxury-minded business traveler. ◆ 5 Embarcadero Center. 788.1234, reservations only 800/233.1234; fax 398.2567

4 One Maritime Plaza Skidmore, Owings, & Merrill's 25-story slab block with exposed diagonal-steel bracing, built in 1967, is one of the few buildings that visually demonstrates its ability to withstand the forces of an earthquake. The entrance lobby is two floors above the street. ◆ Battery St (between Clay and Washington Sts). 397.2339

5 Punch Line They sure don't have to turn on any laugh tracks when the jokes start flying at this comedy club. Part of the "Bill Graham Presents" empire, it has a slick, urbane look. Snacks and meals are served, but food is certainly not the reason for coming. Aspiring comedians are showcased every Sunday night. You must be 18 years of age or older to attend. Seating is on a first-come, first-served basis. ◆ Cover and two-drink minimum. Tickets available at BASS outlets or at the door. Shows daily. Reservations required for dinner on weekends. 444 Battery St (between Clay and Washington Sts), Upstairs. 397.7573

6 Washington/Battery Street Building Built in 1985, **Fee and Munson**'s narrow office block is only 25 feet deep; bay windows capture additional space for tenants. The facade facing east has a large clock. ◆ Washington St (at Battery St)

53

7 Yank Sing ★★★$$ One of the best dim-sum houses of San Francisco, this place just happens to be in the Financial District. Were it not for the food, you'd never guess from the high-tech decor that this is a Chinese restaurant. All the dishes arrive on carts, and virtually everything is delicious. Don't miss the Peking duck, steamed pork buns, chicken wrapped in foil, or the petite custard tarts for dessert. At the end of the meal, they count your plates to tally up the bill. ◆ Chinese ◆ Daily lunch. Reservations required. 427 Battery St (between Clay and Washington Sts). 362.1640. Also at: 49 Stevenson Pl (between First and Second Sts). 495.4510

8 Park Hyatt $$$$ This 360-room hotel is way up on the list of best places to stay in the city, especially if you are in town on business and need such standard extras as two phones and 24-hour room service. Two Mercedes are also available to shuttle you through the downtown area, and the hotel offers a full business center and 14 meeting rooms. Afternoon tea and caviar are served in the lobby lounge. Entertainment runs nonstop daily from 3PM to 11PM. ◆ 333 Battery St (at Clay St). 392.1234, 800/233.1234; fax 296.2919

Within the Park Hyatt:

Park Grill ★★$$$ Chef Charles Lewis offers American fare at this elegant restaurant adorned with rare Australian lacewood, teak and ebony marquetry, and fantastic floral arrangements. Favorite dishes include Dungeness crab cakes, grilled New Zealand lamb chops with vegetables and spiced couscous, oven-steamed Chilean sea bass with stir-fried vegetables, and rosemary free-range chicken with smoked sausage, white beans, and apple-smoked bacon. ◆ American ◆ Daily breakfast, lunch, and dinner. 392.1234

9 Sol y Luna ★★$$ With its relentlessly modern decor and novel approach to food, this tapas restaurant might make you revise your notions about Spanish cooking. The three chefs, all from Spain, start out with traditional ingredients but then take them down unexpected pathways. Tapas served here includes blood sausages seasoned with sweet spices, chicken-liver mousse on toast, and Spanish rice croquettes. At dinner, hungrier souls who order in advance can feast on *paella suprema* (large enough for two to three people). Flamenco dancers perform on Wednesday and Saturday nights. ◆ Spanish ◆ M-Sa lunch and dinner. Reservations recommended. 475 Sacramento St (between Battery and Sansome Sts). 296.8696

10 353 Sacramento Street Handsomely clad in teal- and blue-metal panels, **Skidmore, Owings & Merrill**'s low-scale corner office building is a 1984 reconstruction of a building that previously occupied this location. The result is a strange juxtaposition of styles and forms. The rotated plan of the tower ignores the grid of the street and street wall. ◆ At Battery St

11 Schroeder's ★$$ Heavy German food is served at this popular hangout for Financial District businesspeople. ◆ German ◆ M-F lunch and dinner; Sa dinner. 240 Front St (between California and Sacramento Sts). 421.4778

12 101 California Street With the **Bank of America** building and the **Transamerica Pyramid,** this cylindrical structure by **Philip Johnson** and **John Burgee** acts as the third major landmark in the Financial District. Completed in 1983, its silvery reflective glass looks especially beautiful when seen from the bay at dusk. Although the entrance lobby is rather ungainly, a sloping glass wall slicing across the 90-foot-tall columns makes a dramatic sight. The north-facing plaza on California Street is flanked by two mid-rise blocks cut on the diagonal. ◆ Between Davis and Front Sts

At 101 California Street:

The Atrium ★★$$$ Off the open plaza is this sophisticated restaurant with a menu that changes daily to reflect the freshest offerings of the marketplace. Sample entrées include spicy Creole jambalaya, a grilled thick-cut pork chop with turnip gratin and Gravenstein applesauce, and ancho chili–glazed breast of chicken with garlic mashed potatoes. The sleek dining room, established on several elevated levels, is decorated with black granite, pastel desert colors, and plantation shutters. On sunny days, many diners opt to lunch alfresco. ◆ California ◆ M-F lunch and dinner; Sa dinner. Entrance on Front St. 788.4101

13 Tadich Grill ★★★$$ This is the most famous of the San Francisco fish houses that trace their lineage back for decades, and one of the first to grill fish over charcoal. Order the sand dabs or the petrale sole, or, better yet, ask which fresh fish they received that day; skip anything with an elaborate sauce. The old-fashioned desserts, such as baked apples and custard pudding, are good. Unless you eat in mid-afternoon, be prepared for a long but usually pleasant wait. ◆ American ◆ M-Sa lunch and dinner. 240 California St (between Battery and Front Sts). 391.2373

13 Aqua ★★$$$ Embraced by the see-and-be-seen crowd, this refined restaurant offers lovely-to-behold fish dishes that are imaginatively prepared. The decor is coolly elegant, but sometimes the service could use a little warming up. ◆ Seafood ◆ M-F lunch and dinner; Sa dinner. Reservations recommended. 252 California St (between Battery and Front Sts). 956.9662

14 Industrial Indemnity Building Formerly the **John Hancock Building**, this 1959 structure by **Skidmore, Owings & Merrill** is contemporary with the **Crown Zellerbach Building** (designed by the same architects), but demonstrates more traditional attitudes toward the street and context. It is clad in polished gray granite and has a retail base with a second-level walkway above. ◆ 255 California St (at Battery St)

COURTESY OF CARLOS DINIZ ASSOCIATES

15 First Interstate Center This twin-towered building (pictured above) by **Skidmore, Owings & Merrill** houses a luxury hotel above offices. It was skillfully inserted into the center of the block in 1986 and has an arcade linking Sansome, Battery, and California Streets. The two towers are connected by bridges and capped by two stainless-steel–clad flagpoles. The design represents one of the best examples of modernism and is a stunning addition to the city skyline. ◆ California St (between Battery and Sansome Sts)

Within First Interstate Center:

Mandarin Oriental San Francisco $$$$ Stunningly set atop the twin towers and connected by glass sky bridges, this is the Mandarin Oriental Hotel Group's first US palace. Small and beautifully furnished, it has 158 select rooms and suites with outstanding views of the city and bay; those with marble bathtubs looking out picture windows 40 floors up are incredible. The **Oriental Suite**, on the 38th floor, is a home-away-from-home in grand-luxe style, with a parlor, two bedrooms, two and a half bathrooms, a pantry, and an open-air terrace with a 180-degree view of the bay. The **Taipan Suite**, across the hall, also boasts the same wide vista, as well as a luxurious bedroom, two bathrooms, and a dining room. The secret at this hostelry lies in the personalized service, with a ratio of one staff member to each guest. Particular attention is paid to visiting executives at the lobby-level **Business Center**, which is filled with the latest high-tech office equipment. The sky bridges connecting the towers are worth the admission price. Adjoining the lobby is the **Mandarin Lounge**, where cocktails and hors d'oeuvres are served. ◆ 222 Sansome St (between Pine and California Sts). 885.0999, 800/526.6566; fax 433.0289

Within the Mandarin Oriental San Francisco:

Silks ★★★$$$ Named one of the Top 50 restaurants of 1994 by *Condé Nast Traveler*, this posh restaurant recently underwent a half-million-dollar remodeling. Patterned deep-red and burnt-orange carpeting now covers the floors, elaborate wood lattices adorn the windows, and whimsical paintings and sculptures by local artists enliven the attractive dining area. The beautiful-to-behold entrées are the work of chef Ken Oringer, and vary from being very good to excellent. The menu changes seasonally, but if the braised lamb shanks with Singapore noodles is offered, grab it. Other not-to-be-missed dishes include seared lobster and scallops, seafood and vegetable tempura, fish and chips artfully arranged in a wood basket lined with newspaper, and a divine eggnog or espresso crème brûlée. ◆ Asian/French ◆ Daily breakfast, lunch, and dinner. 986.2020

16 235 Pine Street Note the bronze work above the entrance of this impressive 25-story limestone-clad high rise designed by **Skidmore, Owings & Merrill** in 1990. The 20 relief portrait sculptures, entitled *Called to Rise*, feature individuals who have contributed significantly to the history of San Francisco, including Juan Bautista De Anza, Phoebe Apperson Hearst, Amadeo Peter Giannini, and **Timothy Pflueger.** For more information about these bronze castings and biographies of the people portrayed, ask the person at the front desk in the lobby for a brochure. ◆ Between Sansome and Battery Sts

Use the Ferry Building at the foot of Market Street as your guide to the piers; even-numbered piers are south of the building and odd-numbered piers are to the north.

17 Pacific Coast Stock Exchange Architecturally, **Miller and Pflueger**'s 1930 structure (pictured above) offers a strange combination of classical and Moderne styles. The exchange is the heart of the Financial District and is a little sister to those on Wall Street and in London. ♦ 301 Pine St (at Sansome St)

18 Royal Globe Insurance Building Note the elaborate sculpture in **Howells and Stokes's** 1909 white-marble building with a fine entrance and base. 201 Sansome St (at Pine St)

19 Bank of California Built in 1908 shortly after "The Big One," **Bliss and Faville's** Corinthian-columned temple contains a grand main banking hall. ♦ 400 California St (at Sansome St). 765.0400

20 Federal Reserve Bank of San Francisco Sierra-white marble covers three sides of **George Ketham**'s 1924 building, part of the **Embarcadero Center** complex. The Commercial Street side, which was finished later, is made of glazed terra-cotta brick. The building was renovated as law offices and retail space by **Kaplan/McLaughlin/Diaz** and reopened in 1989. The interior features both real and hand-painted faux marble. Stand across the street for a good view of the eight eagles perched above the entrance. ♦ 400 Sansome St (at Sacramento St)

21 London Wine Bar $$ An excellent selection of two- to three-dozen California (and some imported) wines by the glass awaits you in this cozy English-style bar, which also offers light lunches and evening appetizers. The wine and the convivial atmosphere are the real reasons for coming here. ♦ California ♦ M-F lunch. 415 Sansome St (between Sacramento and Clay Sts). 788.4811

22 Transamerica Pyramid William Pereira and Associates' 853-foot-tall building has become a landmark because of its unusual shape and location at the end of Columbus Avenue. It caused great controversy when it was built in 1972 and, until it gained acceptance, gave credence to the belief that California architecture couldn't be taken seriously. (San Franciscans always hastened to add that a Los Angeles firm designed it.) It's the headquarters of the Transamerica Corporation, founded in 1928 by A.P. Giannini. A public observation area on the 27th floor provides excellent views of such landmarks as the Golden Gate Bridge, **Coit Tower,** and Alcatraz Island, and is open to the public weekdays. The adjoining half-acre **Transamerica Redwood Park** is a pleasant place to sit and gaze up the pyramid's walls or at the lighthearted bronze *Puddle Jumpers* sculpture. Overlooking the park is the pyramid's restaurant and bar, **Cisco Kid Cantina.** ♦ Montgomery St (between Clay and Washington Sts)

23 655 Montgomery Street Architects **Kaplan/McLaughlin/Diaz**'s mixed-use tower contains condominiums above offices. Completed in 1984, its eroded form acknowledges the diagonal of Columbus Avenue. ♦ At Columbus Ave

Within 655 Montgomery Street:

Tommy Toy's
★★★$$$ The owner of this luxurious dining establishment describes the food as "haute cuisine *chinoise*"—and, indeed, it does represent an East/West melding of tastes presented in a palatial setting. The main dining room is fashioned after the 19th-century Empress Dowager's reading room, with ancient powder paintings framed in sandalwood. Ornate carved archways and delicate porcelain bridal lamps are but a few of the opulent touches. The food, essentially Chinese but with a French accent, is as fully satisfying as the ambience, albeit costly. Dishes include such cross-cultural offerings as breast of duckling smoked with camphor-wood and tea leaves served with a plum-wine sauce, whole fresh Maine lobster shelled and sautéed with pine nuts and mushrooms in a peppercorn sauce, and prawns in vanilla-flavored sauce with raisins and fresh melon. ♦ Chinese ♦ M-F lunch and dinner; Sa-Su dinner. Reservations recommended. 397.4888

24 Bank of Canton of California The present building, designed by **Skidmore, Owings & Merrill,** was erected in 1984 to replace the bank's original headquarters, a Financial District fixture since the 1930s. The walls of the 17-story structure are faced with Texas pink granite, and the architects strove for a modern update of the lines and detailing of the adjacent older stone buildings. ♦ 555 Montgomery St (at Clay St)

Within the Bank of Canton of California:
Pacific Heritage Museum This delightful museum, hidden on a side street on the south side of the bank, offers an impressive look at Thai culture through ceremonial objects, murals, photographs, and clothing. A display of Chinese antiquities, including ceremonial vessels that trace the development of Chinese decorative methods over a 4,000-year period, fills the ground floor. ♦ Free. M-F; closed on bank holidays. 608 Commercial St (off Montgomery St, between Sacramento and Clay Sts). 399.1124

25 **505 Montgomery Street** Skidmore, Owings & Merrill's neo-Deco tower houses several offices and the Tokai Bank. Step inside the lobby for a look at the striking pattern of the inlaid-marble floor; the lobby is particularly pretty when it's all decked out during the Christmas season. ♦ Between Sacramento and Commercial Sts

Within 505 Montgomery Street:
Paninoteca Palio d'Asti ★★$ For a great *panino* (sandwich), stop at this offshoot of the popular **Palio d'Asti** restaurant (see entry no. 27, below). Assorted salads, pizzas, weekly specials, pastries, and sweets are also available to savor here or to go. ♦ Italian ♦ M-F breakfast and lunch. 362.6900; fax 362.0700

26 **Jack's** ★★$$$ This has been one of San Francisco's best-known restaurants since 1864, and eating here makes you feel as if you're eating in a dining room untouched by time. An exact replica of the restaurant that stood here before the 1906 earthquake, its grilled meats and fish are good, if unexciting, but service by some of the old-time waiters can be grumpy. Local business titans and political powerbrokers who appear regularly get royal treatment along with their favorite tables. ♦ American ♦ M-F lunch and dinner; Sa dinner. Reservations recommended. 615 Sacramento St (between Montgomery and Kearny Sts). 986.9854

27 **Palio d'Asti** ★★$$ Regional Italian specialties are prepared by chef Craig Stoll in open-display kitchens at this handsome restaurant owned by Gianni Fassio. Dishes from the Piedmont area, which was Fassio's home, are featured, and may include duck-filled *agnolotti* (crescent-shaped pasta) with wild-mushroom sauce, braised rabbit in lemon-egg sauce, and chocolate-amaretto pudding. The lunch and dinner menus are virtually the same, and they change seasonally. ♦ Italian ♦ M-F lunch and dinner;

Sa dinner. Reservations recommended. 640 Sacramento St (between Montgomery and Kearny Sts). 395.9800; fax 362.6002

28 **580 California Street** Architects **Philip Johnson** and **John Burgee's** pseudoclassical 1984 high rise is topped by 12 blank-faced statues that surround the glass mansard roof; the figures allegedly represent the mayor and the 11 members of the board of supervisors. Classically, the design is incorrect: The front facade is divided into an equal number of bays, resulting in a column in the middle of the entry. ♦ At Kearny St

29 **Bank of America World Headquarters** Completed in 1969 by **Wurster, Bernardi, and Emmons Inc.** and **Skidmore, Owings & Merrill,** with **Pietro Belluschi** as design consultant, this is one of the best high-rise office towers ever built—52 stories clad in dark-red carnelian marble. The faceted facade and flush glazing create a changing image depending on the season or time of day. At sunset, the reflection of the sun on the windows makes the building look like a towering inferno; at other times it disappears like a black monolith into the fog. Its asymmetrical profile at the top creates sufficient variety to prevent it from becoming boring. The large lump of abstract black marble at the entryway has been dubbed "Banker's Heart" by irreverent locals. ♦ 555 California St (at Kearny St)

Within the Bank of America World Headquarters:
Carnelian Room ★$$$$ The stupendous view through the floor-to-ceiling glass wall at this spot high above San Francisco is a sight you'll never forget. The food is not memorable, but stop here for a drink—especially when the sun is setting or the fog is rolling in. If you're bent on having a meal here, however, lovers and those who want to be very, very private may reserve the fabulous **Tamalpais Room,** a hideaway within the restaurant seating just two to six; waiters come only when summoned by a bell. ♦ American ♦ Daily dinner. Reservations recommended. Jacket required. 52nd floor. 433.7500

30 **Wells Fargo History Museum** On display in a renovated and expanded 4,400-square-foot space are artifacts from the Gold Rush days, including old mining equipment, gold nuggets, early banking articles, and period photographs documenting Wells Fargo and early state and local history. The star attraction is an authentic 19th-century Concord stagecoach that was once used on old California trails. A reference library is open to the public and tours can be arranged, both by appointment only. ♦ Free. M-F; closed on bank holidays. 420 Montgomery St (at California St). 396.2619

31 Security Pacific Bank Hall In George Kelham's impressive old banking hall, the giant granite Ionic columns outside are matched by faux-marble columns inside. Completed in 1922, the hall's spacious volume is appropriate in scale and grandeur to the traditional forms of banking. ♦ Montgomery St (at California St)

32 250 Montgomery Street Heller and Leake's attractive 1986 office tower is clothed in fiberglass, reinforced concrete, and green granite. ♦ At Pine St

33 Russ Building George Kelham's 1928 Gothic high rise (pictured above) was modeled after the winning entry for the Chicago Tribune Tower competition. Until 1964, it was the tallest building in the city. ♦ 235 Montgomery St (between Pine and Bush Sts)

34 Mills Building and Mills Tower A rare example of the Chicago School west of the Rockies, this 10-story **Burnham and Root** building, completed in 1892, suffered only interior fire damage during the 1906 earthquake. Notice the fine Richardsonian entrance archway on Montgomery Street, the subtly delineated brick planters and strong cornice, and the multifloor frieze. **Willis Polk** supervised the post-fire reconstruction and also designed the adjacent **Mills Tower** on Bush Street. ♦ 220 Montgomery St (at Bush St). 421.1444

35 Kelly's ★★$ Chef/owner Kelly Mills forsook the **Four Seasons Clift Hotel** to set up his own restaurant on Trinity Plaza. It's an upscale, cafeteria-style breakfast and lunch place, and private dinner parties may be booked here. ♦ California ♦ M-F breakfast and lunch. 333 Bush St (at Trinity Plaza, between Kearny and Montgomery Sts). 362.4454

36 Sam's Grill ★★$$ This Old Guard San Francisco restaurant features polished wood, private rooms, and a menu specializing in fish. If you've never eaten here, you've got to try it at least once, and be willing to forgive the indifferent service. The best choices are the simple fish dishes, particularly the rex sole and sand dabs. Jammed for lunch, it's less crowded at dinner if you arrive early. ♦ American ♦ M-F lunch and dinner. Reservations accepted for six or more only.

374 Bush St (between Kearny and Montgomery Sts). 421.0594

37 Belden Place The Financial District's proletarian version of Union Square's Maiden Lane (a tiny pedestrian way filled with umbrella-covered tables during the lunch hour) has a ways to go yet before it catches up to the cachet of its rival. Still, the brick-walled alley between Pine and Bush Streets provides a welcome respite from the hustle and bustle at lunchtime. Closed to traffic from 11AM to 3PM, it offers a melting pot of kitchens to choose from, including **Mariposa** (★$ Chinese), **Vic's Place** (★$ burgers), **Cafe 52** (★$ Mediterranean), **Belden Park Tacquería** (★$ Mexican), and **Oh la la!** (★$ sandwiches and great espresso drinks). Many have alfresco dining during the summer.

A couple of standouts include:

Cafe Bastille ★$ The first restaurant to venture out doors on Belden, it attracts a loyal following with its simple, well-prepared brasserie fare. Choose from salads, soups, crepes, sandwiches, and entrées that range from roasted chicken breast with *pommes frites* to *andouillette* (pork sausage) with sautéed onions. (One question, though: What's a mushroom quesadilla doing on a French cafe menu?) Live jazz is featured three nights a week. ♦ French ♦ M-Sa lunch and dinner. 22 Belden Pl (between Pine and Bush Sts). 986.5673

Cafe Tiramisù ★★$$ The open kitchen at this stylish Italian restaurant turns out fresh pasta, including potato gnocchi with tomatoes and basil, and such entrées as sea bass baked in a sea-salt crust and chicken with a wild-mushroom ragout. Save room for the namesake dessert. The walls were decorated by the same muralists who left their mark on the city's popular **Etrusca** restaurant and the **Stanford Court Hotel**. ♦ Italian ♦ M-F lunch and dinner; Sa dinner. Reservations recommended. 28 Belden Pl (between Pine and Bush Sts). 421.7044

38 Pasta Bene ★★$ This cafeteria-style spot is popular for its fresh pasta made on the premises and desserts that merit breaking your diet. ♦ Italian ♦ M-F lunch. 88 Hardie Pl (off Kearny St, between Sutter and Bush Sts). 989.2222

39 Galleria Park Hotel $$$ One of the small, renovated hotels springing up around town, this has a superb location, adjacent to the **Crocker Galleria** and two blocks from Union Square and the cable cars. The 177 rooms and suites are equipped with bars and refrigerators, and the grand suite offers the comfort of a fireplace and whirlpool. Meeting rooms are available, and there's even a rooftop jogging track and a small fitness facility equipped with a few exercise machines. ♦ 191 Sutter St (at Kearny St). 781.3060, 800/792.9639; fax 433.4409

Within the Galleria Park Hotel:

Bentley's ★★$$$ This grand-scale oyster bar and exhibition kitchen serves fresh seafood from both coasts and features regional recipes and Creole specialties. The Nouveau/Deco setting includes some lovely etched glass. There's live jazz piano on Monday through Thursday from 5PM to 10PM. ♦ Seafood ♦ M-F lunch and dinner; Sa-Su dinner. Reservations recommended. 989.6895

39 John Walker & Co. Liquors This is the largest specialty and import liquor store in the area. If you have questions or need to find that rare cognac, the staff is ready to help. Gift wrapping and shipping are available. ♦ M-Sa. 175 Sutter St (between Montgomery and Kearny Sts). 986.2707

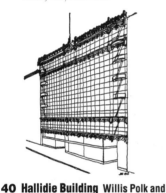

40 Hallidie Building **Willis Polk and Company**'s 1917 building (pictured above) is an architectural favorite. Claiming to be the world's first curtain-wall glass facade, it was built for the University of California and named after Andrew Hallidie, the inventor of the cable car, who was also a university regent. The glass facade is projected a few feet beyond the floor edge and structure. Decorative railings integrate the fire-escape balconies and stairs and create a wonderful silhouette at the top of the building. The sixth floor is the home of the San Francisco chapter of the **American Institute of Architects,** which usually has an exhibit on display in its entryway (free and open to the public). The **US Post Office** occupies most of the ground floor. ♦ 130 Sutter St (between Kearny and Montgomery Sts)

41 Hunter-Dulin Building With the revival of interest in premodern architecture, this 1926 **Schultze and Weaver** building has come to be recognized as one of the finest in the Financial District. Its tripartite division of top, shaft, and base and its rich terra-cotta detailing contrast well with the banality of its more recent neighbors. The style is French château/Romanesque capped by a tile mansard roof. ♦ 111 Sutter St (at Montgomery St)

42 Pacific Telesis Center Whereas the Bank of America World Headquarters represented the then-latest ideas (in 1969) about high-rise towers and their relationship to the urban fabric, **Skidmore, Owings & Merrill**'s design (completed in 1982) embodies a change in architectural thought. It rises sheer from the street without a plaza, and its surface consists of flush two-tone granite panels and mirror glazing. The corners are beveled, emphasizing the wraparound smoothness of the cladding. The matte/glossy granite and mirror glass create changing patterns at different times of the day or night. ♦ 50 Post St (at Kearny St)

Within the Pacific Telesis Center:

Crocker Galleria This ornate, three-level, glass-barrel-vaulted shopping arcade is modeled after Milan's vast Galleria Vittorio Emanuele. Dozens of shops grace this pretty center, including boutiques ranging from **Gianni Versace** to **Polo/Ralph Lauren** and **Marimekko.** You'll also find home furnishings, fresh flowers, cookies, cards, and a range of restaurants, most of them small fast-food places catering to workers in the area. ♦ M-Sa. Entrances are on Post St and Sutter St (between Kearny and Montgomery Sts). 393.1505

Circolo ★★★$$ The third success of the talented restaurateur Fazol Poursohi, this dining spot specializes in homemade pasta (you can see the fresh noodles hanging from racks by the hearth), smoked salmon cut thick instead of traditionally thin, and a gourmet pizza baked in a specially designed wood-burning oven that doubles as a hearth in the elegant dining room. The bar squeezes such fresh juices as apple and carrot. As a bonus, there's a great view of the historic **Hallidie Building** across the street. For all the drama of the peach decor, the atmosphere is cordial and lively and the prices are reasonable. You may enter from the third floor of the **Galleria** or at street level. ♦ California ♦ M-F lunch and dinner; Sa dinner. Reservations recommended. 161 Sutter St (between Kearny and Montgomery Sts). 362.0404

On New Year's Eve, it's a San Francisco tradition in the Financial and Downtown districts to toss calendars out of office windows. The cleanup operation is costly, but locals seem reluctant to give up the practice.

Restaurants/Clubs: Red   **Hotels:** Blue
Shops/ 🌳 **Outdoors:** Green   **Sights/Culture:** Black

COURTESY OF CARLOS DINIZ ASSOCIATES

General Philip Sheridan's success in the Franco-Prussian War. The West had never seen such opulence: seven stories, 800 rooms, and a dining room 150 feet long. The **Grand Court** (now the indoor **Garden Court**) was the stage for a continuing procession of hacks, barouches, and phaetons, from which stepped the wealthy, the powerful, and the famous. The **Palace** has hosted presidents Grant, Teddy and Franklin Roosevelt, Taft, McKinley, Wilson, and Harding, who died here in 1923 while still in office; magnates Morgan, Rockefeller, Carnegie, Vanderbilt, and Pullman; writers Rudyard Kipling and Oscar Wilde; actresses Sarah Bernhardt, Lillie Langtry, and Lillian Russell; royalty from many nations; and countless political figures.

The original structure was rebuilt after the 1906 quake and fire. A 1980s renovation by **Skidmore, Owings & Merrill** established the **Garden Court** as the hotel's focal point. This magnificent room is 120 feet long, 85 feet wide, four stories high, and topped with a glass dome constructed of 80,000 panes (each of which was taken down, cleaned, and repaired during the restoration). Amenities include 550 rooms, a conference area and business center, and a health spa with a skylit, indoor swimming pool, whirlpool, sauna, and exercise room. ♦ 639 Market St (at New Montgomery St). 392.8600, reservations only 800/325.3535; fax 543.0671

Within the Sheraton Palace Hotel

The Garden Court ★★$$$$ The continental cuisine is tasty and lovingly presented here, and the service strives for an old-fashioned attentiveness, but the real star of this restaurant is the room itself. You'll feel as if you've been transported to the elegance of bygone times. Dinner dancing is now offered on Friday and Saturday from 8:30PM to 12:30AM, and the Sunday brunch is a quite extravagant (and costly) affair. ♦ Continental ♦ M-Sa breakfast, lunch, afternoon tea, and dinner; Su brunch, afternoon tea, and dinner. Reservations recommended. 392.8600

Kyo-ya ★★★$$$ Although the prices are steep at this austere and authentic Japanese restaurant, the food is sublime—many think the sushi here is the best in the city. ♦ Japanese ♦ M-F lunch and dinner. Reservations recommended. 392.8600

Maxfield's ★★$$ Don't forget to take in the huge Maxfield Parrish painting, *The Pied Piper* (1909), that adorns the **Pied Piper Bar** as you walk to your table. Hearty portions are dished up in the handsome oak clubroom setting. ♦ Grill ♦ M-F lunch and dinner; Sa dinner; Su lunch. 392.8600

43 88 Kearny Street (San Francisco Federal Savings and Loan) Clad in white concrete and embellished with blue tiles, this 1986 **Skidmore, Owings & Merrill** building (pictured above) has one of the finest entrance lobbies and banking halls in the city. The detailing, materials, and lighting evoke an Art Deco flavor. Notice the reconstruction of the old facade next door, which is on the same axis as Maiden Lane and terminates the vista from Union Square. ♦ At Post St

44 Modernism This gallery features early and contemporary 20th-century art, specializing in avant-garde Russian works. ♦ Tu-Sa. In the Monadnock building, 685 Market St (at Kearny and Third Sts), Second floor, Suite 290. 541.0461

45 Sheraton Palace Hotel $$$$ Originally known simply as the **Palace Hotel,** this is the oldest grand luxury hostelry (illustrated above) in the city and was once the showplace of the Gold Rush town known the world over for outrageous extravagance. Conceived and built by William Sharon, a senator from Nevada, and William C. Ralston, a prosperous Mississippi riverboat carpenter who came to California and founded the Bank of California, the hotel opened its doors in 1875 to fete

46 Hobart Building **Willis Polk and Company**'s 1914 building is part high-rise tower, part mid-rise street block. For many years it was one of the tallest structures on

Market Street; now it is dwarfed by the **Wells Fargo Tower** next door. ♦ 582 Market St (at Second St)

47 Stevenson Place Architects **Kaplan/McLaughlin/Diaz**'s 1986 building was one of the first of the Downtown Plan–generated office towers (the early-1980s Downtown Plan placed restrictions on the height, bulk, and massing of high-rise buildings). With its distinctive gable roof, vertical shaft, and richly detailed granite-clad base, it is in sharp contrast to its flat-topped International-style neighbors. The arcade leads through to a plaza on Jessie Street with a fountain and seasonal landscaping. The design recalls a premodern tradition of tall buildings that respect their context, define the street wall, and maintain the continuity of the urban fabric. At night, the building's copper roof is floodlit. ♦ Stevenson St (bounded by First and Second Sts, and Market and Mission Sts)

48 Citicorp Center The best aspect of this 1984 **William Pereira and Associates** building is the conversion of the old **Banking Hall** (built in 1910 by **Albert Pissis**) into an atrium space that's open to the public during the day. The **Citicorp Cafe** (★$$; 362.6297) and a number of colorful flags help to enliven the space, which previously had an echoing mausoleum-like quality. **Pereira**'s tower is clad in precast concrete. ♦ 1 Sansome St (at Sutter St)

49 130 Bush Street Ten stories high and just 20 feet wide, **George Applegarth**'s 1910 building is surely one of the narrowest high rises ever built. It has slender Gothic lines and a defined top, middle, and bottom. ♦ Between Sansome and Battery Sts

50 The Shell Building One of the city's most beautiful Art Deco towers, **George Kelham**'s structure, built in 1929, was strongly influenced by **Eliel Saarinen**'s entry for the Chicago Tribune Tower competition. Because of its fine proportions—tripartite division of top, shaft, and base—distinctive silhouette, and contextual relationship to the urban fabric, it is now considered an important source of inspiration for the next generation of sky-scrapers. The exterior is sheathed in glazed terra-cotta. ♦ 100 Bush St (between Sansome and Battery Sts)

51 Crown Zellerbach Building Following the example of Lever House in New York City, this 1959 design by **Hertzka and Knowles** and **Skidmore, Owings & Merrill** represented the then-current fashion for treating buildings as isolated objects withdrawn from the street by a belt of landscaping and clad in thin curtain walling. It's ironic to think that in 1981 the suggestion that it might be demolished to make way for a taller building prompted discussion about listing the building as a historic landmark when the time comes.
♦ Market St (between Sansome and Battery Sts)

52 Specialty's Cafe and Bakery ★$ This take-out lunch spot is packed at noontime. Everything's made from scratch—even the sandwich bread comes straight from the oven—and the cookies are heavenly. Try their peanut-butter, banana, and wheat germ sandwich for a change of pace. Catering services are available. ♦ Takeout ♦ M-F breakfast and lunch. 22 Battery St (at Market St). 512.9550. Also at: 312 Kearny St (between Bush and Pine Sts). 788.2254; and 150 Spear St (between Mission and Howard Sts). 788.2254

53 444 Market Street Architects **Skidmore, Owings & Merrill**'s 38-story, aluminum-panel-clad office tower, completed in 1981, has a sawtooth profile. The building steps back on the 33rd, 34th, and 35th floors, opening out onto gardens that overlook the bay. ♦ At Front St

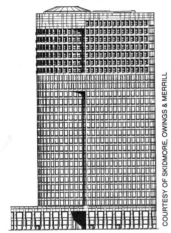

COURTESY OF SKIDMORE, OWINGS & MERRILL

54 388 Market Street One of **Skidmore, Owings & Merrill**'s most refined buildings is this mixed-use, flatiron office tower (pictured above), completed in 1987. The triangular site is occupied to the property lines, in contrast to the **Crown Zellerbach Building** two blocks away on Market Street, designed by the same firm. The building's form consists of a cylinder attached to a triangle. The apartments at the top have deeply recessed windows, while the offices below have flush windows. The facade is a dark-red polished granite, which contrasts with the green window mullions. ♦ Between Pine and Front Sts

55 Federal Reserve Bank Building Carefully scaled to match the adjacent Southern Pacific and Matson buildings, **Skidmore, Owings & Merrill**'s granite-surfaced edifice (completed in 1983) with its grand arcade is an important addition to the formal aspects of Market Street. Take in one of the changing exhibitions in the ground-floor gallery space. ♦ Market St (between Spear and Main Sts)

Chinatown

San Francisco's Chinatown is the largest Chinese community on the West Coast—and the second largest in the US next to New York City's settlement. The tourist area, bounded by **Broadway** and **Stockton, Kearny,** and **Bush Streets**, is home to many of the 120,000 Chinese-Americans living in the Bay Area, but the population extends to North Beach, Russian Hill, and beyond to the Sunset and Richmond districts. Because the pulse of the community remains within the original perimeters of Chinatown—and because traditions are strong—the suburban Chinese come back on Sunday to shop and dine here.

When the first Chinese immigrants arrived, they found a small community huddled around **Portsmouth Square,** still the hub of Chinatown. Once the gold strike was announced, the Cantonese came by the boatload, fleeing famine and the Opium Wars. By 1850 there were more than 4,000 Chinese

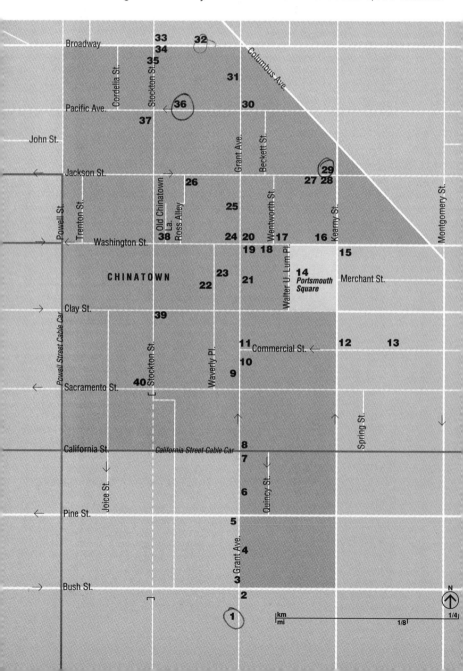

men (and only seven Chinese women) in the area. Chinese "coolies," a term stemming from the word *kuli* (Chinese for bitter toil), were tolerated as long as they performed the tasks other groups scorned—working the mines, building the transcontinental railroad, and, later, planting the Napa vineyards. But when the work dried up in the 1880s, many Caucasian San Franciscans shared Rudyard Kipling's view of Chinatown: "A ward of the city of Canton set down in the most eligible business quarter of the City." A vicious backlash had set in. When hundreds of unemployed whites tried to run them out of town, the Chinese retaliated by organizing *tongs,* or secret associations, for protection, which soon evolved into warring gangs. These organizations turned to selling opium, running extortion rings, and promoting prostitution, with discipline maintained by squads of hatchet men. It wasn't until the 1920s that conflict was banished from Chinatown's streets, but lately, new immigrants are forming gangs once again.

When the area was totally destroyed by the 1906 earthquake and fire, city politicians planned to relocate the Chinese to less valuable property. Instead, the industrious Asians rebuilt with such dispatch that they reclaimed their district before City Hall could act. And the new Chinatown was just as crowded as the old. By World War II, an average of 20 people shared a bath, and there were about 12 people to a kitchen. This same area—18 square blocks—is now struggling to absorb the newest wave of immigrants, the ethnic Chinese from Vietnam.

Chinatown is so much more than the few commercial street-front blocks along **Grant Avenue,** marked by the **Chinese Gate** on Bush Street. It is the back alleys crammed with herb shops; benevolent societies that promote cultural and civic causes; upper-floor residences with balconies; fish hanging on clotheslines; garment sweatshops; the temples; and the action on Stockton Street, which has become the true main street of Chinatown since the tourist trade usurped Grant. Here the food is as much of an attraction as the Grant Avenue trinkets. Fish swimming in tanks, crawling crabs, live chickens awaiting slaughter, hanging ducks, exotic greens, and tempting baked goods you will not see elsewhere can all be found here. It doesn't matter if you can't speak any of the myriad dialects swirling around you. Sign language works very well, and shopping in Chinatown can be a remarkable adventure.

Area code 415 unless otherwise indicated.

1 Dragon House Tasteful Japanese and Chinese antiques are sold in this small, dark shop, which offers all kinds of treasures for the intrepid shopper. Netsukes, decorative figurines, carved snuff bottles, teapots, and other wonders can be found here. ♦ M-Sa. 315 Grant Ave (between Bush and Sutter Sts). 421.3693

2 Hotel Triton $$ The 140 smallish rooms here are stocked with playful and sophisticated modern furniture decorated in a pink-and-gold color scheme. The hotel works hard to ingratiate itself with the fashion and entertainment industry, so expect to see some glitzy folk loitering about. There is no restaurant. ♦ 342 Grant Ave (at Bush St). 394.0500, 800/433.6611; fax 394.0555

3 Grant Avenue Chinatown's tourist shopping street is active, crowded, and fascinating. Restaurants and gift stores line the way from the ceremonial gateway at Bush Street to Broadway. While many of the stores are interchangeable and most sell similar gifts and souvenirs, it's fun to stroll along and sample several of them. Many shops are open until 9 or 10PM every day, so you can have dinner at one of the many restaurants and then browse. Much of Chinatown is best experienced on foot. Don't try driving down Grant or Stockton in this area, as traffic is congested and slow. Instead, leave Grant and wander among the small, narrow alleys and lanes to absorb the sights, sounds, and smells of Chinatown. These little passages hold a hodgepodge of businesses: travel services, temples, groceries, laundries, Chinese book- and newspaper stores, and benevolent associations. The latter are protective organizations, active in the civic and cultural life of Chinese residents. Note how the nondescript buildings are decorated with balconies and doorways painted green, red, yellow, and orange. ♦ Between Bush St and Broadway

4 Tai Nam Yang In the furniture business for more than 30 years, the owners of this shop specialize in ornate rosewood pieces, ceramic *objets,* hand-painted vases and screens, and cloisonné. ♦ M-Sa. 438 Grant Ave (between Bush and Pine Sts). 982.1737

5 Grant Plaza Hotel $ This is probably one of San Francisco's most outstanding values. The lobby has glitzy accoutrements such as a crystal chandelier and generation-spanning Victorian and contemporary sofas in shades of pink and plum. The 72 rooms are small but well decorated. On the sixth floor are a marvelous stained-glass dome and panels, legacies from a nightclub that existed on the premises in the 1920s. There's no restaurant, but being in the heart of Chinatown should make dining out a breeze. ♦ 465 Grant Ave (at Pine St). 434.3883, reservations only 800/472.6899; fax 434.3886

6 Lotus Garden ★$$ This vegetarian restaurant beneath a Taoist temple serves familiar Chinese dishes, but without the meat. ♦ Chinese/Vegetarian ♦ Tu-Su lunch and dinner. 532 Grant Ave (between Pine and California Sts). 397.0707

Within Lotus Garden:

Ching Chung Taoist Temple Take the stairs to the restaurant's top floor with its lovely stained-glass dome, and you'll find yourself in an ornate temple filled with gilded altars, carved furniture, fruit offerings, and smoking incense sticks. Spend a few minutes in appreciative silent contemplation, then leave refreshed for more sight-seeing. ♦ Daily until 6PM. 433.2623

7 Imperial Fashion It's not that the hand-decorated linens and handmade dickeys are any different here than at many other Chinatown shops, but they're particularly well displayed. Prices for the ornate hand-iwork are less than you'd expect to pay for a lot of machine-sewn tablecloths, guest towels, or napkins. ♦ Daily. 564 Grant Ave (at California St). 362.8112

8 Old St. Mary's Church California's first cathedral now functions as a neighborhood parish church, though apparently not for the Chinese Catholic community, which favors a different church offering Mass in Chinese. Built of brick in 1854, it survived both the 1906 and the 1989 earthquakes without structural damage. During wartime, it provided social refuge for soldiers on leave. It operated the first English-language school for the Chinese community. ♦ 660 California St (at Grant Ave)

9 Chinatown Kite Shop Stop here to peruse an incredible assortment of all kinds of kites, including windsock and fish kites in cotton or nylon. Some make wonderful decorations for a child's room; all make great souvenirs. ♦ Daily. 717 Grant Ave (between Sacramento and Clay Sts). 391.8217

10 The Wok Shop Everything you need for creating your own Chinese feast, from cookbooks to utensils, can be found here. ♦ Daily. 718 Grant Ave (between Sacramento and Commercial Sts). 989.3797

10 Eastern Bakery Try the rice candy or some of the Chinese cakes, such as black bean, lotus, and melon. ♦ Daily. 720 Grant Ave (between Sacramento and Commercial Sts). 392.4497

11 Grant Avenue at Commercial Street This corner affords a rare unobstructed view east down to the **Ferry Building.**

12 Hon's Wun Tun House ★$ This tiny, bustling, downscale-looking assemblage of Formica tables and limited counter seating is where the cognoscenti gather when they want a great cheap bowl of noodles or dumpling soup. A glass of tea comes with the meal. It's usually crowded, so expect to share a table. ♦ Cantonese ♦ Daily lunch and dinner. 648 Kearny St (at Commercial St). 433.3966

13 Chinese Historical Society of America Rotating exhibitions of the society's collection of artifacts, photographs, and documents trace the history of the Chinese people in America. Displays are captioned in Chinese and English. ♦ Free. Tu-Sa noon-4PM. 650 Commercial St (between Montgomery and Kearny Sts). 391.1188

14 Portsmouth Square Robert Louis Stevenson spent many hours writing in this square, and his recollections of the area can be found in *The Wreckers.* ♦ Bounded by Walter U. Lum Pl and Kearny St, and Washington and Clay Sts

15 Holiday Inn at Chinatown $$$ Located near North Beach, the Financial District, Union Square, and The Embarcadero, this unique building is the result of an award-winning design by **Clement Chen.** Facilities include 566 rooms with free cable TV, room service until 10PM, a rooftop swimming pool, and five floors of underground parking. There's a cable-car line three blocks away (**California Street**). Altogether, the employees speak 31 languages. ♦ 750 Kearny St (between Washington and Merchant Sts). 433.6600, 800/465.4329; fax 765.7891

Within the Holiday Inn at Chinatown:

Chinese Culture Center A valuable resource and communication center for Chinese culture in the West, this facility offers

changing art shows and entertainment programs in its 650-seat theater. The center also arranges guided tours. ♦ Free. Tu-Sa. Third floor. 986.1822

Lotus Blossom Restaurant ★$ Located on the second floor of the hotel, this restaurant offers an inexpensive all-you-can-eat breakfast and lunch buffet, and the dinner menu features a wide variety of American and Chinese dishes. ♦ Chinese/American ♦ Daily breakfast, lunch, and dinner. 433.6600

15 Wok Wiz Chinatown Tours Shirley Fong-Torres, an author, TV personality, and food critic, created these walking tours to provide an insider's view of Chinatown. Highlights include participating in a private Chinese tea ceremony or tasting, meeting an herbalist, and observing how dumplings are made at a pastry shop. For an extra charge, dim sum at a Chinatown restaurant may be added to the tour. ♦ Daily; call for times and reservations. 750 Kearny St (between Washington and Merchant Sts), Suite 800. 355.9657

16 Buddha's Universal Church This five-story structure was built by hand using an exotic variety of polished woods. The church contains mosaic images of Buddha, bronze doors, and murals on the roof. ♦ Church: daily. Tours: the second and fourth Sunday of every month. 720 Washington St (at Kearny St). 982.6116

17 Sun Hung Heung ★$$ Obviously no one comes to this venerable 1919 establishment for the ambience, a dreary expression of Formica booths and Naugahyde chairs. Still, the food and the modest prices are compelling reasons to return. ♦ Cantonese ♦ M, W-Su lunch and dinner. 744 Washington St (between Grant Ave and Kearny St). 982.2319

18 Silver Restaurant ★★$$ Though lacking charm, this place takes its food seriously and is open around the clock. A tempting row of barbecued ducks hangs in the window. Ginger crab, black beans with clams, and virtually any of the seafood dishes are foolproof here. ♦ Cantonese/Mandarin ♦ Daily 24 hours. 737 Washington St (between Grant Ave and Walter U. Lum Pl). 433.8888

19 Old Chinese Telephone Exchange Building This site used to be home to the *California Star,* the first newspaper in the city and the one that started the rush in 1848 by spreading the cry of "Gold!" The present building, a three-tiered pagoda (pictured above), once housed the operators for Chinatown's telephone system and later the local Pacific Telephone and Telegraph offices. A branch of the Bank of Canton is now located here. ♦ 743 Washington St (between Grant Ave and Walter U. Lum Pl)

20 Li Po Welcome to one of San Francisco's most bizarre bars. From the minute you walk through the golden cave-mouth entrance, you'll know you're not in Kansas anymore. Kitschy Asian furnishings abound, streetwise waitresses move the booze, and Sinatra serenades on the jukebox. Bottoms up. ♦ Daily 2PM-2AM. 916 Grant Ave (between Washington and Jackson Sts). 982.0072

21 China Trade Center Three floors of mall-type shops offer jewelry, linens, clothing, watches, souvenirs, and eyeglasses, among many other types of goods. Dangling from the ceiling above the staircase is a large, fierce-looking dragon. ♦ Daily. 838 Grant Ave (between Washington and Clay Sts). No phone

Within the China Trade Center:

Empress of China ★★$$$ This is one of Chinatown's fancy, expensive restaurants, with a celebrity clientele to match. You'll like the food, but is it significantly better than other nearby Chinese restaurants that charge less than half the price? ♦ Chinese ♦ Daily lunch and dinner. Reservations recommended. 434.1345

The flamboyant green-and-ocher Gateway to Chinatown at Grant Avenue and Bush Street serves as the entrance to the Chinese capital of the Western world. Dragons and lions adorn the gateway, which was erected in 1970.

Early morning, when shopkeepers are busy setting out their wares, is a good time to get a feel for the real (i.e., non-touristy) Chinatown.

Restaurants/Clubs: Red	**Hotels:** Blue
Shops/ ♥ Outdoors: Green	**Sights/Culture:** Black

Dim Sum and Then Some

If you have only one Asian meal in San Francisco, make sure it's dim sum. These small tea pastries came to San Francisco via Hong Kong and became a delicious local institution. Even today, San Francisco and Hong Kong are the only cities in the world with extensive dim-sum restaurants.

Most people eat dim sum for brunch, so the restaurants tend to be open from 9 or 10 in the morning until mid-afternoon. Generally, the food is rolled over to your table on a cart, and you simply choose whatever looks good. Don't worry if the waitresses don't speak English and you don't speak Chinese; when it comes to dim sum it's worth experimenting. When you're done, they count the number of little plates on the table and draw up the bill accordingly. The most

popular dim-sum dishes include *cha siu bow* (steamed buns filled with barbecued pork), *ha gow* (delicate little dumplings stuffed with shrimp), and egg rolls (you haven't eaten an egg roll until you've tried one at a dim-sum restaurant). And for dessert, don't pass up one of those little custard tarts—they'll make you think you're in a Parisian cafe.

Jow Nn Hueng Gai
Chicken lollipops

Chun Guen
Spring rolls

Gee Yoke Go
Savory pork triangles

Pot Sticker (Kou Teh)
Meat-filled dumplings

Four-color Shui Mai
Meat-and-vegetable-filled dumplings

Pot Sticker Triangles
Meat-filled wonton skins

Garlic

Cha Siu Bow
Steamed barbecued pork buns

Sweet and pungent ginger dip

Dow Sah Bow
Sweet bean-paste-filled buns

Gee Cheung Fun
Steamed rice-noodle rolls

Siu Mai
Steamed pork dumplings

Floweret Siu Mai
Meat-filled dumplings

Ha Gow
Shrimp dumplings

Jow Ha Gok
Shrimp turnovers

Cha Siu So
Flaky buns

Fancy Fans
Meat-filled wonton skins

22 Tien Hou Temple Located on the fourth floor of a brightly painted building, this temple is dedicated to Tien Hou, Queen of the Heavens and Goddess of the Seven Seas. Flowers, incense, and intricately carved statues fill the small sanctuary. Its hours are unreliable, so your best bet is to take one of the tours arranged by the **Chinese Culture Center** at the **Holiday Inn at Chinatown** (750 Kearny St; 986.1822) every Saturday at 2PM. But if you're walking past and see clouds of incense swirling down from the balcony, you may assume the temple is open. (There's no elevator, only stairs.) The street it's on—Waverly Place—is known as the "Street of Painted Balconies." It's colorful, crowded, noisy, and redolent with the aroma of exotic foodstuffs and incense. ♦ M-Sa. 125 Waverly Pl (between Washington and Clay Sts), Fourth floor

23 The Pot Sticker ★$$ This appealing little side-street restaurant specializes in the fried and steamed meat-filled dumplings for which it is named. ♦ Mandarin ♦ Daily lunch and dinner. 150 Waverly Pl (between Washington and Clay Sts). 397.9985

24 Chew Chong Tai & Co. The doors opened before 1911, making this the oldest store in Chinatown. It's the place to find calligraphy brushes, ink sticks, and Japanese and Chinese inks. The staff will even mount and frame your completed artwork. ♦ Daily. 905 Grant Ave (at Washington St). 982.0479

25 Ten Ren Tea Co., Ltd. More than 40 different teas are available here, as well as Chinese, Korean, and American varieties of ginseng. Many of the teas and ginseng roots are grown on the company's own farms. This is one of the largest such operations in existence, with 60 branches worldwide. Customers may sample whatever tea is being brewed. ♦ Daily. 949 Grant Ave (between Washington and Jackson Sts). 362.0656

26 Golden Gate Fortune Cookies In addition to the usual crunchy fortune cookies, this small factory located on a side street produces X-rated versions with declarations that would make Confucius blush. ♦ Daily. 56 Ross Alley (off Jackson St). 781.3956

27 Pearl City Seafood ★★$$ This place looks spiffier than many restaurants in the area, with fashionable pink tablecloths and black-lacquer chairs. The huge fish tank on a rear wall attests to the freshness of the seafood dishes. Spiced, salted prawns, and prawns with garlic sauce are among the tempting choices. ♦ Cantonese ♦ Daily lunch and dinner. 641 Jackson St (between Wentworth and Kearny Sts). 398.8383

28 Star Lunch ★$ Very casual counter-service meals are served at this tiny Shanghai-style restaurant. It's a real period piece, with painted wood-planked walls studded with coat hooks. Regulars enjoy the noodles, fried-rice cakes, and perfumed meats. ♦ Shanghai ♦ Tu-Su lunch. 605 Jackson St (at Kearny St). 788.1552

29 Ti Sun Hardware Though this is pretty much like any other hardware shop, it also stocks a particularly nice selection of cleavers, steamers, stirring utensils, cookbooks, and other accoutrements required by professional and amateur Chinese cooks. ♦ Daily. 614 Jackson St (at Kearny St). 982.1948

29 DPD ★$ Inexpensive Shanghai fare is served at this popular restaurant that also does a brisk take-out business. The lunch special, which includes such favorites as peppery cabbage, steamed dumplings with ginger and black vinegar, and plump Shanghai noodles, is a good value. Similar dishes are offered at dinner for slightly more money. ♦ Shanghai ♦ Daily lunch and dinner. 901 Kearny St (at Jackson St). 982.0471

29 House of Nanking ★★★$$ This is one of those hole-in-the-wall Chinese restaurants that are out of this world. Seating is at a half-dozen tables that are crammed together (definitely expect to bump elbows with your neighbors) and at a counter, where you can watch the chef turn the freshest of ingredients (bright purple eggplant, fat green beans, and the like, bought daily at Chinatown markets) into delicious, spicy dishes that never miss. Expect a wait. There's also takeout. ♦ Chinese ♦ Daily lunch and dinner. 919 Kearny St (between Jackson St and Columbus Ave). 421.1429

30 Four Sea Market Barbecued poultry, fresh fish, and live crabs and shellfish are sold at this busy market, typical of many of the spots patronized by fussy home cooks who want the freshest market offerings. ♦ Daily. 1100 Grant Ave (at Pacific Ave). 788.2532

Restaurants/Clubs: Red   Hotels: Blue
Shops/ ♥ Outdoors: Green   **Sights/Culture: Black**

31 New Hop Yick Meat Market Sausages, pork rinds, and whole roast pigs can be found here. The pigs are a particularly good choice when you're looking for an easy way to feed a crowd. ♦ Daily. 1147-49 Grant Ave (between Pacific Ave and Broadway). 989.0247

31 Kwong Jow Sausage This place manufactures its own delicious Chinese sausages, which are displayed hanging on strings. ♦ Daily. 1157 Grant Ave (between Pacific Ave and Broadway). 397.2562

32 Hing Lung Chinese Cuisine ★★$ Very good rice noodles, Chinese fried bread, and many tasty variations of *congee* (a type of rice porridge) are the specialties of this bustling restaurant. It's an only-in-San-Francisco experience (at least outside of China). ♦ Chinese ♦ Daily breakfast, lunch, and dinner. 674 Broadway (between Stockton St and Columbus Ave). 398.8838

33 Yuet Lee Seafood Restaurant ★★$$ Painted an appalling shade of green, this eatery looks like the proverbial greasy spoon, but the food is so good that the lack of ambience is easily overlooked. It's packed every night, so be prepared for a long but worthwhile wait at prime time (it's also one of the very few San Francisco restaurants open until 3AM). Hong Kong–style stir-frying, done over a high flame, is the attraction here. The main specialty is seafood—try the pepper-and-salt roast prawns in the shell or the sautéed clams with pepper-and-black-bean sauce. One of the marvelous pan-fried noodle dishes, crisp on the bottom and covered with your choice of meats and vegetables, is also a must. No alcohol is served, so bring your own beer or wine. ♦ Cantonese ♦ M, W-Su lunch and dinner. Reservations required for five or more. 1300 Stockton St (at Broadway). 982.6020

34 Mon Kiang ★$$ This is one of the few Hakka restaurants in the whole Bay Area. The cooking style is the most down-home of all the Chinese culinary styles and makes generous use of innards and other food Westerners might discard (fish lips and poultry blood, for example). The restaurant has, however, altered some of the dishes to please local palates. Among the specialties is salty baked chicken with pickle sauce. ♦ Hakka ♦ Daily lunch and dinner. 683 Broadway (at Stockton St). 421.2015

35 Stockton Street The street of daily life in Chinatown is no longer exclusively Chinese. Other Asian populations, including Viet-namese, Filipinos, and Koreans, have settled and opened businesses here. Chinatown residents buy goods in the grocery and butcher shops, bakeries, and quaint herb-and-spice stores along this thoroughfare and its side streets. Take note of the many handsome brick structures from the 1850s that were once plush private residences. Francis Pioche, a pioneer financier and bon vivant credited with giving San Franciscans an appreciation of fine food, lived at 806 Stockton. Pioche imported many French chefs and cargoes of vintage wines to the city. ♦ Between Broadway and Sacramento St

36 New Asia ★★$$ Dim sum as good as any you'll find in Hong Kong is served here in a noisy room the size of a football field. Waitresses roll carts up and down the aisles singing over their wares, and you choose what catches your eye. Everything steamed or fried is phenomenal. A trick to beat the wait: Go upstairs, where you share big tables with other diners. ♦ Dim Sum ♦ Daily breakfast, lunch, and dinner. 772 Pacific Ave (between Stockton St and Grant Ave). 391.6666

37 Sang Sang Fish Market If it swims and it's fresh, it's probably for sale here, and at a reasonable price, too. ♦ Daily. 1145 Stockton St (between Pacific Ave and Jackson St). 433.0403

38 Old Chinatown Lane This narrow street was once called the "Street of Gamblers," a reference to Chinatown's enigmatic history. ♦ At Washington St (between Stockton St and Ross Alley)

38 Jade Galore A security officer and two gilded lions guard the entrance to this jewelry shop dealing in Burmese jade and diamonds. ♦ Daily. 1000 Stockton St (at Washington St). 982.4863

39 Celadon ★★$$ Named for the subtle gray-green that accents the refined decor, this restaurant serves very good Chinese food in a classy setting. The lobster dishes are especially recommended. ♦ Cantonese ♦ Daily lunch and dinner. Reservations recommended. 881 Clay St (at Stockton St). 982.1168

40 Cameron House This Presbyterian community center was named after Donaldina Cameron to honor her lifetime of work dedicated to freeing singsong slave girls. The women, mostly Chinese and some Japanese, arrived here thinking they would become brides of the mine workers, but instead were used by businessmen as prostitutes and slaves. Cameron came to be known as "Lo Mo," or the mother. Inside the house are old carved cornices, calligraphy, and paintings. ♦ M-F. 920 Sacramento St (at Stockton St). 781.0408

Nob Hill/Russian Hill

Formerly christened the "Hill of Palaces," Nob Hill vies with Telegraph Hill for the honor of being the best known of San Francisco's many hills. The mansions of the rich are gone now, with the notable exception of James Flood's Edwardian brownstone at 1000 California Street; they've been replaced with luxury hotels, a world-famous cathedral, several exclusive clubs and apartment houses, and upscale condominiums for millionaires.

In the late 1850s, at the site of the **Stouffer Stanford Court Hotel**, Dr. Arthur Hayne cut a trail through the chaparral to survey the land and build the first home on the hill for his bride, actress Julia Dean. Within a few years, men of means followed his trail (a steep route that even their horses found difficult to

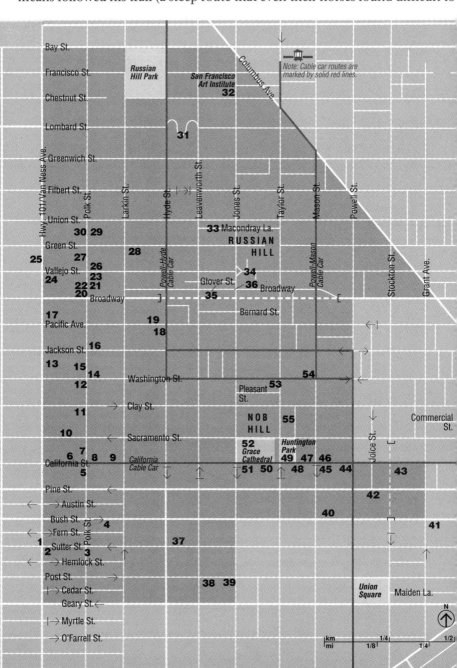

navigate) and began a mass exodus from San Francisco's Rincon Hill and South Park. The advent of the cable car in 1873 encouraged the uphill flow of money, fueling the unbridled ostentatiousness of the homes of the rich and nouveaux riches. Ironically, it was all swept away 30 years later when a massive fire followed the earthquake of 1906.

In a sense, Nob Hill is still the "Hill of Palaces." Fastidious men and women continue to reach their homes or clubs by cable car, though during summer months the riders are almost all tourists. But the reckless display of wealth is gone—the air is more of subdued gentility, although power brokers still make the hill their home. The generally accepted boundaries of Nob Hill are **Bush, Larkin, Pacific,** and **Stockton Streets.**

Russian Hill, next door, is a neighborhood of contradiction, costly and bohemian at the same time. Studded with sleek high-rise apartments attended by porters, it has its share of the rich and famous. But there are also the working singles, struggling writers, and students from the nearby **San Francisco Art Institute** who share apartments, cramming four or five people into two bedrooms—the only way to afford the high rent. Despite the contrasts, it's the kind of place where customers and shop owners know each other on a first-name basis.

Within walking distance of Union Square, the Financial District, and North Beach, Russian Hill is full of picturesque cul-de-sacs, bay views, wooded open spaces, and, of course, that wiggly part of **Lombard Street** that's better known as "the crookedest street in the world." Technically, Russian Hill extends from Pacific to **Bay Street**s and from **Polk** to **Mason Streets,** but its real heart is bordered by **Broadway** and **Chestnut,** Larkin, and **Taylor Streets.**

Area code 415 unless otherwise indicated.

1 American Rag The glad rags here include used retrofashions and new duds from American and European manufacturers. This is the perfect place to find a bowler hat. Although many of the clothes are used, they're not all cheap. ♦ Daily. 1305 Van Ness Ave (at Sutter St). 474.5214

2 Galaxy Theater One of the first movie complexes to be built in the city in a generation, this 1984 **Kaplan/McLaughlin/Diaz** building (pictured above) houses four theaters. It is best seen at dusk, when the neon signs glow rainbow colors. ♦ 1285 Sutter St (at Van Ness Ave). 474.8700

3 Polk Street The stretch between California and Geary Streets is known as Polk Gulch and was the focus of the city's gay population until most of the action moved to the Castro district. Currently, that portion of Polk is in transition, populated by many drifters and young male hustlers. Much of the gloss the street attained in the 1970s has been lost to a proliferation of shops whose wares are in questionable taste. But as strollers head north, beyond California Street, the area's appeal is alive and well, with a mix of old neighborhood food stores, antiques shops, bookstores, restaurants, and several charming specialty shops. ♦ Between Geary and Lombard Sts

4 Alliance Française Here's the educational heart of San Francisco's sizable French-speaking community, and an ideal place to learn how to *parler français*. On the premises is a French cafe. ♦ Cafe: M-Sa lunch. 1345 Bush St (between Polk and Larkin Sts). 775.7755

5 Fields Book Store This shop full of spiritual and esoteric books has been helping its readers solve life's deepest mysteries since 1932. ♦ Tu-Sa. 1419 Polk St (between Pine and California Sts). 673.2027

5 Crustacean ★★$$ The kitchen turns out flavorful crab and other Euro-Asian seafood dishes in this sleek restaurant with its witty, under-the-sea decor. ♦ Seafood ♦ Dinner daily. Reservations recommended. 1475 Polk St (at California St), Third floor. 776.2722

Restaurants/Clubs: Red   Hotels: Blue

Shops/ 🌳 Outdoors: Green   **Sights/Culture:** Black

5 Sushi Paradiso ★★$$ Classical music plays as the chef slices some fine raw fish. The *kozara* (the Japanese version of the Spanish tidbits, tapas) is great, too. ♦ Japanese ♦ M-Sa dinner. 1475 Polk St (at California St), Ground floor. 567.0184

6 Ye Rose & Thistle British beer, darts, pool, and pinball draw Anglophiles and British expatriates to this dark and seedy-looking bar. ♦ Daily until 2AM. 1624 California St (between Van Ness Ave and Polk St). 474.6968

7 Swan Oyster Depot ★★★$$ This restaurant is a favorite among knowledgeable San Franciscans, although you won't find anything fancier than a lunch counter and stools. But the cold fish dishes are fantastic and the servers among the friendliest around. There is also fish to take home. ♦ Seafood/Takeout ♦ M-Sa breakfast and lunch. 1517 Polk St (between California and Sacramento Sts). 673.1101

8 Cordon Bleu ★★$ A perfect choice before catching a movie, this is one of San Francisco's best hole-in-the-wall Vietnamese restaurants, and an unbelievably fine value. Five-spice chicken, a Vietnamese staple, is sumptuous here. ♦ Vietnamese ♦ Tu-Sa lunch and dinner; Su dinner. 1574 California St (at Polk St). 673.5637

9 Emerald Garden ★★★$$ This charming little restaurant was created in an alleyway between two buildings. The narrow space has been transformed with lovely original artwork, Asian sculpture, and a profusion of tropical blooms. What keeps people coming back, besides the appealing decor and prices, is the outstanding Vietnamese food prepared with a California touch. Grilled stuffed chicken roll and macadamia-nut chicken are among the numerous possibilities. ♦ Vietnamese/California ♦ M-F lunch and dinner; Sa-Su dinner. Reservations recommended. 1550 California St (between Polk and Larkin Sts). 673.1155

10 Acquerello ★★★$$$ Giancarlo Paterlini and Suzette Gresham, who operate this sophisticated restaurant, serve marvelously inventive contemporary dishes in a soothing, pastel-hued dining room decorated with original watercolors. The small menu, which changes frequently, might include salmon-and-scallop ravioli in dry vermouth, fillet of beef with balsamic vinegar and shallots, or breast of chicken rolled in pancetta with sage and Madeira sauce. ♦ Italian ♦ Tu-Su dinner. Reservations recommended.

1722 Sacramento St (between Van Ness Ave and Polk St). 567.5432

11 Double Rainbow Some aficionados claim the rich and creamy ice cream at this shop is the best in San Francisco. The ultrachocolate flavor certainly is tops! ♦ Ice Cream ♦ Daily. 1653 Polk St (at Clay St). 775.3220. Also at: 3933 24th St (at Sanchez St). 821.3420; 407 Castro St (at Market St). 621.2350; 1724 Haight St (at Cole St). 668.6690; 2133 Chestnut St (between Pierce and Steiner Sts). 922.3920

12 Adriatic ★★$$ This charming corner restaurant is most people's idea of what a French bistro should look like. It has bentwood chairs, lace curtains, and lots of brass accent pieces arranged in an intimate green-and-white setting. The food is reliably good, although not wildly exciting, and the prices are right. ♦ French ♦ Tu-Su lunch and dinner. 1755 Polk St (at Washington St). 771.4035

13 House of Prime Rib ★★★$$ A favorite among beef eaters with big appetites, this grill offers handsome decor, comfortable booths, soft lighting, and generous servings of excellent prime rib that are carved at the table. There are even seconds for those who can go the distance. Good grilled salmon is offered as a non-beef alternative. All in all, it's a great value. ♦ American ♦ Daily dinner. Reservations recommended. 1906 Van Ness Ave (between Jackson and Washington Sts). 885.4605

14 Buffalo Exchange The young crowd loves the new and recycled clothing stocked here, and many keep their wardrobes going by regularly exchanging what they have for something they like better. ♦ Daily. 1800 Polk St (at Washington St). 346.5726. Also at: 1555 Haight St (between Clayton and Ashbury Sts). 431.7733; 2512 Telegraph Ave, Berkeley. 510/644.9202

15 Tibet Shop Just entering this small, exotic shop puts many customers into a meditative state. Antiques, jewelry, curios, and clothing from Tibet, Nepal, Bhutan, and Afghanistan are terrific buys here. If you must have some silver bangles or little lapis-lazuli skulls in your jewelry box, this is the place to find them. ♦ Daily. 1807 Polk St (between Washington and Jackson Sts). 982.0326

15 Birkenstock In the neighborhood for more than 15 years, this store sells the comfy, albeit homely, footwear once favored by the counterculture but now popular with the mainstream as well. ♦ Daily. 1815 Polk St (between Washington and Jackson Sts). 776.5225

The east end of Lombard Street is the crookedest street in the world, with eight turns in one block.

15 Naomi's Antiques to Go A paradise for nostalgiaholics, this place stocks lots of American dinnerware, pottery, and china from the 1920s to the 1950s. ◆ Tu-Sa. 1817 Polk St (between Washington and Jackson Sts). 775.1207

16 The Bell Tower ★★$ This handsome new bar and restaurant is quickly becoming a neighborhood favorite, serving low-priced standards such as burgers, hot dogs, and chicken wings. Also on the menu are inexpensive nontraditional dishes like fried catfish sandwiches; tequila-lime-and-cilantro-marinated Chilean sea bass, served on a bed of black beans; and salmon pasta with herb cream, red onions, and capers. It's the perfect place to take a break and chat with the locals. ◆ California/American ◆ Daily lunch and dinner until midnight. 1900 Polk St (at Jackson St). 567.9596

16 Fioridella One of San Francisco's most creative (and, yes, expensive) florists; its designs are much favored by the socially prominent. ◆ M-Sa. 1920 Polk St (between Jackson St and Pacific Ave). 775.4065

16 J. Goldsmith Antiques This cute general store stocks American collectibles—with special emphasis on toys—and sells them at slightly lower-than-market prices. ◆ Daily. 1924 Polk St (between Jackson St and Pacific Ave). 771.4055

17 Harris' Restaurant ★★$$$ There's no doubt that this steak-and-prime-rib house means business—a glass refrigerator full of its stock is on prominent display to passersby and for sale to those who would rather cook at home. Mrs. Harris herself, who has a cattle-ranching background, presides over the restaurant. Top-quality meats are served in two substantial dining rooms decorated with roomy booths and wood. Lighter suppers are served in the bar. It's reminiscent of a comfortable, old-money ranchers' club. ◆ Steakhouse ◆ Daily dinner. Reservations recommended. 2100 Van Ness Ave (at Pacific Ave). 673.1888

18 Hyde Street Bistro ★★★$$ There's little in the way of ambience at this casual, friendly bistro, but the food is great and the desserts are works of art. The menu, emphasizing roasted meats and luscious pastas, changes regularly, and, like the chef/owner, reflects an Austrian viewpoint that is wonderfully compatible with the Northern Italian food. Expect dishes such as strudel and spaetzle here. ◆ Austrian/California ◆ Daily dinner. Reservations recommended. 1521 Hyde St (at Pacific Ave). 441.7778

19 Ristorante Milano ★★★$$ This small, stylish restaurant serves some of the best Northern Italian dishes in town at moderate prices. The waiters are polite and knowledgeable; the contemporary decor is an interesting mix of Japanese woodwork and Milanese design in charcoal gray and off-white. With plenty of repeat customers and reservations limited to parties of four or more, expect a crowd and possibly a long wait unless you dine early or very late. ◆ Italian ◆ Tu-Su dinner. 1448 Pacific Ave (between Hyde and Larkin Sts). 673.2961

20 Johnny Love's ★★$$$ The bar at this new nightclub/restaurant overflows with decked-out singles. Co-owner Johnny Love remains involved in a number of local success stories, including the **Blue Light Cafe.** Try the calamari, which comes with three excellent dipping sauces, and the mini-pizzas. Expect long lines at the bar entrance—live music starts nightly at 10:30PM. ◆ California ◆ Daily dinner. Reservations recommended for dinner (use the side entrance on Polk St for dining-room access). 1500 Broadway (at Polk St). 931.6053

20 Pasha ★$$$ Fine Middle Eastern fare and a sensuous, exotic ambience are the drawing cards at this Moroccan restaurant. Don't hesitate to tuck dollar bills into the belly dancer's waistband as she (or he) undulates by. Other temptations include rack of lamb with pomegranate and honey, and quail with lime and sage. ◆ Moroccan ◆ Tu-Su dinner. Reservations recommended. 1516 Broadway (between Polk St and Van Ness Ave). 885.4477

21 The Real Food Company This supermarket of organic foods (affectionately referred to by neighborhood residents as "The Real Expensive Food Company") features an excellent produce section. Check the center aisle for fresh bread delivered daily by the Bay Area's best bakeries, and hidden in back is a very good meat-and-fish counter. ◆ Daily. 2140 Polk St (between Vallejo St and Broadway). 673.7420. Also at: 1023 Stanyan St (between Carl St and Parnassus Ave). 564.2800; 3939 24th St (between Noe and Sanchez Sts). 282.9500; and 1240 Sutter St (between Van Ness Ave and Polk St). 474.8488

¡WA-HA-KA!

22 WA-HA-KA! Oaxaca Mexican Grill ★$
This casual, hip Polk Street place packs 'em in, not just because the food is great, but because it's fresh, fast, and inexpensive. Place your order at the counter, grab a table, and wait to be called to pick up your delicious food—try the fish taco, shrimp fajitas, or WA-HA-KA! burrito with grilled steak. Sangria and Mexican beer are available to wash it all down. The cooks proudly proclaim they never use lard in the food. Everything is available to go, too. ♦ Mexican ♦ Daily lunch and dinner. 2141 Polk St (between Vallejo St and Broadway). 775.1055. Also at: 1489 Folsom St (at 11th St). 861.1410

23 The Real Food Deli ★★★$ Take a number to reserve your place in line as soon as you walk through the door, then ogle at all the savory salads, specials, and divine desserts on display. The soups and made-to-order sandwiches are first-rate, and everything is prepared with very fresh, often organically grown ingredients. Don't pass up the creamy arborio rice pudding, the lemon tartlets, or the banana bread pudding—they're worth breaking your diet for. Great breads, olives, and cheeses are also sold here. Takeout is also available. ♦ Deli ♦ Daily breakfast, lunch, and dinner. 2164 Polk St (at Vallejo St). 775.2805. Also at: 1001 Stanyan St (at Carl St). 564.1117

24 Babylon ★★$$$ A place for the well-heeled 20- and 30-something crowd to meet and mill, this spot combines a bar and dance club with a restaurant serving surprisingly good Mediterranean food—all fixed up in a neo-Greco-Roman motif. Most people are dressed to the nines, but you can get by with a leather jacket and jeans if you've got attitude. ♦ Mediterranean ♦ Tu-Su dinner. 2260 Van Ness Ave (at Vallejo St). 567.1222

25 North China Restaurant ★★★$ Don't let the nearly empty dining room fool you—this Chinese restaurant may lack ambience, but it serves great food. The spicy Kung-Pao shrimp is a must. Take-out orders are available, too. ♦ Chinese ♦ M-Sa lunch and dinner. 2315 Van Ness Ave (between Vallejo and Green Sts). 673.8201

26 Russian Hill Antiques There are two floors of pine furniture, jewelry, and gift items here; most are from early 20th-century America and Europe. ♦ Tu-Sa. 2200 Polk St (at Vallejo St). 441.5561

27 Green's Sports Bar If you think San Francisco sports fans aren't as enthusiastic as those on the East Coast, just try getting a drink (or getting *in*, for that matter) during a 'Niners game—it's a spectacle worth checking out. Between games, however, this place transforms into a pleasant neighborhood bar. ♦ Daily. 2239 Polk St (between Vallejo and Green Sts). 775.4287

28 Le Petit Cafe ★★$$ This is the perfect neighborhood cafe for a breakfast of creamy oatmeal or steamed eggs. Linger over a cappuccino, browse the bookshelves, and watch the artsy crowd come and go. At night, white linens and candles cover the wood tables, and the menu switches to simple, satisfying Italian fare—fettuccine, polenta, grilled chicken, and fish. Come early for the weekend brunch—before the BMW crowd flocks in from other neighborhoods. ♦ American/Italian ♦ Daily breakfast and lunch; Tu-Sa dinner. 2164 Larkin St (at Green St). 776.5356

29 La Folie ★★★★$$$$ Gourmets adore this place, and with good reason. The superb food ranks among the best French fare offered in the city. A plus (or a deficit, depending on one's point of view) is that it's served in a fairly relaxed setting. There is no dress code, and patrons may be dressed to the teeth or utterly casual. Banquette seating doesn't allow for too many intimate exchanges, but most of the satisfied sighs here are inspired by the food. Offerings might include such refined and inventive choices as sweetbreads with shiitake mushrooms or *rôti* of quail and squab wrapped in crispy potato strings. The five-course Discovery Menu is the best way to experience the genius of the kitchen here. Another plus is the free valet parking. ♦ French ♦ M-Sa dinner. Reservations recommended. 2316 Polk St (between Green and Union Sts). 776.5577

29 Little Thai ★$ Beneath the spreading branches of a large fake coconut tree, diners are served some inexpensive and often memorable dishes. Among the many choices are *param long srong* (a sliced-pork creation with spinach in a sweet peanut sauce), *larb ped* (ground duck with lemon sauce), and *yum plamuk* (spicy calamari with mint and lemon). ♦ Thai ♦ Daily dinner. 2348 Polk St (between Green and Union Sts). 771.5544

30 Casablanca ★$$ North of the nighttime hubbub on Polk Street is this lively international restaurant decorated with bentwood chairs, antique pieces, swirling overhead fans, Oriental carpets, and nicely framed photographs of Humphrey Bogart. Daily specials showcase the best of the kitchen's offerings, although such regular standards as pepper steak and roast duck are also favored choices. Live dinner music is played nightly from 7PM to 9PM; at 9:30PM the sound gets friskier with a pianist and bass player offering jazz, blues, and pop tunes. There's free valet parking. ♦ International ♦ Tu-Su dinner. Reservations recommended. 2323 Polk St (between Green and Union Sts). 441.2244

31 Lombard Street Nicknamed "the crookedest street in the world," this section of Lombard (pictured above) was designed in the 1920s to respond to the slope's extreme steepness. Faced with brick pavers and landscaped with flowers, shrubs, and hedges, the street is a fine example of the art of road engineering integrated into the urban fabric. There is an ongoing discussion about limiting vehicular traffic on the street, but so far nothing has happened. If you plan to drive down it, prepare yourself for a line of visitors waiting to do the same thing—especially on Saturday and Sunday. ♦ Between Hyde and Leavenworth Sts

---

Restaurants/Clubs: Red   **Hotels:** Blue
Shops/ ♥ Outdoors: Green   **Sights/Culture:** Black

32 San Francisco Art Institute This 1871 establishment is the oldest cultural institution in the West. Home to three galleries, the institute has played a central role in the development of contemporary art in the Bay Area. Student work is displayed in the **Diego Rivera Gallery;** the **Walter/McBean Gallery** shows work by professional artists; and the **Still Lights Gallery,** adjacent to the photography studios, has photographic exhibitions. **Paffard, Keatings, Clay**'s 1969 extension to the art institute, designed with great verve, is a rare example of the Corbusian *béton brut* style in California. It contains a lecture theater, a conference room, studios, workshops, exhibition spaces, and a cafe. ♦ Tu-Sa during the school year. 800 Chestnut St (at Jones St). 771.7020

33 Macondray Lane The condominiums by **Bobbie Sue Hood** fit successfully into the traditional San Francisco bay-windowed residential style on this two-block pedestrian street on the steep north face of Russian Hill. ♦ Between Union and Green Sts, and Leavenworth and Taylor Sts

34 1000 Block of Vallejo Street One of the city's most attractive residential neighborhoods, this block consists of three narrow residential streets—Vallejo Street (which is approached from Jones Street by ramps designed by **Willis Polk), Russian Hill Place,** and **Florence Street. Polk** built four Mediterranean-style villas between 1915 and 1916, and **Charles F. Whittlesey** designed the three to the south on Vallejo Street. All are private residences. ♦ Vallejo St (between Jones and Taylor Sts)

35 Glover Street Duplex One of the **Dan Solomon–Paulette Taggert** team's beautifully designed San Francisco houses, this consists of two units interlocked one above the other on a 25-foot-wide lot. The front facade (pictured at right) is an interesting mixture of traditional bay-window elements and a classical portico with a severely detailed triangular pediment. The modernist windows and gateway make the 1982 design of this private residence both Rationalist and Contextual. ♦ 15 and 17 Glover St (between Jones and Leavenworth Sts)

COURTESY OF SOLOMON, INC.

36 Allegro Ristorante Italiano ★★$$ Nestled on Russian Hill, this restaurant has an intimate dining room designed in jewel-box shades of mauve and pink. Italian-born owner Angelo Quaranta prepares the food himself, emphasizing the dishes of central and southern Italy. ♦ Italian ♦ Daily dinner. Reservations recommended. 1701 Jones St (at Broadway). 928.4002

37 York Hotel $$ Moderately priced and centrally located, this is one of the many small hostelries that has been spiffed up. The 96 rooms are attractive, and there are trendy extras such as chauffeured-limousine service, a complimentary breakfast, and an executive gym. There is no on-premises restaurant. ♦ 940 Sutter St (between Hyde and Leavenworth Sts). 885.6800, 800/227.3608; fax 885.2115

Within the York Hotel:

The Plush Room Big-name as well as up-and-coming entertainers play at this unique, aptly named cabaret. Among those who've performed here are Michael Feinstein, Charles Pierce, Jim Bailey, Margaret Whiting, and Andrea Marcovicci; most recently a popular, long-running comedy revue has occupied the stage. Note the spectacular stained-glass ceiling. ♦ Cover. Hours vary according to show times. 885.6800

38 Hotel Bedford $$ This 17-story, 144-room inn has a stunning dining room, a friendly lobby, and intimate bedrooms that have the feeling of a private home. Hotel guests are invited to a complimentary wine bar every evening, and room service is available for breakfast and dinner. Another plus: It's just three blocks from Union Square and very close to galleries, theaters, and transportation. ♦ 761 Post St (at Leavenworth St). 673.6040, 800/227.5642; fax 563.6739

39 Hotel Beresford Arms $ One of the finest small hotels in the theater district provides a friendly atmosphere and personal service. Many of the 95 rooms have whirlpool baths and wet bars. Senior citizens get discounts and children under 12 may stay free. There is an unusually attractive lobby for entertaining your guests, but no restaurant. ♦ 701 Post St (at Jones St). 673.2600, 800/533.6533; fax 474.0449

40 Cafe Mozart ★★★★$$$$ One of Nob Hill's best restaurants, this refined establishment with intimate dining on three levels produces food that arrives so beautifully arranged on the plate, it's hard to decide whether it should be photographed or eaten. Gourmets who can't make up their minds should choose the *menu dégustation,* which provides samplings of many different dishes that change regularly to reflect the freshest products in the market. The ambience here is cozy and traditional, with Corots and Monets gracing the walls. A fireplace glows in the main dining room, and only Mozart is played in the background. The wine list is pricey. ♦ French ♦ Tu-Su dinner. Reservations recommended. 708 Bush St (between Mason and Powell Sts). 391.8480

41 Aioli ★$$ Chef Sebastian Urbain concocts imaginative dishes that meld Italian, French, California, and Creole influences. The menu is fairly limited, but good. ♦ Italian ♦ Daily lunch and dinner. Reservations recommended. 469 Bush St (at Grant Ave). 249.0900

42 Nob Hill Lambourne $$ This business-oriented hotel includes a fax machine and a personal computer in all 20 rooms. There also is voice mail, full secretarial support, desktop publishing, and boardroom facilities, but no restaurant. The guest rooms are decorated in contemporary and period styles. ♦ 725 Pine St (between Powell and Stockton Sts). 433.2287, 800/274.8466; fax 433.0975

43 The Ritz-Carlton San Francisco $$$$ A relative newcomer to Nob Hill's noble hotel scene, this hostelry occupies a renovated 1909 Neo-Classical building that used to house Metropolitan Life Insurance. It has 336 beautifully furnished rooms and suites, including a concierge floor with such amenities as complimentary breakfast. The multilingual staff offers impeccable, old-fashioned service, and there's an indoor lap pool and fitness center. An elegant afternoon tea is available daily in the lobby lounge from 2:30PM to 5PM. ♦ 600 Stockton St (between Pine and California Sts). 296.7465, 800/241.3333; fax 986.1268

Within the Ritz-Carlton San Francisco:

The Dining Room ★★★$$$$ Chef Gary Danko, formerly of Château Souverain in Sonoma, brings his special brand of California-French-Continental cuisine to this lovely, formal restaurant, which made *Condé Nast Traveler*'s Top 50 list in 1994. The kitchen prides itself on the breadth and imaginativeness of the menu. ♦ French ♦ M-Sa dinner. Reservations required. 296.7465

The Terrace Restaurant ★★$$$ Chef Stephan Marshall offers very good Mediterranean cuisine at **The Dining Room's** less formal cousin. The Sunday brunch features live jazz. ♦ Italian ♦ M-Sa breakfast, lunch, and dinner; Su brunch and dinner. 296.7465

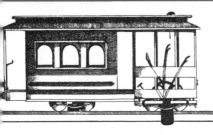

Streetcars of Desire

San Francisco's beloved cable-car system made its maiden voyage on 1 August 1873. With its Scottish inventor, Andrew Hallidie, at the grip, the car successfully tackled five hilly blocks along Clay Street to Portsmouth Square in Chinatown.

Hallidie, a mine-cable designer during the Gold Rush days, decided to invent the system after witnessing an unfortunate accident on a steep hill: A horse-drawn wagon had rolled backward, dragging the helpless horses behind. Hallidie's system was safer, and it opened up areas in the city previously thought unsuitable for building homes.

Just before the 1906 earthquake, cable cars had reached their peak, with 600 cars traveling a 110-mile route. But the system sustained heavy damage during the quake and fire, and many lines were not rebuilt. Electric trolleys took over some of the lines, and the number of cable cars dwindled over the next 50 years. But in 1955 the city voted to preserve the famed hill-climbers, and in 1964 they became the first moving National Historic Landmark in the United States.

Starting in 1984, at a cost of more than $60 million, the system underwent two years of head-to-toe renovations. Old track and cable vaults were pulled up and replaced. For extra strength, deeper grooved rails and more flexible curves were installed. The track was also realigned or moved to avoid interfering with traffic, and the pulleys and depression beams that guide each cable were replaced. The historic Washington-Mason car barn was completely renovated and its traditional appearance preserved. The cars themselves were given a shiny coat of maroon, blue, and gold paint, as well as new brakes, seats, and wheels.

Today you can choose from three lines: the **Powell-Mason Line;** the **Powell-Hyde Line,** which is said to offer the best views and the most thrilling curves; and the **California Line.** There are 44 cable cars in all, with 27 used at peak times. An average of 13 million passengers travel on the 17 miles of track in a year—about 35,616 people a day.

Each six-ton car attaches itself to a cable beneath the street, moving along at a steady 9.5 miles per hour by the turning of 14-foot wheels located in barns. A cable-car operator starts and stops the car by mechanically gripping the cable to make the car go forward and by releasing it to stop the car. Tension can be adjusted if necessary to keep the cable from slipping.

44 Stouffer Stanford Court Hotel $$$$
America's top executives often rank this
hotel (pictured above) as their favorite in San
Francisco. The attractive decor is combined
with the amenities of a European-style
hostelry. Each of the 402 rooms and suites
has individually controlled air conditioning, a
marble bath with a dressing room, a color TV
well hidden in an armoire, and heated towel
racks. Many have canopied beds. Coffee,
newspapers, and overnight shoe shines are
among the complimentary services. Mercedes
and Rolls-Royce limousines are available for
hire from 7AM to 8PM.

It was built on the site of railroad magnate
Leland Stanford's mansion, later the location
of a 1912 apartment building, which was
gutted to create the hotel. The only remainder
from the Stanford days is a 30-foot-high wall
surrounding the property, although the design
borrows something from the original house.
For example, the Stanfords had a circular
vestibule illuminated by an amber glass dome
three stories above. A similar effect has been
achieved in the hotel by covering the central
courtyard and fountain with a lofty stained-
glass canopy; tea and cocktails are served
here. There's also indoor valet parking and a
multilingual staff. ♦ 905 California St (at
Powell St). 989.3500, 800/HOTEL.1; fax
391.0513

Within the Stouffer Stanford Court Hotel:

Fournou's Ovens ★★★$$$$ The most
distinctive places to dine in this multilevel
restaurant are in the glass-enclosed
conservatory area, which is pleasant for
breakfast and lunch, or at the "oven" level,
which boasts a magnificent open hearth
decorated with Portuguese tiles and a floor-
to-ceiling wine cellar. The chef does an
exemplary job with roasts from the oak-fired
ovens, and fresh vegetables, which are
prepared in an appealingly contemporary
style. Organic produce, meats, game, and
local seafood are emphasized on the seasonal
menu. Breads and pastries—including some
of the best sourdough loaves in town—are
baked on the premises. ♦ American ♦ Daily
breakfast, lunch, and dinner. Reservations
recommended. 989.3500

**45 Mark Hopkins Inter-Continental San
Francisco** $$$$ Ever since its opening in
1926, this 392-room hotel (familiarly known
as "The Mark") has been well regarded
internationally. It was host to officials during
the formation of the United Nations, and a
vacation site for presidents Hoover and
Eisenhower and countless other celebrities. In
1939, the 19th floor (once the private
apartment of copper magnate D.C. Jackling)
was remodeled and opened as the **Top of the
Mark.** It is the foremost skyroom cocktail
lounge anywhere, with a 360-degree view of
the bay and hills. Designed by **Timothy
Pflueger,** it was one of the first examples of
this now commonplace hotel feature. The
huge glass panels can supposedly withstand
120-mile gales (although no winds have ever
reached that velocity in San Francisco). Over
the years, the famous **Peacock Court** and
Room of the Dons have been chosen for San
Francisco's society weddings, debuts, and
charity parties. Amenities include 24-hour
room service, one-day laundry and valet
services, terry-cloth robes, in-room movies,
video messages posted on the TV screen,
minibars, baby-sitting and concierge services,
and a health club. There is also a business
service center. ♦ 1 Nob Hill (at California and
Mason Sts). 392.3434, 800/327.0200; fax
421.3302

Within the Mark Hopkins Inter-Continental
San Francisco:

Nob Hill Restaurant ★★$$$$ The
atmosphere is formal at this handsome, oak-
paneled restaurant, which may help explain
why it has never quite caught on with the
locals, although the food is quite well
prepared and seasoned with herbs grown in
the hotel's own garden. The extensive wine list
includes bottlings from 34 states. During the
day, the menu emphasizes California cuisine;
by night, the accent is decidedly French. There
is a Japanese dish on the menu at all meals.
♦ California/French ♦ Daily breakfast, lunch,
and dinner. Reservations recommended.
616.6944

Lower Bar This congenial drinking spot with
a vaulted Tiffany-style skylight and colorful
murals serves cocktails all day and afternoon
tea from 2:30PM to 5:30PM. ♦ Daily.
392.3434

Restaurants/Clubs: Red	**Hotels:** Blue
Shops/ 🌳 Outdoors: Green	**Sights/Culture:** Black

46 The Fairmont $$$$ This hotel was constructed on the property of Senator James "Bonanza Jim" Fair, and the foundations of the palace he had planned to build were later incorporated into the hotel. Son-in-law Hermann Oeirichs planned and began construction of the hotel, to the consternation of the city fathers, who could not understand placing any hotel so far from the center of town. New owners took over before the building was completed, hoping to open it in 1906. Although the frame withstood the earthquake, the subsequent fire ate up the interior and work had to begin all over again. When Senator Fair's daughter offered to take the property back, the disheartened owners jumped at the chance. On 18 April 1907, Mrs. Hermann Oeirichs kicked off the opening of the hotel with a magnificent banquet symbolizing the rebirth of the city one year after the earthquake.

Today, with the addition of a 22-story tower, this grand hotel has 600 rooms and suites, six restaurants, six lounges (including the **Fairmont Crown,** the highest public-observation point in the city, and the **New Orleans Room,** with nightly live jazz), two orchestras, international supper-club talent, and an almost one-to-one ratio of guests to employees. ♦ 950 Mason St (at California St). 772.5000, 800/527.4727; fax 789.3929

Within the Fairmont:

Crown Room Top of the Tower ★$$$ Sunday brunch, a light lunch, and a buffet dinner are accompanied by what many consider the all-time best view of San Francisco. ♦ American ♦ M-Sa lunch and dinner; Su brunch and dinner. 772.5211

Masons Restaurant ★★$$$$ For those who don't have adventurous palates, this smart-looking and comfortable restaurant serves elegant American food that's imaginative but not intimidating. The lounge, with live piano music, is popular with the city's social set. ♦ American ♦ Daily dinner. Reservations recommended. 772.5233

Tonga Restaurant and Hurricane Bar $$; Disneyland meets the South Pacific in this unintentionally high-camp restaurant that serves exotic drinks and mediocre Polynesian food. It's a one-of-a-kind experience worth trying (without the food), as there are regular tropical thunderstorms (with real water) that pour down around a pool. Go during "Happy Hour," Monday through Friday from 5PM to 7PM, when the drinks are cheaper and the greasy hors d'oeuvres are free. ♦ Polynesian ♦ Daily dinner. 772.5278

Bella Voce Ristorante & Bar $$; This is definitely not the best Italian restaurant in town, but it's a lot of fun in the evening. Waiters and waitresses with well-trained voices, many of them waiting to be

"discovered," sing opera and show tunes with vigor. ♦ Italian ♦ Daily breakfast, lunch, and dinner. Reservations recommended. 772.5199

47 The Pacific-Union Club Remodeled by **Willis Polk** in 1908 after the quake and fire, this Edwardian brownstone was originally built in 1886 for James C. Flood, one of the city's railroad kings. He reputedly spent $1.5 million on the house alone, an enormous sum for the times. Polk added the attic story and the entrance tower, which somewhat mar the original classical lines. The building is now used as a very, very private social retreat for male members of "the Establishment." ♦ 1000 California St (at Mason St)

48 The Huntington Hotel $$$ Small, elegant, impeccably groomed, and located on the peak of Nob Hill, this 140-room hotel is the kind of place that has such a loyal following that advertising is unnecessary. This is partly due to the permanency of its staff, which does much to preserve the Huntington brand of personal hospitality. No two rooms are alike; they all look as if they might well belong in a private residence, and all have a view of either the city or the bay. Suites are equipped with a complete kitchen or a wet bar. Complimentary limousine service to the Financial and shopping districts and tea or sherry served upon your arrival are among the amenities. ♦ 1075 California St (between Taylor and Mason Sts). 474.5400, 800/652.1539 in CA, 800/227.4683; fax 474.6227

Within the Huntington Hotel:

The Big Four ★$$$ Named in tribute to four railroad magnates of San Francisco—Collins P. Huntington, Charles Crocker, Mark Hopkins, and Leland Stanford—this restaurant features decor that brilliantly evokes the late 1800s with such touches as etched beveled-glass panels and polished woods. The restaurant features a combination of French and nouvelle California cuisine, highlighting seafood and wild-game dishes. ♦ French/California ♦ Daily breakfast and dinner; M-F lunch. Reservations recommended. 474.5400

49 Huntington Park This delightful oasis atop Nob Hill has a central fountain that replicates Rome's 16th-century Tartarughe Fountain. ♦ Taylor St (between California and Sacramento Sts)

50 Masonic Temple Auditorium This 3,165-seat auditorium is large, but the sight lines are terrible. Orchestras, dance groups, and lectures appear on the thrust stage. ♦ 1111 California St (between Taylor and Jones Sts). 776.4917

51 Vanessi's ★★$$$ In business since 1936, and at this sleek location for almost a decade, this Northern Italian restaurant has charmed generations of San Franciscans with its homemade ravioli and tortellini, fresh veal and fish dishes, and classy Caesar salad (put together tableside). Newer restaurants have overshadowed its cooking style, but this dining spot still remains a favorite. ♦ Italian ♦ M-F lunch and dinner; Sa-Su dinner. Reservations recommended. 1177 California St (at Jones St). 771.2422

52 Grace Cathedral Lewis P. Hobbart's fine neo-Gothic cathedral, modeled after Notre Dame in Paris, took 53 years to build and was finally consecrated in 1964. Notice the beautiful rose window, completed by Gabriel Loire in Chartres, and the spectacular entry, with its *Doors of Paradise,* taken from the same mold used for the entrance to Ghiberti's Baptistry in Florence. There is also a magnificent organ and a not-to-be-missed boys' and men's choir. ♦ 1051 Taylor St (bounded by Taylor and Jones Sts, and California and Sacramento Sts). 776.6611

The Long and Winding Roads

Lombard Street has long laid claim to being the crookedest street in the world, but it seems the famed San Francisco roadway has a little competition. The good citizens of Burlington, Iowa, insist the honor belongs to their own Snake Alley, a brick-laid street that was constructed in 1894 and consists of seven curves on a 16 percent grade. They say that although Lombard boasts more switchbacks and an 18.2 percent grade, it is broken up into a series of short increments, whereas Snake Alley maintains a sinuous stretch of continuous curves. Then again, some San Franciscans claim that the crookedest-street title may really belong to yet another curvaceous roadway: **Vermont Street,** in San Francisco's **Potrero Hill** district. The street has only six curves and a measly 14.3 percent grade, but its muscle-straining, hair-raising turns are much sharper than those of the other contenders.

San Francisco has other winding ways worth exploring, including the following favorites:

Twin Peaks Drive up the hill at the intersection of **Clarendon Avenue** and **Twin Peaks Boulevard,** then wind down the 12 curves (in a 9,000-foot stretch) to **Portola Drive.** The view, 910 feet above sea level, is spectacular.

O'Shaughnessy and Teresita Boulevards Begin at the intersection of Portola Drive and O'Shaughnessy Boulevard, heading southeast. Arrows shaped like C's warn you of the curves—20 of them in 12,000 feet. Turn right on **Brompton Avenue** and again on **Joost Avenue.** Then turn right on **Foerster Street** for two blocks and again at Teresita Boulevard. The following block—which alone has nine curves—is lined with charming, colorful houses.

Telegraph Hill Four curves—and, unfortunately, a passel of traffic jams—in 2,400 feet lead to the landmark **Coit Tower.** On a clear day, the view of **Alcatraz** and the city is tremendous and worth the effort.

53 Venticello ★★★$$ Often favorably compared to New York City's neighborhood Italian restaurants, this spot serves excellent, if rather rich, Italian food in a trattoria-like atmosphere. The tables are crowded together, the service can be brusque and the dining room quite noisy, but the food will make you forgive all that. The imaginative pasta dishes are perfectly prepared, and the pizza is a slice of heaven. ♦ Italian ♦ Daily dinner. Reservations recommended. 1257 Taylor St (at Washington St). 922.2545

54 Cable Car Museum The winding house for the underground cables that control the cars, known as the **Cable Car Barn** (pictured above), was constructed in 1887, then rebuilt after it was badly damaged in the 1906 quake. When the cable-car system was renovated in the early 1980s, the barn was reinforced, but the exterior was left alone. The museum now has an underground viewing room where you may watch the cables work. Photographs and memorabilia are also on display, including three vintage cable cars and scale models of all the cars ever used. ♦ Free. Daily. Washington and Mason Sts. 474.1887

55 Nob Hill Café ★★$ This family-run bistro, where owner Michael Deeb and his friendly staff go out of their way to make you feel at home, is tucked into a charming, quiet corner of Nob Hill. It's a neighborhood favorite, and paintings by local artists adorn the walls. The menu offers traditional Italian cuisine and an array of California-tinged specials at prices uncommonly low for the area. Try the *crostini di polenta* (topped with mozzarella and pesto), a pizza Margherita, or any of the chef's nightly creations. Be prepared to wait—there are only eight tables and reservations are not accepted. ♦ Italian ♦ Daily lunch and dinner. 1152 Taylor St (between Sacramento and Clay Sts). 776.6500

Russian Hill was named after a graveyard (long since removed) for Russian seamen.

Dianne Feinstein
United States Senator

I'm a native San Franciscan and terribly in love with my city. Selecting a favorite place is consequently very difficult, since there are simply miles and miles of pleasures and delights packed into our 47-square-mile area.

However, caveats aside, I always recommend that visitors to San Francisco stroll through **Golden Gate Park,** with its more than 1,000 acres of magnificent trees, plants, and greenswards. The park also houses our renowned **Japanese Tea Garden,** a special park within a park whose ambience is unmistakably Eastern—a wonderful place to reflect and relax.

Some of San Francisco's finest museums are also located within **Golden Gate Park**—the **Asian Art Museum,** the **M.H. de Young Memorial Museum (Fine Arts Museum),** the **Academy of Sciences,** and the **Steinhart Aquarium.**

I also highly recommend visiting San Francisco's **Chinatown**—one of the largest outside of Asia—where you can eat exquisitely for very low prices and shop for virtually anything.

And don't forget to ride one of San Francisco's **cable cars.** The city, with tremendous support from the private sector, has rehabilitated this century-old transportation system—America's only moving national monument—and it remains a great way to see San Francisco's incredibly hilly streets and spectacular views.

Visit **Fisherman's Wharf,** too, and sample our incomparable Dungeness crab, sourdough bread, and succulent seafood. Be sure to take a boat ride on **San Francisco Bay,** one of the world's most beautiful deep-water bodies. You can sail right under the **Golden Gate Bridge**—as well as the equally impressive **Bay Bridge.** Views of San Francisco from the bay are breathtaking.

As for restaurants, we have more per capita than any city in America and they range fully across the world's most exciting cuisines. We have food for literally every palate!

Shopping is also excellent, particularly in **Union Square,** one of the nation's leading retail centers, located in the heart of downtown San Francisco.

My final recommendation is probably the most important one: Be sure to meet our citizens. San Francisco is a cultural cornucopia of the world's people, most of whom are friendly, helpful, and eager to share their insights about life in San Francisco.

"Nob Hill, the hill of palaces, must certainly be counted the best part of San Francisco. It is there that the millionaires who gathered together, vying with each other in display, look down upon the business wards of the city."

Robert Louis Stevenson

Herbert Gold
Writer

San Francisco is America's great metropolitan village. The many spots like **Caffè Puccini** in North Beach, **Le Petit Cafe** on Russian Hill, or **Cafe Picaro** in the nouveau-beatnik Mission district enable me to bump into, and sometimes get to know, fellow orphans of the world. All of those strangers out there, fellow choristers in the 175-year-long operetta of San Francisco, are part of a kind of "maxifamily."

Theaters such as the **Roxie,** the **Clay,** or the **Lumiere** mean I can stand in line in the fog and often see films until the end in the company of my "maxifamily." The walk home in this walled city—walled by water—is always an option. More than once I've forgotten my automobile because I hardly need it except to cross one of the bridges.

I like breathing the air of the sea lions who gather near **Pier 39,** although I wish they would brush their teeth. On quiet nights I can sometimes hear them barking from my home on Russian Hill.

Leon F. Litwack
Professor of History, University of California, Berkeley and recipient of 1980 Pulitzer Prize in History

The first place I take a visitor is unquestionably **Fort Point,** under the **Golden Gate Bridge.** (Park at **Crissy Field** in the **Marina** and walk to the point—the spot where Kim Novak leapt into the bay in Hitchcock's *Vertigo.*) Then, drive through the **Presidio** on Lincoln Boulevard, gaze at the vistas on the way to the **Palace of the Legion of Honor,** cut across to Geary Street and proceed down to the Pacific Ocean and (at the windmill) into **Golden Gate Park.** Within two hours you will have come to know what makes this city so magic, so spectacular, so irresistible.

Lunch: dim sum at **Yank Sing** (Battery Street) in Chinatown.

Clement Street. For the atmosphere, the people, the cafes, and **Green Apple Books.**

Telegraph Hill and **Coit Tower.** On a clear day or night, it's well worth the climb (or drive).

Cocktail hour: the **Redwood Room** at the **Clift Hotel** or the bar at **Stars Restaurant.**

Dinner: **Stars** (reservations advised; ask to be seated in the Club section).

To round out the night, visit the **Tosca Cafe** on Columbus Avenue (preferably weekdays when the disco next door is closed) for a cappuccino, and **City Lights Bookstore** (across the street) for browsing and rubbing shoulders with the memories of the Beat authors and poets who immortalized this cultural landmark in the 1950s.

East Bay. Drive to **Berkeley** (or take **BART**), walk through the university campus (preferably on weekdays when classes are in session), experience **Telegraph Avenue.**

North Beach/Fisherman's Wharf/Telegraph Hill

The North Beach district was named after a beach that once extended from Telegraph Hill to Russian Hill, but has long since been built up by landfill. The community guards its reputation against the creeping encroachment of the neon, skin shows, and drag queens of nearby **Broadway**, as well as the skyrocketing real-estate prices that threaten the stability of its long-standing ethnic mix. But somehow the old ingredients of the melting-pot neighborhood survive, along with certain remnants of the life that made this area the birthplace of the "Beat Generation." Although North Beach is synonymous with "Little Italy," Italians were not the first nor the last to arrive. Chilean prostitutes came first, in the 1850s, attracted by the Gold Rush, only to be chased out by the Irish, who were eventually replaced by other Latin Americans. On a site first occupied by a Russian Serbian Greek Orthodox Church, the **Washington Square Theater** presented Enrico Caruso in concert. Later this theater became the **Pagoda Palace**, featuring Chinese movies. Supplemented by small colonies of Basques, young working people, and bohemians, the Chinese began crossing Broadway from Chinatown in the 1960s. Today the North Beach population is

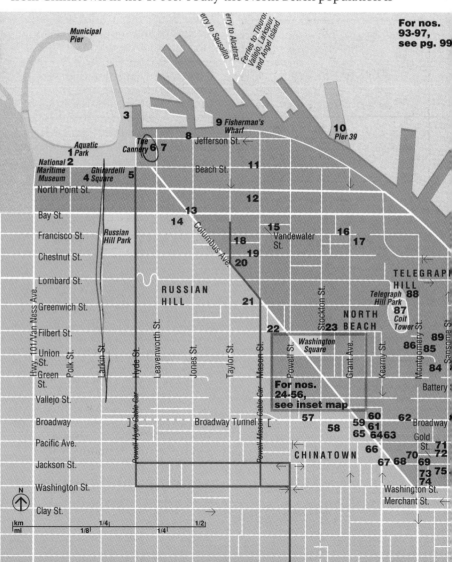

For nos. 93-97, see pg. 99

For nos. 24-56, see inset map

approximately 50 percent Chinese—and growing—although new Italian immigrants are also settling here once again. The perfect place to sample the tempo of this neighborhood is **Washington Square.** Relax on a park bench here and let the gossip in Chinese and Italian swirl around you while old men and women practice T'ai Chi and kids and drifters hang out on the grass.

Bordering North Beach is Telegraph Hill, with its quaint cottages and vine-covered lanes, flowering gardens, stunning views, and impossible parking. Artists and writers once lived here, but now it's mostly the affluent and established who've made it home. The "Hill," as residents call it, looked quite different in the days of the Gold Rush. Although its height is the same (284 feet), the east slope used to be smooth and round and covered with grazing goats. The barren, jagged cliff you see today was created by sailors digging out ballast for their empty ship holds back when water lapped at the hill's base. The area went through several names, but after the Morse Code Signal Station was set up in 1853, the current name stuck. Although most of North Beach burned in the post-earthquake fire of 1906, the Italians managed to save a number of the old wooden cottages on the hill with a bucket brigade, using barrels of homemade red wine. The tiny shacks, built by early fishermen, now sell for hundreds of thousands of dollars. Crowning the hill is **Coit Tower,** named for Lillie Hitchcock Coit, who provided the funds to build it.

Fisherman's Wharf, also bordering North Beach, is one of the city's most popular tourist attractions. Seafood houses stand where crab fishers once hauled in their catch, and there are enough souvenir shops to keep the locals away. It's best to get to the area by cab or bus, and once you're there, plan on doing a lot of walking.

Not much more than a legend remains of the **Barbary Coast,** the once-notorious neighborhood extending between **Pacific, Montgomery, Washington,** and **Kearny Streets.** Aptly named for the equally unsavory pirate headquarters in North Africa, this was where the term "shanghai" originated, describing the practice of drugging a hapless seaman and shipping him out as a crew member for an understaffed ship. The Barbary Coast was a gathering place for hoodlums—a word coined here during the early 1900s, when the city had a worldwide reputation for viciousness. The area was finally shut down after World War I. In the 1950s it was renamed **Jackson Square** by the decorators who renovated the old buildings, exposing handsome brick walls and restoring the mid-19th-century structures. As a result, these few blocks became the city's first designated historic site.

Area code 415 unless otherwise indicated.

1 Aquatic Park This terraced park over-looking the bay sits adjacent to **Ghirardelli Square.** Historic ships managed by the **San Francisco Maritime National Historic Park System** are docked at nearby piers. There is swimming for hardy types, fishing off the scenic **Municipal Pier,** a small beach for wading, and plenty of grass for picnicking with a view. ♦ Beach St (at Polk St). 556.3002

2 National Maritime Museum Part of the **San Francisco Maritime National Historic Park System,** this museum documents maritime history through displays of ship models, photographs, and memorabilia. The fascinating miniatures include passenger liners, freighters, US Navy ships, and a model of the *Preussen,* the largest sail-powered ship ever built. Tours by rangers are available daily. ♦ Free. Daily. Aquatic Park (at Polk St). 556.3002

3 Hyde Street Pier As San Francisco is first and foremost a seaport, no visit to the area would be complete without a tour along the waterfront. Several vessels are docked at this pier (where ferries once carried passengers to Sausalito and Berkeley), which is part of the **San Francisco Maritime National Historic Park System.** The three that are open to the public, the *C.A. Thayer,* the *Eureka,* and the *Balclutha,* hold artifacts, photography collections, and displays that help bring their exciting pasts alive. ♦ Admission; seniors and children under 12 free. Daily. Hyde St (at Jefferson St, at the west end of Fisherman's Wharf)

At Hyde Street Pier:

C.A. Thayer Built in 1895, this schooner (pictured above) was the Pacific Coast's last commercial sailing ship. It transported lumber, served in two wars, and was most recently employed by the fishing industry.

Eureka This was the last diesel-powered ferry to operate in the US. Built in 1890, this vessel (pictured at bottom of page) hauled freight and passengers for the **San Francisco and Northern Pacific Railroads.**

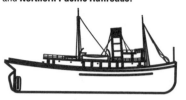

Hercules Berthed beside the *Eureka,* this frigate (pictured above) is under restoration and not open to the public. Built in 1907, the oceangoing tug hauled cargo, crippled ships, barges, and even materials for the Panama Canal.

Balclutha A favorite city landmark, this is a classic square-rigged, three-masted sailing ship. Built in Scotland in 1883, it sailed the Cape Horn route for many years, bringing European goods to the West Coast and taking California grains back home. After the turn of the century, it served as a lumber ship, a salmon cannery in Alaskan waters, and finally a carnival ship and Hollywood movie prop.

4 Ghirardelli Square During the Civil War this was the site of a woolen mill, but it was the famous chocolate factory built here by Domenico Ghirardelli that gave the square its name. The factory was converted into the most attractive commercial complex in the city by **Wurster, Bernardi & Emmons Inc.** and **Lawrence Halprin & Associates** from 1962 to 1967. Their innovative renovation (pictured on page 85) set the stage for retail conversions of Faneuil Hall Market Place in Boston and New York's South Street Seaport, as well as other adaptive-reuse architectural projects around the nation. The location is blessed with views of the bay, and at night the buildings are illuminated with strings of lights. The *Mermaid Fountain* in the central plaza, designed by local artist Ruth Asawa, is a good resting and meeting place. There is usually free entertainment somewhere within the square, which contains dozens of specialty shops, galleries, and restaurants. Among the many interesting places to browse are **Folk Art International;** the **Xanadu Gallery,** which specializes in tribal art; and the **California Crafts Museum,** which exhibits and sells contemporary crafts on the second floor of the **Chocolate Building. Operetta** carries unique men's and women's Italian fashions;

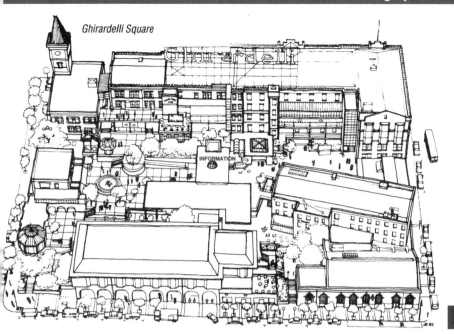

Ghirardelli Square

Something/Anything is a good place to find interesting jewelry and California crafts; and **Goosebumps** sells humorous contemporary gifts. The **Information Booth** has a detailed guide to shops and restaurants. ♦ 900 North Point St (across from Aquatic Park). 775.5500

Within Ghirardelli Square:

McCormick & Kuleto's ★$$ Famed restaurant designer **Pat Kuleto** has put his distinctive stamp on this terrific fish restaurant. The decor is tasteful and plush, the views are astounding, and the seafood menu is one of the most extensive in the city. There's a fresh crab/oyster bar, and a pianist plays jazz on weekend nights. ♦ Seafood ♦ Daily lunch and dinner. Reservations recommended. 929.1730

Mandarin ★★★$$$ This pricey, pretty restaurant with a view of the bay has exceptional Chinese cuisine. The smoked tea duck is excellent, as is the Beggar's Chicken, which you must order 24 hours in advance. The pot stickers are also of the highest quality. ♦ Chinese ♦ M-Sa lunch and dinner; Su dim sum, lunch, and dinner. Reservations recommended. 673.8812

Gaylord India Restaurant ★★$$$ Part of a worldwide chain, this dining spot is beautiful and elegant, and the food is quite good. Tandoori dishes suspended in a clay oven are its specialty. Ask for a window table for a spectacular view of the bay. ♦ Indian ♦ Daily lunch and dinner. Reservations recommended. 771.8822

Compadres Mexican Bar & Grill $$ Sit your tired fanny at a table on the outside balcony, skip the menu completely, and ask for some chips, salsa, and a *grande* margarita or two. Now sit back, relax, and enjoy the spectacular view of the bay and the pleasant sound of live acoustical music that often emanates from below. ♦ Daily lunch and dinner. 885.2266

Ghirardelli Chocolate Manufactory This old-fashioned ice-cream parlor and candy store sells luscious hot-fudge sundaes and five-pound chocolate bars. Take a look at the display of some original chocolate-making machinery in the back. ♦ Daily. 771.4903

Greenpeace Environmental Store Owned and operated by Greenpeace, which reaps the proceeds, this shop stocks environmentally correct merchandise ranging from jewelry and clothing to ornaments and videotapes. ♦ Daily. 474.1870

In 1907, famous escape artist Harry Houdini put on a show at San Francisco's Aquatic Park. While submerged in the frigid waters of the bay, he unshackled himself from chains in just 57 seconds.

Restaurants/Clubs: Red **Hotels:** Blue
Shops/ 🌳 **Outdoors:** Green **Sights/Culture:** Black

5 The Buena Vista $$ Always jammed with tourists and locals, this is the place where Irish coffee got started, and it's still a specialty. There's food, too (American fare, such as burgers and chicken), but do a snack tour of nearby **Ghirardelli Square** instead, and have Irish coffee as the finale. ◆ American ◆ Daily breakfast, lunch, and dinner. 2765 Hyde St (at Beach St). 474.5044

6 The Cannery Originally constructed in 1909 as the Del Monte Fruit Company's peach-canning plant, this building was remodeled in 1968 by **Joseph Esherick & Associates** following the success of **Ghirardelli Square**. Unlike that complex, this structure looks in on itself rather than outward toward its scenic surroundings. The three-story complex contains shops, restaurants, a comedy club, galleries, and a movie theater. Its sunken courtyard filled with flowers and century-old olive trees hosts mimes, musicians, and other talented street performers. Treasures from the estate of newspaper tycoon William Randolph Hearst have been installed in some of the facilities. The interior of the **American Traditions** souvenir shop, for example, has a 90-foot-long hall, a carved fireplace, and a Jacobean staircase originally built in the early 1600s by **Inigo Jones**—England's first true Renaissance architect—for Queen Elizabeth I's ambassador to France. The ceiling in the **San Francisco Museum**, also retrieved from Hearst's warehouse, is a 13th-century Byzantine mosaic of hand-carved and hand-painted wood. ◆ 2801 Leavenworth St (at Jefferson St)

Within the Cannery:

Best Comics and Rock Art Gallery From Richie Rich to Pink Floyd, rediscover your youth through every comic book and rock poster imaginable. ◆ Daily. S Bldg, First floor. 771.9247

Cobb's Comedy Club Belly laughs are induced here nightly. Patrons get three hours of validated parking at the nearby **Anchorage Garage.** Dinner is available from the adjoining **Cafe Rigatoni** (★$; 771.5225). ◆ Cover. Shows daily. S Bldg, Courtyard entrance. 928.4320

The Gourmet Market Shop for yourself or for gifts at this popular spot, which features imported cookware, kitchen accessories, and gourmet treats, from candy to coffee. ◆ Daily. N Bldg, First floor. 673.0400

Cannery Wine Cellars This liquor market is huge. It has an astounding selection of wines and other alcoholic beverages—probably more than you've ever seen before in one place. ◆ Daily. N Bldg, First floor. 673.0400

7 The Anchorage Heavy on souvenir shops, this complex is downstream from **Ghirardelli Square** and **The Cannery**. ◆ Daily. 2800 Leavenworth St (between Jefferson and Beach Sts). 775.6000

8 Lou's Pier 47 Everyone from swabbies on shore leave to local blues aficionados checks out the blues, rock, jazz, or whatever's playing at this club owned by Curtis Lawson. ◆ Shows daily. 300 Jefferson St (between Jones and Leavenworth Sts). 771.0377

9 Fisherman's Wharf The wharf was once the center of San Francisco's commercial fishing fleet, and while the boats are still here, this is now heavy tourist territory. Locals who remember when the business here really was the fishing industry are not pleased with the direction the area has taken and will not be found in significant numbers at the many seafood restaurants, few of which provide much cause for gastronomic rejoicing. ◆ Taylor St (at The Embarcadero)

At Fisherman's Wharf:

Pampanito Submarine This World War II original is docked at the pier. ◆ Admission. Daily. At the pier. 929.0202

Guinness Museum of World Records See the smallest book, the largest guitar, and other record-breaking wonders. ◆ Admission. Daily. 235 Jefferson St (at Taylor St). 771.6226

Ripley's Believe It or Not! Museum Tour two floors of oddities collected by cartoonist Robert L. Ripley. ◆ Admission. Daily. 175 Jefferson St (at Taylor St). 771.6188

Boudin Sourdough French Bread Bakery Frenchman Isadore Boudin opened the city's first bakery on Grant Avenue in 1849 and became one of the first to bake sourdough bread. Now there are 10 Boudin bakeries in San Francisco, including this one, which provides a glimpse of the mysterious sourdough process. ◆ Daily. 156 Jefferson St (at Taylor St). 928.1849

Sheraton at Fisherman's Wharf $$$ This handsome complex of redwood, brick, and greenery has 525 guest rooms interspersed with courtyards. The **Mason Beach Grill** features a breakfast buffet and a nightly seafood buffet. ◆ 2500 Mason St (at Beach St). 362.5500, 800/325.3535; fax 956.5275

Pier 39

Upper Level

A European Heritage
Chic's Place
Eagle Cafe
Good News Stand
Picture San Francisco
B Fun Stitch
Kite Flite
Alamo Flags
Lotus Earrings
C Old Swiss House
D Only in San Francisco
SF Tea & Coffee
Company
E Animal Country
Behind the Wheel
Swing Song
F Cartoon Junction
Midsummer Nights
Fashions Limited

G Brass Boutique
Pacific West Gallery
Bellissima
Swiss Louis
H SF Shirt
Emporium
Trademarks
I House of Reptile
J Dreamweaver Imports
The Marine Mammal
Interpretive Center
National Park Store
K Ballena Bay
Pewtersmiths
Bay View Cafe
Neptune's Palace
Scrimshaw Gallery

L The Beat Goes On
For Effect
M Country San Francisco
Cook Currency
Exchange
Vannelli's
Yet Wah
N Dante's Sea Catch
Designs in Motion
Poster Prints
Vito's Bar
O Juggling Capitol
San Francisco Gold
Company

P Krazy Kaps
Harry Mason Design
Studio
Perestroika
NFL for Kids
The Sweater Gallery
SF Gift Source
Sweats Ltd.
Q NFL Shop
The SF Experience

Lower Level

A The Burger Cafe
Chowders
One Hour Photo
Only in San Francisco
Sal's Pizzeria
B Blue Chip Cookies
ConeCept
Pepe's Tacoria
Showtime Photos
D Chocolate Heaven
On the Road Again
Travel Wear

E On the Road Again—
The Traveler's Store
SF Bay Wear
Scandals
Whittler's Mother
F Le Carousel
The Pier Market
G College Shop
Impostors Jewelry
The Sock Market
Kid's Cottage
H International Sausage
Leather Blues
Naturesque
The Pearl Factory
Puppets on the Pier
I Apple Annie's

J Beach Bums
Sunglass Hut
Wound About
K The Disney Store
The Fudge House
Magnet P.I.
What's A Churro?
L Hollywood USA
Aunt Fanny's Hot
Pretzels
SF Tea & Coffee Co.
M Alcatraz Bar & Grill
Alcatraz Bar & Grill
Gifts
The Candy Store
Turbo Ride
Li'l Reader
Kitty City
N Cable Car Hallmark
Over the Candlestick
Champions
Shirtique

Walk America
Poster Prints
O The Crystal Shop
Encyclopaedia
Britannica
Left Hand World
Pacific Time
We Be Knives
P The Cable Car Store
SF City Wear
The Pearl Factory
Ready Teddy
SF Music Box
Sausalito Accessories
Shell Cellar
Victorian Shoppe
Q Boudin Sourdough
French Bread
Breyers Ice Cream
Music Tracks
Namco Cyber Station
NFL Shop
Stamp-a-teria
Vlahos Fruit Orchard

TraveLodge at the Wharf $$ If you're looking for peace and quiet, this is exactly the wrong place to go. But if you want clean, tastefully decorated rooms at a reasonable price, this above-average chain motel with 250 rooms is right on the money. Amenities include a pool, restaurant, and lounge, free parking, and, for a few dollars more, a balcony overlooking **Alcatraz Island.** It's also within steps of Fisherman's Wharf. ♦ 250 Beach Street (at Taylor St). 392.6700, 800/255.3050; fax 986.7853

10 Pier 39 America's third-most-visited amusement attraction (Disney takes the top spots), this two-level shopping street, particularly popular with families, runs along the north waterfront near Fisherman's Wharf (see the map above). It's the northernmost point of the San Francisco peninsula, thus providing superb views of Alcatraz, the Golden Gate Bridge, the bay, and the city skyline. It opened in 1978 after being transformed from a cargo pier into a fictional image of a turn-of-the-century San Francisco street scene, although it resembles a village on Martha's Vineyard more than a West Coast city. It includes shops, waterfront restaurants serving a variety of cuisines (including more than 20 specialty restaurants for families on a budget), the **Blue & Gold Fleet** (sight-seeing boats), the multimedia presentation *San Francisco Experience,* a waterfront park, a 350-berth marina, a double-deck carousel, and an amusement area. The controversial **Underwater World,** a 50,000-square-foot aquarium exhibiting indigenous northern California marine life, was scheduled to open at press time (critics argue that it will steer visitors away from the excellent **Steinhart Aquarium** in Golden Gate Park).

Among the pier's stores are those specializing in kites, music boxes, teddy bears, and merchandise for left-handed people. Other attractions include the wildly popular sea lions that have taken over part of the marina on the west side of the pier, and the street performers who play daily free of charge at **Stage I,** at **Center Stage,** or by the carousel. The **Pier 39 Cable Car Company** operates a fleet of motorized trolleys—replicas of cable cars—for city tours and charters.

Restaurants include the **Alcatraz Bar & Grill** ($; 434.1818), which gives diners an overview of the rich history of the penal island; **Chic's Place** ($$; 421.2442), with its Art Nouveau decor; the **Eagle Cafe** ($; 433.3689), a San Francisco landmark that has been in business since 1928 (it was once a longshoremen's hangout that was originally located on the site of what is now the garage, until it was lifted and moved to its present location); **Neptune's Palace** ($$; 434.2260), a seafood restaurant; the **Old Swiss House,** one of the better places to eat on the pier, with a great view (★$$; 434.0432); and the **Swiss Louis Italian Restaurant** ($$; 421.2913), which was long established in North Beach before relocating here. A parking garage is located across from the pier on Beach Street (the entrance is on Powell Street). The **Blue & Gold Fleet**'s sight-seeing bay cruises depart from the pier; call 781.7877 for the ferry schedule. ♦ Beach St (at The Embarcadero). 981.8030; 981.PIER (recording)

11 The Wharf Inn $ Granted, it's not the Ritz (and there's no restaurant), but for its location (a block from Fisherman's Wharf) and price (most of the 51 rooms are under $100 a night), this utilitarian hotel is an understated bargain. Add to this free parking and the "no extra person charge," and suddenly one can learn to live with the green-and-mustard decor. ♦ 2601 Mason St (at Beach St). 673.7411, 800/548.9918

12 The Tuscan Inn $$$ This 220-room inn is the first new-construction hotel to be developed by entrepreneur Bill Kimpton, better known for renovating older properties downtown. It follows the successful Kimpton formula, offering style and personal service. Complimentary services include wine every evening and daily coffee or tea by the wood-burning fireplace in the lobby, and limousines to the Financial District weekday mornings. There's in-house parking, room service, same-day valet/laundry service, and programs for children. A collection of Gold Rush artifacts unearthed during the hotel's construction is displayed in the lobby. ♦ 425 North Point St (at Mason St). 561.1100, 800/648.4626; fax 561.1199

Adjoining the Tuscan Inn:

Cafe Pescatore ★★$$ Modeled after a classic Italian trattoria, this attractive, informal restaurant may be the best dining choice in the Fisherman's Wharf area, where pickings are plentiful but culinary excitement is hard to find. Floor-to-ceiling windows open in warm weather to provide semi-alfresco dining. Miniature boats, peppers, and sausages dangle from the ceiling. The exhibition kitchen has a wood-burning pizza oven. Specialties include oak-roasted chicken, risotto with seafood, and Italian seafood stews. ♦ Italian ♦ M-F lunch and dinner, Sa-Su dinner. Reservations recommended. 2455 Mason St (at North Point St). 561.1111

13 San Francisco Marriott Fisherman's Wharf $$$$ One of the most elegant hotels in the wharf area blends apricot marble, comfortable leather, and an abundance of greenery. There are 256 rooms and suites complete with writing desks and cable TV. **Spada's,** the hotel restaurant, specializes in Angus beef and fresh seafood. The lobby lounge features a complimentary buffet. ♦ 1250 Columbus Ave (at Bay St). 775.7555, 800/228.9290; fax 474.2099

14 635 Bay Street This apartment building boasts a charming trompe l'oeil exterior that includes painted-on moldings and a giant "keyhole." It's a private residence. ♦ At Jones St

15 Vandewater Street In this short, narrow alley between Powell and Mason Streets are several architectural firms and some interesting housing examples—notably **No. 55,** a condominium development designed by **Daniel Solomon & Associates** in 1981. Its beautifully proportioned facade is adorned with a gently curved arch at the top and a palette of pinks and beiges. **No. 33** next door, designed in 1981 by **Donald MacDonald &**

Restaurants/Clubs: Red   Hotels: Blue
Shops/ 🍢 Outdoors: Green   Sights/Culture: Black

Associates, is a simpler version, painted white. **No. 22** is an apartment block that the architecture firm **Esherick, Homsey, Dodge & Davis** designed in 1976.

16 210 Francisco Street This 25-foot-wide structure is a modern reinterpretation of the traditional San Francisco row house. **Backen, Arrigoni & Ross**'s 1985 design has all the essential elements—the curved bay window, the false facade—but is constructed out of contemporary materials, including white porcelain enamel panels, glass blocks, and poured-in-place concrete. It's a private residence. ♦ At Grant Ave

COURTESY OF BACKEN, ARRIGONI & ROSS

17 Telegraph Terrace **Backen, Arrigoni & Ross**'s award-winning group of expensive Spanish-style condominiums (pictured above) climbs the steep hillside and looks out over ornamental details that make it fit into its context. The private residences were built in 1984. ♦ Francisco St (at Grant Ave)

18 Albona ★★$$ This is the West Coast's only restaurant serving food of the Istrian Peninsula, the body of land that pokes out below Trieste and is across the Adriatic Sea from Venice. The restaurant is named after a city on the peninsula that was once Italian, then Yugoslav, and now belongs to Slovenia, and the food reflects the Italian and Central European influences of that region. This may be the only establishment in the country that makes cheese-and-nut-filled *crafi Albonesi* (Albonese ravioli). All the desserts, including a knockout apple strudel, are made on the premises. The small dining room is intimate and cozy. ♦ Italian/Slovenian ♦ Tu-Sa dinner. Reservations recommended. 545 Francisco St (at Taylor St). 441.1040

19 San Remo Hotel $ The only budget-priced hotel in North Beach, this lovingly restored Italianate Victorian building was constructed in 1906 by A.P. Giannini, Bank of America's founder. The 62 rooms all share immaculate baths with charming Victorian fixtures. Each of the guest rooms is furnished with antiques or would-be antiques, and some have sinks. There are no telephones or TVs, and the hotel lacks a restaurant, but there is abundant charm. ♦ 2237 Mason St (at Chestnut St). 776.8688, 800/352.7365

20 Campbell-Thiebaud Gallery This gallery specializes in contemporary Bay Area artists. Co-owner Paul Thiebaud is the son of painter Wayne Thiebaud. ♦ Tu-Sa. 647 Chestnut St (between Taylor and Mason Sts). 441.8680

21 Buca Giovanni ★$$$ *Buca* means "cave" in Italian, and you reach the dining room here by descending a stairway to the lower level. The menu offers at least 11 daily specials in addition to its unusually large selection (54) of classic Italian dishes. On any given evening, the dishes presented might include ravioli stuffed with eggplant and gorgonzola in a light basil cream sauce or linguine with fresh porcini mushrooms; the restaurant is also known for using home-smoked rabbit in many pasta dishes. ♦ Italian ♦ Tu-Sa dinner. Reservations recommended. 800 Greenwich St (between Taylor and Mason Sts). 776.7766

22 Graffeo Coffee Roasting Co. You can smell the dark beans roasting several blocks away at this long-established firm, which turns out a daily grind. There's no brewed coffee, however. ♦ M-Sa. 733 Columbus Ave (at Filbert St). 986.2429, 800/222.6250

23 Maybeck Building This office building was constructed in 1909 around a courtyard with apartments on the upper floors. It was once the Old Telegraph Hill Neighborhood Center Building (the oldest neighborhood center in the city). ♦ 1736 Stockton St (between Greenwich and Filbert Sts)

24 Moose's ★★★$$$ Less than three years after their retirement from **Washington Square Bar & Grill,** restaurateurs Mary Etta and Ed Moose are back at it again, this time with the help of chef Lance Dean Velásquez, formerly of **Campton Place** and the **Ritz-Carlton.** This spacious, well-lit grill has been the "who's who" headquarters since the day it opened, serving Italian/Mediterranean-style cuisine. Try the crisp polenta appetizer served with gorgonzola cream sauce and nuggets of grilled pears, followed by an entrée of grilled salmon on a bed of pureed potatoes. While the friendly, attentive servers are entertaining, the main attraction is Ed himself, who can usually be found bounding from table to table seven nights a week, to make sure you're absolutely satisfied with everything. ♦ Italian/Mediter-ranean ♦ Daily lunch and dinner; Su brunch. Reservations recommended. 1652 Stockton St (between Filbert and Union Sts). 989.7800

Angel Island, also known as the "Ellis Island of the West," served as an immigration and quarantine station until November 1940. It's the largest island in the bay.

24 The Washington Square Inn $$ Each of the 15 rooms at this European-style hostelry, located in the heart of North Beach midway between **Fisherman's Wharf** and Union Square, is individually decorated and furnished with English and French antiques. Four of the rooms share two full baths. The hotel overlooks Washington Square and the **Church of St. Peter and St. Paul.** Continental breakfast, afternoon tea and cookies, and wine and finger sandwiches are included in the price of a room, but there's no restaurant. ♦ 1660 Stockton St (between Filbert and Union Sts). 981.4220, 800/388.0220; fax 397.7242

25 Washington Square Located halfway along Columbus Avenue, this plaza is the center of the Italian North Beach community. On the north side is the **Church of St. Peter and St. Paul;** on the east, next to the post office, is the **Italian Athletic Club.** Lunching at **Caffè Malvina** (★$; 391.1290) on the corner of Stockton and Filbert Streets is a pleasant way to watch life go by. ♦ Bounded by Filbert, Union, Powell, and Stockton Sts

26 Washington Square Bar & Grill ★$$ Jammed with locals as well as tourists, this North Beach hangout is especially popular with media mavens and is beloved more for its scene than for its food. The best dishes here are seafood, especially the calamari. ♦ Italian ♦ Daily lunch and dinner. 1707 Powell St (at Union St). 982.8123

27 Little City Antipasti Bar ★$$ This airy, attractive dining room is a perfect place to meet friends for drinks and a snack. In fact, a whole meal can be made of the antipasti. ♦ Daily lunch and dinner. 673 Union St (at Powell St). 434.2900

27 Gira Polli ★★$ No one does chicken better than this stylish 10-table restaurant, with 18 spits whirling in the wood-fired rotisserie. The Sicilian menu is small, simple, and to the point. Chicken is served with luscious Palermo-style potatoes (boiled in chicken stock and baked with white wine and herbs). The homemade pasta is also richly rewarding, as is the sensational lemony cheesecake. The place does a brisk take-out and delivery business. ♦ Italian/Takeout ♦ Daily dinner. Reservations recommended. 659 Union St (at Powell St). 434.4472. Also at: 590 E Blithedale Ave, Mill Valley, Marin County. 383.6040

28 Susie Kate's ★★★$$ Homey, friendly, and redolent with the smells of authentic southern home cookin', this spot looks like a Norman Rockwell painting come to life. Try the shrimp-and-cheese grits, chicken with dumplings, or shrimp-and-duck jambalaya—although you can't go wrong with anything here. One hint: If you want the made-in-heaven fried chicken, order it right when you sit down, since it takes about 20 minutes to prepare. Save room for dessert. ♦ Southern ♦ M-Sa dinner; Su brunch and dinner. Reservations recommended. 655 Union St (at Columbus Ave). 981.5283

29 Mario's Bohemian Cigar Store ★$ You'll hear lots of Italian spoken at this tiny, friendly spot, where the clientele hunkers down over a few tables. It's smaller and plainer than other coffeehouses in the area, but many swear it has the best espresso and focaccia sandwiches. It was a cigar store in the 1960s, but you won't find any stogies here anymore. ♦ Coffeehouse ♦ Daily. 566 Columbus Ave (at Union St). 362.0536

30 Ristorante Castellucci ★★$$ Homemade pastas and carefully grilled meats draw enthusiastic diners to this pleasant, tiled restaurant. ♦ Italian ♦ M-Sa dinner. 561 Columbus Ave (between Union and Green Sts). 362.2774

30 Il Pollaio $ No pasta is served here, just charbroiled meats prepared Argentinean style. As the name (which means "the chicken coop") would suggest, chicken is a specialty, but other meats are on the menu, too, including rabbit and lamb. Each meal is prepared to order. ♦ Italian/Argentinean ♦ M-Sa lunch and dinner. 555 Columbus Ave (between Union and Green Sts). 362.7727

30 Gold Spike ★$ Catering to big eaters since 1920, this restaurant, decorated with eclectic clutter, dishes out hearty six-course family-style dinners. There's a crab cioppino feast on

Friday. ♦ Italian ♦ M-Tu, Th-Su dinner. 527 Columbus Ave (between Union and Green Sts). 421.4591

31 Amelio's ★★$$$$ This upscale restaurant features the innovative cooking of chef and co-owner Jacky Robert, who dazzles diners with his contemporary interpretations of French cuisine. Try the baby abalone to start, then order the sautéed, encrusted Chilean sea bass with tomatoes and basil, served with fresh pasta. ♦ French ♦ Daily dinner. Reservations required. 1630 Powell St (between Union and Green Sts). 397.4339

32 Grifone Ristorante ★$$ You'll find good northern Italian cuisine and Caesar salad at this family-run establishment. ♦ Italian ♦ Daily dinner. Reservations required. 1609 Powell St (at Green St). 397.8458

33 Capp's Corner ★$ If you have a hungry family or group with not-so-discriminating tastes and not-so-unlimited funds, head for the corner that's belonged to Capp since who knows when. Here you'll learn what Italian "family dining" is all about: back-to-back Sinatra tunes, endless glasses of headache-quality Chianti, and brusque but cheery service. Granted, the food isn't tops, but if you order the mussels marinara, you'll at least leave pleasantly stuffed. ♦ Italian ♦ M-F lunch and dinner; Sa-Su dinner. 1600 Powell St (at Green St). 989.2589

34 Club Fugazi Steve Silver's popular cabaret-style show, *Beach Blanket Babylon,* has been playing here in various incarnations for years. The show's theme changes annually, but it invariably features outrageous costumes, zany hats, and an earnest, high-energy, talented cast bent on making the lowbrow material seem funny. No one under 21 is admitted except for the Sunday matinee. ♦ Admission. Shows daily. Reservations required three to four weeks in advance. 678 Green St (between Powell St and Columbus Ave). 421.4222; fax 421.4817

35 North Beach Museum The history of North Beach, Chinatown, and Fisherman's Wharf is presented in old photos and artifacts. ♦ Free. M-F. 1435 Stockton St (between Green and Vallejo Sts), Mezzanine. 626.7070

36 U.S. Restaurant ★$$ Huge portions, low prices, and good roasts, pastas, and nightly specials make the brusque service tolerable. ♦ Italian ♦ Tu-Sa breakfast, lunch, and dinner. 431 Columbus Ave (between Green and Vallejo Sts). 362.6251

For a walk that will literally take your breath away, head over to Filbert Street, the steepest street in San Francisco. It boasts a whopping 31.5 percent grade between Hyde and Leavenworth Streets—enough to make even the most shipshape soul sweat.

37 Stella Pastry & Caffe Try the famous *sacrapantina,* a scrumptious frozen concoction of zabaglione and cake layers. ♦ Coffeehouse ♦ Daily. 446 Columbus Ave (between Green and Vallejo Sts). 986.2914

37 Millefiori Inn $$ A European-style hostelry far above the commonplace, this is one of a few interesting places to stay in the area. The name means "a thousand flowers," and great care has gone into the design of the 15 rooms—each featuring a different flower. The sophisticated style is a bit of a surprise in the midst of the down-home clatter of Columbus Avenue, the main artery of Italian North Beach. Continental breakfast is served in an adjoining patio that connects to **Caffè Roma.** ♦ 444 Columbus Ave (between Green and Vallejo Sts). 433.9111

37 Calzone's ★$$ Savor trendy pizzas from a wood-burning brick oven while people-watching through the large picture windows. For a real winner, try chicken-liver pasta. The management dispatches a free limousine to the Financial District to pick up lunchtime customers. ♦ Italian ♦ Daily lunch and dinner. 430 Columbus Ave (between Green and Vallejo Sts). 397.3600

38 Caffè Roma ★$ The atmosphere of North Beach is perfectly captured in this coffeehouse where the walls are decorated with charming cupid murals. The kitchen makes an excellent pizza. On a sunny day, head for a table in the courtyard in the back. ♦ Italian ♦ Daily breakfast, lunch, and dinner. 414 Columbus Ave (between Green and Vallejo Sts). 391.8584

39 Caffè Greco ★$ Ultra-friendly owners Sandy and Hanna Suleiman and their family quickly made this North Beach coffeehouse popular. It's always crowded, and on warm days and evenings conversation spills onto the street through open picture windows. The desserts, including tiramisù and chocolate cheesecake, are worth every sinful bite. There are also focaccia sandwiches and salads. ♦ Italian ♦ Daily breakfast, lunch, and dinner. 423 Columbus Ave (between Green and Vallejo Sts). 397.6261

39 Caffè Puccini ★$ Minimal operatic-themed decor graces this invariably full coffeehouse favored by local residents, who sip their selections while overlooking the Columbus Avenue scene. ◆ Coffeehouse ◆ Daily. 411 Columbus Ave (between Green and Vallejo Sts). 989.7033

40 Victoria Pastry Co. Try the delicious St. Honoré cake here, as well as the biscotti, *corcini* (chocolate cake), and other types of pastries. ◆ Daily. 1362 Stockton St (at Vallejo St). 781.2015

41 Molinari's This landmark Italian deli has been a local monument since 1896 and offers a huge selection of Italian sausages, among other typical fare. ◆ M-Sa. 373 Columbus Ave (at Vallejo St). 421.2337

42 Cafe Europa $ There is a cafe downstairs, and upstairs seating overlooks Columbus Avenue. In addition to the usual espresso and pastry selection, the cafe can liven up your breakfast with steamed eggs and fruit, or serve a full dinner of hot pasta dishes. ◆ Italian ◆ Daily breakfast, lunch, and dinner. 362 Columbus Ave (at Grant Ave). 986.8177

43 The Stinking Rose ★$$ You won't find a vampire in sight at this popular restaurant and bar, where everything from the eggs in the morning to the cocktails at night contains traces of the stinking rose—a nickname for garlic. There's a small store hawking garlic paraphernalia, too. ◆ Italian/American ◆ Daily lunch and dinner. Reservations recommended. 325 Columbus Ave (between Vallejo and Broadway Sts). 781.ROSE

44 Caffè Trieste ★$ This quintessential San Francisco coffeehouse is a haven for artists, writers, and gawkers. There are live opera performances and slightly higher drink prices Saturday afternoons. ◆ Coffeehouse ◆ Daily. 609 Vallejo St (at Grant Ave). 392.6739

45 Mo's ★$ Some say they turn out the best burgers in the city, or maybe the whole state, here. They might be right. ◆ American ◆ Daily lunch and dinner. 1322 Grant Ave (between Green and Vallejo Sts). 788.3779

46 La Bodega ★$ On the well-beaten path of Grant Avenue, this rustic Spanish restaurant (the only one in North Beach) is a leftover from the Beat Generation's heyday and still delights customers with its inexpensive paella and flamenco dancing to live guitar. ◆ Spanish ◆ Daily dinner. 1337 Grant Ave (between Green and Vallejo Sts). 433.0439

47 Dianda's Elaborate, award-winning Italian cakes and pastries, heavy on the cream fillings and icing, may be enjoyed on the premises or taken home. The rum cakes are especially wonderful if calories are not an issue. ◆ Daily. 565 Green St (between Stockton St and Grant Ave). 989.7745

48 Caffè Sport $$ Expect a long wait, rude service (though waiters have sometimes been known to be friendly), and garlic-laced food served in a roomful of kitschy decor. Although this place is popular among many tourists, the food is nothing to write home about. The Sicilian-style seafood creations, however, are served in huge portions. ◆ Italian ◆ Tu-Sa lunch and dinner. 574 Green St (at Columbus Ave). 981.1251

49 Golden Boy Pizza ★★$ Prize-winning thick-crusted pizza is dished out in a real greasy-spoon ambience. This is a good place for a fast, no-frills snack. ◆ Pizza ◆ Daily lunch and dinner. 542 Green St (between Stockton St and Grant Ave). 982.9738

49 Danilo Bakery North Beach cooks patronize this place for its Italian and French breads, pizzas, panettone, and Italian cookies. ◆ Daily. 516 Green St (between Stockton St and Grant Ave). 989.1806

50 Bocce Cafe ★$$ One of the better bargains in North Beach, this spacious Italian restaurant serves somewhat respectable cuisine at competitive prices. Try its best dish, the *linguine pescatore* (with a seafood sauce), wash it down with some cheap Chianti, and try not to fall asleep on the sinfully comfortable pillowed booths, constructed of river rocks cemented together. Avoid Friday night, when the band shows up and ruins everyone's meal. ◆ Italian ◆ Daily lunch and dinner. 478 Green St (at Grant Ave). 981.2044

Maykadeh

50 Maykadeh ★★$$ Very popular and very good, this attractive restaurant serves exotic Persian cuisine in a mauve, California-like setting. The lamb dishes are a delight. ◆ Persian ◆ Daily lunch and dinner. Reservations recommended. 470 Green St (at Grant Ave). 362.8286

51 The Shlock Shop Specialty hats and collectibles crammed into a small, well-aged store have been attracting shoppers for more than 25 years. This is the very place to find a dusty aviator helmet, cowboy hat, or bowler. ◆ Daily noon-11PM. 1418 Grant Ave (between Union and Green Sts). 781.5335

51 Primal Art Center They import primitive statues, masks, and carvings from Africa and Papua New Guinea here. ♦ Daily. 1422 Grant Ave (between Union and Green Sts). 391.3836

51 Savoy Tivoli $ This long-established, charmingly decrepit North Beach hangout with a sidewalk cafe and recreation room is a great place for meeting the locals. ♦ Italian ♦ Tu-Su 3PM-2AM. 1434 Grant Ave (between Union and Green Sts). 362.7023

52 Quantity Postcards As its name implies, this shop is packed with postcards, postcards, and more postcards. You'll find everything from standard shots of the Golden Gate Bridge to 1950s-type kitsch and some extremely bizarre images (better make sure the folks back home have a sense of humor before dashing off one of these). ♦ Daily; F-Sa until 1AM. 1441 Grant Ave (between Union and Green Sts). 986.8866

Won't You Let Me Take You on a Bay Cruise?

When the sun god smiles and it's not too windy, there's no more exhilarating way to view San Francisco than by boat. Here are some of the companies that will let you play on the bay.

Blue & Gold Fleet Refreshments are served on board during one-hour-and-15-minute narrated tours of the bay. Departure point: Pier 39, West Marina (Grant Ave at The Embarcadero). 781.7877

A Day on the Bay The oldest charter service in San Francisco, this business has boats for rent or charter, and also gives sailing lessons. There are 18 sailboats and powerboats in the fleet, most of them character boats (1920s- and 1930s-style wooden pleasure craft). Departure point: San Francisco Marina (Marina Blvd at Webster St). 922.0227

Hornblower Yachts Luxury party boats are available for lunch cruises, champagne brunch cruises, and dinner/dance cruises. Prepaid reservations are necessary. Departure point: Pier 33 (Bay St at The Embarcadero). 394.8900 ext 7

The Oceanic Society These nine-and-a-half-hour boat tours to the Farallon Islands are not for the faint of heart—the water is often choppy and you're confined to the boat the entire time. However, you will enjoy some great bird and marine-mammal watching. No children under 10 are allowed. Sa-Su June-Nov. Departure point: Scott St and Marina Blvd (near the Harbor Master's Office). 474.3385

Red & White Fleet A 60-minute, six-language audio tour of the Bay Area is a part of this cruise around the bay and past Sausalito and Alcatraz Island. Departure point: Pier 43½ at Fisherman's Wharf. 542.2628, 546.2805, 800/229.2784 in CA

Restaurants/Clubs: Red   **Hotels:** Blue
Shops/ 🌳 Outdoors: Green   **Sights/Culture:** Black

53 Cafe Jacqueline ★★$$ Costly soufflés, both sweet and savory, are the raison d'être of this cute little cafe, where sharing the airy creations is a good idea unless you really want a huge portion all to yourself. ♦ French ♦ W-Su dinner. 1454 Grant Ave (at Union St). 981.5565

53 R. Iacopi and Co. Widely regarded as one of the best butcher shops in North Beach, this store also has a good deli stocked with Italian goodies. ♦ Daily. 1462 Grant Ave (at Union St). 421.0757

54 North Beach Pizza ★★$ The variety of toppings at this jam-packed pizza parlor is impressive, and the minestrone is good. You may order food to go or have it delivered. ♦ Italian ♦ Daily lunch and dinner. 1499 Grant Ave (at Union St). 433.2444. Also at: 1310 Grant Ave (at Green St). Same phone

55 Italian French Bakery This bakery's breads and breadsticks have won top awards in North Beach culinary competitions. ♦ Daily. 1501 Grant Ave (at Union St). 421.3796

56 Yoné Sift through a veritable gold mine of beads, buttons, and jewelry; you could even make yourself a necklace or a pair of earrings with what's available here. ♦ Th-Sa. 478 Union St (at Grant Ave). 986.1424

57 Des Alpes ★$$ This is one of the oldest (it first opened its doors in 1908) of several family-style Basque restaurants in San Francisco. Plain, informal, untrendy, but utterly reliable, the place pleases big eaters with staggering quantities of food served over seven courses. The prices are reasonably low and the food, though not fancy, is tasty and satisfying. ♦ Basque ♦ Tu-Su dinner. Reservations recommended. 732 Broadway (between Powell and Stockton Sts). 391.4249

58 Columbus Italian Food ★★$ Hearty, tasty made-to-order home cooking at not-to-be-missed prices has kept this place a favorite among locals who care more about food than about ambience. The setting is spare, but proprietor May Ditano keeps things friendly. Roasts are delicious and regulars await the daily specials, which range from tripe on Monday to lamb shanks and polenta on Saturday. ♦ Italian ♦ Daily lunch and dinner. 611 Broadway (between Grant Ave and Stockton St). 781.2939

59 Broadway This brash strip has been a monument to man's mammary fascination since 1964, when Carol Doda first performed her topless act at the **Condor Club**. Once a family street with Italian grocery stores, it became a center for bootlegging in the 1930s, and in the 1940s was dotted with brothels and pool halls. Then, in the 1950s, the strip began to clean up its act when the likes of Lenny Bruce and Barbra Streisand played here at the

Hungry i, Johnny Mathis sang at Ann's 448, and folk musicians strummed at On Broadway. The entertainment boom went bust as high-paying Vegas clubs wooed the big names. By the mid-1960s, the street had turned raunchy again. Loud barkers lured leering tourists into the 20 topless clubs, which featured expensive cover charges, lightly liquored drinks, and a parade of breasts. The strip is more subdued now. Most of the surviving topless clubs do not have liquor licenses, and many of the new businesses are restaurants. ♦ Between Grant Ave and Sansome St

59 Condor Bistro $$ San Francisco's moral minority let out a cheer in 1991 when the **Condor Club**'s Carol Doda sign (a larger-than-life rendering of the city's most famous stripper) was torn down and the landmark topless bar became a bistro. Despite the expensive spit and polish, the result is a rather bland place that will surely keep the sailors away. ♦ French ♦ Daily lunch and dinner. 300 Columbus Ave (at Broadway). 781.8222

60 Columbus Books Browse through new and used books at discount prices. ♦ Daily; F-Sa to midnight. 540 Broadway (between Grant Ave and Kearny St). 986.3872

60 Finocchio's For more than 50 years, tourists have blushed and giggled at the irrepressible and quite tame drag show here. The revue features 10 female impersonators, flashy costumes, slightly ribald humor, and some unusual specialty acts. Sophisticates will not be shocked, maybe not even amused, and no one under 21 is admitted. ♦ Cover. Shows W-Sa. 506 Broadway (between Grant Ave and Kearny St). 982.9388

61 Little Joe's and Baby Joe's ★$ Virtually an institution in North Beach, this is the best of the no-frills, low-cost Italian establishments. The cooks are masters of sautéing and have been known to sing opera arias as they rattle their pots and pans in view of diners. They do wondrous things with dishes such as squid cooked in its own ink and a simple but superb hamburger served on crusty Italian bread. ♦ Italian ♦ Daily lunch and dinner. 523 Broadway (between Columbus Ave and Kearny St). 433.4343

62 Helmand ★★★$$ San Francisco's premier Afghan restaurant has an exotic menu that includes such intriguing choices as *kabuli* (rice baked with lamb tenderloin and raisins), *mourgh challow* (chicken sautéed with spices and yellow split peas), and *theeka kabab* (charbroiled beef tenderloin marinated in yogurt, baby grapes, and herbs). All dishes are deftly prepared and complex in their spicing, but not fiery hot. ♦ Afghan ♦ M-Sa lunch and dinner. Reservations recommended. 430 Broadway (between Kearny and Montgomery Sts). 362.0641

BRANDY—HO'S

62 Brandy Ho's ★★$ This is one of the best Hunan restaurants in the city, especially for those whose palates are up to the challenge of lots of chili peppers and garlic. The deep-fried dumplings with garlic sauce, onion cakes, smoked ham with garlic, and lamb with crispy rice noodles are but a few of the many pungent temptations available. No MSG is used in the kitchen. This is a glamorous offshoot of the owner's first restaurant, located just a few blocks away, and the improved atmosphere is worth the tiny difference in price. Architecturally, this newer restaurant combines aspects of the Chinese and Italian cultures that coexist along Broadway. A golden water dragon graces the rear dining room, where windows reveal the cliffs of Telegraph Hill. ♦ Hunan ♦ Daily lunch and dinner. 450-452 Broadway (between Kearny and Montgomery Sts). 362.6268. Also at: 217 Columbus Ave (between Broadway and Pacific Ave). 788.7527

63 Tommaso's Restaurant ★★$$ In business since 1935 and still pleasing customers a great deal more than the X-rated businesses that surround it, this Neapolitan restaurant is best known for its brick-oven pizzas. The other hearty, traditional dishes served here are deftly prepared. ♦ Italian ♦ Tu-Su dinner. 1042 Kearny St (between Broadway and Pacific Ave). 398.9696

64 Campo Santo ★$$ Step into this one-of-a-kind restaurant and you'll think you've died and gone to heaven: It's covered top to bottom with a colorful Mexican Day of the Dead motif. Still, the effect is fun and lively, not maudlin. The Latin food (fajitas, tequila prawns, fried calamari, etc.) is very good, especially the fresh fish tacos. ♦ Latin ♦ Tu-F lunch and dinner; Sa-Su dinner. Reservations recommended. 240 Columbus Ave (between Broadway and Pacific Ave). 433.9623

64 Tosca Cafe ★$ Media types, socialites, and a cross section of the city's creative community all love to hang out at this unassuming cafe. Visiting celebrities have been known to pop up as impromptu bartenders. A coffeeless cappuccino made with steamed milk, brandy, and chocolate is the specialty drink. ♦ Coffeehouse ♦ Daily. 242 Columbus Ave (between Broadway and Pacific Ave). 391.1244

65 City Lights Booksellers & Publishers More than any other bookstore, this one, especially beloved by night owls, evokes the atmosphere and accomplishments of literary San Francisco. Owned by poet Lawrence Ferlinghetti, the shop's heyday was the Beat era of the 1950s. Many of the writers who immortalized that time—Allen Ginsberg, Gregory Corso, Michael McClure, Jack Kerouac, and Ken Kesey—are featured, and there's a marvelous poetry section. ♦ Daily; F-Su to midnight. 261 Columbus Ave (between Broadway and Pacific Ave). 362.8193

65 Vesuvio If it's bohemian atmosphere you're after, this is the place. This landmark North Beach bar is still frequented by artists and poets from the Beat era, in addition to more current representatives of the scene. The walls are covered with objets d'art. ♦ Daily. 255 Columbus Ave (between Broadway and Pacific Ave). 362.3370

66 San Francisco Brewing Company $ Allen Paul's brewery, the last of the Barbary Coast saloons, now gets customers who mine their gold in the nearby Financial District. By law, food is served, but the attraction here is the 20 types of domestic and imported beers from small specialty breweries, along with several brewed by the owner on the premises. The interior, dating from 1907, is graced by a solid mahogany bar trimmed with brass, as well as a tile spittoon. Babyface Nelson was captured in what is now the women's room, and Jack Dempsey was a bouncer here for a short time. The management organizes beer tastings and brew-pub crawls sporadically. There's live blues Monday, Wednesday, and Thursday, and jazz on Saturday. ♦ American ♦ Daily lunch and dinner. 155 Columbus Ave (at Pacific Ave). 434.3344

67 Caffè Macaroni ★★$$ This very small, very good, very Italian restaurant has a menu that changes daily to accommodate the market's freshest selections; choices can range from baked stingray to classic pasta dishes. ♦ Italian ♦ M-F lunch and dinner; Sa dinner. Reservations recommended. 59 Columbus Ave (at Kearny St). 956.9737

68 Thomas Brothers Maps Browse through an extraordinary selection of maps, from pocket- to wall-size, as well as globes, atlases, and guides, in this shop that's also known as the Map House. The hanging brass lamps complement the Victorian premises. ♦ M-F. 550 Jackson St (at Columbus Ave). 981.7520

68 Cypress Club ★★★$$$ It's Ali Baba meets Roger Rabbit at this outrageously decorated restaurant owned by John Cunin, the former maître d' at **Masa's**. The overall atmosphere is playfully elegant, the service is polished, and the eclectic, often daring food can range from good to sublime. The desserts are a work of art (and sometimes taste as good as they look). ♦ California ♦ M-F lunch and dinner; Sa-Su dinner. Reservations recommended. 500 Jackson St (at Columbus Ave). 296.8555

69 William Stout Architectural Books One of the few great architectural bookstores in America, this shop has grown from a handful of books available at Bill's apartment to a collection of more than 10,000 volumes of rare books, magazines, and portfolios. European and Japanese volumes are available. ♦ M-Sa. 804 Montgomery St (at Jackson St). 391.6757

70 Ernie's ★$$$$ Immortalized by director Alfred Hitchcock in his classic *Vertigo,* this well-established, expense-account restaurant has been charming food fanciers since 1934. You won't see the famous red-silk interior anymore—the formal, comfortable dining room is now replete in champagne colors. Chef David Kinch turns out innovative dishes with a light touch, such as lobster with grapes and sabayon, polenta croquettes, and crab timbale with asparagus. In tune with these cost-conscious times, a prix-fixe, four-course dinner for $30 is served Monday through Thursday from 6PM to 7:30PM. ♦ French ♦ M-Sa dinner. Reservations recommended. 847 Montgomery St (between Jackson St and Pacific Ave). 397.5969

71 Pacific Avenue Interesting shops include **LIMN** architectural and graphic furniture (457 Pacific at Sansome St. 397.7475) and **Thomas Cara Ltd.** (517 Pacific at Sansome St. 781.0383), an old establishment selling coffee, espresso machines, and kitchenware. ♦ Between Kearny and Sansome Sts

72 Bix ★★★$$$ Located in a historic building that can be difficult to find, this lively neo-Deco restaurant is popular with movers and shakers. The handsome interior space includes columns and a mezzanine level. Classic American fare, such as rack of lamb and chicken hash, is served with friendly professionalism. Live jazz plays nightly. ♦ American ♦ M-F lunch and dinner; Sa-Su dinner. Reservations required. 56 Gold St (between Sansome and Montgomery Sts). 433.6300

73 Hotaling Place This block-long alley leads from Jackson Street, between Montgomery and Sansome Streets, right into the base of the **Transamerica Building** on Washington

Street. There are two old warehouses that were distilleries in the Barbary Coast days.

73 Jackson Square Historic District Designated the city's first historic district, this area contains the only group of downtown business buildings to survive the 1906 earthquake and fire; most date back to the 1850s. Some buildings sustained additional damage in the 1989 quake, but all survived. Most are brick and have been carefully restored and remodeled to become the city's fabric and furniture showroom center; many are open to the trade only. ♦ Bounded by Montgomery and Sansome Sts, and Jackson and Washington Sts

74 722 Montgomery Street This three-story brick building is registered as a historic landmark. The first meeting of Freemasons in California was held here on 17 October 1849. It now houses the elaborate, Victorian-style offices of San Francisco's celebrated lawyer Melvin Belli. ♦ At Washington St

75 Arch Drafting instruments and supplies are imaginatively displayed in this beautifully designed architectural-supply store. It's conveniently close to

the popular architectural bookstore, **William Stout,** and within easy reach of the many architectural offices in the neighborhood, which explains the crowd at lunchtime. ♦ M-Sa. 407 Jackson St (between Montgomery and Sansome Sts). 433.2724

76 US Appraiser's Building This government building occupies the same block as the **US Custom House,** and both represent contrasting attitudes toward federal architecture. Erected by **Gilbert Stanley Underwood** in 1941, this building represents the aesthetics of the WPA era with its stripped-down Moderne styling. It was reclad in 1988 by **Kaplan/McLaughlin/Diaz** with precast concrete and a new polished-granite base. The same firm redid the windows in 1992. ♦ Battery and Jackson Sts

77 US Custom House Older than the **US Appraiser's Building** on the same block, this classical Baroque building has a massive rusticated base, an elaborate cornice line, and a generously proportioned entrance hall. It was constructed from 1906 to 1911 by **Eames & Young.** Room 504 on the fifth floor houses the USGS offices, which sell maps of every part of the US and *Apollo 11* maps of the moon. ♦ 555 Battery St (at Jackson St)

78 Ciao ★$$ This glittering contemporary restaurant was one of the first high-tech Italian establishments to open in the US. The specialty is the fresh pasta, but the kitchen does a consistently good job with most dishes. ♦ Italian ♦ M-Sa lunch and dinner; Su dinner. Reservations recommended. 230 Jackson St (at Battery St). 982.9500

79 MacArthur Park ★$$ This quintessentially Californian watering hole serves excellent barbecue fare, although some of the kitchen's other offerings can be disappointing. The meats, cooked in an oak-fueled smoker, come out succulent and tender. There's a fine, reasonably priced California wine list. ♦ American ♦ M-F lunch and dinner; Sa-Su dinner. Reservations recommended. 607 Front St (at Jackson St). 398.5700

80 Square One ★★★$$$ Opened by Joyce Goldstein, who got her culinary start at **Chez Panisse,** this restaurant is one of the jewels in San Francisco's restaurant crown. The innovative menu, which changes daily, can lead to an ever-interesting, but inconsistent, culinary performance. Yet when it's good, it's very, very good. ♦ California/Mediterranean ♦ M-F lunch and dinner; Sa-Su dinner. Reservations recommended. 190 Pacific Ave (between Front and Davis Sts). 788.1110

81 Bricks Bar & Grill This all-American local bar with matchbook covers lining the walls has burgers that can't be beat. ♦ American ♦ Daily breakfast and lunch. 298 Pacific Ave (at Battery St). 788.2222

82 Hunan ★★$$ When San Francisco first fell in love with fiery Hunanese food, this restaurant was here to heat up willing palates. It began as a small Chinatown business but grew into these larger quarters. ♦ Chinese ♦ Daily lunch and dinner. Reservations recommended. 924 Sansome St (off Broadway). 956.7727

83 Remodeled Warehouses Some old warehouses, most built in the 1930s, have been turned into offices for architects, graphic artists, and TV companies. Of particular note are **855 Battery Street,** for **Channel 5/ Westinghouse TV,** remodeled by **Gensler and Associates** (1980-81); **243 Vallejo,** by **Marquis Associates** (1972); **220 Vallejo,** by **Kaplan/McLaughlin/Diaz** (1978); and **101 Lombard Street,** by **Hellmuth, Obata & Kassabaum,** completed in 1979. There are fine old brick warehouses on Battery between Union and Green Streets, plus the old **Ice House,** which is now an office complex, on Union Street between Sansome and Battery Streets. ♦ From Broadway to Lombard St (between Battery and Sansome Sts)

84 Kahn House Similar to his Lovell House in Los Angeles, this 1939 building by **Richard Neutra** steps down the hill and offers its occupants superb views of the bay. It's a private residence. ♦ 66 Calhoun Terr (between Union and Green Sts)

85 1360 Montgomery Street Featured in the Humphrey Bogart movie *The Maltese Falcon,* this 1937 apartment house is designed in the Moderne style, with exterior murals and a fine glass-block facade leading to the entrance lobby. It's a private residence. ♦ At Alta St

86 The Shadows ★★$$$ One of the most romantic settings in San Francisco can be found in this French restaurant, bathed in shades of pink, with mirrored walls and a fabulous bay view. You may sample French and continental classics as well as more innovative dishes on the seasonally changing menu. ♦ French ♦ Sa dinner. Reservations recommended. 1349 Montgomery St (between Filbert and Union Sts). 982.5536

JOHN ELLIS

87 Coit Memorial Tower Located at the top of Telegraph Hill, this 1934 tower (pictured **above**) by **Arthur Brown Jr.** marks the point where the first West Coast telegraph sent messages notifying the arrival of ships from the Pacific. Messages were then signaled downtown by a semaphore tower. Lillie Hitchcock Coit, who as a girl of 15 had been the mascot of the crack firefighter company Knickerbocker No. 5, left funds to beautify the city in 1929. An incorrect story persists that the tower was shaped to look like a firehose nozzle to commemorate her interest in the fire department. Inside are restored spectacular murals depicting California workers. Painted as a Public Works of Art Project, the murals, some of which lean politically to the left, created a stir when they were first unveiled. Take the elevator to the top for a spectacular view of the city and bay. The tower's base, from which there are panoramic views, is accessible all day. ♦ You must buy a ticket to ride the elevator. Daily. At the end of Telegraph Hill Blvd

88 Julius' Castle ★$$$$ Noteworthy alone for its eccentric architecture and fabulous view of the bay, this place has always been favored by out-of-towners. The menu features well-presented French and Northern Italian dishes, paying particular attention to pastas, seafood, and veal. There's valet parking—a necessity on Telegraph Hill. ♦ French/Italian ♦ Daily dinner. Reservations required. 1541 Montgomery St (at Lombard St). 362.3042

89 Filbert Steps Down the east side of Telegraph Hill, the terrain is so steep that Filbert Street becomes Filbert Steps—a series of precariously perched platforms and walkways with some of the city's oldest and most varied housing. A beautifully landscaped walkway climbs down the hill and gives access to the lanes on either side—Darrell Place, Napier Lane, Alta Street. **No. 228** Filbert Steps, built in the 1870s, is a fine example of Carpenter Gothic style. These are private residences. ♦ Between Montgomery and Sansome Sts

90 Levi's Plaza In 1982 **Hellmuth, Obata & Kassabaum** built this enormous three-building development for the Levi Strauss Company. The architects reduced the vast scale by stepping back the profiles of the buildings so they blend into the shape of Telegraph Hill. All the buildings are clad in brick tiles that match the adjoining **Ice House,** a converted office complex. Not quite as successful is the integration of the glazed atrium space at the entrance facing the plaza. Lawrence Halprin landscaped the plaza. This is also the home of the San Francisco branch of HarperCollins Publishers. ♦ Sansome and Battery Sts (between Union and Greenwich Sts)

Within Levi's Plaza:

Il Fornaio ★★$$ This enormously popular restaurant is the last word in trendy decor and dining, and though not each dish the kitchen produces is a roaring success, most are—especially at breakfast, with Italian adaptations of oatmeal and French toast and a knockout fruit-filled calzone. The premises include a pastry shop, pizzeria, *rosticceria,* cafe, and bar, all incorporated into what management calls *gastronomia Italiana.* Sandwiches at lunch are made with great herb breads. Also available most of the day are wonderful spit-roasted meats and pizzas baked in a brick oven. Sit on the patio when the weather's warm. ♦ Italian ♦ Daily breakfast, lunch, and dinner. Reservations recommended. 986.0100. 927.4400

The first criminals to sit behind bars in Alcatraz weren't gangsters like Al Capone or murderers like Robert "The Birdman" Stroud. They were Confederate sympathizers, out-of-line soldiers, suspected war spies, and disorderly Native Americans.

Restaurants/Clubs: Red   **Hotels:** Blue
Shops/ ♥ Outdoors: Green   **Sights/Culture:** Black

91 Fog City Diner ★★$$ The diner concept merely served as design inspiration for this ultrasleek restaurant filled with polished stainless steel, chrome, and neon. A creative, eclectic menu of California cuisine offers something for everyone, from crab cakes and grilled sesame chicken to quesadillas and Asian prawns. The pickles are homemade. It's operated by the same restaurateurs who own the popular **Mustards Grill** in Napa Valley and **Buckeye Roadhouse** in Mill Valley. ◆ California ◆ Daily lunch and dinner. Reservations recommended. 1300 Battery St (off The Embarcadero). 982.2000

92 Pier 23 Cafe ★★$$ "Excuse me, do you mambo?" Well, after a few pitchers of sangria at this bayside restaurant and dance club, you will. It's great fun even for people who can't dance (and you know who you are), and the food's good, too. Come early and try the spicy meat loaf with mashed potatoes or the crab-and-shrimp quesadilla before squeezing onto the dance floor. When the weather's nice, the alfresco dining is unbeatable. Friday is mambo night, and Saturday is reggae. ◆ California ◆ Tu-Sa lunch and dinner; Su brunch. Reservations recommended. Pier 23 (near the end of Lombard St). 362.5125

Islands in the Bay

The rocky islands in **San Francisco Bay** are home to a once-notorious prison, naval training stations, and wildlife refuges teeming with sea lions and birds. Tours of **Alcatraz, Angel,** and **Treasure Islands** can be arranged, or you may cruise by on one of the ferries that dock at **Fisherman's Wharf.**

93 Angel Island This square mile of rocky land rising to a summit of 781 feet is the largest island in the bay. It was also the place Lieutenant Juan Manuel de Ayala initially anchored in 1775 during the first European expedition to sail through the Golden Gate. In 1863 it was occupied by the US Army and used as a fortification. It served as a prison camp for Native Americans in the 1870s; and from 1888 to 1935 it acted as a quarantine station for immigrants and ailing military personnel returning from duty. Between 1860 and 1890, the island's **Camp Reynolds** operated as a Civil War outpost and later as a staging area for soldiers engaged in Indian fighting. It is the only remaining garrison of its type from the Civil War. During the Spanish-American War and World Wars I and II, the island served as a debarkation and discharge point for troops.

From 1910 to 1940 it was regarded as the "Ellis Island of the West," serving mostly Asian immigrants. It became an internment camp for Italian and German prisoners in World War II.

Today the State Park Service maintains the island, and it's a perfect spot for a day of hiking, bicycling, or beachcombing. Trails meander along rugged slopes on a five-mile route. There are nine environmental campsites on the island (only charcoal fires allowed; pit toilets and picnic tables are available to campers; you must carry in your own gear and bring out your trash. For more information call 435.5390, for reservations 800/444.7275). There are also picnic and barbecue facilities, a snack bar during the summer months, and a souvenir kiosk. The **Visitor's Center** offers 20-minute video tours year-round and guided tours of historic sites from April through October. For a schedule, call 435.1915. ◆ Park: daily 8AM-sunset. Ferries: Daily in summer, weekends only in winter. The island is accessible by two routes: the **Red & White Fleet** runs ferries from San Francisco (542.2628, 546.2805, 800/229.2784 in CA), and the **Angel Island/Tiburon Ferry Company** departs from Tiburon (435.2131).

DETAIL FROM THE 10" x 40" FULL-COLOR OFFICIAL MAP & GUIDE TO ALCATRAZ, FOR SALE AT FISHERMAN'S WHARF, ALCATRAZ ISLAND, AND BOOKSTORES THROUGHOUT THE BAY AREA. DESIGN: REINECK & REINECK, SAN FRANCISCO

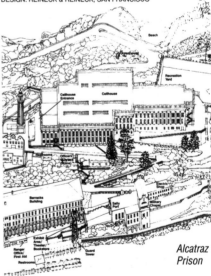

Alcatraz Prison

94 Alcatraz Island When Lieutenant Juan Manuel de Ayala discovered the island in 1775, he named it *Isla de los Alcatraces* (Island of the Pelicans) after the colony of pelicans roosting here. The first lighthouse on the West Coast was installed here in 1854. The island's strategic and isolated position made it ideal for use as a defensive and disciplinary installation. The first cell block was built by the US Army, and from that time on, the island was fated to be a prison facility. Crude stockades held unruly soldiers convicted of crimes in the 1860s, and Indians who proved troublesome were detained here in the 1870s. The island served as a quarantine post for soldiers returning from the Spanish-American War, and after the 1906 earthquake and fire, prisoners from the crumbled San Francisco jails were temporarily held here. In 1934 it became a federal maximum-security prison (illustrated on page 98). The fame of the "Rock" spread as it became home to such notorious criminals as Al Capone, Machine Gun Kelly, and Robert Stroud, the "Birdman of Alcatraz" (who never actually kept birds here). There is no evidence that any of the many attempted escapes were successful. The prison was closed in 1963. Between 1969 and 1971 a political protest and occupation by about a hundred Native Americans put the island in the headlines. Today it is part of the **Golden Gate National Recreation Area** (although some San Franciscans are lobbying hard to turn it into a casino, albeit without much luck so far). An excellent cell-house audio tour (recorded by former inmates and wardens), ranger-led programs, and a slide show are available daily. Dress warmly and plan to stay about two hours. ♦ Ferry fare. Daily ferry departures. Reservations recommended. Pier 41, Powell St (at Fisherman's Wharf). **Red & White Fleet:** 542.2628, 546.2805, 800/229.2784 in CA

95 Treasure Island This artificial island was created to serve as the site of the **Golden Gate International Exposition of 1939-40.** After the awe-inspiring effort to simultaneously construct two of the largest bridges in the world (the Golden Gate and Bay Bridges, completed within a few months of each other), it seemed fitting to celebrate by building an artificial 400-acre island for the fair. Later it was slated to become the **San Francisco Airport.** Of course, it was found to be too small and much too close to the Bay Bridge, and with the outbreak of World War II, the Navy acquired the island as a base. The Navy will close the base in September 1997. Who will acquire this hotly contested property remains to be seen, but in the meantime it's still worth a visit for the spectacular views of San Francisco and both bridges. ♦ To reach the island, take the Bay Bridge to the Treasure Island exit or take an **AC Transit** *T* bus.

On Treasure Island:

Treasure Island Museum Located just inside the main gate, the museum has exhibitions on the history of the Navy, Marines, and Coast Guard in the Pacific arena. There is an interesting exhibition on the **Golden Gate International Exposition of 1939-40.** ♦ Free. Daily. Bldg 1. 395.5067

96 Yerba Buena Island This island connects and anchors the cantilever and suspension sections of the Bay Bridge. Known in early days as "Wood Island" to seafarers, it was officially named *Yerba Buena* (good herb) after the wild mint that grew here. For years, goats were kept on the island, so it was also called "Goat Island." Historically, Indians used to paddle across the water in barges made of bundles of reeds and used the island as a fishing station. Remains of a village and cremation pits have been dug up, along with buried contraband from smugglers, portions of a shipwrecked Spanish galleon, and graves of soldiers, pioneers, and goatherds. Today, the island is a **Coast Guard Reservation** and **Naval Training Station.** It is connected to Treasure Island by a 900-foot causeway.
♦ The Coast Guard offers tours of the island by reservation only. 399.3449

97 Farallon Islands In 1872, this chain of craggy islands located 32 miles from Point Lobos was incorporated into the city and county of San Francisco. The name *Farallon* is derived from the Spanish expression for small, rocky, pointed islands. Inhospitable to humans, these islands today are closed to the public. They are home to crowds of sea lions and birds, and were declared a bird sanctuary in 1909. There is, however, a Coast Guard station on **South Farallon** (the island most visible from San Francisco's shores), and from the 1850s until 1968, a handful of stoic families lived there. Lighthouse keepers had to climb a steep zigzag path 320 feet up to the light, sometimes crawling on their hands and knees during the onslaught of a gale or storm. Today an automated lighthouse and foghorn warn ships to stay away from the treacherous rocks. To many San Franciscans, the significance of the Farallon Islands is meteorological, demonstrated by the expression "On a clear day you can see the Farallon Islands." They are best viewed from Ocean Beach or Point Reyes in Marin County.

SAN FRANCISCO BAY ISLANDS

San Francisco Bay

Marin

93 Angel Island

Alcatraz Island 94

Treasure Island 95

97 to the Farallon Islands

Fisherman's Wharf

96 Yerba Buena Island

Oakland

San Francisco

N

For nos. 1-92, see pg. 82

km 5 10
mi   5

Restaurants/Clubs: Red   Hotels: Blue
Shops/ ♦ Outdoors: Green   Sights/Culture: Black

Pacific Heights/Marina

When a cable-car line was built in the Pacific Heights district in 1878, this area quickly became an enclave of San Francisco's nouveaux riches. They moved into huge, gray Victorians, monuments to the bonanza era, and attempted to outdo the wooden castles on Nob Hill with Gothic arches, Corinthian pillars, Norman turrets, Byzantine domes, mansard roofs, and enough stained glass to outfit several cathedrals. Their houses lined **Van Ness Avenue**, which was five feet wider than Market Street and considered the Champs-Elysées of San Francisco.

But the magnificence on Van Ness Avenue was short-lived. The earthquake of 1906 reduced the exquisite homes to shambles, and the area never fully recovered. However, eastern Pacific Heights, like Russian and Nob Hills, was rebuilt with luxury apartment houses, and a substantial number of the original Victorians still remain. Today the Pacific Heights and Marina areas, along with **Cow Hollow** and **Presidio Heights**, hold more college graduates, professionals, and families earning upper-middle and higher incomes than any other city district. There are more mansions per city block as well, with handsome examples of the work of architects **Bernard Maybeck, Willis Polk, Ernest Coxhead,** and **William Knowles** on the streets feeding into **Broadway**. One of the oldest is at **2727 Pierce Street**. The city's most photographed group of dainty Victorians is along the south side of **Alta Plaza Park**. The fine collection of Victorian houses on **Union Street** has been turned into a shopper's dream, with more than 300 boutiques, restaurants, antiques stores, and coffeehouses. A drive out Broadway to the **Presidio Gate** will give you a capsule glimpse into the privileged lives of years past and present. Private ownership of such enormous buildings was destined to die out, and many of the more impressive mansions now house schools, consulates, and religious orders, or have been converted into apartments.

Although technically part of the Richmond district, Presidio Heights is philosophically, socially, and economically akin to its neighbor, Pacific Heights. It's a low-density area, filled with elegant private houses. **Sacramento Street**, which starts at **The Embarcadero**, turns into a chic commercial enclave between **Divisadero** and **Spruce Streets**. In this restrained, exclusive neighborhood, more than a whiff of affluence wafts across the few blocks of expensive specialty shops and antiques stores, some of which are open by appointment only.

Cow Hollow, the area north of Pacific Heights, was named for the 30 dairy farms established there in 1861. A tiny lagoon, **Laguna Pequeña** (also known as **Washerman's Lagoon**), was used as a communal wash basin for the city's laundry. In the late 1800s, tanneries, slaughterhouses, and sausage factories appeared because of the dairies and fresh water from the lake and springs. But pollution from open sewage, industry, and the cows forced the city to banish livestock forever and to fill the putrid lagoon with sand from the dunes on Lombard Street.

After the devastating 1906 earthquake and fire, to show the world it was a city that refused to die, San Francisco proceeded to stage one of the most spectacular fairs of all time—the Panama-Pacific International Exposition of 1915. The excuse was the opening of the Panama Canal, and the exposition was the springboard for a citywide open house that drew more than 18 million visitors. On the bay north of Cow Hollow, 600 acres of marshland were filled in, a seawall was built running parallel to the shoreline, and sand was pumped up from the ocean bottom to serve as fill. The dredging produced enough deep water to build the **San Francisco Yacht Harbor**, the present site of the **St. Francis Yacht Club,** and enough land to create the Marina district. One of the exhibition's buildings, the monumental **Palace of Fine Arts,** is now home to the **Exploratorium,** a very popular family science museum and auditorium. However, the landfill proved to be a dangerously shaky foundation during the 7.1 quake that rocked the city in October 1989. Many Marina residents lost their homes; others were evacuated for more than two months before utilities were restored. Throughout the Marina, 35 buildings were declared unsafe and uninhabitable, an additional 92 were damaged, and 10 were demolished.

The Marina, still in the process of rebuilding after the earthquake, reflects the Mediterranean-revival architecture popular in the 1920s, with mostly pastel, single-family dwellings and large, well-maintained flats along the curving streets. Although **Chestnut Street** offers fine neighborhood restaurants and interesting shops, **Lombard Street,** or "Motel Row," is generally considered a blight on the cityscape from Van Ness Avenue to the entrance to the Golden Gate Bridge. The **Marina Green,** which borders the harbor, is often full of kite flyers, volleyball players, sunbathers, joggers, and boaters. Nearby **Fort Mason,** planned by the Spanish in 1797 as a gun battery for the protection of **La Yerba Buena** anchorage, now functions as a giant community center offering theaters, workshops, the **Mexican Museum,** exhibition space, galleries, classes, and **Greens,** the best-known vegetarian restaurant in San Francisco.

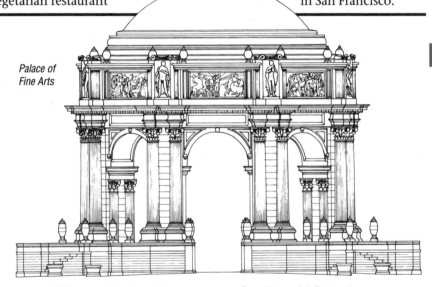

Palace of
Fine Arts

Area code 415 unless otherwise noted.

1 Palace of Fine Arts Originally built in 1915 for the Panama-Pacific Exposition, the palace (pictured above) houses the **Exploratorium,** a science museum for kids and adults, and an auditorium used for lectures and film presentations. Architect **Bernard Maybeck**'s building was the pièce de résistance of his career as well as of the exposition. It has a great stage set consisting of a classical Roman rotunda with two curved colonnades, behind which is the curved exhibition shed. The setting is in the midst of a small park, complete with an artificial lake and waterfowl (including two swans). The palace became so popular that the buildings were retained and completely rebuilt after the Exposition ended. Restoration was completed in 1969, the year the **Exploratorium** opened as a science museum. The museum was conceived on the premise that one learns by doing, and the more than 650 exhibits require visitor participation. You can pull, push, and manipulate various objects to demonstrate principles of prisms, sound, electricity, lasers, plant behavior, and more. The special **Tactile Gallery,** which some private groups have explored in the nude, has a separate admission charge and requires reservations (call 561.0362). ◆ Admission; children five and under free; free the first Wednesday of every month. Tu, Th-Su. 3601 Lyon St (between Jefferson and Bay Sts). 563.7337

2 Liverpool Lil's ★$ The cozy, pub-like atmosphere and reasonably priced food bring locals and enlisted folks from the Presidio back again and again. A hearty specialty for the hungry is the Manchester Wellington—ground round wrapped in ham and a flaky crust. This is a great place for a late supper. ♦ English ♦ Daily lunch and dinner. Reservations recommended. 2942 Lyon St (at Lombard St). 921.6664

3 St. Francis Yacht Club This Spanish-style building overlooks the bay and the Marina yacht harbor. Badly damaged by a fire on Christmas day in 1976, the private club was completely remodeled by **Marquis Associates,** only to once again sustain heavy losses after the 1989 quake. ♦ Marina Blvd (at Baker St)

4 Marina Green Area residents jog, bike, skate, fly kites, and sun-worship along this green swath of park that runs from the yacht harbor to **Fort Mason.** It's a glorious place to drink in the magnificent scenic beauty surrounding the bay. ♦ Marina Blvd (between Scott and Webster Sts)

5 Fort Mason Center Dating from the mid-1800s, when it served as a command post for the army that tamed the West, this proud reserve was added to by WPA workers in the 1930s. Today the area is part of the **Golden Gate National Recreational Area (GGNRA)** and houses theaters, classes, workshops, a restaurant, and art galleries, as well as trade shows and special exhibitions. ♦ Marina Blvd (entrance at Buchanan St). 441.5706

Within Fort Mason Center:

San Francisco Museum of Modern Art Rental Gallery An arm of the **San Francisco Museum of Modern Art,** this gallery focuses on works of lesser-known, emerging northern California artists. It has frequently changing exhibitions. Artwork is offered for sale and/or rent. ♦ Free. Tu-Sa. Bldg A. 441.4777

San Francisco Craft & Folk Art Museum Exhibitions of contemporary crafts, American folk art, and traditional ethnic art from home and abroad are on display. ♦ Nominal admission; free Saturday 10AM-noon and the first Wednesday of each month. Tu-Su. Bldg A. 775.0990

Young Performers Theatre This theater produces children's classics, adaptations, and new works, with children working alongside professional adult actors. The theater school offers classes year-round for children preschool age and up. Parties are held after weekend shows (it's a perfect place for birthday celebrations). ♦ Bldg C, Third floor. 346.5550

J. Porter Shaw Library Part of the **San Francisco Maritime National Historic Park System,** this is a treasure trove of marine-related books. ♦ Tu-Sa. Bldg E, Third floor. 556.9870

The Magic Theatre This experimental playhouse (founded in 1967) has achieved international recognition for its contribution to American theater. New plays by such writers as Pulitzer Prize winner Sam Shepard and poet/playwright Michael McClure have been produced here, as well as innovative works by emerging playwrights. ♦ Bldg D. 441.8822

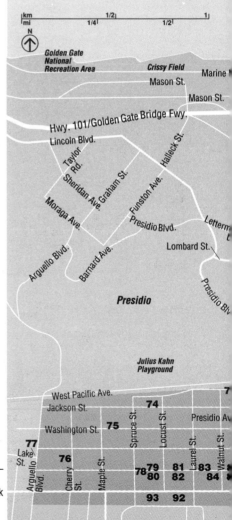

Restaurants/Clubs: Red   **Hotels:** Blue

Shops/ 🌳 Outdoors: Green   **Sights/Culture:** Black

Bayfront Theater This theater hosts the best works of local and national theater groups, and it's the site of a variety of music and dance concerts. ♦ Bldg B. 441.5706

Cowell Theater One of the Bay Area's most exciting performance spaces, its elegant design takes advantage of the architectural character of the more-than-75-year-old pier. ♦ Pier 2. 441.5706

African-American Historical and Cultural Society This resource center provides accurate accounts of the culture and history of African-Americans. The society has art exhibitions, a museum, and a gift shop. ♦ Donation. W-Su. Bldg C. 441.0640

Museo Italo-Americano Dedicated to researching, preserving, and displaying the works of Italian and Italian-American artists, this museum also strives to foster the appreciation of Italian art and culture. ♦ Donation. W-Su. Bldg C. 673.2200

Mexican Museum This museum collects, exhibits, and translates works of Mexicano (Mexican, Mexican-American, and Chicano) as well as Latino artists in an attempt to generate new perspectives on American culture. ♦ Nominal admission. W-Su noon-5PM. Bldg D. 441.0445

Greens ★★★$$$ San Francisco's finest vegetarian restaurant is run by dedicated disciples of Zen Buddhism. Its opening in 1979 made vegetarianism stylish, and it's easy to see why. You won't find any ordinary vegetables-stirred-in-a-wok here; only tasty culinary creations so interesting you'll forget you're not eating meat. The soups, homemade breads, and salads can't be matched. The black-bean chili, herb-flavored potatoes baked in parchment, and Green Gulch salad with lettuces, Sonoma goat cheese, pecans, and oranges are all excellent. As an added bonus, you'll have a beautiful view of the bay and the

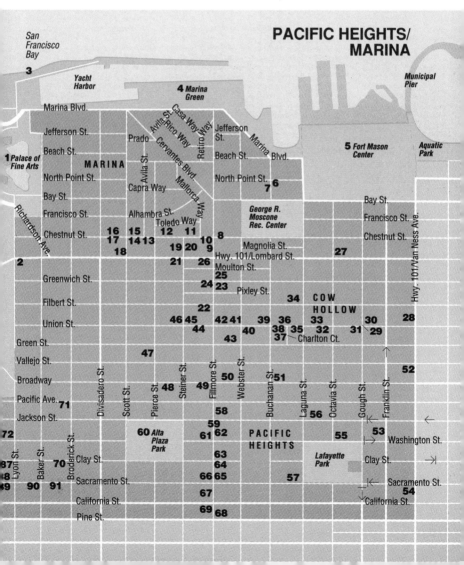

Golden Gate Bridge. Check out the bathrooms—they belong in an architectural guidebook. ♦ California/Vegetarian ♦ Tu-Sa lunch and dinner; Su brunch. Reservations recommended. Bldg A. 771.6222

6 San Francisco Gas Light Company Building This fine late-19th-century building (pictured above), which originally held storage tanks for the San Francisco Gas Light Company, has been converted into offices. Notice the corner turret and consistent brick and stone detailing throughout. ♦ 3600 Buchanan St (at North Point St)

7 The Buchanan Grill ★★$$ Low-key and comfortable, this spot dishes up tasty California cuisine—often to hungry local singles on the prowl. It's also a nice place to have drinks. ♦ California ♦ Daily lunch and dinner; Su brunch. Reservations recommended. 3653 Buchanan St (between Bay and North Point Sts). 346.8727

8 Chestnut Street Between Fillmore and Divisadero Streets, Chestnut becomes a main shopping artery for Marina residents. In marked contrast to trendy Union Street just a few blocks away, it is characterized by ordinary groceries, drugstores, small restaurants, and bars. However, several chichi shops and cafes have sneaked in recently, making this a street definitely worth a stroll. ♦ Between Fillmore and Divisadero Sts

• Cafe Adriano •

9 Cafe Adriano ★★$$ Chef Adriano Paganini, imported from a village outside of Milan, has brought his international cooking experience to this small, charming neighborhood cafe nestled in the heart of the Marina district. The result is a modest yet impressive, reasonably priced menu with such refined dishes as duck and mixed-greens salad tossed with balsamic vinaigrette; risotto with lobster, snap peas, and herbs; *gnocchi al*

gorgonzola (potato dumplings with gorgonzola cheese sauce); and grilled fillet of salmon with red onions and citrus vinaigrette. Be sure to save room for the peaches marinated in champagne and lemon that come with vanilla-bean ice cream or the equally divine chocolate terrine with orange sauce. ♦ Italian ♦ Tu-Su dinner. Reservations recommended. 3347 Fillmore St (between Chestnut and Lombard Sts). 474.4180

10 House of Magic If hocus-pocus is your thing, you'll enjoy this old-fashioned magic and joke store. ♦ Daily. 2025 Chestnut St (between Fillmore and Steiner Sts). 346.2218

11 La Pergola ★★$$ Northern Italian specialties here include homemade pastas and grilled veal marinated with rosemary—all served in a comfortable, charming dining room. ♦ Italian ♦ Daily lunch and dinner. Reservations recommended. 2060 Chestnut St (between Steiner St and Mallorca Way). 563.4500

12 The Body Shop Satin-smooth celebrities, as well as regular folk, are rumored to stock up on body and bath products from this London-based firm. Try the peppermint foot lotion—it's heavenly on tired feet. ♦ Daily. 2106 Chestnut St (between Steiner and Pierce Sts). 202.0112

12 Lucca Delicatessen One of the city's many fabulous Italian delis, this place sells fresh cheese, cold cuts, pasta, salads, and frittatas, plus imported canned goods. The staff also makes savory sandwiches on delicious bread. ♦ Daily. 2120 Chestnut St (between Steiner and Pierce Sts). 921.7873

13 Johnny Rockets ★$ A nostalgic re-creation of a 1950s diner with countertop jukeboxes (they're cheap to play, too), this fountain makes the best milk shake in town and is a good place for a late bite. ♦ American ♦ Daily lunch and dinner. 2203 Chestnut St (at Pierce St). 931.6258. Also at: Fisherman's Wharf, 81 Jefferson St (at Mason St). 693.9120; and 1946 Fillmore St (at Pine St). 776.9878

14 The Chestnut Street Grill $$ Hamburgers and fanciful sandwiches are named after the faithful clientele at this lively neighborhood restaurant and bar. There's garden seating in the rear. ♦ American ♦ Daily lunch and dinner. 2231 Chestnut St (between Pierce and Scott Sts). 922.5558

14 The Caravansary $ This versatile establishment houses a gourmet deli, store, and restaurant under one roof. ♦ Middle Eastern/California ♦ Daily lunch. 2257 Chestnut St (between Pierce and Scott Sts). Restaurant and store 922.2705; deli 921.0534

15 E'Angelo ★★$$ Ignore the meat dishes and try the really fine pasta in this bustling, family-run place. The fettuccine carbonara, *tortellini papalina* (stuffed with veal in a cream sauce with prosciutto and peas), and lasagna draw raves. ♦ Italian ♦ Tu-Sa dinner. No credit cards. 2234 Chestnut St (between Pierce and Scott Sts). 567.6164

15 Jack's Here's the place to find out-of-town newspapers, magazines, paperbacks, and tobacco. ♦ Daily. 2260 Chestnut St (between Pierce and Scott Sts). 567.0175

15 Judy's Cafe ★★$ This country-cute cafe, with lemon-colored walls and a balcony, is a hot spot for breakfast. Omelettes, sandwiches, and wholesome salads at modest prices are the principal attractions. ♦ American ♦ Daily breakfast and lunch. 2268 Chestnut St (between Pierce and Scott Sts). 922.4588

16 Bechelli's Coffee Shop ★★$ Homemade desserts and more than 25 varieties of omelettes, along with traditional coffeehouse chow, are the draw at this charming little restaurant. Sit at the counter or in the green upholstered booths. ♦ American ♦ Daily breakfast and lunch. 2346 Chestnut St (between Scott and Divisadero Sts). 346.1801

17 Marimba Cafe ★★$$ Open a trendy restaurant in a trendy neighborhood and sure enough, they will come. Which partly expains why this place has been a hit with the locals since the day it opened (reservations aren't taken, so expect to wait an hour or more for a table). The specialty of the house—*mole negro* of Oaxaca—is great, as is the taco bar (try the spiced octopus, shrimp, or snapper tacos). Mexican standards, such as enchiladas and quesadillas, round out the menu. ♦ Mexican ♦ Daily dinner; Tu-F lunch; Sa-Su brunch. 2317 Chestnut St (between Scott and Divisadero Sts). 776.1506

17 Citrus Cafe and Grill ★★$$ Choose from counter seating, a pleasant garden patio, or additional mezzanine seating in this restaurant that looks deceptively small from the outside. Though you'd never guess it from the name, the food is Moroccan with French accents, and just to keep things international, all-American apple pie is served for dessert. The lamb dishes are particularly fine. ♦ Moroccan ♦ Daily dinner; Sa-Su brunch. Reservations recommended for dinner. 2373 Chestnut St (between Scott and Divisadero Sts). 563.7720

18 Scott's Seafood Grill ★★$$ People are almost always overflowing out of the door of this restaurant, which has one of the most interesting bar scenes in the Bay Area. The fish is grilled with a knowing hand, and the cioppino is excellent. It is many cuts above most of the Fisherman's Wharf seafood houses, and is much in favor with local aficionados, both for the culinary expertise and for the comfortable interior, decorated with lots of brass and warm wood. ♦ Seafood ♦ Daily lunch and dinner. 2400 Lombard St (at Scott St). 563.8988. Also at: 3 Embarcadero Center. 981.0622

19 Izzy's Steaks & Chops ★★$$$ This lively, informal, 1930s-style steakhouse turns out big, satisfying meals. The 21-day, dry-aged New York steak is a winner, but for those with cholesterol concerns, there's a good selection of seafood. Wonderful creamed spinach accompanies the orders. ♦ Steak/Seafood ♦ Daily dinner. Reservations recommended. 3349 Steiner St (between Lombard and Chestnut Sts). 563.0487

20 Village Pizzeria ★$ Good pizza is available by the slice or whole pie. ♦ Pizza ♦ Daily lunch and dinner. 3348 Steiner St (between Lombard and Chestnut Sts). 931.2470

20 Barney's Gourmet Hamburgers ★$ For a quick, cheap bite to eat, nothing beats this joint, which offers all kinds of burgers— from big and beefy to turkey to vegetarian, chicken sandwiches, and a variety of salads. ♦ American ♦ Daily lunch and dinner. 3344 Steiner St (between Lombard and Chestnut Sts). 563.0307

20 Hahn's Hibachi ★$ You'll find good Korean-style barbecued pork, chicken, and beef to go at this small take-out place, which also has a delivery service and five small tables for those who want to eat on the spot. ♦ Korean/Takeout ♦ M-Sa lunch and dinner. 3318 Steiner St (between Lombard and Chestnut Sts). 931.6284. Also at: 1710 Polk St (at Clay St). 776.1095

21 Gatip Classic Thai Cuisine $ This restaurant may look like a winner from the outside, but the food is inconsistently prepared—sometimes it's quite good and sometimes quite bad. ♦ Thai ♦ M-Sa lunch and dinner; Su dinner. 2205 Lombard St (at Steiner St). 292.7474

22 La Canasta ★★★$ The Bay Area's *best* burritos are made here. A variety of other delicious Mexican food is available, too, but all of the food is for takeout only. ♦ Mexican/Takeout ♦ M-Sa lunch and dinner. 2219 Filbert St (at Fillmore St). 921.3003. Also at: 3006 Buchanan St (between Union and Filbert Sts). 474.2627

The first public school in the United States opened in San Francisco on 3 April 1848.

23 Pierce Street Annex Drinking Establishment This infamous member of "The Triangle," a bar-studded intersection in the Marina district that was named after this bar, the **Balboa Cafe,** and the **Golden Gate Grill,** is your typical singles hangout. In addition to its vivacious clientele, it shows football games during the season, and features a DJ and dancing nightly. ♦ Daily until 2AM. 3138 Fillmore St (between Greenwich and Filbert Sts). 567.1400

23 Baja Cantina ★$$ Good-sized portions of Mexican food are served here. Eat on the patio when the weather is warm, and don't miss the giant (and expensive) "Top Shelf" margaritas. ♦ Mexican ♦ Daily lunch and dinner. 3152 Fillmore St (at Greenwich St). 885.2252

24 Balboa Cafe ★$$ What used to be a hamburger place in the back room of a bar has been turned into an adventure in American cooking. But the elongated, juicy hamburger, tucked into a baguette, is still around, and is the one memorable item on the frequently changing menu. The place is usually filled with socialites by day and lovelorn singles in the evening. ♦ California ♦ Daily lunch and dinner. 3199 Fillmore St (at Greenwich St). 921.3944

25 Golden Gate Grill ★$ This restaurant and bar is equipped with a large-screen TV and maintains a low-key profile during the week with games like liars' dice and backgammon. On the weekend, however, the scene is much rowdier; expect a long line of singles after 10PM. ♦ American ♦ Daily dinner; Sa-Su brunch. 3200 Fillmore St (at Greenwich St). 931.4600

26 Blues Owner Max Young claims that this is "the only real dark, dingy blues club in the city." The music is live. ♦ Cover. M-Sa until 2AM. 2125 Lombard St (between Fillmore and Steiner Sts). 771.2583

27 Marina Inn $$ Ideally located for family sight-seeing, this attractive 40-room inn features the Early American theme. **Fort Mason** and Fisherman's Wharf are both nearby. Continental breakfast is included, although there is no restaurant. ♦ 3110 Octavia St (at Lombard St). 928.1000, 800/274.1420; fax 928.5909

28 Mick's Lounge It's a crapshoot as to whether the band is worth listening to, but at least you can't go wrong with the pool table, dart boards, and hefty draft beers. It's a casual, unpretentious place, best suited for a beer or two with a good friend. There's live music on Monday, Thursday, Friday, and Saturday. ♦ Daily. 2511 Van Ness Ave (between Union and Filbert Sts). 928.0404

29 Union Street In the 19th century this district was known as Cow Hollow because it was used as grazing land for the city's dairy cows.

Since the 1950s the six-block stretch from Gough to Steiner Streets has undergone a dramatic metamorphosis, from neighborhood stores to chic shops and swinging bars. The streets are lined with cleverly remodeled Victorian houses transformed into boutiques, art galleries, and cafes. Not all nearby residents are happy with the change, however; crowds can make parking difficult. (There's parking garage at Buchanan and Union Streets, and buses run frequently along here. ♦ Between Gough and Steiner Sts

30 Mudpie Shop here for casual upscale clothing for children and newborns, including lots of European designerwear for the budding fashion-conscious. ♦ Daily. 1694 Union St (at Gough St). 771.9262

31 Octagon House Home of the National Society of Colonial Dames, this beautifully preserved 19th-century house is now a museum, built on the strength of the once popular belief that eight-sided houses were lucky. It has been moved across the street from its original location and the lower-floor plan has been changed, but the upper floor displays the original layout, with square bedrooms on the major axes and bathrooms and service areas in the remaining triangular spaces. ♦ Admission. Second Su, second and fourth Th of every month; closed in January. 2645 Gough St (at Union St). 441.7512

32 Medioevo Taverna del Borgo ★★$$ Okay, so it's a bit hokey, with overenthusiastic waiters in striped tights and jesters' hats negotiating around hay bales and rough-cut wooden tables, but kids will enjoy the re-creation of a medieval dining hall, complete with heraldic figurines, terra-cotta tiles, and a wine cave. Of course, none of this works unless the Italian food is good, which, thanks to chef Vincenzo Cucco, formerly of the **Fairmont Hotel,** it is. The menu offers various types of pasta, with cream or marinara sauce; veal, rabbit, chicken, or sausage, prepared in classic Italian style; one delicious special is sea bass flavored with white wine, lemon, and fennel. ◆ Italian ◆ Tu-Su dinner. 1809 Union St (between Octavia and Laguna Sts). 346.7373

32 Pasand ★★$$ Southern Indian food is served to the sounds of live American music, from swing and rhythm and blues to jazz and pop. *Dosas* (wonderful lacy crepes), curries, and vegetarian and meat dishes are offered in a setting reminiscent of the 1960s. ◆ Indian ◆ Daily lunch and dinner; music until 1AM. 1875 Union St (between Octavia and Laguna Sts). 922.4498

33 Oggetti, Inc. Stunning hand-marbled Italian papers and desk accessories are the specialties at this store. ◆ Daily. 1846 Union St (between Octavia and Laguna Sts). 346.0631

34 Art Center Bed & Breakfast $$ Three suites and one studio are available in this smoke-free, New Orleans–style building; each has a color TV, radio, private bathroom, and heating pads. The three suites have microwave ovens and refrigerators stocked with breakfast food; two have fireplaces. Croissants are delivered to all guests in the morning. A deck garden is available for sunbathing. This is an excellent value in a prime location, with good bus service just one block away. ◆ 1902 Filbert St (at Laguna St). 567.1526

35 Bus Stop In business since 1900, this plain neighborhood bar provides an inkling of what the street was like before it was gentrified. The place draws a lot of local sports fans who just want an honest drink without having to come up with clever, sociable conversation. ◆ Daily. 1901 Union St (at Laguna St). 567.6905

35 Joji's ★$ Established in 1972, this unpretentious 20-seat restaurant has a faithful following of local people who like the low prices, French toast, and tasty teriyaki dishes. It's probably the best food value in the area. ◆ Japanese/American ◆ Daily breakfast, lunch, and dinner. 1919 Union St (between Laguna and Buchanan Sts). 563.7808

36 Perry's ★$$ It's boy meets girl at this popular, long-established Union Street watering hole, with a bar that's always jammed and some of the most genial bartenders in town. Owner Perry Butler, who opened the business in 1969, escaped from Madison Avenue with the intention of re-creating an East Side New York–style saloon in San Francisco. Those who just want to eat, rather than make new connections, head for the restaurant in back, where hearty, unpretentious American food is served in generous quantity. Magazines and newspapers hang on a brass rail for those who like to eat and read. A blackboard menu describes what's available. The hamburger is classically wonderful, and there's a memorable corned-beef hash. ◆ American

◆ M-F breakfast, lunch, and dinner; Sa-Su brunch and dinner. 1944 Union St (between Laguna and Buchanan Sts). 922.9022

36 Yankee Doodle Dandy This American folk-art gallery features one of the largest collections of pre-1935 quilts in the country. Established in 1967, it's one of the oldest businesses on Union Street—although over the years it's had different names and different merchandise. ◆ Daily. 1974 Union St (between Laguna and Buchanan Sts). 346.0346

36 The Deli ★$ Located in a cluster of Victorians, this deli, which would be unrecognizable as such to most New Yorkers, is one of the stalwart restaurants on the street. The overstuffed sandwiches may be eaten in an atrium area or in the wood-paneled rooms decorated with stained glass. ◆ Deli ◆ Daily lunch and dinner. 1980 Union St (between Laguna and Buchanan Sts). 563.7274

37 Bed and Breakfast Inn $$ Located on a quiet mews in the Union Street area, this was the forerunner of the bed-and-breakfast epidemic in the city. The word must have spread about its romantic atmosphere and excellent service—you'll have to reserve one of the 11 rooms (four with shared bath) well in advance. There is even a library and a garden for guests. ◆ 4 Charlton Ct (off Union St, between Laguna and Buchanan Sts). 921.9784

38 Blue Light Cafe ★★$$ This cafe offers Cajun cuisine in a modern interior gussied up with galvanized-metal walls and glass panels etched with bayou scenes. The place is invariably crowded with young singles. The kitchen turns out a hearty, spicy meat loaf with mashed potatoes, a commendable pot roast, and tasty barbecued ribs. ◆ Cajun ◆ Daily dinner. 1979 Union St (between Buchanan and Laguna Sts). 922.5510

39 Prego ★$$ Trendy but informal contemporary Italian restaurants are the rage in San Francisco, and this spot was one of the pacesetters. It's beautifully decorated, airy, and lively, but many say the quality of the food has fallen off in recent years. ◆ Italian ◆ Daily lunch and dinner. 2000 Union St (at Buchanan St). 563.3305

The variable weather of San Francisco is often more noticeable in Pacific Heights, with the fog funneling through the Golden Gate Bridge and flowing around the shoreline and hills. At almost any time of year, you can climb up a gray hillside to the sound of foghorns and stare down onto a sun-drenched view of the other side.

Restaurants/Clubs: Red   Hotels: Blue
Shops/ 🌳 Outdoors: Green   **Sights/Culture: Black**

Union Street Shopping Map

VAN NESS AVENUE

	UNION STREET	
The Coffee Merchant		
First Nail Care		
S.F. Fitness		La Salle Gallery *furniture*
The Great Frame Up		
Printer Service		
Mikes Antiques		Pacific Heights Inn
Union Garage		
Post Box		
Sherman Market		

FRANKLIN STREET

Union St. Hair Company
Fanyela's Skin Care Clinic

Pacific Framing Company
The Fitting Room Alterations

Heads First Salon
Italian deli Corsagno Bakery

Union St. Graphics
children's clothing Mudpie

GOUGH STREET

Shaw's Rugs	Hong Kong Restaurant *Chinese*
Union French Cleaners	Georgiou *women's clothing*
Canyon Beachwear	Brownie's *tan and fitness*
Forget-Me-Knots	T.C. Jeweler
gems St. Eligius	Bouvardia *florist*
Kinder Toys	Cow Hollow Shoe Repair
Hespe Gallery	Zuni Pueblo *Native-American artifacts*
Mömen Futon	Lamperti Associates *kitchen-bath showroom*
manicures Best Nails	Donato Rollo *men's clothing*
	Arte Forma *home furnishings*
Images of the North Gallery	Sushi Chardonnay
A Touch of Asia Gallery	Crepe' N Coffee *restaurant and cafe*
clothing Dantone	David Wang & Sons *antique Chinese carpets*

OCTAVIA STREET

	UNION STREET	
Fox Photo Lab		Fenzi Uomo *men's clothing*
Sanuk Asian Collectables		B & A Estate *jewelry*
housewares The Cottage Shoppe		Medioevo Taverna del Borgo *Italian restaurant*
hair salon Salon di Moda		Sunny-Side Up *gifts*
women's clothing Girlfriend's		
SF Familiar Gifts		Discovery Shop *women's clothing*
American restaurant What's Cooking?		
jewelry Baby Moon		Colours *casualwear*
Italian restaurant Antipasta		Pavillon de Paris *crystal and glass*
men's clothing Spaccio		Hourion Gallery
Oggetti, Inc.		Robert Dana Gallery
shops The Courtyard		Alley Cuts *hair salon*
Dynasty Gallery		Luisa's *Italian restaurant*
sportswear Body Options		Union Nails *manicures*
men's clothing Sy Aal		C.P. Shades *women's clothing*
David Clay Jewelers		Jason Adam *antiques*
Sauers Antiques		Pasand *Indian restaurant*
Comics, Etc.		Harbor View *Armenian cafe*
greeting cards Papyrus		The Enchanted Crystal *gifts*
Copy Mat		Starbucks Coffee

LAGUNA STREET

Wells Fargo Bank	Bus Stop *bar*
Bepple's Pie Shop	Union St. Goldsmith
American restaurant and bar Perry's	La Petite Boulangerie *bakery*

Shopping map continues on the next page

Union Street Shopping Map, continued

jewelry **Paris 1925**
women's clothing **PeLuche**
Art's Beauty World
Artisans Picture Framing
gifts **Yankee Doodle Dandy**
The Deli
coffee shop **Coffee Cantata**
hair salon **St. Tropez**
bar and restaurant **Union Ale House**
cosmetics **Bath Sense**
gifts **Aud's**
children's clothing **Thursday's Child**
Phoenix Florist
men's clothing **Casanova**

Joji's Japanese restaurant
Helen René salon
Glamour jewelry
John Wheatman, Inc. interior design
Puffins jewelry
Dreamy Angeles Boutique women's clothing
Union Garden Cafe
Patronik Designs jewelry
Kicks women's hosiery and socks
Union Gent hair salon

Mimi Tam clothing
S & B women's clothing
Blue Light Cafe
Earthly Goods women's clothing and shoes
Bank of America

UNION STREET

BUCHANAN STREET

Italian restaurant **Prego**
Banyan Restaurant
jewelry **The Jewel Box**
men's clothing **Spaccio**
French restaurant **L'Entrecôte de Paris**
Victorian Court
Cut Cut Hair Studio
Fog City Leather
delicacies **Papillon**
Solar Light Books
Japanese fashions **UKO**
cosmetics **Body Time**
men's and women's shoes **Kenneth Cole**
athletic shoes **Foot Locker**
clothing **Armani Exchange**

Fumiki Asian Arts
Shaw Shoes women's shoes
Union St. Plaza shops
Farnoosh women's clothing
Amici's Pizzeria
The Ocularium glasses
Jest Jewels jewelry
Metro Theatre
Dosa clothing
Z Gallerie gifts and posters
The Wherehouse records, CDs, and tapes
Bebe women's clothing

WEBSTER STREET

athletic shoes **The Athlete's Foot**
home furnishings **Gordon Bennett**
Hairs Alive Salon
Pierra Accessories
clothing **Fashion Crew**
women's clothing **Vivo**
alterations **Zaki**
Mexican restaurant **La Cucina**
bar **Tarr & Feathers**
Roamin' Pizza
Union St. Travel
upholstery **Van Galen**
furnishings **Z Gallerie**
Valentine & Riedinger Florist
cards and stationery **Union St. Papery**
Thriftway Market
bakery **La Nouvelle Patisserie**
deli **City Pantry**
liquor **Michaelis**

Opticians eyeglasses
Maud Frizon shoes
Hair Design by Kamiran
Mimi's women's clothing
The Bombay Company furniture
Foliot wristwatches
Tampico women's clothing
Nail Today manicures
Lorenzini men's clothing
Trojanowska Gallery
American Girl in Italy women's clothing
Amerasian Cafe Chinese and American
Artiques Gallery
Old & New Estates Jewelry

Three Bags Full women's clothing
Nice Cuts hair salon
Eyes in Disguise glasses
Coffee Roastery

FILLMORE STREET

florist **The Bud Stop**
women's clothing **Carnevale**

Dave's Pharmacy

Dance Shop
women's clothing **Cocos**
Thackerey & Robertson Gallery
Two Sisters Nail Salon
florist **Bed of Roses**
children's books **Charlotte's Web**
Sun Days Tanning Salon
Italian bakery **Il Fornaio**

Union St. Music Box Company gifts
Images For Hair hair salon
Le Bouquet florist
Nails 2001
Doidge's American restaurant
Ristorante Bonta Italian restaurant
Union St. Inn

Fazy's meats

Robert Henri Travel
Kelly 1 Salon hair salon
Marina Submarine

UNION STREET

109

39 Original Cow Hollow Farmhouse Marked by a big palm tree in front, this Victorian-era former farmhouse contains a complex of shops. In the rear is what was once the barn (the hayloft is still obvious); it's now a gallery. ♦ 2040 Union St (between Buchanan and Webster Sts)

Adjacent to the Original Cow Hollow Farmhouse:

L'Entrecôte de Paris ★$$ This restaurant gives a fresh California twist to French fare; the house favorite is steak with *pommes frites.* Live piano and sax on Friday and Saturday evenings evoke a cabaret atmosphere. ♦ French/California ♦ Daily lunch and dinner. Reservations recommended. 2032 Union St (at Buchanan St). 931.5006

40 Writer's Bookstore This is the only used and discounted bookstore located in Cow Hollow. ♦ Daily. 2848 Webster St (at Union St). 921.2620

41 Yoshida-Ya ★★$$ Yakitori is a whole different form of Japanese food, featuring all sorts of combinations of fish, meat, and vegetables put on skewers and charcoal-grilled at your table. Here you can get such dishes as mushrooms stuffed with ground chicken and asparagus wrapped in sliced pork. The atmosphere in this beautifully decorated restaurant is relaxed and pleasant. ♦ Japanese ♦ Daily dinner. 2909 Webster St (at Union St). 346.3431

42 La Nouvelle Patisserie Dieters beware! Elegant, divinely decadent French pastries are yours to eat on the premises or to take home. ♦ French Bakery/Takeout ♦ Daily. 2184 Union St (between Fillmore and Webster Sts). 931.7655. Also at: San Francisco Centre, Fifth St (at Market St). 979.0553

43 Sherman House $$$$ Built in 1876 by Leander Sherman, founder and owner of the Sherman Clay Music Company, this structure (illustrated above) was reopened as a luxury hotel in 1984 after being thoroughly refurbished by interior designer Billy Gaylord. Chiefly Italianate in style, although heavily influenced by the Second Empire style of French architecture, it is considered one of the most handsome and well-preserved examples of its period. The house was awarded historical landmark status in 1972. Each of the 14 rooms and suites is unique, individually furnished in French Second Empire, Biedermeier, or English Jacobean motifs. The carriage house, tucked away behind formal gardens and cobblestoned walkways, contains three suites, one of which opens onto its own private garden with a gazebo. Another suite has its own roof deck. All rooms have wood-burning fireplaces, views of the Golden Gate Bridge and the bay, and modern amenities such as wet bars, wall safes, TVs and stereo systems, and mini-TVs and whirlpool baths in the black-granite bathrooms.

The large west wing consists of a three-story music and reception room with a grand piano and a ceiling enlivened by an ornate lead-glass skylight. This room has hosted such greats as Caruso, Tetrazzini, Victor Herbert, and Lillian Russell. Now only a family of finches serenades you from their small château—a large cage created especially for them, inspired by Château Chenonceau in the Loire Valley, France. A double staircase from the music room leads up to a comfortable parlor where cocktails are served in the evening. Downstairs, classic French and nouvelle-style food is served. The discreet service and attention to minute details make the hotel popular with such celebrities as Shirley MacLaine, Ted Kennedy, and Bill Cosby. There is 24-hour room service, secretarial and translation services, valet parking, and chauffeured travel in vintage automobiles. ♦ 2160 Green St (between Webster and Fillmore Sts). 563.3600; fax 563.1882

44 Doidge's ★★$$ One of the most popular brunch spots in San Francisco offers perfectly cooked omelettes, eggs Benedict and other egg dishes, and marvelous French toast with fresh fruit. ♦ American ♦ Daily brunch. Reservations recommended. 2217 Union St (between Fillmore and Steiner Sts). 921.2149

44 Bonta ★★★$$ Intimate and friendly, this tiny, well-regarded trattoria serves rustic Italian fare and fine homemade pastas such as ravioli stuffed with sea bass and angel-hair pasta with tomatoes and garlic. Also recommended are the grilled mozzarella with mushrooms and the grilled beef with radicchio served in a balsamic-vinegar sauce. ♦ Italian ♦ Tu-Su dinner. Reservations recommended. 2223 Union St (between Fillmore and Steiner Sts). 929.0407

44 Union Street Inn $$$ The elegance of a 19th-century Edwardian home is combined with personal attention typical of a fine European pension. This six-room inn has a small but exquisite garden where breakfast, tea, and coffee are served, plus a parlor well stocked with books and magazines. The carriage house on the far side of the garden has a special suite with a Jacuzzi. Other rooms have private vanities, but share baths. ♦ 2229 Union St (between Fillmore and Steiner Sts). 346.0424

Il Fornaio

45 **Il Fornaio** Beautifully decorated and jammed with breads and pastries that will make you want to order one of everything, this is an Italian bakery you have to see to believe. Not all the food tastes as good as it looks, but the croissants, pizzas, and some of the breads are superb. ♦ M-Sa. 2298 Union St (at Steiner St). 563.3400

46 **Pane e Vino** ★★★$$ Many Italian food fanciers rave over the pasta at this quaint trattoria. Excellent grilled meats and fish also emerge from the open kitchen. ♦ Italian ♦ M-Sa lunch and dinner; Su dinner. Reservations recommended. 3011 Steiner St (at Union St). 346.2111

47 **Casebolt House** Built in the mid-1860s, this noteworthy Italianate-style house is one of the oldest in Pacific Heights. It's also a private residence. ♦ 2727 Pierce St (between Green and Vallejo Sts)

48 **Pacific Heights Mansions** Some of the finest Victorian mansions grace the tree-lined streets that run along the crest of the hill, offering spectacular views north across the bay and to Golden Gate Bridge. The 1700 to 2900 blocks of Broadway have houses in Italianate, Stick, Georgian, Queen Anne, and Dutch Colonial styles. Look for Queen Anne houses on the 1600 to 2900 blocks of Vallejo Street, and mansions on Divisadero and Jackson Streets and Clay Street at Steiner Street. At **2776 Broadway** is a very contemporary home dramatically different from its neighbors; it was the first custom-designed solar home in San Francisco. All are private residences. ♦ Between Pierce and Steiner Sts, and Broadway and Pacific Ave

49 **Apartment Towers** Pacific Heights has many splendid towers in many different styles. Most of the apartments, built in the 1920s, have elaborate marble-faced entrance lobbies complete with doormen. The penthouses create interesting silhouettes along the skyline. ♦ Broadway (between Steiner and Fillmore Sts). Also at: Washington and Steiner Sts

50 **Convent of the Sacred Heart** The former Flood Mansion, built in the Spanish Renaissance style by **Bliss and Faville** in 1916, is now an exclusive private school for girls. The building may be rented for private functions. ♦ 2222 Broadway (between Fillmore and Webster Sts). 563.2900

51 **2000 Broadway** Backen, Arrigoni, and Ross's 1973 design is a modern version of the great apartment towers built along Broadway during the 1920s. This is a private residence. ♦ At Buchanan St

52 **Golden Turtle** ★★$$ Every Vietnamese dish prepared by owner/chef Kim Quy Tran exudes freshness in this cousin of the well-established haute spot just off Clement Street. The sauces are light but intense, and all dishes are garnished with Chinese parsley, mint, basil, cucumbers, and raw carrots right from the garden. Don't miss the imperial rolls, lemon-grass beef, or fresh crab in ginger-and-garlic sauce. The dining-room walls are lined with exotic, carved-wood murals. ♦ Vietnamese ♦ Tu-Su lunch and dinner. 2211 Van Ness Ave (between Broadway and Vallejo Sts). 441.4419. Also at: 308 Fifth Ave (between Geary Blvd and Clement St). 221.5285

53 **Haas-Lilienthal House** One of the most grandiose Stick-style houses in the city, this 1886 confection (picture above) is a great Romantic pile of forms with elaborate wooden gables and a splendid Queen Anne–style circular corner tower. Inside, it has a series of finely preserved Victorian rooms complete with authentic period furniture. Walking tours of surviving pre–World War I mansions in Pacific Heights take place every Sunday, sponsored by the Foundation for San Francisco's Architectural Heritage. The group departs from here at 12:30PM; call 441.3000 for details. Docent-led tours of the house are given on Wednesdays and Sundays. It may also be rented for private functions (call 441.3011). ♦ Admission. W, Su. 2007 Franklin St (between Jackson and Washington Sts). 441.3004

54 Hard Rock Cafe ★$$ This lively, trendy spot, which attracts a young crowd with its ear-splitting rock music, serves classic American fare—ribs, burgers, fries, and rich, old-fashioned desserts—at reasonable prices. The decor features cars smashing through walls and a 1950s diner motif, with waitresses dressed like carhops. Other branches are in London; Los Angeles; Chicago; Dallas; Washington, DC; and New York City. The public can now buy a piece of the Rock—on the New York Stock Exchange. ♦ American ♦ Daily lunch and dinner. 1699 Van Ness Ave (at Sacramento St). 885.1699

55 Spreckels Mansion Called the "Parthenon of the West," this is the grandest home in San Francisco. It occupies a full block, bordered by Jackson, Gough, and Octavia Streets. Architect **George Applegarth** built the white Utah limestone mansion in 1913 for German immigrant Claus Spreckels, a sugar czar in the Gold Rush era. Years later, moviegoers saw the mansion as the opulent nightclub Chez Joey in the 1957 film *Pal Joey,* and again in the 1969 movie *The Eye of the Cat.* Romance writer Danielle Steel bought the house in 1990, reportedly for $8 million. The garden was sold separately. ♦ 2080 Washington St (at Octavia St)

56 Whittier Mansion This red-brown sandstone mansion was completed in 1896 for William Whittier, a prosperous paint manufacturer. It's a private residence. ♦ 2090 Jackson St (at Laguna St). 567.1848

57 Pacific Heights Conference Center & Culinary Arts Institute This landmark building is the only private residence built by the renowned architect **Arthur Page Brown**, whose other projects include the **Ferry Building.** The 1895 structure's interior incorporates 17 different woods. It is now used for private functions, including conferences. ♦ 2212 Sacramento St (at Laguna St)

57 Mansion Hotel $$$ Built by Utah senator Richard C. Chambers in 1887, this twin-towered Queen Anne is a museum of eccentric Victorian memorabilia that includes tapestries, art, clothing, toys, and curios. Each of the 21 guest rooms honors a celebrated San Franciscan. The garden displays the largest collection of Benny Bufano statues in the world. Rates include breakfast and whimsically wacky Magic Concerts (a cabaret-magic show held nightly). An elegant dining room serving continental fare overlooks the gardens. Garage spaces are available. ♦ 2220 Sacramento St (between Laguna and Buchanan Sts). 929.9444

58 Jackson Fillmore ★★★$$ The name of this enormously popular, invariably crowded little trattoria is a play on words, as it's at Fillmore and Jackson Streets. Originally it was called Jack's on Fillmore, but the owners of Jack's downtown protested and the present

compromise was reached. Customers hunker down to wonderfully rustic Italian food served in a utilitarian setting that makes the flavors the focal point of the evening. ♦ Italian ♦ Daily dinner. Reservations required for three or more. 2506 Fillmore St (between Jackson and Pacific Sts). 346.5288

59 Fillmore Street This street has developed from a nondescript, slightly seedy area into a smart thoroughfare of upscale boutiques, interesting resale shops, and trendy restaurants, easily rivaling those on Union Street. ♦ Between Jackson St and Geary Blvd

60 Alta Plaza Park One of a series of urban parks laid out when Pacific Heights was first developed, this green is set on the top of the hill with magnificent terraces stepping down to Clay Street. The park offers superb views south and east to **St. Mary's Cathedral** and the **Civic Center.** Around it is an interesting mixture of mansions, apartment towers, and false-front Italianate row houses. ♦ Bounded by Scott and Steiner Sts, and Jackson and Clay Sts

61 Pauli's Cafe ★$$ Almost always crowded, this bright, cheerful space is the perfect setting for breakfast or lunch. Breakfasts feature standard American cuisine with a twist—such scrumptious dishes as Grand Marnier French toast, eggs Florentine, and blueberry pancakes with old-fashioned maple syrup. At lunch, try the sandwich of grilled lamb sausage on focaccia, lamb stew, or crab cakes; at dinner, there are 11 types of pasta, including fettuccine with smoked salmon, horseradish, capers, and sour cream, or sample the hearty center-cut pork chop in a red wine–lemon sauce with mashed potatoes. ♦ California ♦ M lunch; Tu-F lunch and dinner; Sa brunch and dinner; Su brunch. Reservations recommended for dinner. 2500 Washington St (at Fillmore St). 921.5159

62 Yountville—Clothes for Children Look here for sophisticated sportswear for children. ♦ Daily. 2416 Fillmore St (at Washington St). 922.5050

63 Victorian Annex Thrift Shop Used clothing and bric-a-brac are sold by volunteers to benefit the nearby **California Pacific Medical Center.** ♦ M-Sa. 2318 Fillmore St (at Clay St). 923.3237

64 La Posada ★★$$ Good margaritas, tasty salsa, and large platters of flavorful Mexican food are offered in a curiously non-Mexican setting that's heavy on Victoriana. ♦ Mexican

♦ M-Sa lunch and dinner; Su brunch and dinner. 2298 Fillmore St (at Clay St). 922.1722

65 Next-to-New Shop Mostly women's clothing, along with some household items and menswear, is sold at this resale shop run by the Junior League of San Francisco and stocked principally by its enthusiastic members. Proceeds benefit community programs. ♦ M-Sa. 2226 Fillmore St (between Sacramento and Clay Sts). 567.1628

65 D&M Liquors You'll find an incredible selection of California wines here. The specialties are champagne and sparkling wines—250 different varieties. ♦ Daily. 2200 Fillmore St (at Sacramento St). 346.1325

66 Repeat Performance Thrift Shop This thrift shop is run by volunteers, with proceeds benefiting the **San Francisco Symphony.** There's often a good supply of evening wear. ♦ M-Sa. 2223 Fillmore St (between Sacramento and Clay Sts). 563.3123

66 Hillcrest Bar & Cafe ★★$$ The unpretentious menu has regional American accents and offers a great variety of dishes with a fresh approach. Don't miss the homemade soups (Louisiana corn chowder, Italian artichoke, and five-onion), hearty hamburgers, hot sausage and corned beef, and mesquite-grilled fish with a dazzling choice of sauces. The beige two-story dining room is relaxing, with interesting watercolors and soft lighting. A cozy bar in the corner gives the feeling of being in a private home and offers an extensive selection of California wines. The dessert menu has tortes, tarts, cakes, and pies; some choices change daily. Appetizers and desserts are served until 2AM for post-movie patrons. ♦ American ♦ Daily lunch and dinner; Su brunch. 2201 Fillmore St (at Sacramento St). 563.8400

66 R.H. Reminiscent of an English cottage, this quaint shop is known for its excellent selection of topiary creations. ♦ Daily. 2506 Sacramento St (at Fillmore St). 346.1460

67 Fillamento Furniture and housewares, all on the cutting edge of design, are offered at this modern shop. ♦ Daily. 2185 Fillmore St (between Sacramento and California Sts). 931.2224

67 Vivande Porta Via ★★$$$ Italian chef Carlo Middione's popular restaurant has marvelous homemade pastas and desserts; his equally popular deli has the city's best selection of Italian cheeses. You'll enjoy just browsing around this Sicilian equivalent to the popular French charcuterie. ♦ Italian ♦ Restaurant: daily lunch and dinner. Deli: daily. 2125 Fillmore St (between Sacramento and California Sts). 346.4430

67 Le Chantilly Chocoholics will delight in these excellent chocolates and sophisticated, decadent pastries. ♦ M-F. 2119 Fillmore St (between Sacramento and California Sts). 441.1500

68 Harry's Bar ★★$ Renowned for the sociable scene, it features lots of dark mahogany and brass, a white-tile floor, a grand piano, and great hamburgers. The owner, genial Harry Denton, is one of San Francisco's beloved characters. ♦ American ♦ Daily dinner. 2020 Fillmore St (between California and Pine Sts). 921.1000

68 Chestnut Cafe ★$ A pleasant place for a cheap feed, this cafe serves sandwiches, soups, and salads with an organic touch, as well as great energy drinks. ♦ American ♦ Daily breakfast and lunch. 2016 Fillmore St (between California and Pine Sts). 922.6510

68 The Brown Bag This complete stationery store for desk fanatics has a good selection of cards, ribbons, and gold paper clips. ♦ M-Sa. 2000 Fillmore St (at Pine St). 922.0390

69 The Elite Cafe ★★$$ Many San Franciscans first discovered the cholesterol-rich pleasures of New Orleans cooking at this lively restaurant, designed with cozy wooden booths and a green-tile floor. The busy raw bar is a great lure for shellfish aficionados. Blackened redfish, blackened filet mignon, and some of the most interesting brunch dishes to be found anywhere in town keep the crowds coming to this stylish and reasonably priced restaurant. The seafood chowder, bread pudding, and pecan pie are not to be missed. ♦ Creole/Cajun ♦ Daily dinner; Su brunch. 2049 Fillmore St (between California and Pine Sts). 346.8668

Restaurants/Clubs: Red	**Hotels:** Blue
Shops/ ♥ Outdoors: Green	**Sights/Culture:** Black

Fillmore Street Shopping Map

JACKSON STREET

Spinelli Coffee Company	**Mayflower Market** *grocery store*
Juicy Newstand	**Hueston's Appliance Service**
Mail Boxes Etc.	**S.F. Boot and Shoe Repair**
Pacific Heights Cleaners	**Maureen's** *hairdresser*
	Bond Cleaners
	Pacific Heights Pharmacy
L.P. Nail Care	**Paint Magic** *art store*
	Mark Wilner *jewelry*
	GJ Mureton's Antiques
	Yountville — Clothes for Children
	Hedy's Hair Salon
Pauli's Cafe	**Eugene Anthony Interior Design**
	Zoe *women's clothing*

FILLMORE STREET

WASHINGTON STREET

Pets Unlimited	**Belmont Florist**
	In-Shape *aerobics studio*
	Cottage Industries *exotic imports*
	Victorian House Thrift Shop
	Bank of America
American restaurant and bar **Fillmore Grill**	**Broemmel Pharmacy**

CLAY STREET

Clay Theatre	**La Posada** *Mexican restaurant*
home furnishings **International Market Gallery**	**Seconds To Go** *thrift store*
hair salon **Architects & Heroes**	**Via Veneto** *Italian restaurant*
women's clothing **Jim-Elle**	**Dean's** *women's clothing*
Japanese restaurant **Ten-Ichi**	**Next To New Shop**
clothing **Cielo**	**Starbucks Coffee**
S.F. Symphony Thrift Shop	**Body Options** *sportswear*
Mad Hatter Tea & Cheshire Cheese	**La Mediterranée** *Lebanese restaurant*
Worden's Custom Framing	**Kyo's Flowers**
Hillcrest Bar & Cafe	**D & M Liquors**

SACRAMENTO STREET

Sugar's Broiler	**Mike Furniture**
Browser Books	
housewares **Fillamento**	**Pascual's** *furniture*
women's clothing **Bebe**	**Metro 200** *women's clothing*
Italian market & restaurant **Vivande Porta Via**	**Jet Mail** *mail service*
Connocine Cafe	**The Beauty Store** *beauty products*
women's clothing **Scarlett's**	**Dover-Foxcroft, LTD** *frame store*
desserts **Le Chantilly**	**Vintage Boutique** *clothing*
beauty products **The Face Place**	
women's shoes **Footwear First**	**De Paula's** *Brazilian restaurant*
greeting cards **Papyrus**	
Express 1 Hour Photo	**Wells Fargo Bank**
Dino's Pizza	

CALIFORNIA STREET

Rolling Pin Donuts	**Bi-Rite Liquors**
Marquise Jewelers	**Wash Palace Laundry**
The Elite Cafe	**Mrs. Dewson's Hats**
natural foods **The Straw, The Jar, and The Bean**	**Nail Gallery & Hair Too**
women's clothing **Mio**	**Cavanaugh Gallery** *home furnishings*
women's clothing **Rag Trade**	**Departures from the Past** *clothing*
women's clothing **Betsey Johnson**	
men's clothing **J & G**	**Harry's Bar**
home furnishings **British Country Style**	**Chestnut Cafe**
ice cream **Rory's**	
exotic birds **Spectrum**	**The Brown Bag** *office supplies*
Pacific Heights Bar & Grill	

FILLMORE STREET

PINE STREET

Pacific Heights Market	**Johnny Rockets** *diner*
Cedonna Artful Living	**Avant Premiere** *women's clothing*
Japanese restaurant **Osome**	**Trellis** *women's clothing*
Fabricare Dry Cleaners	**Fillmore Glass and Hardware**
	Shopping map continues on the next page

Fillmore Street Shopping Map, continued

Asian and Italian restaurant **Oritalia**	**Main Line Gifts**

WILMOT ALLEY

women's clothing **The Company Store**	
Leon's Bar-B-Q	
Perfect Cleaners	**Coup de Chapeau** *hat boutique*
Invision Eyewear	**Maruya Sushi**
upholstery **It's My House**	**Narumi** *Japanese antique dolls*
women's clothing **We Be Bop**	**Beads & Clasps Craftshop**
clothing **Crossroads Trading Company**	**Vogue Nails**

BUSH STREET

Walgreens		**Delanghe Patisserie**
		Fleurtations *florist*
	F	**Trio Cafe**
	I	
	L	**Photomotion** *film development*
	L	**J.T. Nails** *nail salon*
	M	**Barry for Pets**
	O	**Alonso Eyewear**
	R	
	E	
bedding **Duxiana**		**Kay's Elegant Treats** *gifts*
Mexican cafe **Hot Chihuahua**	STREET	

69 Rory's Try homemade ice cream in a turquoise-and-pink-neon parlor. This place specializes in "twist-ins"—swirls of nuts, chocolate, and other treats spun into the ice cream—and delicious homemade waffle cones. ♦ Ice Cream ♦ Daily. 2015 Fillmore St (between California and Pine Sts). 346.3692

69 Spectrum It's fun to look at and talk to this choice collection of exotic birds, even if you aren't buying. ♦ Daily. 2011 Fillmore St (between California and Pine Sts). 922.7113

70 William Sawyer Gallery Contemporary paintings and sculpture by West Coast artists are featured at this gallery. Look for an off-white house with no sign. ♦ Tu-Sa. 3045 Clay St (between Broderick and Baker Sts). 921.1600

71 El Drisco Hotel $$ This San Francisco landmark has hosted many distinguished guests—including presidents Eisenhower, Truman, and Nixon—because of its discreet ambience and unique location (it was Pacific Heights's only hotel for decades). Some of the 25 elegant rooms have spectacular views. There's no restaurant, but continental breakfast is included in the room rate. ♦ 2901 Pacific Ave (at Broderick St). 346.2880; fax 567.5537

72 Swedenborgian Church Arthur Page Brown built this church in 1884, and **Bernard Maybeck** and **A.C. Sweinfurth,** who were in Brown's office, worked on the designs, as you can see by the beautiful Craftsman-style detailing. The church is adjacent to a fine walled garden that is raised up above the surrounding street and contains trees, flowers, and shrubs from every continent on earth. Inside the church is a large fireplace, as well as stained-glass windows by Bruce Porter and furniture by Gustav Stickley. ♦ 2107 Lyon St (at Washington St)

73 3200 Block of Pacific Avenue One of the most unusual groups of houses in the city, this complex is located on a wedge-shaped lot that steps downhill. The entire block is clad in brown shingles and contains some of the city's best turn-of-the-century domestic architecture. Each house retains its own special identity with distinct window or doorway detailing while maintaining the unity of the entire block. **Nos. 3203** and **3277** are by **Willis Polk**; No. 3233 is by **Bernard Maybeck;** and **Nos. 3232** and **3234** are by **Ernest Coxhead. No. 3232** is of particular interest for its fine doorways and bizarre balcony. All of the homes are private residences. ♦ Between Walnut St and Presidio Ave

74 Roos House This 1909 structure by **Bernard Maybeck** is a highly personalized example of English Tudor with typical **Maybeck** window and eaves detailing. It is a private residence. ♦ 3500 Jackson St (between Spruce and Locust Sts)

75 3778 Washington Street A mixture of Bay Area and International styles, this house was built in 1952 by **Eric Mendelsohn.** Early **Mendelsohn** details such as the rounded corner bay and the porthole windows characterize this private residence. ♦ At Maple St

76 Lem House Daniel Solomon & Associates built this stucco-clad row house with an imposing Palladian window and rusticated base in 1986. It is a private residence. ♦ Cherry St (between Sacramento and Clay Sts)

The three-tiered staircase in Alta Plaza Park is still chipped and cracked from the manic car chase featured in Peter Bogdanovich's film *What's Up, Doc?* The damage upset residents and enraged city officials.

77 Temple Emanu-El This stunning structure is the spiritual center for California's oldest Jewish congregation, founded in 1850. Built by **Arthur Page Brown** in 1926, it is northern California's largest synagogue, with a sanctuary that seats 2,000. The dome was inspired by Constantinople's Hagia Sofia, a sixth-century Byzantine masterpiece. The temple was restored to its original grandeur in 1989. ♦ Docent tours M-F. Arguello Blvd (at Lake St). 751.2535

78 Sacramento Street A mixture of auto garages, movie theaters, ice-cream parlors, gift and antiques shops, boutiques, and a store that is open only two months each year to present an incredible selection of Christmas ornaments are located along this less overwhelming, less touristy version of Union Street. ♦ Between Baker and Spruce Sts

79 Dottie Doolittle If you've got plenty of money to spend on little clotheshounds, you'll like these fine kids' clothes, mainly European imports. ♦ Daily. 3680 Sacramento St (between Spruce and Locust Sts). 563.3244

79 Tortola ★$$ Established in 1922 (at a different location), this is one of the oldest restaurants in the city. In its current incarnation, it looks very trendy, with a contemporary interior and abstract artwork. It used to be known as a restaurant that served "early California" food; now the culinary emphasis is southwestern. ♦ Southwestern ♦ Tu-Sa lunch and dinner; Su dinner. Reservations recommended. 3640 Sacramento St (between Spruce and Locust Sts). 929.8181

79 Tuba Garden ★$$ Although the food doesn't approach the finesse of the setting, this remains one of the most delightful places for an alfresco lunch or brunch. Garden statuary and a fountain decorate a charming garden abloom with flowers. Indoor seating is equally pleasant in the adjoining Victorian house. Omelettes, sandwiches, and salads are the best bets. ♦ American ♦ M-F lunch; Sa-Su brunch. Reservations recommended. 3634 Sacramento St (between Spruce and Locust Sts). 921.TUBA

79 Bath Sense This shop stocks all kinds of soothing, fragrant products for bath and body, including gift items created by local artists. ♦ M-Sa. 3610 Sacramento St (between Spruce and Locust Sts). 567.2638

80 Beyond Expectations ★★★$ This is everything a cafe should be. The food, served cafeteria-style, is excellent, with most of it made from scratch on the premises (the morning cheese pie with blueberries is a dish to dream about). The coffee is terrific, as are the wonderful sandwiches, fluffy quiches, fresh salads, soups, and homemade baked goods. There are periodicals for reading, and a view of a pretty little garden from the back dining area. ♦ American ♦ M-Sa breakfast and lunch. 3613 Sacramento St (between Spruce and Locust Sts). 567.8640

80 Rosemarino ★★$$ This popular neighborhood haunt serves well-prepared Mediterranean food in a cheerful, if somewhat cramped, setting. Try for a courtyard seat on a sunny day. ♦ Mediterranean ♦ Daily lunch; Tu-Sa dinner; Su brunch. Reservations recommended. 3665 Sacramento St (between Spruce and Locust Sts). 931.7710

81 Jonathan-Kaye by Country Living Cluttered and dedicated to quality, this shop offers a charming selection of children's furnishings and toys. ♦ Daily. 3548 Sacramento St (between Locust and Laurel Sts). 563.0773

ＳＡＮＴＡ ＦＥ

82 Santa Fe Antique Navajo blankets, Indian pots and baskets, early Hispanic ranch furniture, weavings and folk art, silver and turquoise jewelry, and vintage cowboy collectibles are among the items to be found in this shop, which also features the work of artists who find inspiration in traditional southwestern art forms and designs. At press time, it was scheduled to change its name to **Arts of the Americas** and its location to 2797 Union St (at Baker St). ♦ Daily. 3571 Sacramento St (between Locust and Laurel Sts). 346.0180

83 Elliot Lucca Browse through the impressive collection of imported travel accessories, shoes, jewelry, and handbags. ♦ Daily. 3484 Sacramento St (between Laurel and Walnut Sts). 771.8251

84 Ken Groom's Pet Supplies & Gifts Everything from basic collars to Burberry raincoats for the pampered dog, cat, or bird is on display at this well-stocked shop. ♦ M-Sa. 3429 Sacramento St (between Laurel and Walnut Sts). 673.7708

85 Marilyn Brooks You'll find amusing sportswear and unusual jewelry from Toronto. ◆ M-Sa. 3376 Sacramento St (between Walnut St and Presidio Ave). 931.3376

85 Elaine Magnin Needlepoint All the needlework accoutrements are sold here, including patterns for pillows that carry the words "Living Well Is the Best Revenge"—a notch above the old bromide "Home Sweet Home." Lessons are available, too. ◆ M-Sa. 3310 Sacramento St (between Walnut St and Presidio Ave). 931.3063

86 Kouchah's This shop carries imported handicraft and decorative items, and specializes in Persian tribal rugs. ◆ Daily. 3369 Sacramento St (between Walnut St and Presidio Ave). 928.7388

86 Town School Clothes Closet Clothing from some of San Francisco's wealthiest households can be found at this resale shop. Proceeds benefit a private school. ◆ M-Sa. 3325 Sacramento St (between Walnut St and Presidio Ave). 929.8019

86 Return to Tradition These naturally dyed Dobag carpets are woven in a Turkish cooperative. ◆ Daily. 3319 Sacramento St (between Walnut St and Presidio Ave). 921.4180

87 Celebrations One of the best one-stop party shops in town, it features custom gift wrapping, printing, party planning, balloon delivery, and helium-tank rentals. There is also a very large assortment of party favors in stock. ◆ M-Sa. 340 Presidio Ave (between Sacramento and Clay Sts). 885.2117

88 Forrest Jones Check out the culinary ware and piles of exotic-looking baskets here. ◆ Daily. 3274 Sacramento St (between Lyon St and Presidio Ave). 567.2483

89 Brava Strada Fabulous leather accessories and many one-of-a-kind pieces await those who don't mind paying big prices for a very individual look. The shop itself is a beauty, with adobe-style walls hung with local art. ◆ M-Sa. 3247 Sacramento St (between Lyon St and Presidio Ave). 567.5757

89 Osteria ★★★$$ The kitchen at this popular neighborhood restaurant knows how to please its clientele. Green *tagliarini* pasta with shrimp and garlic, and linguine with tomatoes and clams are two of the excellent pasta possibilities. Veal and fish are also featured. ◆ Italian ◆ M-Sa dinner. 3277 Sacramento St (at Presidio Ave). 771.5030

90 American Pie This place, which smells delightful, bills itself as "a contemporary general store," and so it is. Candy, toiletries, coffees, candles, and stationery are among the items sold. You'll find things here you never knew you needed, but suddenly can't live without. ◆ Daily. 3101 Sacramento St (between Lyon and Baker Sts). 929.8025

91 V. Breier You'll find playful and charming contemporary and American decorative arts here. ◆ M-Sa. 3091 Sacramento St (between Broderick and Baker Sts). 929.7173

91 Sue Fisher King Chic tableware and home accessories that are aimed at upmarket households are sold at this elegant shop. ◆ M-Sa. 3067 Sacramento St (between Broderick and Baker Sts). 922.7276

92 Quinby's This store sells children's books, videos, records, and arts and crafts. ◆ Daily. 3411 California St (between Locust and Laurel Sts). 751.7727

92 Laurel Village Cafe ★$ Stop by here for a sandwich and a frozen yogurt. ◆ Cafe ◆ Daily breakfast and lunch. 3415 California St (between Locust and Laurel Sts). 751.4242

92 Peet's Coffee & Tea One of the Bay Area's best-regarded coffee chains features beans and brews for serious coffee and tea connoisseurs. ◆ Coffeehouse ◆ Daily. 3419 California St (between Locust and Laurel Sts). 221.8506. Also at: 2156 Chestnut St (between Steiner and Pierce Sts). 931.8302; 54 W Portal Ave (in Forest Hill). 731.0375; 2257 Market St (at Sanchez St). 626.6416; and 2139 Polk St (between Vallejo St and Broadway). 474.1871

92 Fantasia Bakery & Confections Throw your diet to the wind at this sensational Austrian bakery. The Sacher torte is the best in town. ◆ Daily. 3465 California St (between Locust and Laurel Sts). 752.0825

93 La Rocca's Oyster Bar ★$$ Another of the delightful, authentic San Francisco Italian seafood restaurants, this eatery serves only the freshest fish in a casual setting. The specialties here are fish native to the Bay Area, such as rex and petrale sole, sand dabs, Dungeness crab, and salmon. ◆ Seafood ◆ M-Sa breakfast and lunch. 3519 California St (between Locust and Spruce Sts). 387.4100

93 Young Man's Fancy Shop here for conservative, well-tailored clothing for boys of all ages. ◆ M-Sa. 3527 California St (between Locust and Spruce Sts). 221.4230

93 Imaginarium This marvelous toy shop brings out the playful spirit in all its customers. ◆ Daily. 3535 California St (between Locust and Spruce Sts). 387.9885

Restaurants/Clubs: Red	**Hotels:** Blue
Shops/ ◆ Outdoors: Green	**Sights/Culture:** Black

The Haight/Japantown

The Haight is a district of extremes, an amalgam of subcultures that includes **Golden Gate Park, Buena Vista Hill, Ashbury Heights, Edgewood,** and the celebrated neighborhood of **Haight-Ashbury.** There are villas and ghetto flats, new developments and Baroque mansions, as well as what is probably the oldest house in San Francisco (at **329 Divisadero Street**), which was shipped around the Horn in sections as a gift for a homesick bride.

All this was once part of a 4,000-acre land grant to a man named José de Jesus Noe, the last *alcalde* (mayor) of San Francisco when the city was still known as Yerba Buena and belonged to Mexico. The area was developed somewhat later than the one around Alamo Square just to the east (traditionally known as the Western Addition), so the houses have more of the ornate character of the 1890s. The Haight (as Haight-Ashbury is often known) was everything a proper 19th-century neighborhood should be, with more than a thousand

Victorian houses (many still standing), the beginnings of an enormous park, and a landscaped strip for promenading called the **Panhandle**, which looked something like Boston's Commonwealth Avenue, except for the difference in the architecture of the homes.

The names of other nearby streets honor the men who worked to make **Golden Gate Park** possible: **Cole**, **Clayton**, **Shrader**, **Stanyan**, and **Ashbury**. The neighborhood's decline began in 1917, when the Twin Peaks tunnel encouraged people to move out toward the Sunset district, and it continued through the 1950s. The big houses were divided into flats and then divided again. Then there was "the Happening"—the blossoming of the flower children and the hippie movement, which, depending on one's sociological viewpoint, either continued the decline or marked the neighborhood's rebirth. The flower children disseminated the values of their counterculture all around **Haight Street**, but idealism mixed with drugs and unemployment ultimately proved an ineffective formula for social improvement. The area fell into a state of marked decay and became a place where only the streetwise could walk comfortably. But with the rise in real-estate values around the city, a gentrification trend soon reached the Haight. While many drug-dazed drifters can still be seen asking for spare change and toting their bedrolls to and from **Golden Gate Park**, the neighborhood has become home to middle- and upper-middle-class professionals. The young execs and the New Wavers rub shoulders with washed-out, homeless remnants of the 1960s, resulting in an often tense bustle of eclectic eccentrics, tailor-made for brave people-watchers.

From **Masonic Avenue** to Stanyan Street, Haight Street is lined with some of the city's most interesting shops, bookstores, nightclubs, and cafes. It's a haven for vintage-clothing aficionados and those interested in the occult. And the rebellious spirit hasn't been silenced completely. In 1988 a chain drugstore was burned to the ground during the construction stage, and a decision (probably a wise one) was made to avoid building in a part of town where such enterprises were so obviously unwelcome. Farther east along Haight Street, the area known as **Lower Haight** is also experiencing a renaissance, with many unique small shops and restaurants.

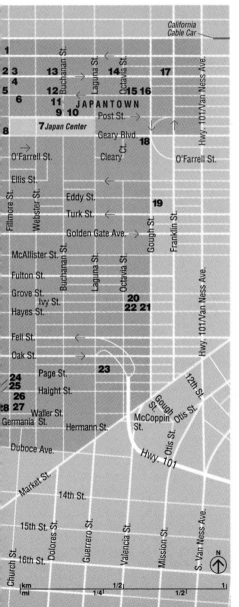

Japantown, *Nihonmachi* to its residents, is a surprising oasis—a pristine village located within the approximate boundaries of **Octavia** and **Fillmore Streets**, and **California Street** and **Geary Boulevard.** Ever since the end of World War II, when the city's Japanese-Americans returned from internment camps to find their former homes occupied, the greatest proportion have lived in other neighborhoods. Only about four percent of San Francisco's Japanese-Americans actually live in Japantown now, but most return here regularly for shopping and for social and religious activities. The construction of the **Japan Center** in 1968 inspired a community-renewal program, with residents and merchants of *Nihonmachi* working together to beautify the surrounding blocks. As you approach the center's main entrance from the north, the block-long **Buchanan Mall,** landscaped with flowering trees, resembles a meandering stream, with fountains by noted sculptor Ruth Asawa. On many weekends, especially during the spring Cherry Blossom Festival and the summer months, you can see a variety of Japanese cultural activities, from tea ceremonies and martial-arts presentations to flower arranging and musical performances. In the gardens along the neat rows of Victorians, you will see shrubs crafted into exotic shapes and a stone lantern here or there in well-tended grounds, planned with obvious respect for the tea-garden tradition.

Area code 415 unless otherwise noted.

1 Pacific Heights Bar & Grill ★★$$ This California-cuisine grill, with its tasteful, modern decor, offers several fish dishes. Favorites include spinach fettuccine with alderwood-smoked salmon, and sautéed prawns over saffron couscous with artichokes and Dijon-mustard sauce, as well as daily specials. Many cognoscenti think it has the best oyster bar in town. ◆ California ◆ Daily dinner; W-Sa lunch; Su brunch. Reservations recommended. 2001 Fillmore St (at Pine St). 567.5226

2 Osome ★★★$$ For years this place has maintained its reputation as one of the top sushi bars and Japanese restaurants in San Francisco. The impeccably prepared food is served in a comfortable, unpretentious setting of Formica-topped tables and blond-wood chairs with rush seats. *Yousenabe* (a seafood stew) and *ton katsu* (pork cutlet) are among the many highly recommended dishes served here. ◆ Japanese ◆ Daily dinner. 1923 Fillmore St (between Bush and Pine Sts). 346.2311

2 Oritalia ★★★$$ The cooking in this restaurant represents an ingenious and original melding of Asian and Italian culinary styles. It makes sense, since pasta was supposed to have come from China. Portions are modest and meant to be shared, enabling diners to sample and savor many of the menu's excellent offerings. Possibilities might include Korean barbecued beef with lettuce wrap; *enoki*, shiitake, and oyster mushrooms in a sake-batter ginger sauce; and Japanese linguine with *unagi* (eel). ◆ Asian/Italian ◆ Daily dinner. Reservations recommended. 1915 Fillmore St (between Bush and Pine Sts). 346.1333

2 Leon's Barbecue ★$ Designed like a 1950s diner, this place offers chicken, hot links, ribs, and homemade sweet-potato-and-pecan pie and peach cobbler for dessert. As barbecue goes, it's just OK—fans of this down-home cuisine won't be dazzled. ◆ Barbecue ◆ Daily lunch and dinner. 1911 Fillmore St (between Bush and Pine Sts). 922.2436. Also at: 2800 Sloat Blvd (at 46th Ave). 681.3071

3 Maruya ★★$ The take-out sushi at this modest establishment offers good value for the price. ◆ Japanese/Takeout ◆ Daily lunch and dinner. 1904 Fillmore St (between Bush and Pine Sts). 921.2929

3 Narumi Antiques This intriguing shop specializes in Japanese antiques, particularly 18th- and 19th-century dolls and stained glass. ◆ M-Sa. 1902B Fillmore St (between Bush and Pine Sts). 346.8629

4 Patisserie Delange You'll find fine French pastry at this friendly shop. ◆ Tu-Su. 1890 Fillmore St (at Bush St). 923.0711

5 Duxiana Swedish bedding and linen are the specialties here, as well as the Dux bed, which has two sets of inner springs, and adapts to the contours of your body to help keep your spine straight while sleeping. ◆ Daily. 1803 Fillmore St (at Sutter St). 673.7134

6 Cafe Kati ★★★$$$ Get ready for some unusual combinations in this eclectic and daring neighborhood restaurant. The kitchen starts out innocently enough with basic main ingredients—duck, lamb, chicken, rabbit, and fish—and then throws in papayas, Asian spices, or other exotica to give the food a distinctly Pacific Rim flavor. The presentations are gorgeous; the decor, artsy and sophisticated. ◆ California/Pacific Rim

♦ Tu-Su dinner. Reservations recommended. 1963 Sutter St (between Fillmore and Webster Sts). 775.7313

7 Japan Center This five-acre shopping, dining, and entertainment complex is packed into three square blocks, the commercial and cultural center for northern California's more than 12,000 Japanese-American residents. Designed by **Minoru Yamasaki,** the center consists of three main commercial buildings: the **Miyako Hotel,** the **Kabuki 8 Cinema,** and the **Webster Street Bridge of Shops** (an Asian Ponte Vecchio), as well as several other smaller buildings. Designed as a miniature Ginza, the two-level shopping area encloses pedestrian malls, Japanese gardens, shops, restaurants, art galleries, and sushi bars. ♦ Bounded by Geary Blvd and Post St, and Laguna and Fillmore Sts. 922.6776

Within Japan Center:

Kabuki Hot Spring Japanese-style communal baths—including a giant hot tub, large cold tub, walk-in sauna, steam room, Japanese-style washing area, and Western-style showers—leave customers feeling relaxed and squeaky clean. Shiatsu (Japanese pressure-point massage) is the specialty. ♦ Daily. 1750 Geary Blvd (at Fillmore St). 922.6002

Miyako Hotel $$$ Eastern and Western traditions merge in the 218 rooms and suites of this hotel. Most rooms are furnished in Western style with a few Japanese touches, such as authentic shoji screens, hand-painted and lacquered *fusuma* screens, and niches for flowers and art objects.

There is a variety of deluxe accommodations here. Ten luxury suites have private saunas. Two rooms and one suite combine traditional American and Japanese accommodations and are ideal for families. One area has a king-size bed, while a second partitioned space is carpeted with heavy tatami mats and traditional down-filled futon bedding. The **Club Floor** has a private entryway and includes 14 deluxe rooms and suites, a whirlpool in every room, and a spacious lounge.

Within the hotel are convention and meeting facilities, the **Elka** restaurant (which serves international and Japanese specialties), and a cocktail lounge. Children 18 years old and under may stay free in their parents' room. ♦ 1625 Post St (at Laguna St). 922.3200, 800/533.4567; fax 921.0417

Kinokuniya Book Store Books about Japan in English and Japanese, as well as Japanese publications and recordings, are this store's focus. ♦ Daily. Kinokuniya Bldg, 1581 Webster St (at Post St). 567.7625

The Peace Pagoda The focal point of the center, the pagoda rises 100 feet in five tiers from the reflecting pool in the middle of the **Peace Plaza.** It was designed by **Yoshiro Taniguchi** of Tokyo, an authority on ancient Japanese structures.

Mifune ★★$ The Japanese version of fast food is served here, with every sort of noodle dish you could think of—and then some. ♦ Japanese ♦ Daily lunch and dinner. Restaurant Mall, Kintetsu Bldg, 1737 Post St (at Webster St). 922.0337

Mikado Look here for an impressive collection of items that accessorize a kimono, from obis to tassels to footwear. There are also Japanese dolls, toys, and chinaware. ♦ Daily. Kintetsu Bldg, 1737 Post St (at Webster St). 922.9450

Isobune ★★$$ Sushi boats float past customers seated around an oblong bar as chefs launch their creations from the center. If you don't see what you want right away, wait until another boat sails by. ♦ Japanese ♦ Daily lunch and dinner. Restaurant Mall, Kintetsu Bldg, 1737 Post St (at Webster St). 563.1030

Koji Osakaya ★★$$ Japanese curry is among the specialties of this small eatery, which has a pleasant Asian ambience. ♦ Japanese ♦ Daily lunch and dinner. Kintetsu Bldg, 1737 Post St (at Webster St). 922.2728

Asakichi This shop offers a good selection of antique *tansu* chests and decorative objects. ♦ Daily. Kinokuniya Bldg, 1581 Webster St (at Post St). 921.2147

Isuzu ★★★$$ Seafood, including sushi, is the specialty at this elegant Japanese restaurant, which was a favorite of the late actor Raymond Burr. ♦ Japanese ♦ M, W-Su dinner; M, Th-Su lunch. Kinokuniya Bldg, 1581 Webster St (at Post St). 922.2290

Kimono Shige Nishi Guchi The excellent selection here makes this store great for browsing as well as for buying vintage kimonos. ♦ Daily. Kinokuniya Bldg, 1581 Webster St (at Post St). 346.5567

Kinokuniya Stationery & Gifts This shop stocks lovely Japanese greeting cards and imported paper. ♦ Daily. Kinokuniya Bldg, 1581 Webster St (at Post St). 567.8901

Murata Pearls You'll find a huge selection of pearls at attractive prices. ♦ Daily. Kintetsu Bldg, 1737 Post St (at Webster St). 922.0666

Ikenobo Ikebana Society This branch of Japan's largest flower-arranging school is its North American headquarters. On Saturday, from about 10AM to noon, you might be able to see the experts creating the weekly floral window displays. Call for a class schedule. ♦ Kintetsu Bldg, 1737 Post St (at Webster St). 567.1011

Mr. Dandy Petite clotheshounds will find men's and some women's fashions in small sizes here. ♦ Daily. Kintetsu Bldg, 1737 Post St (at Webster St). 929.8633

Oshare Corner Small-size fashions for women are carried here. ♦ Daily. Kintetsu Bldg, 1737 Post St (at Webster St). 922.9744

8 Jack's Bar Home of the **Deacon Jones Blues Band,** this place has, since 1932, been "where the blues cats hang out." Earl King, John Lee Hooker, and Wolfman Jack have made appearances, and if you wear your **Jack's** T-shirt, you won't have to pay a cover charge. Sandwiches are served at the bar. ♦ Cover. Daily until 2AM. 1601 Fillmore St (at Geary Blvd). 567.3227

9 Sanppo ★★$$ Elegant Japanese food is served in a setting that's better than most. Try the excellent *gyoza* (a Japanese-style pot sticker) or barbecued eel *unajyu,* steamed in its own iron pot. ♦ Japanese ♦ Tu-Su lunch and dinner. 1702 Post St (at Buchanan St). 346.3486

10 Soko Hardware This is a great place to find rice cookers, Japanese garden tools, kitchen utensils, and even a state-of-the-art toilet. ♦ M-Sa. 1698 Post St (at Buchanan St). 931.5510

11 Sushi-A ★★★$$ The quality of the food at this popular sushi bar is high, perhaps because the chef/owner was trained in Japan. ♦ Japanese ♦ M, W-Su lunch and dinner. 1737 Buchanan Mall (at Sutter St). 931.4685

11 Benkyodo Confectioners ★$ The social hub of Japantown, this place specializes in Japanese confections and light lunches served at a counter. ♦ Japanese ♦ M-Sa breakfast and lunch. 1747 Buchanan St (at Sutter St). 922.1244

12 Best Western Miyako Inn $$ This eight-story, 125-room hotel is comfortable and reasonably priced. Sixty of the rooms are equipped with steam baths, and **Cafe Mums** offers Eastern and Western cuisine. ♦ 1800 Sutter St (at Buchanan St). 921.4000; fax 563.1278

13 Restored Victorian Row Houses These painted ladies were moved from their former sites when the Western Addition was being destroyed in the name of urban renewal. They have been carefully restored and given front gardens, in contrast to their previous condition, when the houses were located on the street front. ♦ Bush St (between Fillmore and Gough Sts)

14 La Fiammetta ★★$$$ This intimate little spot serves interesting Italian food, including linguine with prawns and scallops in a fra diavolo sauce, and grilled portobello mushrooms with garlic and fresh herbs on a bed of mixed greens. Most notable are the appetizers and the skillfully grilled meats. ♦ Italian ♦ Tu-Su dinner. Reservations recommended. 1701 Octavia St (at Bush St). 474.5077

15 Queen Anne Hotel $$ Although this is one of the largest bed-and-breakfasts in town, no two of the 49 rooms or suites are decorated alike. Each has a private bath, telephone, color TV, and king- or queen-size bed. Ten have fireplaces, and all are furnished with English and American antiques. Although there's no restaurant, a continental breakfast is served in the salon, and tea and sherry are offered every afternoon. Of architectural interest are the oak paneling in the hall, the carved Spanish-cedar staircase, and the fine inlaid floors. The structure was originally built by Senator James Fair, one of the Comstock silver kings, to house a girls' school. It served in turn as an elite gentlemen's club, a home for young working women, and finally a hotel. ♦ 1590 Sutter St (at Octavia St). 441.2828, 800/227.3970; fax 775.5212

16 Hotel Majestic $$$ This hostelry has a long history, and, according to an 1888 document, it just might be the city's oldest surviving hotel. It was untouched by the 1906 earthquake and fire, and at that time was used as a shelter for the homeless. During the 1930s, actresses (and sisters) Joan Fontaine and Olivia de Havilland reputedly lived here. Today, its 58 rooms (including nine luxurious suites) are replete with furniture from the French Empire and English manor houses, fine paintings, hand-painted four-poster beds, and many fireplaces. The lobby has been restored far beyond its initial grandeur. ♦ 1500 Sutter St (at Gough St). 441.1100, 800/869.8966; fax 673.7331

Within the Hotel Majestic:

Cafe Majestic ★★$$$$ Voted the city's most romantic restaurant four years running by the readers of *Epicurean Rendezvous* magazine, this restaurant serves modern interpretations of classic European dishes in a setting of Edwardian grandeur. (Note the butterfly collection that surrounds the more-than-150-year-old, horseshoe-shaped bar.) Chef Marc Glassman turns out such tasty fare as roast breast of Sonoma duck with shiitake mushrooms and hoisin sauce, and fillet of salmon stuffed with prawn mousse and served in puff pastry. ♦ Continental ♦ Daily breakfast and dinner; Tu-Su lunch. Reservations recommended. 776.6400

17 Audium This theater was constructed specifically for audiophiles, in part with a grant from the National Endowment for the Arts. Listeners sit in concentric circles and are surrounded by speakers in sloping walls, the floating floor, and the suspended ceiling. A tape director feeds compositions through a console to any combination of 136 speakers. ♦ Admission. F-Sa. Children under 12 years of age not permitted. 1616 Bush St (at Franklin St). 771.1616

18 St. Mary's Cathedral Built in 1971 by **Pietro Belluschi, Pier Luigi Nervi,** and **McSweeney, Ryan and Lee,** this modern cathedral consists of four hyperbolic paraboloids creating a 190-foot roof over a square plan on a podium. It seats 2,500 people around a central altar and is similar to other contemporary cathedrals in Liverpool and Brasília. ♦ Geary Blvd (at Gough St). 567.2020

19 St. Paulus Lutheran Church This 1872 edifice (pictured above) seems more like a cathedral than the one up the street. The front entrance porches were modeled after those at Chartres. ♦ Eddy St (at Gough St). 673.8088

20 Cafe Sinfonia ★★★$ Chef/owner Tony Nika is Albanian, the food is Milanese, the prices are incredibly reasonable, and the result is a culinary treasure. *Pasta sinfonia* (linguine with Italian sausage, white wine, and mushrooms) is outstanding, as are the scallops sautéed in a delectable lemony sherry sauce. There's no wine list, but the house wine is decent. This tiny, gazebolike place is close to the **Civic Center,** and frequented by the performing-arts crowd. ♦ Italian ♦ M lunch; Tu-F lunch and dinner; Sa dinner. 465 Grove St (between Gough and Octavia Sts). 431.7899

21 Pendragon Bakery & Cafe Coffee, espresso, delicious scones, pastries, and light lunches are the order of the day. ♦ Cafe ♦ Daily until 5PM. 400 Hayes St (at Gough St). 552-7017

22 Geva's ★★$$ Customers get a warm welcome at this intimate restaurant close to the **Performing Arts Center.** The flamingo-pink walls of the dining room are a perfect backdrop for the spicy food. Don't miss the terrific barbecued ribs. There's alfresco dining in an adjoining garden. ♦ Contemporary Caribbean ♦ Daily dinner. Reservations recommended. 482A Hayes St (between Gough and Octavia Sts). 863.1220

23 294 Page Street Designed by architect **Henry Geilfuss,** this 1885 Victorian Stick-style house, a private residence, has been beautifully preserved. ♦ At Laguna St

24 The Mad Dog in the Fog This brew pub is a comfortable place to knock back a few pints of bitter, throw some darts, and indulge in a genuine shepherd's pie. ♦ English/Irish ♦ Daily lunch and dinner. 530 Haight St (between Fillmore and Steiner Sts). 626.7279

24 Spaghetti Western ★$ The Wild West meets the even wilder Haight, and together they rustle up some decent grub. Where else can you eat red snapper for breakfast, lunch, and dinner? The place has been described as a "day" nightclub. ♦ California ♦ Daily breakfast and lunch; Tu-Sa dinner. 576 Haight St (between Fillmore and Steiner Sts). 864.8461

25 Toronado Belly up to the bar and ask for your favorite brew—they're bound to have it at this friendly watering hole that proudly boasts 44 top-notch draft beers, one of the largest selections in the city. ♦ Daily until 2AM. 547 Haight St (between Fillmore and Steiner Sts). 863.2276

Restaurants/Clubs: Red   **Hotels:** Blue
Shops/ 🌳 Outdoors: Green   **Sights/Culture:** Black

25 Noc-Noc A New Wave bar featuring black walls and buzzing TV sets, this place serves, as one patron says, "a clientele so relentlessly hip as to make the South of Market trendies look like geriatric polyesteroids." For those young, hip, and brave enough to handle the crowds and the attitudes, this is a fun place to spend the evening. ♦ Daily 5PM-2AM. 557 Haight St (between Fillmore and Steiner Sts). 861.5811

26 Body Manipulations At this place (possibly the weirdest entrepreneurial effort in San Francisco), customers who like a primitive look may be pierced anywhere they want to be (yes, anywhere), ears being the tamest option. Scarring and branding are also offered for those who want to take bodily embellishments to their skin-deep limits, although you need to make an appointment for this service and are requested to bring your own design or at least have an idea of what you want. There's a tattoo studio upstairs, and the owners say that a professional medical consultant advises them. ♦ Daily. 254 Fillmore St (at Haight St). 621.0408

27 Skin & Bones, Sticks & Stones This shop peddles oddball jewelry, animal bones, artifacts, and other weird and fascinating whatnots. ♦ Daily. 210 Fillmore St (between Haight and Waller Sts). 864.2426

27 Kit Shickers Both sexes will get a kick out of the custom-made boots, shoes, belts, and other leather apparel at this shop. Styles range from the staid to the exotic. ♦ F-Su; M-Th by appointment. 206 Fillmore St (between Haight and Waller Sts). 431.5487

28 Thep-Phanom ★★$ This intimate, attractively decorated restaurant serves a great combination of bright tastes and striking textures. Particularly good is the *tom kha ghi* (chicken soup with coconut milk and ginger). Other entrées include *kiew warm ghi* (green curry chicken) and *sam kasatr* (a fiery pork curry). Every dish is a wonderful bargain. ♦ Thai ♦ M-Sa lunch and dinner; Su dinner. 400 Waller St (at Fillmore St). 431.2526

29 Germania Street Houses Donald MacDonald built these two minuscule dwellings in 1984. Each occupies a 20-by-20-foot footprint and proves that it is possible to build affordable housing in San Francisco. They have basic detailing and an almost cartoonlike form. ♦ At Steiner St

30 601 Steiner Street Constructed in 1891, this Queen Anne house, a private residence, boasts elaborate carving and a fine turret. ♦ At Fell St

The sun shines in San Francisco an average of 65 hours out of every 100 hours.

31 700 Block of Steiner Street The six identical houses (pictured above) by **Matthew Kavanaugh** have been carefully restored and painted. With the backdrop of the city's Financial District skyline, this late 19th-century row is often featured in tourist photographs of the city. All are private residences. ♦ Between Grove and Hayes St

32 The Archbishop's Mansion Inn $$$ This has to be one of the most spectacular bed-and-breakfast inns in San Francisco. Built for an archbishop in 1904, the handsome building has been lovingly restored by its present owners. It features a three-story open staircase covered by a 16-foot-tall stained-glass dome, 18 fireplaces with magnificently carved mantelpieces, and Belle Epoque furnishings with Victorian and Louis XIV chandeliers. There are 15 guest rooms in all, each with a private bath; 10 rooms have fireplaces and several are suites. A continental breakfast is included, and there is a private dining room available for catered functions. ♦ 1000 Fulton St (at Steiner St). 563.7872, 800/543.5820

33 1198 Fulton Street Stop here to ogle one of the grandest and most beautiful Victorian mansions in the city. It's a private residence. ♦ At Scott St

34 Prince Neville's ★$$ This restaurant serves the unique and truly delicious cuisine of Jamaica. Tropical murals, reggae music, and the eager, friendly service help foster the illusion that you are really on the island. The best bets are the seafood dishes—fresh, spicy, and prepared with delicacy and care. Other choices are fried plantains and, for the more adventurous, curried goat. The beer and wine list is extensive. ◆ Jamaican ◆ W-Sa lunch and dinner. 1279 Fulton St (at Divisadero St). 567.1294

35 Victorian Inn on the Park $$ This Queen Anne–style mansion, once known as Clunie House, was built in 1897 (Queen Victoria's jubilee year) and is now a registered city and county landmark. All 12 rooms are furnished with antiques and large beds smothered in down comforters and pillows; several still have the original fireplaces, with turn-of-the-century handmade tiles. Fresh flowers are everywhere, and stunning old photographs provide a glimpse into the 19th century. Homemade baked goods are served for breakfast in the oak-paneled dining room, and wine is poured in the evening in the parlor. The top floor has a suite in the belvedere tower. ◆ 301 Lyon St (at Fell St). 931.1830, 800/435.1967

36 Country Cheese You'll find excellent buys on dried fruit, cheeses, grains, and nuts—great for party givers. ◆ M-Sa. 415 Divisadero St (between Fell and Oak Sts). 621.8130

36 Ujama Run by Nigerians, this shop specializes in well-priced African clothing and arts and crafts. ◆ M-Sa. 411 Divisadero St (at Oak St). 252.0119

37 1111 Oak Street Completed in 1860, this is one of the oldest houses in San Francisco. It has been beautifully restored, and is now used for office space. Nearby buildings from the same era have also been converted for commercial use. ◆ Between Broderick and Divisadero Sts

38 San Francisco Stained Glass Works Beautiful stained glass is made to order on the premises. The store also does repairs and provides classes for stained-glass hobbyists. ◆ M-Sa. 345 Divisadero St (between Page and Oak Sts). 626.3592

38 Cookin' The recycled gourmet kitchen gear sold here has been a subculture secret. Cooks will be thrilled by the variety of wares, including oodles of cookie cutters, molds, vintage cherry pitters, grinders, and the like. ◆ Tu-Su. 339 Divisadero St (between Page and Oak Sts). 861.1854

38 Gamescape The only serious game store in town carries everything from board games to fantasy games. You can find used games, too. ◆ Daily. 333 Divisadero St (between Page and Oak Sts). 621.4263

38 329 Divisadero Street The oldest house in San Francisco is well hidden in the middle of the block. Built in 1850, it has been moved

twice, and a glimpse of it can be caught on Oak Street at Divisadero. It is a private residence. ◆ Between Page and Oak Sts

38 The Metro Hotel $ This 23-room Victorian hotel is a well-kept secret, but known by some visiting Europeans. In the past, it was a residential hotel that was reputedly a home to shady ladies; in its current incarnation, the high-ceilinged rooms are full of innocent charm. There's a pleasant garden in the back that guests may use, a nice little adjoining coffee shop called **La Dolce Vita Cafe,** and off-street parking. ◆ 319 Divisadero St (between Page and Oak Sts). 861.5364; fax 864.5323

38 Comix Experience Fans of the genre will enjoy perusing this collection of new and used comic books. ◆ Daily. 305 Divisadero St (at Page St). 863.9258

39 Spencer House $$ This magnificently restored Queen Anne–style mansion is one of the most handsome homes in the Haight district, furnished with fine antiques and European fabrics. There are six guest rooms with private baths, and a full breakfast, served in a private dining room, is included. ◆ No credit cards. 1080 Haight St (between Baker and Broderick Sts). 626.9205; fax 626.9208

40 Buena Vista Park The park affords a wonderful view of the Coast Range Mountains as far as Mount Tamalpais to the north, Mount Hamilton to the south, and Mount Diablo to the east. ◆ Haight St (between Buena Vista Ave E and Buena Vista Ave W)

41 Park Hill Condominiums Architects **Kaplan/McLaughlin/Diaz** converted the **St. Joseph's Hospital** building into residences in 1986. The former chapel is now a recreation center and the whole scheme has been repainted in warm, pastel shades. ◆ 355 Buena Vista Ave E (off Duboce Ave)

42 Spreckels Mansion Not to be confused with the other, grander **Spreckels Mansion** on Washington Street, this elegant edifice (pictured above) was built in 1887 and is situated on a hill next to **Buena Vista Park.** Formerly a bed-and-breakfast (Ambrose Bierce and Jack London were celebrated guests), it has been converted into a private residence. ◆ 737 Buena Vista Ave W (between Frederick St and Central Ave)

43 Bound Together The hours of business at this anarchist collective bookstore and meeting place tend to be irregular, befitting the political philosophy. ♦ Daily. 1369 Haight St (between Central and Masonic Aves). 431.8355

43 Recycled Records Rare and hard-to-get tapes, CDs, and records are bought, sold, and traded here. ♦ Daily. 1377 Haight St (between Masonic and Central Aves). 626.4075

44 Pipe Dreams *The* smoke shop of the 1960s, it offers an eclectic assortment of nontraditional smoking accoutrements, such as water pipes, in addition to Egyptian jewelry, crystals, and T-shirts. ♦ Daily. 1376 Haight St (between Masonic and Central Aves). 431.3553

44 Dish ★★$$ This appealing restaurant is on the site of what was one of Haight-Ashbury's most notorious businesses in the 1960s. In those psychedelic times, it was a cafe called the **Drogstore,** and well-tended marijuana plants were on view in its window boxes. The current management serves fantastic breakfasts and brunches—the most popular meals here—which include not-to-be-missed macadamia-nut waffles with fruit toppings. The restaurant's name was inspired by the dozens of mismatched plates that decorate the walls. ♦ American ♦ M-F breakfast, lunch, and dinner; Sa-Su brunch and dinner. 1398 Haight St (at Masonic Ave). 431.3534

45 The Pork Store Cafe ★$ Once a butcher shop, with a porker immortalized in a stained-glass window to prove it, this place now draws locals to its counter for breakfast and burgers. ♦ American ♦ Daily breakfast and lunch. 1451 Haight St (between Ashbury St and Masonic Ave). 864.6981

46 Sugartit Exquisite vintage clothing and Art Deco objects are featured at this pricey shop. ♦ Daily. 1474 Haight St (between Ashbury St and Masonic Ave). 552.7027

47 Touch Stone All kinds of essentials for making magic, from oils and incense to amulets and crystals, can be found here. Custom jewelry is also crafted in this fascinating store. ♦ Daily. 1601A Page St (at Ashbury St). 621.2782

48 Artery This shop sells primitive art, such as African and Asian masks, tapestries, and jewelry. ♦ Daily. 1510 Haight St (between Ashbury and Clayton Sts). 621.2872

Restaurants/Clubs: Red   **Hotels: Blue**

Shops/ 🌳 Outdoors: Green   **Sights/Culture: Black**

48 Mendel's Art Supplies and Stationery/Far-Out Fabrics An incongruous assortment of fascinating fabrics, feathers, buttons, and a vast variety of shoulder pads share retail space with office supplies. ♦ M-Sa. 1556 Haight St (between Ashbury and Clayton Sts). 621.1287

49 Dharma The fashion of the counterculture, essentially clothing from Third World countries, is sold here at reasonable, but definitely First World, prices. ♦ Daily. 1600 Haight St (at Clayton St). 621.5597

50 Wasteland Vintage and contemporary clothing is dramatically displayed in what was once a theater. Notice the impressive facade graced with colorful gargoyles. ♦ Daily. 1660 Haight St (at Belvedere St). 863.3150

51 The Red Victorian Bed & Breakfast Inn $$ The only surviving hotel on Haight Street (pictured above) was purchased in 1977 by artist Sami Sunchild, who strives to preserve the unique history and character of the building (circa 1904) in the form of an art gallery, human-relationships center, and bed-and-breakfast. The 18 guest rooms are quite nice—and each one is decorated in its own fanciful (sometimes eccentric) way. A continental breakfast is included, served in a private dining room. ♦ 1665 Haight St (between Cole and Belvedere Sts). 864.1978

52 La Rosa Vintage tuxedos and dresses from the 1920s and 1930s are sold or rented to those who want to make a deliberate out-of-style statement. ♦ Daily. 1707 Haight St (at Cole St). 668.3744

52 Forma Described by its owner as "a general store for the terminally insane," it hawks religious icons, candles, toys, jewelry, housewares, and art. ♦ Daily. 1715 Haight St (between Cole and Shrader Sts). 751.0545

52 Red Vic Movie House A worker-owned-and-operated haven for art-film lovers. ♦ 1727 Haight St (between Cole and Shrader Sts). 668.3994

53 Cha Cha Cha ★★★$$ Most people come for tapas and the spicy grilled meats, washed down by excellent sangria. The food here reflects Spanish, Cajun, and Caribbean influences, including traditional dishes such as black-bean soup, Cajun shrimp, and fried calamari. Bright decor (including a collection of *santería* altars), friendly service, and reasonable prices make this restaurant one of Haight Street's best bets. Be prepared to wait for a table, although it has recently doubled its seating capacity. ♦ Latin ♦ Daily lunch and dinner. No credit cards. 1801 Haight St (at Shrader St). 386.5758

53 Thirsty Swede Local and out-of-town bands play all kinds of music, including contemporary rock and New Wave. A DJ takes over on Wednesday and Friday and plays funk. On "Sushi Sunday" there's live music, no cover charge, and lots of fresh raw fish. ♦ Cover. Daily. 1821 Haight St (between Shrader and Stanyan Sts). 221.9008

53 Rock 'n' Bowl Even those folks who normally balk at bowling line up to knock the pins down here—where nonstop music videos are played on a 9- by 12-foot screen and above every lane on a 25-inch TV. Music blasts from a mega–sound system while lots of amateur bowlers balance a ball in one hand, a beer in the other, and twist and shout their way down the alley attempting to hit a strike. It's one big party—and particularly popular with large groups of friends. ♦ Fee. Th-Sa. Reservations recommended. At Park Bowl, 1855 Haight St (between Stanyan and Shrader Sts). 826.2695

54 Skates on Haight This is one of the few places near **Golden Gate Park** to rent (or buy) in-line skates, roller skates, and all the pads you need to help cushion those inevitable tumbles. ♦ Daily. 1818 Haight St (between Stanyan and Shrader Sts). SKATE.75

54 Club Boomerang Another hip Haight Street hangout, this smoky, dark dancin' and drinkin' club replaced the once popular **Rockin' Robins** nightspot. Call for the latest lineup of live tunes. ♦ Cover W-Sa. Daily. 1840 Haight St (between Stanyan and Shrader Sts). 387.2996

55 Tools of Magick Uma, the proprietor, sells incense, oils, and other paraphernalia to magicians and soothsayers from all over the country. ♦ Tu-Sa. 1915 Page St (between Shrader and Stanyan Sts). 668.3132

56 Stanyan Park Hotel $ Another stylish establishment near **Golden Gate Park,** this building exhibits the designers' elegant style of transition from Queen Anne to Beaux Arts classicism. The hotel has 30 rooms and six

suites; the suites have fireplaces and bay windows overlooking the park. A continental breakfast, and tea and cookies in the afternoon, are served in a private dining room. ♦ 750 Stanyan St (at Waller St). 751.1000; fax 668.5454

57 Neptune Society Columbarium This domed building, which holds the ashes of 10,000 early San Franciscans, is one of the hidden secrets of the city. It was originally built for the **Oddfellows Cemetery** by **B.J. Cahill** in 1897, and has been restored to its original splendor, with stained glass, artwork, and silver and gold urns. Names of prominent families, many of whom have streets named after them, are everywhere. Free architectural tours with refreshments are given. ♦ Tu-Sa mornings. 1 Loraine Ct (off Anza St, between Stanyan St and Arguello Blvd). 221.1838

58 Straits Cafe ★★$ This is one of the only restaurants in San Francisco to offer Singaporean cuisine, which is known for being spicy and subtly sweet. Specialties include the *kway pai ti* appetizer (pastry filled with vegetables and prawns), chicken and beef satay, chili crab, and basil chicken. A banana-leaf brunch is served on Sunday. ♦ Singaporean ♦ Daily lunch and dinner; Su brunch. Reservations recommended. 3300 Geary Blvd (at Parker Ave). 668.1783

59 San Francisco Fire Department Museum The colorful history of the early days of the fire department is recounted in displays of memorabilia and photos in this small museum. Horse-drawn fire wagons and the city's first fire bell are star attractions. ♦ Free. Th-Su afternoons. 655 Presidio Ave (between Bush and Pine Sts). 861.8000

60 Monte Cristo Bed and Breakfast $ Located in a building that dates back to 1875, the inn's 14 rooms (three with shared bath) are simply but tastefully furnished with authentic period pieces. Better yet, it's just two blocks from bustling Sacramento Street and near transportation to downtown. A buffet breakfast is served in the private dining room. ♦ 600 Presidio Ave (at Pine St). 931.1875

61 Rasselas ★★$ Named after the hero of a Samuel Johnson story, this place is both a good Ethiopian restaurant and a cushy jazz club (there's no cover charge) that's popular, crowded, and the scene of some great music. ♦ Ethiopian ♦ Daily dinner. Reservations recommended. 2801 California St (at Divisadero St). 567.5010

The Mission/Potrero Hill

Early in the 1800s, the sunny, fog-free valley that is part of today's Mission district became a rural locale for San Francisco's resort activities. When a private franchise was granted permission to construct a 40-foot-wide planked toll road from present-day **Third Street** to **16th Street**, gambling houses, saloons, dance halls, pleasure parks, and racetracks sprang up among the farmhouses and country homes to take advantage of the increased traffic. Over the next 30 years, the number of people here grew from 23,000 to 36,000, and except for the adobe **Mission Dolores**, founded in 1776, not a trace of the area's previous Spanish influence remained. Instead, colorful Victorian row houses were built everywhere. Yankees, Germans, and Scandinavians moved in, and after the 1906 earthquake and fire ravaged

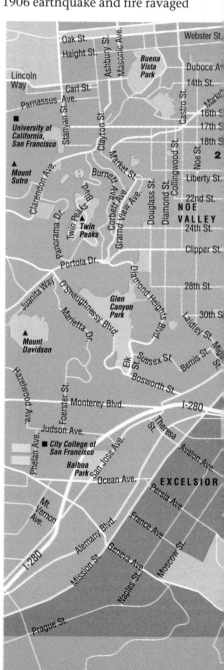

the North Beach and South of Market areas, the homeless Italians and Irish followed. It was then that the residents began cultivating a kind of Spanish revival. Palm trees were planted along **Dolores Street**, turning it into a handsome boulevard; the mission's stucco was repaired; a pseudo-Spanish church was built alongside it; and red-tiled roofs appeared on buildings. Latinos began to pour into the area, and today the Hispanic population continues to expand, and restaurants and markets catering to their tastes thrive here.

You'll find heavy traffic, palms, and a few parks in this area. (There are more children concentrated in this part of the city than anywhere else, so some streets serve as playgrounds.) Residential hotels are refuges for the impoverished elderly, and the district is a haven for followers of alternative lifestyles—**Valencia Street** caters quietly to feminists and lesbians. Many art groups have also made their homes in the area. There are many clubs in the district; most open in early afternoon and the beat goes on until 2AM. Blended into the Latino neighborhood are Filipinos, Samoans, Southeast Asians, most of the city's Native Americans, and remnants of the earlier Irish community.

The Spanish dubbed the land stretching south from the Mission *Potrero Nuevo* (new grazing ground). When industry expanded here from the Mission, marshlands were bridged to provide additional access and a five-mile streetcar line was added, making this area the city's first suburb. Today Potrero Hill is a community of small and colorful houses, with a few contemporary apartments basking in the sun while the rest of the city shivers—a place where some of the cottages have *banyas* (Russian steambaths) in the backyard. This is not tourist country. Instead of chic boutiques, you'll see utilitarian shops. At the foot of the hill are early-19th-century warehouses, including **Showplace Square**, which houses one of the largest wholesale furnishing centers in the West. The neighborhood remains working-class and heterogeneous, although there are signs of growing gentrification. The agreeable climate and sweeping views have attracted artists and professionals whose lifestyles range from bohemian to deluxe. The thriving community gardens adjoining **McKinley Square**, where neighbors work side by side, are proof of Potrero Hill's ability to assimilate many different ethnic groups.

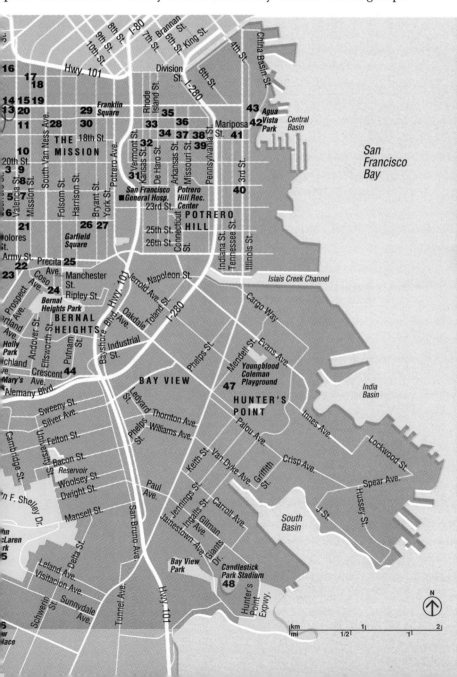

The less congested **Outer Mission** is dotted with single-family homes. The land here was originally part of a Spanish land grant. In the **Excelsior** district, many of the original farmhouses rub shoulders with 1930s-style homes. **Bay View/Hunter's Point**, to the east of Highway 101, represents the largest concentration of African-Americans in the city, although in recent years lower housing prices have attracted Latino and Pacific Rim families as well. Hunter's Point is the most unsafe district in San Francisco—crime is rampant here, so if it's an area you want to survey, be very cautious. This district grew up around shabbily and hastily constructed temporary housing after World War II, when the largest shipyard on the West Coast stood at the water's edge.

Candlestick Park Stadium, home of the **San Francisco Giants** and the **San Francisco 49ers**, is nearby. The fact that a World Series game was taking place at "the Stick," as the ballpark is known, may have saved many lives when the 1989 earthquake struck. It has been estimated that were it not for that game, many more commuters would have been on the Bay Bridge and Interstate Highway 880, which were both severely damaged.

Area code 415 unless otherwise noted.

1 Mission Dolores Spanish settlers led by Captain José Moraga founded San Francisco's first mission in 1776 (illustrated above), on the site of an Indian village, just five days before the signing of the Declaration of Independence. Formally called the **Mission San Francisco de Assisi,** this is the sixth of the 21 missions built by Franciscans along El Camino Real, the Spanish road linking the missions from Mexico to Sonoma, California. Though the mission was dedicated to St. Francis de Assisi, it became better known by its current name after a nearby lagoon called Lake of Our Lady of Sorrows (*dolores* is Spanish for "sorrow"). The city's oldest building, its structure has withstood four major earthquakes and is the only one of the original missions that has not been rebuilt. Its four-foot-thick adobe walls have survived the years without serious decay or extensive restoration.

Mission Dolores Basílica, the larger church next door, was rebuilt in 1918 and was declared a basilica in 1952 by Pope Pius XII. In addition to several historical figures, more than 5,000 native Costanoan Indians are buried in the cemetery garden (most died from diseases transmitted by white settlers). ♦ Daily. Dolores St (at 16th St). 621.8203

1 Star Wash One of the most glamorous laundromats in town, this clean and friendly spot shows video movie classics to relieve the washday blues. ♦ Daily. 392 Dolores St (at 16th St). 431.2443

2 Dolores Park This green oasis on the fringes of the Mission district is where tennis players, dog walkers, and sun worshipers gather for neighborhood recreation. ♦ Bounded by Church and Dolores Sts, and 18th and 20th Sts

3 Liberty Street The blocks from Castro to Valencia Streets contain some of the best Italianate houses in San Francisco, unspoiled since the last century. **No. 159**, built in 1878, is where Susan B. Anthony—whose dollar coin we now seem to have forgotten—used to visit her fellow suffragists. **No. 109** was built in 1870. ♦ Between Castro and Valencia Sts

4 Flying Saucer ★★$$$ This ordinary-looking little storefront restaurant is short on ambience but big on culinary satisfaction. Sophisticated dishes typically presented in much more luxurious places are prepared here by two talented chefs who once worked at the chic Auberge du Soleil in Napa Valley. The menu changes frequently, but might include such offerings as fish ragout, lamb shanks with white beans, or duck on a bed of lentils. ♦ California/French ♦ W-Su dinner. Reservations recommended. 1000 Guerrero St (at 22nd St). 641.9955

5 Lucca Ravioli Co. Great buys on imported cheeses are reason enough to patronize this deli, but there are also very good ravioli, tortellini, and other noodles, and tasty sauces to go with them. A tempting line of Italian cold cuts and other delicacies is available, too. ♦ M-Sa. 1100 Valencia St (at 22nd St). 647.5581

5 Saigon Saigon ★★$ Low prices and high quality make this upscale Vietnamese restaurant a neighborhood favorite. Try the lemon pork, papaya-beef salad, garlic crab, or black-pepper catfish. ♦ Vietnamese ♦ Daily lunch and dinner. 1132-34 Valencia St (between 22nd and 23rd Sts). 206.9635

6 Good Vibrations You can probably find out everything you've always wanted to know about sex—and then some—at San Francisco's most utilitarian sex store. With an emphasis on health, education, quality, and fun, this one-of-a-kind retail and mail-order emporium valiantly tries to take the smut out of sex shops. ♦ Daily. 1210 Valencia St (at 23rd St). 974.8980; mail order 974.8990

7 El Oso ★$$$ One of San Francisco's few authentic Spanish restaurants is more upscale and dressier than most Mission establishments, with a kitschy decor that incorporates lots of stained glass. There's live piano nightly, flamenco every Sunday at 7PM, and, invariably, patrons who like to dance while they eat their dinner. The paella is a crowd pleaser, but prices are high for the caliber of cooking. Tapas at the bar are a good way to enjoy the atmosphere without feeling financially strained. ♦ Spanish ♦ Daily lunch and dinner. Reservations recommended for dinner. 1153 Valencia St (between 22nd and 23rd Sts). 550.0601

8 Old Wives' Tales Women's Books More than 13,000 titles by and about women and people of color, with a particularly large section on lesbianism, are for sale here. ♦ Daily. 1009 Valencia St (at 21st St). 821.4675

8 Woman Crafts West As the name implies, porcelain, jewelry, and textiles handmade by women are this store's stock in trade. ♦ Tu-Su. 1007½ Valencia St (at 21st St). 648.2020

8 Val 21 ★★$$ Yet another of San Francisco's current crop of restaurants to knock down culinary borders, this place offers everything from egg rolls to tiny pizzas, blackened chicken to prawns with pesto. The decor is sleek and modern, with bold splashes of color and some tasty art on the walls. Service is adept and friendly. ♦ California

♦ M-F lunch and dinner; Sa-Su brunch and dinner. Reservations recommended. No smoking allowed. 995 Valencia St (at 21st St). 821.6622

9 La Rondalla ★★$$ It's nothing to look at, but this is a hugely popular, extremely lively Mexican restaurant known for mariachi music, good margaritas, and year-round Christmas decor. The menu goes far beyond the usual tacos and enchiladas. You can get interesting grilled-pork creations and Mexican egg dishes for a fine late-night snack. And if you hanker for goat meat, this place has it. ♦ Mexican ♦ Tu-Su lunch and dinner. 901 Valencia St (at 20th St). 647.7474

10 Chameleon A young, artsy crowd frequents this club. Everything from rock records, tapes, and videos to live music is played on Friday and Saturday from 10PM to 1AM. ♦ Cover. Daily. 853 Valencia St (between 19th and 20th Sts). 821.1891

11 Elbo Room This is the Mission district's version of upper Market Street's popular **Cafe Du Nord,** filled with an eclectic, alternative crowd and a suitably cool atmosphere. Wear lots of black or vintage clothing, order an imported beer, and you'll fit right in. ♦ Daily. 647 Valencia St (between 17th and 18th Sts). 552.7788

12 16th Street From Dolores Street east toward Mission Street and beyond, this thoroughfare is a microcosm of the Mission district's diverse flavors, including some Asian restaurants, Hispanic influences, and offbeat bookstores, cafes, and clubs. ♦ Between Dolores and Folsom Sts

13 Cafe Macondo ★$ A popular hangout, this place has wooden floors, mismatched wooden tables and chairs, and lots of flyers and posters about the Third World. Espresso, light meals, and snacks with a Hispanic accent are served. Chilean empanadas, *licuados* (Mexican fruit drinks), and even a Greek dish or two have found their way onto the menu. ♦ Latin ♦ Daily lunch and dinner. 3159 16th St (between Guerrero and Valencia Sts). 863.6517

13 La Estrella All kinds of cookies and pastries to tempt any sweet tooth are offered at this Mexican bakery. The *churros* (cylindrical, sugar-coated doughnuts) and Mexican breads are specialties. ♦ Daily. 3141 16th St (at Albion St, between Guerrero and Valencia Sts). 431.4161

13 Albion There's live music—could be blues, acoustic rock, or whatever the person who's grabbed an open mike is offering—at this gaudy but intriguing bar. A young and artsy crowd, who scrutinize the rotating displays of art and wait their turn at the pool table, fills the place nightly. ♦ Daily to 2AM. 3139 16th St (at Albion St, between Valencia and Guerrero Sts). 552.8558

131

13 The Roxie This vintage movie house (with seating for about 280) specializing in classic and esoteric movies is film-buff heaven. ♦ 3117 16th St (between Valencia and Guerrero Sts). 863.1087

13 The Abandoned Planet Bookstore If you like browsing through used-book stores, you'll love this one, with plenty of well-worn, comfy chairs and a large selection of affordable hardbound classics and poetry. ♦ M-Sa. 518 Valencia St (between 16th and 17th Sts). 626.2924

13 Bombay Bazar Just about every spice you could possibly need to flavor an Indian dish is sold here, in addition to dried peas, beans, and Indian groceries and videos. ♦ Tu-Su. 548 Valencia St (between 16th and 17th Sts). 621.1717

14 New Dawn ★$ The decor is surreal at this counterculture cafe, a good place for a snack, light meal, or coffee, and a chat with some of the locals. ♦ Cafe ♦ Daily breakfast and lunch; W-Su dinner. 3174 16th St (between Valencia and Guerrero Sts). 553.8888

14 Adobe Bookstore You'll find used books, with an emphasis on Aquarian titles and first editions, at this shop. Poetry readings, mostly by local artists, are held frequently. ♦ Daily; F-Sa until 11PM. 3166 16th St (between Valencia and Guerrero Sts). 864.3936

14 Clubhouse In the evening, a DJ spins music from world beat to reggae to hip-hop for a dressed-down crowd. This place is packed on weekends. ♦ Daily to 2AM. 3160 16th St (at Albion St, between Valencia and Guerrero Sts). 621.5877

14 Cafe Picaro ★$ Many people come to this combination bookstore/cafe just to hang out and read the stacks of underground newspapers and fascinating bulletin-board entries. The self-service operation offers ample portions of wholesome chow for very little money. ♦ Cafe ♦ M-Sa breakfast, lunch, and dinner. 3120 16th St (between Valencia and Guerrero Sts). 431.4089

15 Esta Noche At San Francisco's first Latin drag-queen bar, some think the "ladies" are better-looking than those who perform at the famous North Beach drag clubs. There's disco dancing to a salsa beat in the evenings. ♦ Cover. Daily. 3079 16th St (at Mission St). 861.5757

16 Levi Strauss & Co. The world's oldest blue-jeans manufacturing plant was built after the earthquake of 1906. The company conducts group tours of the plant by appointment. ♦ 250 Valencia St (at Brosnan St, between Duboce Ave and 14th St). 565.9153

16 Pauline's ★★$$ Gourmet pizza is served in a variety of eclectic, eccentric expressions, from pesto pizza to a little number covered with chèvre. There's no atmosphere to speak of—just great pizza few Italians would recognize as their native food. Takeout is available. ♦ Pizza ♦ Tu-Sa dinner. 260 Valencia St (at Brosnan St, between Duboce Ave and 14th St). 552.2050

17 Mission Street This is the Mission district's great commercial artery, with the heaviest concentration of activity that's of interest to strollers stretching from approximately 15th to Army Streets. The street buzzes with entrepreneurial energy, and the small businesses supply the neighborhood with produce (much of it geared toward Hispanic recipes). There are clothing shops for budget-minded buyers; furniture stores with some of the most garish, overwrought designs imaginable; small restaurants reflecting the area's diverse Hispanic populations; and butchers, bakers, and candlestick makers offering votive lights and other illumination to those who use candles in prayer, meditation, and spell-casting. ♦ Between 15th and Army Sts

18 Rainbow Grocery and General Store Collectively owned and operated, these two-stores-in-one reflect strong environmental positions and countercultural tastes. The grocery stocks a sizable assortment of organic produce and health foods, while the general store carries a staggering variety of items, from housewares, toiletries, and natural-fiber clothing to toys and gemstones. Vitamins and cast-iron ware are offered at particularly attractive prices. Customers are encouraged to bring their own bags and jars for packing foodstuffs. An ever-changing bulletin board keeps tabs on Third World and community activities. ♦ Daily. 1899 Mission St (at 15th St). 863.9200

19 Theatre Rhinoceros Gay and lesbian issues are explored in the offbeat productions staged at this 112-seat theater. ♦ 2926 16th St (between Mission St and S Van Ness Ave). 861.5079

20 La Cumbre Taquería ★★$ Renowned for huge, tasty burritos, this place serves what amounts to a full meal wrapped in a napkin-size tortilla. Several kinds of meat and poultry fillings are available; all are delicious, but the *carne asada* (beef that's cooked on the grill while you wait) is a must. There's usually a line, but it moves briskly. Selections may be eaten at small wooden tables or taken home. ♦ Mexican/Takeout ♦ Daily lunch and dinner. 515 Valencia St (between 16th and 17th Sts). 863.8205

Restaurants/Clubs: Red   **Hotels:** Blue
Shops/ 🌳 Outdoors: Green   **Sights/Culture:** Black

21 La Traviata ★★★$$ You don't expect to find Italian restaurants in the Mission district, particularly one so good that it draws not only customers from neighborhoods across town but world-famous opera stars as well. Pictures of divas and great tenors line the walls, and opera plays constantly. The pastas are marvelous, and the chicken and veal dishes are first-rate. ♦ Italian ♦ Tu-Su dinner. Reservations recommended. 2854 Mission St (between 24th and 25th Sts). 282.0500

22 Cesar's Latin Palace Things start jumping around 10PM at this club offering Latin jazz, salsa, and tango on Sunday. Whether you're looking for the scene or the sounds, it's not to be missed. ♦ Cover. F-Sa until 5AM. 3140 Mission St (at Army St). 648.6611

22 El Río Dance to the beat of Latin, Cuban, and Brazilian salsa and African world music. There are live shows on Thursday, Saturday, and Sunday. A wonderful courtyard awaits out back. ♦ Cover Th, Sa-Su. Daily. 3158A Mission St (at Army St). 282.3325

23 Manora's Thai Cuisine ★★$$ One of the best Thai restaurants in San Francisco, this unassuming, pleasant little spot packs in the crowds and maintains an admirable level of excellence and consistency. Daily specials augment the dishes on the menu. The spices are complex and the presentation is appealing. ♦ Thai ♦ Tu-Su dinner. 3226 Mission St (at Valencia St). 550.0856. Also at: 1600 Folsom St (at 12th St). 861.6224

24 170-80 Manchester Street Built on the slopes of Bernal Heights in 1986 by **William Stout,** these modern, stucco-clad houses capture the spirit of the white architecture of the modern movement. They are private residences. ♦ At Bernal Heights Park (south end of Folsom St)

25 Mission District Murals Painted by Mexican-American artists and other residents, these murals are a colorful example of community spirit. The artists have brightened and humanized their urban environment with vivid wall paintings dispersed throughout the neighborhood between Mission and York Streets and 14th and Army Streets, adorning banks, restaurants, schools, housing projects, and community centers. Some of the murals are inside buildings. Sightseers may take a self-guided walk or a two-hour, eight-block walking tour given by the **Precita Eyes Mural Arts Center** every Saturday at 1:30PM. Group tours can be arranged at other times with advance notice. Forty murals are covered on the tour. Maps are available from the center, in addition to a checklist of all Mission-district murals. ♦ Nominal fee; discount for seniors, students, and children. Arts Center: 348 Precita Ave (at Folsom St). 285.2287

26 La Victoria Mexican Bakery and Grocery For more than 30 years, this place has been turning out Mexican specialties, including sugary wedding confections and custardy cones. ♦ Daily. 2937 24th St (at Alabama St). 550.9292

26 China Books and Periodicals This shop specializes in imported and American books on China's history and politics, with some of the works in Chinese and many in English. There is also a selection of Chinese peasant paintings and handicrafts. ♦ M-F. 2931 24th St (between Alabama and Florida Sts). 282.2994

27 Galeria de la Raza/Studio 24 Since its founding in 1970, this nonprofit gallery exhibiting works of Latino artists has gained renown worldwide. The adjoining studio supports the work of the gallery with sales of crafts representing contemporary and traditional arts of Latin American countries. ♦ Tu-Sa. 2857 24th St (at Bryant St). 826.8009

27 Roosevelt Tamale Parlor ★$ This place built its reputation around its crowd-pleasing tamales, which have drawn customers since 1922. Other traditional Mexican dishes are offered as well. Customers are an enthusiastic mix of gringos from north-of-Market neighborhoods and locals who share a common interest in a good, cheap feed. ♦ Mexican ♦ Tu-Su lunch and dinner. 2817 24th St (between Bryant and York Sts). 550.9213

27 St. Francis Candy Store Not much has changed in this soda fountain since it opened its doors in 1918. It sells homemade ice cream and peanut brittle and has cases filled with candies that will take you back to your childhood. ♦ Daily. 2801 24th St (at Bryant St). 826.4200

28 New Performance Gallery Experimental music, theater, and dance are presented at this 200-seat theater. ♦ Daily. 3153 17th St (at Shotwell St, east of S Van Ness Ave). 863.9834

29 Byron Hoyt Sheet Music Service This shop has the biggest selection of sheet music in the city. ♦ Tu-Sa. 2525 16th St (between Harrison and Bryant Sts). 431.8055

30 Theatre Artaud This popular multidisciplinary theater showcases contemporary work by local, national, and international performers. The 300-seat space was formerly an American Can Company factory. ♦ Call for performance schedule. 450 Florida St (at 17th St). 621.7797

31 Vermont Street The view is nice and the absence of mobs even nicer at southern San Francisco's answer to Lombard Street. ♦ South of 20th St to Mariposa St

Stretching 7.29 miles, Mission Street is San Francisco's longest thoroughfare.

32 610 Rhode Island Street Designed for **Kronos Quartet** members Pat Gleeson and Joan Jeanrenaud, this contemporary home amid rows of traditional 19th-century houses became an object of controversy. Critics maintained that its industrial look was out of context in the neighborhood. The 24-foot-high living space covered in black asphalt shingles is visible to passersby. This private residence was built in 1989 by **Daniel Solomon.** ♦ At 18th St

33 Basic Brown Bears This small stuffed-animal factory has taken Elvis's advice and chosen the teddy bear as its official mascot. Don't miss the free 30-minute tour. ♦ Daily. Tours M-F 1PM, Sa 11AM and 2PM, Su 3PM. 444 De Haro St (at Mariposa St). 626.0781

34 Anchor Brewing Co. It's San Francisco's version of a Dickens tale: Fritz Maytag, a young, carefree college student who also happens to be heir to a washing-machine company, stops into his local beer hall, orders his first pint of Anchor Steam, and instantly becomes smitten with the rich amber brew, forgetting all about the family business. Meanwhile, Lawrence Steese is struggling to keep his old Anchor brewery out of bankruptcy and is desperately in need of a deep-pocketed partner. This is where our hero Fritz steps in and saves the day, much to the delight of beer aficionados around the world. For a tour of the delightfully anachronistic brewery and a tasting of what many consider one of the few *real* beers left, make reservations as far in advance as possible (at *least* two weeks in advance, although you might get lucky and fill in a no-show). ♦ Free. Daily; reservation only. 1705 Mariposa St (at De Haro St). 863.8350

35 Garibaldi Cafe ★★$$ Those who have an inside track on good places to dine are buzzing about this restaurant. The dining room is a fascinating conglomeration of white-and-gray high-tech furnishings set amid corrugated-metal walls. Lunchtime salads are excellent, and dinner always includes special seafood and pasta entrées. The menu changes every six months and aims for creativity; the portions are generous. A take-out annex next door serves interesting dishes. ♦ California ♦ M lunch; Tu-F lunch and dinner; Sa dinner. Reservations recommended. 1600 17th St (at Wisconsin St). 552.3325

36 The Bottom of the Hill ★$ This is the kind of neighborhood bar you always dreamed about: friendly bartenders, good bands playing every night, a well-maintained pool table, cushy bar stools, outdoor seating, a fireplace, good burgers and kabobs, and a $2, all-you-can-eat barbecue on Sunday from 4PM to 8PM. Are you swooning yet? ♦ Daily. 1233 17th St (at Missouri St). 626.4455

37 Asimakopoulos ★★$$ A contemporary version of a Greek restaurant, this place is set up cafe style, with small wood tables and a long wooden counter. The look is clean, sunny, and uncluttered, and the food is flavorful. Classic Greek specialties such as marinated and skewered meats and poultry and flaky, spinach-filled pastry are well prepared. ♦ Greek ♦ Daily dinner; M-F lunch. 288 Connecticut St (at 18th St). 552.8789

38 San Francisco Bar-B-Que ★★$ Despite its limited menu and simple presentation, this restaurant always comes through with tasty, honest, addictive Thai-style barbecue dishes at modest prices. The chicken and pork ribs are the most popular, cooked to lean succulence and flavored with a medium-hot sweet-sour Thai sauce. ♦ Thai ♦ Tu-F lunch and dinner; Sa-Su dinner. 1328 18th St (between Missouri and Pennsylvania Sts). 431.8956

39 300 Pennsylvania Street Situated on top of Potrero Hill, this was one of a series of mansions built as the city grew south of Market Street. A private residence, it was constructed in 1868. ♦ At 18th St

40 Massimo's ★★★$ This small lunch spot is a well-guarded San Francisco secret. You won't find much ambience, just some of the best pasta in the city, pure and simple. Try some with fresh crabmeat in a brandy-cream sauce or veal-stuffed tortellini in marinara sauce. The menu features daily specials and interesting cold plates, but Massimo himself will probably tell you what to order—even if you don't ask. Takeout and catering are available. ♦ Italian ♦ M-F lunch. 1099 Tennessee St (at 22nd St). 550.6670

Moshi Moshi

41 Moshi Moshi ★★$ Tucked into a wasteland of warehouses, this place serves good Japanese food at prices that are more than fair. The decor is simple—almost spare—with bleached-wood tables and chairs and pale-green walls. The back porch has been turned into an outdoor dining area. If you're really hungry, start with a generous order of *gyoza* (Japanese-style dumplings). The menu offers all the classic favorites: chicken and steak teriyaki (served quite rare, as it should be), shrimp tempura and yakitori, as well as excellent sushi. For dinner there are more seafood dishes. The overall quality and value are hard to beat. ◆ Japanese ◆ Daily dinner; M-F lunch. Reservations required for six or more. 2092 Third St (at 18th St). 861.8285

42 The Ramp ★★$$ Although hidden away in a boatyard, this place's reputation has spread by word of mouth, and an eclectic crowd of suits, gays, and boat workers gathers here for a good time. The inside dining room has a loud jukebox and no atmosphere; most people prefer to dine alfresco on the large deck overlooking the bay. Hamburgers, salads, daily specials, and creative stews are the culinary attractions. There's also live music in the summer—jazz, salsa, rock—Thursday through Sunday, as well as an outdoor weekend barbecue. ◆ American ◆ Daily dinner; M-F lunch. 855 China Basin St (at the end of Mariposa St). 621.2378

42 Mission Rock Resort ★$ Tucked away on the docks of the China Basin is one of the choicest bars and hamburger joints in San Francisco, with a terrace overlooking the slips and dry docks. The bar keeps going long after the kitchen closes, and there is live music on the deck on Sunday from 2PM to 6PM, weather permitting. ◆ American ◆ Daily breakfast and lunch. 817 China Basin St (at the end of Mariposa St). 621.5538

43 ESPRIT Outlet The popular San Francisco–based manufacturer has a huge clothing outlet here, frequented by the teen set and the young at heart. ◆ Daily. 499 Illinois St (at 16th St). 957.2500

43 Caffe ESPRIT ★★$$ This convenient lunch spot offers fresh, organically grown salads, gourmet pizzas, and generous, creative sandwiches. ◆ California ◆ M-Sa lunch. 499 Illinois St (at 16th St). 777.5558

44 Farmers' Market Saturday is the big shopping day at this open-air market where California farmers sell their seasonal produce at prices lower than those in most supermarkets. Pickings are sparse during the week; try to come on a Friday or Saturday. ◆ Tu-Sa. 100 Alemany Blvd (between Crescent and Putnam Sts). 647.9423

45 John McLaren Park The city's second-largest park was named for the man who created its biggest one, **Golden Gate Park.** Several residential districts make use of the rugged, wooded tract: Bayshore, Portola Valley, Bay View, and the Outer Mission. The steep slopes offer good views of Visitacion Valley and the San Bruno Mountains. ◆ Bounded by Moscow and Delta Sts, and Felton St and Geneva Ave

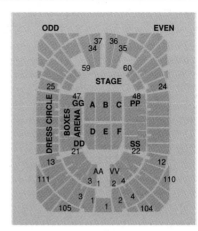

46 Cow Palace Everything from livestock shows to the Beatles has been booked here (see the floor plan illustrated above). With a seating capacity of 10,300 to 14,300, it offers an ever-changing series of events. ◆ Geneva Ave (at Santos St), Daly City. 469.6000

47 The Bayview Opera House San Francisco's oldest theater opened its doors in 1888. Seating 300, it has been renovated and provides the community with a variety of plays, dance concerts, and musical theater. ◆ Call for information on shows. 4705 Third St (at Oakdale Ave). 824.0386

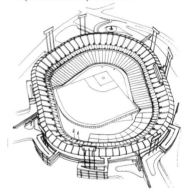

48 Candlestick Park Stadium The home of the **San Francisco 49ers** and the **San Francisco Giants,** with seating for up to 60,000 people, was built in 1960 by **John S. Bolles and Associates.** Situated on a rocky promontory overlooking the bay, the site suffers from exposure to bitter cold winds and occasional flooding, and is widely regarded as one of the most uncomfortable places in which to watch—or play—a game. It was the first major-league baseball stadium (pictured above) to be constructed entirely of reinforced concrete, and there is movable seating for the switch between baseball and football. ◆ Take Candlestick Park Exit off Hwy 101 S, to Giants Dr at Gilman Ave. Giants tickets 467.8000. 49ers tickets 468.2249

Restaurants/Clubs: Red   **Hotels:** Blue
Shops/ ◆ Outdoors: Green   **Sights/Culture:** Black

Noe Valley/Castro/ Upper Market

The Noe and **Eureka Valley**s snuggle below the protective eastern slopes of **Twin Peaks** and share much of the same history, climate, and architecture. Both also underwent dramatic population shifts in the 1970s, as escalating real-estate prices in fashionable, white-collar neighborhoods north of **Market Street** drove hordes of young professionals to the more affordable southern reaches of San Francisco. For many, it was their first trip across the main Market Street artery that had for years bisected sociologically distinct parts of the city. Both valleys are quaint neighborhoods of Victorian storefronts and homes, and were originally called Horners'

Addition after Mormon Gold Rush pioneers Robert and John Horner, who made their fortune selling food to gold diggers. (A street named Horner was renamed **23rd Street** in 1861.)

Noe Valley, separated from Eureka Valley by the ridge of **22nd Street**, was historically part of the 4,000-plus-acre land grant given to the last Mexican mayor of San Francisco, José de Jesus Noe, by California governor Pio Pico in the 1840s. Noe's ranch house was one of the first buildings in the district and stood at the corner of 22nd and Eureka Streets. The area was once filled with blue-collar German and Irish families. Later, a sprinkling of gay residents moved in and the neighborhood gained a somewhat bohemian outlook. More recently, Noe Valley has been called San Francisco's Greenwich Village, although continued gentrification suggests movement in a more conservative direction. It still includes an eclectic mix of families and bohemians who moved from other parts of the city. While it's technically part of the greater Mission district, residents, who consider themselves a breed apart, have always insisted they live in Noe Valley. In this relaxed urban village, residents frequently spot raccoons in their backyards, gather for an annual picnic and a local history day at the library, and spend the weekends fixing up their old houses. Between **Dolores** and **Diamond Streets**, **24th Street** is a lively shopping area dispensing the stuff of everyday life, with supermarkets, coffeehouses, and ethnic delis where you can buy a burrito, a knish, and a quiche, all within a two-block range. **Church Street**, named for the many houses of worship that once stood there, is fast developing as another commercial thoroughfare, with most of the shops concentrated between 24th and **30th Street**s. To preserve the small-town atmosphere, with people shopping and chatting together, one residential group has promoted a hard stance against establishments selling liquor. In **Upper Noe Valley**, steep streets and hills create truly spectacular housing sites.

At the same time that double-income heterosexual couples were flocking to Noe Valley, Eureka Valley was becoming a magnet for gays from everywhere in the country. **Castro Street** is the main thoroughfare, and so strong is its impact that the area is commonly known as the Castro district rather than Eureka Valley. This center of San Francisco's gay social life is a crowded collection of unique shops, bars that stay open until 2AM, and restaurants, mostly concentrated on Castro between Market and **20th Street**s. The gay influence extends to the Upper Market area, which was also part of Noe's land grant in the early 1800s. San Francisco's gay and lesbian population is well organized, and it has been said that no politician can win an election in the city without gay support. Legislation is always being put forth to test the limits and tolerance of the nongay community, making San Francisco a bellwether of social change. Although the scourge of AIDS has caused more than 11,500 deaths here, it also has united the gay community, focusing its political spokespeople on finding government funding for research, and banding it together in efforts to offer solace and assistance to the afflicted.

Area code 415 unless otherwise indicated.

1 The Willows Inn $ Popular with the gay and lesbian community, this quiet, 11-room bed-and-breakfast inn housed in a 1904 Edwardian is central to the Castro, the Mission, and downtown and near easy connections to **BART** and **MUNI**. The graceful California Gypsy Willow furniture (made of bentwood) was designed specifically for each room, and the place has a restful, European-country look. There is a telephone, washbasin (guests share the bathrooms), and kimono in each room, and a continental breakfast is served along with a morning paper. Complimentary sherry and truffles are left in each room in the evening. ♦ 710 14th St (at Church St). 431.4770

2 Cafe Du Nord For those in the know, this basement-level, windowless club/cafe is the place to see and be seen. Moody lighting, a stylish crowd, and intriguing live music combine to create an interesting scene. A small dinner menu consisting of the soup of the day, green salads, small pizzas, pan-fried trout, steamed mussels, chicken, and desserts is served four nights a week. ◆ Cafe ◆ Cover. Daily; W-Sa dinner. 2170 Market St (between Church and Sanchez Sts). 861.5016

3 Scandinavian Delicatessen/Restaurant ★$ Plain, homey, and as trusting as they get in a big city, this long-established restaurant works on the honor system. You order whatever you want, remember what you've eaten, and report what it was to the cashier on the way out. Scandinavians have known about this place for years, and now others have discovered it. Favorite Scandinavian salads, fish, meatballs, and pork are always available. It isn't the most sophisticated fare you'll find, but it's like eating in Grandma's kitchen (if Grandma was Scandinavian), and the management's trusting nature just makes you feel good. ◆ Scandinavian ◆ M-F lunch. 2251 Market St (between Sanchez and Noe Sts). 861.9913

4 Cafe Flore $ For coffee, snacks, or just people watching, this is the ultimate Upper Market hangout. Everyone in the city's counterculture seems to end up here eventually, sipping and schmoozing under the corrugated-metal roof. It's a favorite haunt of authors, would-be authors, film buffs, punks, and just about any other bohemian type who wants to be where the action is. ◆ Cafe ◆ Daily. 2298 Market St (at Noe St). 621.8579

5 La Mediterranee ★★★$ It's easy to understand why the owners have succeeded: The food is good—and cheap. The "Mediterranean Meza," made for two or more, gives a pretty good overview of the kitchen by presenting 10 Middle Eastern specialties, all quite wonderful, on a large platter. There is also reasonably priced party catering. ◆ Middle Eastern ◆ Tu-F lunch and dinner; Sa-Su brunch and dinner. 288 Noe St (at Market and 16th Sts). 431.7210. Also at: 2210 Fillmore St (between Sacramento and Clay Sts). 921.2956; 2936 College Ave, Berkeley. 510/540.7773

6 Joseph Schmidt Confections This small shop is where chocoholics go to worship. Joseph Schmidt, who has mastered chocolate sculpture, creates bowls, flowers, sports equipment, animals, bottles, and automobiles in his edible medium. He also makes the best chocolate truffles in town—maybe anywhere. ◆ M-Sa. 3489 16th St (between Church and Sanchez Sts). 861.8682

7 Ixia When daisies just won't do, this unusual florist specializes in exotic, esoteric plants and flowers. ◆ M-Sa. 2331 Market St (between Castro and Noe Sts). 431.3134

8 The Names Project This is the visitor's center for those who create the panels of remembrance that form the AIDS quilt. The quilt has been exhibited around the world to commemorate those who have died of AIDS and to draw attention to the toll the epidemic has taken. ◆ Daily. 2362 Market St (between Castro and Noe Sts). 863.1966. Administrative offices: 310 Townsend St, Suite 310. 882.5500

9 Inn on Castro $$ One of the smaller guesthouses in the city (five rooms, each with private bath), this inn's intimate surroundings make it truly a home away from home. Although located in an Edwardian town house, its interiors are contemporary: white walls, track lighting, classic Modern furniture, brilliant flowers, and the original art of one of the owners. Upstairs, breakfast is served every morning on an extensive and ever-changing collection of imported china and stoneware dishes. ◆ 321 Castro St (at Market St). 861.0321

10 The Randall Museum The emphasis at this nature and history museum is on participation, with live animals and a petting corral, a ceramics room, a woodworking shop, a seismograph, and biology classes. An environmental learning garden is currently under construction. Many special workshops and events are offered, especially during the summer. ◆ Free. Tu-Sa. 199 Museum Way (at Roosevelt Way). 554.9600

11 Twin Peaks Always lively, always friendly, this was the first gay drinking establishment in San Francisco to come out of the closet by having large picture windows where clients could see and be seen. ◆ Daily. 401 Castro St (off Market St). 864.9470

11 The Bead Store All kinds of nifty beads and unique pieces of jewelry are displayed for those who want to do things themselves, or have their adornment done by someone else with lots of talent. ◆ Daily. 417 Castro St (off Market St). 861.7332

11 Bare Necessities You'll find a variety of natural skin-care products here, from herbal deodorant to vegetable-oil soaps from Provence. ◆ Daily. 421 Castro St (off Market St). 621.6206

11 Castro Theatre San Francisco officialdom dubbed this structure the finest example of a 1930s movie palace in the city. Designed by **Pflueger/Miller** in 1922, the 1,600-seat theater has earned its reputation because of its remarkable Spanish colonial architecture. The auditorium ceiling is probably the most noteworthy feature, an extraordinary affair cast in plaster to resemble a giant cloth canopy tent, complete with swags, ropes, and tassels. And in what better setting could you enjoy an ever-changing series of movies from Hollywood's heyday? Anybody who swoons over *Camille* or drools over the exquisite timing in *Bringing Up Baby* will want to take in a flick at this classic theater. ◆ 429 Castro St (off Market St). 621.6120

Castro Street Shopping Map

MARKET STREET

Bank of America	Twin Peaks *bar*
Marcello's Pizza	Double Rainbow *ice cream*
Louie's Barber Shop	Castro Smoke House *cigarettes and magazines*
Rossi's Deli	Rococoa's Faerie Queen Chocolates
casual clothing In-Jean-Ious	The Bead Store
Cove Cafe	Bare Necessities *natural skin-care products*
Thailand Restaurant	The Castro Cheesery *cheese, coffee,*
bar The Bear	*and chocolate*
California Federal Bank	Castro Theatre
men's clothing and shoes Rolo	Eureka Bank
bar Castro Station	Take One Video
American restaurant Without Reservations	Sliders Diner
American restaurant Welcome Home	Mrs. Field's Cookies
Mueller's Delicatessen	All American Boy *men's clothing*
Valley Pride Market	Tattoo Attitude
bar Phoenix	Headquarters *bar*
Walgreens	Cliff's Variety *hardware and fabrics*
	A Different Light Bookstore
	Village Deli Cafe
	Rolling Pin Donuts
	Presto Prints 1-Hour Film Processing

(vertical label: CASTRO STREET)

18th STREET

bar Elephant Walk	Bank of America
Spinelli Coffee Co.	
Castro Computers, Inc.	The Sausage Factory *Italian restaurant*
pizza Escape from New York	Castro Video
gifts Mainline	Jerusalem Shoppe *international clothing*
Crown Books	Patio Cafe *American*
Chinese Canton Restaurant	Sid's Pipes Dreams *tobacco shop*
Browser's Nook Antiques	Under Cover *undergarments*
men's clothing Citizen	
Books etc.	Quality Shoe Repair
Mexican/Cuban/Caribbean restaurant Pachá	Headlines for Women *cards and clothing*
Always Tan and Trim	Headlines *gifts*
cards and wrapping paper Castro Place	Prima Facie *facial salon*
optometrist For Your Eyes Only	Notorious for Hair *salon*
Great Earth Vitamins	Orion Travel *travel agency*
American Castro Gardens Restaurant	Skin Zone *skin care and cosmetics*
Suzanne's Muffins	Anchor Oyster Bar & Seafood Market
greenhouse Hortica	Grand Central Station Antiques
Brand X Antiques	Bruno Hair Design
Liquor Express	China Court *restaurant*
men's used and new clothing Worn Out West	
mailbox services PO Plus	
optometrist Eye Gotcha	
Chinese Medicine/Herbs/Acupuncture	
Buffalo Whole Food & Grain Company	
health foods	

19th STREET

men's clothing High Gear	

11 Cliff's Variety This Castro Street institution is actually two shops side by side. One carries all manner of fabrics, spangles, and feathers for making costumes or embellishing a smashing drag getup; the other sells straightforward household needs, such as hardware and paint. It's beloved for its folksy merchandising approach and cordial staff. ♦ M-Sa. 471-479 Castro St (between Market and 18th Sts). 431.5365

11 A Different Light The only store in San Francisco devoted to *both* gay and lesbian literature. ♦ Daily until 11PM. 489 Castro St (at 18th St). 431.0891

12 Marcello's Pizza ★$ In San Francisco, this is as close as you're likely to come to a New York–style pizza. There's a smattering of small, crowded tables, but most customers grab a slice to go. It's one of the few places nearby where you can find sustenance late at night. ♦ Pizza/Takeout ♦ Daily lunch and dinner; M-Th, Su until 1AM, F-Sa until 3AM. 420 Castro St (off Market St). 863.3900

12 Rolo Definitely not for the introverted, this shop offers fashions for men who like to push the outer limits of style. ♦ Daily. 450 Castro St (between Market and 18th Sts). 626.7171. Also at: 2351 Market St (between Castro and Noe Sts). 431.4545; 1301 Howard St (at Ninth St). 861.1999; 438 Miller Ave, Mill Valley, Marin County. 383.4000

13 Mu Chacha's ★★★$$ Regional Mexican food is served in a highly stylized, stage-set dining room reminiscent of both the Aztec and the Flintstones. Fanciful presentations commingle with interesting flavors. Among the recommended dishes are the *sopa de lima* (lime soup), soft Oaxacan tacos, and marinated flank steak. ♦ Mexican ♦ Tu-Su dinner. Reservations recommended. 4238 18th St (between Collingwood and Diamond Sts). 861.8234

13 Ryan's ★★★$$ This charming restaurant rambles through several appealingly decorated rooms in an old house. The inventive menu changes seasonally and offers nightly specials. Some of the outstanding dishes include baked chocolate pudding and Jamaican barbecued baby back ribs. A ground-level charcuterie offers food to go, and there's a balcony that's popular with the lunch and brunch crowds. ♦ California ♦ M, W-Sa lunch and dinner; Tu lunch; Su brunch. Reservations recommended. 4230 18th St (between Collingwood and Diamond Sts). 621.6131

14 Cafe Lupann's ★★$$ Down-home American standards such as pot roast and grilled pork chops are offered in this attractive upstairs restaurant set in an oddly sophisticated, generously mirrored space. ♦ American ♦ Daily dinner. Reservations recommended (call after 4PM). 4072 18th St (between Castro and Noe Sts). 552.6655

15 Does Your Mother Know? *We* won't tell her if you shop here for unusual, outrageous, and funny greeting cards. ♦ Daily. 4079 18th St (between Castro and Noe Sts). 864.3160

15 Bad Man Jose's ★★$ Tasty Mexican health food is prepared without using preservatives or chemicals for those who want a fast, healthy, filling meal. ♦ Mexican ♦ Daily lunch and dinner. 4077 18th St (between Castro and Noe Sts). 861.1706

15 Body Citizen Rather revealing men's sportswear for the let-it-all-hang-out crowd is in this shop. ♦ Daily. 4071 18th St (between Castro and Noe Sts). 861.6111

15 The Midnight Sun Boy meets boy at this popular gay video bar, sleekly designed with a galvanized-metal exterior. ♦ Daily to 2AM. 4067 18th St (between Castro and Noe Sts). 861.4186

15 Hot 'N' Hunky ★★$ This is the original of two popular hamburger stands with a Castro flavor. Among the choices are burgers called "The Swisher," "Ms. Piggy," "Macho Man," and "I Wanna Hold Your Ham." ♦ American ♦ Daily lunch and dinner. 4039 18th St (between Castro and Noe Sts). 621.6365. Also at: 1946 Market St (at Duboce Ave). 621.3622

15 Rosie's Cantina ★★$ A much-favored Mexican spot for fast, inexpensive food catering to gringo tastes, this place is pleasantly decorated with pigskin chairs. ♦ Mexican ♦ Daily lunch and dinner. 4001 18th St (at Noe St). 864.5643

16 Jerusalem Shoppe Fabulous ethnic jewelry by well-known artisans and imported clothing are offered at affordable prices. ♦ M-Sa. 531 Castro St (between 18th and 19th Sts). 626.7906

16 Patio Cafe ★$$ It's fun to discover a place that surprises you as this one does. Located at the back of a small shopping mall is a brick-walled room that opens onto a charming garden, where patrons usually prefer to dine. Though the food isn't a great attraction—you won't be disappointed as long as you keep things simple—the setting is a real winner. Breakfast and lunch are the best meals here. ♦ American ♦ Daily breakfast, lunch, and dinner. Reservations required for parties of six or more. 531 Castro St (between 18th and 19th Sts). 621.4640

16 Headlines This store sells cards, accessories, and clothing, and is a ticket outlet to boot. ♦ Daily. 557 Castro St (between 18th and 19th Sts). 626.8061. Also at: 838 Market St (between Powell and Fifth Sts). 956.4872; 549 Castro St (between 18th and 19th Sts). 776.4466; 2301 Chestnut St (at Scott St). 441.5550

Restaurants/Clubs: Red   **Hotels:** Blue

Shops/ 🌴 Outdoors: Green   **Sights/Culture:** Black

16 Skin Zone All kinds of toiletries and soaps are sold here to enhance the body beautiful. ♦ Daily. 575 Castro St (between 18th and 19th Sts). 626.7933

16 Anchor Oyster Bar & Seafood Market ★★$$ When you have a yen for chowder and shellfish, this neat little place, with a counter and a few tables, satisfies it nicely. And if you get a hankering for an "oyster shooter" (an oyster in a shot glass with Bloody Mary mix, Worcestershire sauce, a touch of Tabasco, and a squeeze of lemon), you'll find that here too. ♦ Seafood ♦ Daily dinner; M-Sa lunch. 579 Castro St (between 18th and 19th Sts). 431.3990

17 Buffalo Whole Foods & Grain Company Health foods, organic produce, vitamins, and Chinese remedies for whatever ails you are available here. ♦ Daily. 598 Castro St (at 19th St). 626.7038. Also at: 1058 Hyde St (between California and Pine Sts). 474.3053

17 PO Plus This handy-dandy little service business deals with very 20th-century needs in a quaint, converted Victorian house. The folks here rent mailboxes, handle shipping and packing, sell labels and boxes, and will fax or notarize documents. ♦ M-Sa. 584 Castro St (between 18th and 19th Sts). 864.5888; fax 621.5592

17 Brand X Antiques A lovely selection of antique and estate jewelry and collectibles is on display. It's not cheap, but it's awfully nice. ♦ Tu-Su. 570 Castro St (between 18th and 19th Sts). 626.8908

17 Hortica When your rooms look empty but you don't have the money for furniture, try plants instead. The horticultural accomplishments here are quite artful. ♦ Daily. 566 Castro St (between 18th and 19th Sts). 863.4697

17 Castro Gardens ★$ From the street, this little restaurant doesn't look particularly distinctive, but a walk through the dark, narrow dining room reveals additional seating on a wonderful landscaped patio. Simple dishes, such as quiches and salads, are the best bets. ♦ American ♦ Daily breakfast and lunch. 558 Castro St (between 18th and 19th Sts). 621.2566

17 Books Etc. Bibliophiles will find a fair selection of new and mostly used books. ♦ Daily; F-Sa until midnight. 538 Castro St (between 18th and 19th Sts). 621.8631

17 Canton Restaurant ★★$ The decor may be uninspired, but the food at this cafeteria-style Chinese restaurant is fresh and tasty. It's good if you want to eat quickly but don't want the usual fast-food offerings. There's also take-out service. ♦ Cantonese ♦ Daily lunch and dinner. 524 Castro St (between 18th and 19th Sts). 626.3604

18 Java Road They carry about 30 varieties of well-displayed coffees here, plus chocolates for those who want to indulge all their minor vices at once. ♦ Daily. 4117 19th St (between Castro and Collingwood Sts). 626.5573

18 Castro Village Wine Company More than 400 California wines are stocked here. The shop offers wine tastings, and shipping is available. ♦ Daily. 4121 19th St (between Castro and Collingwood Sts). 864.4411

18 Isak Lindenauer Mission-style furniture and lighting from 1895 to 1916 are the specialties here, with an emphasis on California decorative pieces. ♦ W-Su; other days by appointment. 4143 19th St (between Castro and Collingwood Sts). 552.6436

19 Nobby Clarke's Folly This attractive, eclectic construction was built in 1892 by Alfred Clarke, who worked as a clerk in the police department. It was alleged to have cost $100,000—a fortune then—and originally included a 17-acre estate. Today it is an apartment house. ♦ 250 Douglass St (at Caselli Ave)

COURTESY OF BJ DROUBI REAL ESTATE

20 3733-3777 and 3817-3871 22nd Street The panels framing the plaster floral arrangements and the banded laurel (which looks like the letter X) are trademarks of builder **John Anderson**. These private residences (pictured above) were built in 1905 and 1906. ♦ Between Castro and Sanchez Sts

21 3780 23rd Street Constructed in 1865, this white Italianate Victorian is believed to be the oldest house in Noe Valley. It's a private residence. ♦ At Church St

22 Noe Valley Ministry This Presbyterian church also functions as a community center, offering a concert series and an eclectic assortment of courses ranging from belly dancing and yoga to solstice celebrations. ◆ 1021 Sanchez St (at 23rd St). 282.2317

23 Noe's Nest $$ There are five rooms to let at this private residence: a self-contained unit with a kitchenette; a garden room with a private deck and a fireplace; a room with a Jacuzzi; a room with a 1920s brass bed; and a penthouse with a dynamite view and a steam room. Each unit has a TV, a VCR, and a phone. The owner, Sheila Rubinson, offers a buffet breakfast. She speaks French, Hebrew, and a little Japanese, and is a legitimate massage therapist. Her quarters represent excellent value for those who want a homey place away from home. ◆ 3973 23rd St (between Sanchez and Noe Sts). 821.0751

COURTESY OF BJ DROUBI REAL ESTATE

24 1051 Noe Street Constructed in 1891, this home (pictured above) is one of the 387 tower houses built in San Francisco. The tower was generally unconstructed within and is there just for show, although it's in dire need of a paint job. This is a private residence. ◆ At Elizabeth St (between 23rd and 24th Sts)

25 San Francisco Mystery Bookstore This entire store is devoted to new and used whodunits. ◆ F-Su. 746 Diamond St (at 24th St). 282.7444

26 Meat Market Coffeehouse $ One of the longest-established hangouts in Noe Valley, this place opened in the 1970s, and its clientele hasn't changed much since. There's a time-warp quality to the ambience. Customers are invited to check the bulletin board and peruse the stacks of alternative newspapers as they enjoy coffee and a light snack. ◆ Coffeehouse ◆ Daily breakfast and lunch. 4123 24th St (between Diamond and Castro Sts). 285.5598

26 Little Italy Ristorante ★★$$ A bustling, happy place to eat dinner, this looks lately as if some remodeling and general freshening up are in order. The portions are huge, the vegetable platters should be shared, and the garlic is applied with a generous hand. The chicken, steak, and sausage *contadino* is a wonderful, rustic dish, but you'll reek of garlic for days. Early birds who dine between 5:30PM and 6:30PM get 20 percent off the cost of their entrée. ◆ Italian ◆ Daily dinner. Reservations recommended for three or more. 4109 24th St (between Diamond and Castro Sts). 821.1515

26 Mary's Clothing Exchange You'll find samples, irregulars, and seconds at this women's consignment boutique. ◆ Daily. 1302 Castro St (at 24th St). 282.6955

26 Peek-a-bootique New and lots of used clothing and toys for infants and children line the shelves of this pleasant shop. ◆ Daily. 1306 Castro St (between 24th and 25th Sts). 641.6192

26 Allure They buy, sell, and trade used women's clothing at this shop. Some new, contemporary clothes are also offered. ◆ Daily. 1320 Castro St (between 24th and 25th Sts). 282.0722

27 Out of Hand You'll find high-quality American contemporary crafts here. ◆ Daily. 1303 Castro St (at 24th St). 826.3885

27 Natural Resources This support center for pregnant women and new mothers provides information, referral services, and educational events. ◆ M-Sa. 4081 24th St (between Castro and Noe Sts). 550.2611

27 Ocean Front Walker Whimsical 100-percent-cotton clothing for adults is this store's specialty. ◆ Daily. 4069 24th St (between Castro and Noe Sts). 550.1980. Also at: 1458 Grant Ave (between Union and Green Sts). 291.9727

28 Rat & Raven This friendly neighborhood bar carries just about every brand of beer imaginable. There's a pool table, a dart board, and, on weekends, a DJ. ◆ Daily. 4054 24th St (between Castro and Noe Sts). 285.0674

28 Star Magic This unusual shop sells space-age gifts, including kaleidoscopes, New Age music, yoga videos, wands, holograms, crystals, and other offbeat items. ◆ Daily. 4026 24th St (between Castro and Noe Sts). 641.8626

Lights, Camera, Action: The SF Movie Scene

San Francisco has always been a director's dream. If you count the early silent days, when the city was a major filmmaking center, literally hundreds of movies have been filmed here. What follows is a selective roster of important films shot entirely (or partially) in this city by the bay.

Greed (1923) Erich von Stroheim directed, and the (long-lost) uncut version ran nine and a half hours. It's considered one of the greatest films of all time.

The Barbary Coast (1935) Howard Hawks's brawling, period adventure film starred Edward G. Robinson and Miriam Hopkins.

San Francisco (1936) Clark Gable, Jeanette MacDonald, and Spencer Tracy find plenty of adventure in turn-of-the-century San Francisco. The Great Quake provides a shattering climax and a terrific special-effects scene.

Charlie Chan at Treasure Island (1939) This episode, with Sidney Toler as the wisdom-spouting detective, is one of the best of the Chan series.

The Maltese Falcon (1941) So popular is this P.I. classic that a Dashiell Hammett walking tour has been put together following Humphrey Bogart's footsteps. For information, call 707/939.1214.

Dark Passage (1947) Humphrey Bogart and Lauren Bacall court and spark in an atmospheric thriller set in the foggiest Frisco you ever saw.

Out of the Past (1947) Arguably the greatest film noir ever made, this features Robert Mitchum as a cynical detective and Jane Greer as the lethally attractive woman who proves his cynicism inadequate.

I Remember Mama (1948) Irene Dunne gives a memorable performance in this sentimental favorite.

Raw Deal (1948) This hard-boiled tale of revenge among gangsters was directed by Anthony Mann.

The Lady from Shanghai (1949) See Orson Welles and Rita Hayworth stroll through **Steinhart Aquarium!** This pyrotechnic thriller was mostly shot in studios, but sharp-eyed viewers will spot several fascinating location sequences.

It Came from Beneath the Sea (1955) A monster destroys the city, courtesy of special-effects wizard Ray Harryhausen.

Pal Joey (1957) This cleaned-up screen version of Rodgers and Hart's great musical features Frank Sinatra and Kim Novak.

The Lineup (1958) A crime thriller, this motion picture was directed by action ace Don Siegel, with Eli Wallach and Robert Keith.

Vertigo (1958) James Stewart stars as an obsessed lover trying to remake Kim Novak into the dead Madeleine in this Hitchcock classic. It was shot at some of the city's most popular locales.

Days of Wine and Roses (1962) Under Blake Edwards's direction, Jack Lemmon and Lee Remick give memorable performances as they battle with the bottle.

Guess Who's Coming to Dinner (1967) This socially conscious interracial comedy was directed by Stanley Kramer, with Spencer Tracy, Sidney Poitier, and Katharine Hepburn. Katharine won an Oscar.

Point Blank (1967) John Boorman's existential thriller features Lee Marvin as a gangster bent on revenge and Angie Dickinson as his faithless wife.

Bullitt (1968) Cars go flying in the definitive San Francisco chase sequence. Steve McQueen plays a police detective; Peter Yates directs.

Petulia (1968) Julie Christie, George C. Scott, and Shirley Knight star in Richard Lester's sad, moving love story about life in the 1960s. It's highly regarded by critics.

Psycho-out (1968) Early performances by Jack Nicholson and Bruce Dern are highlights of this cult item, set during the Summer of Love.

Dirty Harry (1971) This action masterpiece from director Don Siegel stars Clint Eastwood as mean Inspector Callahan. Siegel's brilliant visuals show San Francisco to fine advantage.

Harold and Maude (1972) A swinging septuagenarian (Ruth Gordon) and suicidal youngster (Bud Cort) fall in love in Hal Ashby's popular black comedy.

What's Up, Doc? (1972) Peter Bogdanovich's screwball remake of Howard Hawks's *Bringing Up Baby* features Barbra Streisand, Ryan O'Neal, and some of the funniest car chases ever filmed.

Freebie and the Bean (1973) This comic cops-and-robbers movie stars James Caan and Alan Arkin, plus flying cars—all directed by Richard Rush.

Magnum Force (1973) This *Dirty Harry* sequel feels the loss of director Siegel, but has amusing moments.

The Conversation (1974) Gene Hackman stars in Francis Coppola's masterpiece of paranoia, probably the director's best film.

Foul Play (1978) Peter Hyams directs Chevy Chase and Goldie Hawn in their klutzy antics.

Invasion of the Body Snatchers (1978) Bay Area filmmaker Philip Kaufman concocted this stylish remake of Don Siegel's scary original.

48 Hours (1982) Cop Nick Nolte and prisoner Eddie Murphy team up to solve a crime, incidentally wreaking havoc with a **MUNI** bus and provoking much violence.

A View to a Kill (1985) Roger Moore, in his last James Bond role, must save Silicon Valley from destruction by villain Christopher Walken. The **Golden Gate Bridge** sets the scene for the obligatory heart-stopping climax.

Star Trek IV (1986) William Shatner, Leonard Nimoy, and the *Enterprise* crew drop into **Golden Gate Park** in the 1980s. There are fantastic shots of 23rd-century San Francisco.

28 Elisa's Health Spa Here's a legitimate place to get the knots worked out of your body. Massage, an outdoor hot tub, a sauna, and a steam room are offered. Prices are discounted from noon to 4PM. ♦ Daily. 4026½ 24th St (between Castro and Noe Sts). 821.6727

28 Panos' ★★$$ With lots of mirrors and comfortably upholstered banquettes, this is about as upscale as restaurants get in Noe Valley, although the clientele tends to remain casually dressed. The kitchen makes a good hamburger and *spanikopita* (spinach pie). Early birds who dine between 5:30PM and 6:30PM (5PM-6PM on Sunday) get 20 percent off the cost of their entrée.
♦ Greek/American ♦ Daily lunch and dinner; Su brunch. 4000 24th St (at Noe St). 824.8000

29 Streetlight One of the largest selections of used CDs in the Bay Area can be found here. The store also carries a wide array of mainstream and unconventional music from classical to Cajun, used videos, and out-of-print and collectible 45s and LPs. The staff is notably helpful. ♦ Daily. 3979 24th St (between Sanchez and Noe Sts). 282.3550

29 The Chef Caviars, cheeses, pâtés, coffees, and other delicacies tempt you at this enticing store. ♦ Daily. 3977 24th St (between Sanchez and Noe Sts). 550.7982

29 Aquarius Records New and used records, tapes, and CDs by independent producers are the specialties here. ♦ Daily. 3961 24th St (between Sanchez and Noe Sts). 647.2272

29 Colorcrane A marvelous hand-painted floor depicting a bird's-eye view of downtown is a main attraction at this office- and art-supply shop that also provides photocopying services. ♦ Daily. 3957 24th St (between Sanchez and Noe Sts). 285.1387

29 Noe Valley Tien Fu ★★$ This Chinese restaurant is particularly noted for its green-onion pancakes, though the vegetable dishes and spicy garlic shrimp are also excellent.
♦ Hunanese/Szechuan/Cantonese ♦ Daily lunch and dinner. 3945 24th St (between Sanchez and Noe Sts). 282.9502. Also at: 3011 Fillmore St (at Filbert St). 567.0706

Every year a fire hydrant at 20th and Church Streets is painted gold. It's believed to be the only hydrant in the city that continued to function during the 1906 earthquake and fire, and is credited with saving the area. A memorial plaque in the sidewalk next to the hydrant reads: "Though the water mains were broken and dry on April 18, 1906, yet from this Greenberg hydrant on the following night there came a stream of water allowing the firemen to save the Mission District. . . .
Presented to San Francisco by the Upper Noe Valley Neighborhood Council, April 18, 1966."

29 The Real Food Company Get real with the groceries and very high-quality organic produce sold here. ♦ Daily. 3939 24th St (between Sanchez and Noe Sts). 282.9500. Also at: 1023 Stanyan St (between Carl St and Parnassus Ave). 564.2800; 1234 Sutter St (between Van Ness Ave and Polk St). 474.8488; 2140 Polk St (between Vallejo St and Broadway). 673.7420

29 Panetti's Gifts An eclectic, oftentimes amusing selection of gift items and handmade jewelry is for sale here. ♦ Daily. 3927 24th St (between Sanchez and Noe Sts). 648.2414

29 Courtyard Cafe ★★$ Interesting salads, pastas, and Middle Eastern and Moroccan dishes make for an unusual light meal. There's outdoor seating, and a host of magazines is for sale. ♦ American/Middle Eastern ♦ Daily breakfast and lunch. 3913 24th St (between Sanchez and Noe Sts). 282.0344

30 Spinelli Coffee Co. Serious coffee for caffeine addicts is poured daily. The store does its own roasting, too. ♦ Daily. 3966 24th St (between Sanchez and Noe Sts). 550.7416. Also at: 919 Cole St (between Carl St and Parnassus Ave). 753.2287; 2455 Fillmore St (at Jackson St). 929.8808; 504 Castro St (at 18th St). 241.9447; 2255 Polk St (at Green St). 928.7793

30 Cover to Cover Booksellers This neighborhood bookstore is known for its excellent children's section and knowledgeable staff. Your kids will love it. ♦ Daily. 3910 24th St (at Sanchez St). 282.8080

30 Global Exchange A nonprofit organization that's in partnership with handicraft cooperatives around the world sells their wares out of this narrow shop. ♦ Daily. 3900 24th St (at Sanchez St). 648.8068

24 th St. CHEESE CO.

31 24th St. Cheese Co. Three hundred different cheeses are offered along with excellent pâtés, fine wines, and specialty food items. ♦ Daily. 3893 24th St (at Sanchez St). 821.6658

Restaurants/Clubs: Red   Hotels: Blue
Shops/ ♥ Outdoors: Green   Sights/Culture: Black

31 Tuggey's Noe Valley's beloved hardware store offers personal service to do-it-yourselfers. It's been in the neighborhood since the early 1900s and hasn't changed much since. In fact, the place still closes for a half-hour lunch during the week. ◆ M-Sa. 3885 24th St (between Sanchez and Church Sts). 282.5081

32 Holey Bagel Ex–New Yorkers rejoiced when this business opened in Noe Valley. Here's the place to find those foods dear to a Jewish-food lover's heart: bagels made daily, smoked fish, pickled tomatoes, and knishes. ◆ Deli ◆ Daily breakfast and lunch. 3872 24th St (between Sanchez and Church Sts). 647.3334. Also at: 3218 Fillmore St (between Lombard and Greenwich Sts). 922.1955; 1206 Masonic Ave (at Haight St). 626.9111; 308 Strawberry Village (at Redwood Hwy), Mill Valley, Marin County. 381.2600

32 Matsuya ★★★$$ San Francisco's first sushi bar, this little hole-in-the-wall establishment has been serving many of the same people for over 30 years. The chef prepares some of his own secret concoctions. Trusting customers simply ask him to do something special and he takes it from there. ◆ Japanese ◆ M-Sa dinner. 3856 24th St (between Sanchez and Church Sts). 282.7989

33 Noe's A neighborhood tavern with a vaguely pub-like appearance, this place specializes in Irish coffee. It opens pretty early for those who hanker for a drink along with their sunshine. ◆ Daily at 9AM. 1199 Church St (at 24th St). 282.4007

34 Rami's Caffè ★$$ This attractive little restaurant, which draws a clientele beyond the boundaries of Noe Valley, offers fresh fish, pork, chicken, pasta, and vegetables incorporating California and Mediterranean touches. House specialties include trout stuffed with goat cheese, pine nuts, spinach, and mushrooms, and sesame-chicken pasta. A changing collection of work by local artists adorns the walls. Weekend brunchers can dine alfresco on the patio. ◆ California/Mediterranean ◆ M-F lunch and dinner; Sa-Su brunch and dinner. Reservations recommended. 1361 Church St (between Clipper and 26th Sts). 641.0678

35 What's for Dessert? One of the best pastry shops in the city is owned by Mervyn Mark, who apprenticed with the well-known master Jim Dodge. Only the best ingredients are used. Special-occasion cakes, which are works of art, can be made to order. Other temptations include the fruit tarts, princess cake, and chocolate-fudge cake. Customers can enjoy a piece of pastry with espresso on the premises. And if you want to be really wicked, there's Ben & Jerry's ice cream to top everything off. ◆ Pastry ◆ Tu-Su. 1497 Church St (at 27th St). 550.7465

36 Lady Sybil's Closet Vintage linens, laces, doilies, and dresser scarves are but some of the treasures Sybil tenders. The tea cozies are hand-knit in England. ◆ Th-Su. 1484 Church St (at 27th St). 282.2088

37 Homes of Charm Reasonably priced Victorian furniture, lighting, hardware, and bric-a-brac are carried in this shop, which has been around since 1964. It also stocks lots of stuff for creating a country kitchen. ◆ Tu-Su. 1544 Church St (at Duncan St). 647.4586

38 Speckmann's Restaurant ★$$ Up front is an excellent German bakery and deli counter; behind it is a restaurant serving hearty German food. You'll find such entrées as *konigsberger Klopse* (meatballs with a caper sauce), Wiener schnitzel, and a fine Hungarian goulash. ◆ German ◆ Daily lunch and dinner. 1550 Church St (at Duncan St). 282.6850

39 Lehr's German Specialties German imports of all kinds, including cosmetics, magazines, records, gourmet foods, and beer steins, make it fun to browse here. ◆ Daily. 1581 Church St (at 28th St). 282.6803

40 One Stop Party Shop Stock up on cards, glitter, gift bags, banners, balloons, and all the other stuff that makes a party fun. It's the only store of its kind in Noe Valley. ◆ Tu-Su. 1600 Church St (at 28th St). 824.0414

41 Drewes Market This friendly meat-and-fish market has been at the same location since it was established as the Fairmount Market in 1888 by German immigrant Frederick Drewes and his partner, Otto Dierks. It has had only two names and three owners since it opened. ◆ M-Sa. 1706 Church St (at 29th St). 821.0555

Bests

Steve Silver
Producer, Beach Blanket Babylon

Dinner at **Stars,** dinner at **Moose's.**

Lunch at **LuLu's.**

Chez Panisse in **Berkeley** for dinner.

View of the city from the end of **Vallejo Street.**

Shopping **Wilkes Bashford.**

The **Armani** store architecture (most beautiful).

Anticipating the opening of the new **Museum of Modern Art.**

Tonga Room at **Fairmont Hotel.**

The **Rotunda** at **City Hall.**

The blossoms blooming at the **Japanese Tea Garden** in **Golden Gate Park.**

A walk in **Muir Woods** (any time of the year).

Visit to **Sonoma.**

The **Swedenborgian Church** on Lyon Street.

A drive through the **Presidio.**

The lights on the **Embarcadero Center** buildings during Christmas.

Sunset/Twin Peaks

The heart of San Francisco's fog belt encompasses a large expanse lined with row after row of single-family, pastel-colored, look-alike houses, and is thought by some to be the best place in the city to raise children. **Golden Gate Park** is to the north; **Stern Grove**, the **San Francisco Zoo**, and **Lake Merced** are to the south; and the **Pacific Ocean** lies to the west.

During the 1920s and 1930s, the Sunset emerged as a residential neighborhood, with most of the houses financed by the Federal Housing Administration (FHA). Developer Henry Doelger paved over the sand dunes and built two houses a day throughout the Depression, selling them for $5,000 each. Many of the San Franciscans who first settled here are now retired. The general image of the district is of conservative, white, middle-

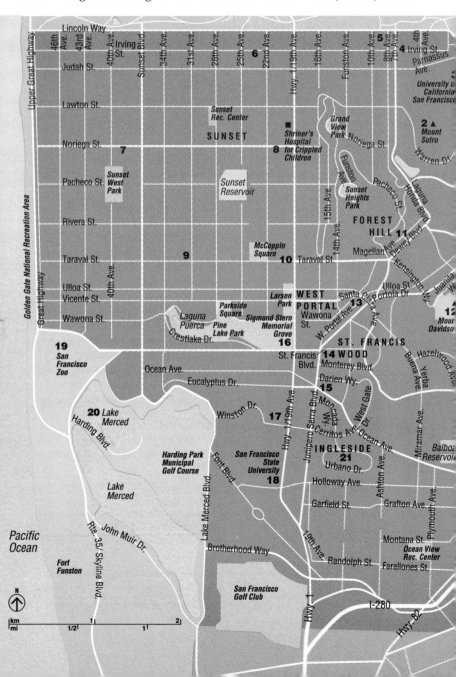

class families, although international stirrings are gradually being felt with the advent of a number of Asians and a young Irish colony. The **Ingleside** area, the site of one of San Francisco's early racetracks, is predominantly African-American and Latino. And on **Irving Street** in the so-called **Inner Sunset**, cafes and clubs offer different kinds of ethnic dancing and entertainment, as well as restaurants and shops with an international flavor. This area is home to the **San Francisco Conservatory of Music, Shriners Hospital**, and **San Francisco State University**. Also here is Lake Merced, originally named **Lake of Our Lady of Mercy** and part of a surrounding ranchero granted by José Castro to José Antonio Galino in 1835. Today it is a standby reservoir for the city, as well as its "backyard fishin' hole."

Stern Grove comes alive on Sunday during the summer, when thousands settle in for picnics and free jazz and classical-music concerts. Beautiful **St. Francis Wood** is an expensive development of large homes with gates and fountains designed by Beaux Arts architect **John Galen Howard**. Nearby is sedate, middle-class **West Portal**, whose diagonal and curving streets make it look somewhat like a Swiss village. It lies at the foot of three hills: **Mount Davidson, Forest Hill**, and **Edgehill Heights**. Land here was originally part of a Spanish land grant.

Twin Peaks, an area containing the second- and third-highest hills in the city, offers wonderful 360-degree panoramas of the Bay Area. Even view-crazy San Franciscans left the area alone until World War II, but today it is a very popular neighborhood, with spectacular houses the size of great villas and many apartment complexes. On the south side, single-family homes face the **San Bruno Mountains** and the ocean. The upscale neighborhood known as Forest Hill, which was planned in 1913 and had racially restrictive covenants until the 1950s, remains a generally conservative and stable family bastion, full of handsome houses and lush landscaping. Tucked away in **Glen Park**, a neighborhood with the feeling of a small village, lies **Glen Canyon**, where, according to old-timers, Russian smugglers once hid their contraband.

Twin Peaks, once known as *Los Pechos de la Chola* (The Breasts of the Indian Girl), offers a 360-degree view of the entire Bay Area.

Area code 415 unless otherwise indicated.

1 Twin Peaks The Costanoan Indians believed that these peaks were created when the Great Spirit separated a quarreling couple with a clap of thunder in order to have peace. Spanish explorers named them "Breasts of the Indian Girl." Then unimaginative Americans changed the name to Twin Peaks. The steep, grassy slopes are a wonderful, if windy, lookout point, providing a 360-degree view of the entire bay—the best vista in San Francisco. At night, the crest is surrounded by a sea of twinkling lights spreading in every direction. It was from this spot that **Daniel Burnha**m conceived his city plan in 1905. Today the view provides cause for reflection on civilization and the effects of "progress"; too often the panorama is marred by smog from polluted air, and you can see how the hills have been carved up and nearly obliterated by stacks of housing developments. Take a sweater; the winds here are chilly even in the summer. ♦ Off Twin Peaks Blvd

2 Sutro TV Tower In 1968 this tower was built on top of Mount Sutro; it supports TV antennae for several of San Francisco's stations. Once a controversial design because of its tripod form and size, it is now an accepted part of the landscape. ♦ Off Warren Dr

3 University of California, San Francisco Adolph Sutro contributed the land that became the 107-acre **Parnassus Campus** of one of the world's great centers for biomedical research. Professional schools of medicine, pharmacy, nursing, and dentistry, as well as a separate graduate studies division, are here. The campus also includes the **Langley Porter Psychiatric Institute and Hospital,** which was the city's first psychiatric hospital and training center, and the **Medical Center,** composed of **Moffitt/Long Hospitals** and the **Ambulatory Care Center.** In addition, the campus contains two of the country's major social- and public-policy institutes, and at least 600 community outreach programs, some of which operate on a statewide level. The medical center pioneered the study and treatment of infant respiratory distress syndrome. On campus, the **Cole Hall Cinema** presents weekly movies and stages lectures and entertainment for the general public (call 476.2542 for details). ♦ Entrance at 513 Parnassus Ave (bounded by Parnassus Ave, Fourth Ave, Crestmont Dr, Clarendon Ave, and Stanyan St). Weekly campus tours 476.4394

4 Irving Street This is a main shopping thoroughfare for residents of the Sunset district. Stores, cafes, and small restaurants (with a heavy emphasis on Asian cuisines) are concentrated between Fifth and 26th Avenues. The area is not chic, but serves the day-to-day needs of the locals.

5 Stoyanof's Cafe & Restaurant ★★$ One of the best informal restaurants in the area, this attractive, family-run place offers a garden area for lunch, although comfortable weather for alfresco dining is a rarity in the fogbound Sunset. The menu offers Macedonian dishes (a kissing cousin to Greek cuisine), all impeccably prepared from scratch. The moussaka and the Mediterranean appetizer platter are highly recommended. Don't pass up the spectacular homemade pastries. During the day, it's a cafeteria; at dinner, there's table service. It's conveniently located near one of the **Golden Gate Park** entrances, where you can walk off some calories. ♦ Macedonian ♦ Tu-Su lunch and dinner. 1240 Ninth Ave (between Irving St and Lincoln Way). 664.3664

6 Marnee Thai ★★★$ Diners from far beyond the Sunset district flock here for the terrific Thai food. Don't miss the ginger chicken, spicy duck, or deep-fried prawns. ♦ Thai ♦ M, W-Su lunch and dinner. Reservations recommended. 2225 Irving St (at 23rd Ave). 665.9500

7 Polly Ann Ice Cream Here's an ice-cream parlor that marches to the beat of a different drummer. Indecisive customers can spin the flavor wheel and put their fate in Polly's hands (just hope it doesn't land on "durian," which smells a bit like unleaded gasoline). Asian flavors are the specialty here, including taro root (not bad), litchi, rose, and dozens more. Oh, and bring your pooch—they'll give the lucky pup a free Doggie Cone. ♦ Ice Cream ♦ Daily. 3142 Noriega St (between 38th and 39th Aves). 664.2472

8 Casa Aguilar ★★★$$ Considered by many to be the finest Mexican restaurant in the city, this place has won a loyal following with its inventive, well-prepared food, large portions, and festive atmosphere. Giant paper fruits and colorful icons are scattered about the small dining room. The chicken mole and *puerco de Morelos* (pork, salsa, potatoes, tomatoes, onions, and jalapeño peppers) are especially recommended. The no-reservations policy ensures a long wait, but the food really is incredible. ♦ Mexican ♦ Daily breakfast, lunch, and dinner. 1240 Noriega St (at 20th Ave). 661.5593

Patty "Tania" Hearst and the Symbionese Liberation Army (SLA) made headlines with their holdup of the Hibernia Bank at 1450 Noriega Street (now a Security Pacific Bank).

Restaurants/Clubs: Red   **Hotels:** Blue
Shops/ 🌳 Outdoors: Green   **Sights/Culture:** Black

9 Ristorante Marcello ★★$$ For those tired of trendy food, ultracontemporary decor, and steep prices, this long-established neighborhood restaurant is a refreshing change. Hearty Tuscan cooking is served with a generous hand. The homemade ravioli and cannelloni *della casa* are delectable. ♦ Italian ♦ Tu-Su dinner. Reservations recommended. 2100 Taraval St (at 31st Ave). 665.1430

10 Taraval Street Another of the Sunset's main shopping streets, this one is less lively than Irving Street. Most of the activity is concentrated between 14th and 23rd Avenues.

11 Forest Hill This upscale community, planned in 1913 by **Mark Daniels**, who also designed Sea Cliff (a well-to-do neighborhood near the Presidio), follows the contours of a hill and is favored by those who like big homes and don't mind a lot of fog. A triangular piece of manicured lawn and a huge urn, located before Magellan Avenue, suggest a sense of formality for the area. ♦ Main entrance is on Pacheco St (off Dewey Blvd)

11 Forest Hill Association Clubhouse Rented out for weddings and other events, this Tudor-inspired building was built, along with the gardens, by neighborhood volunteers in 1919. **Bernard Maybeck** was the architect. ♦ 381 Magellan Ave (at Montalvo Ave). 664.0542

12 Mount Davidson Part of Adolph Sutro's 12,000-acre estate, this is the highest spot in San Francisco, rising 938 feet. A great white concrete-and-steel cross looms 103 feet above the summit. George Davidson, surveyor for the US Coast and Geodetic Survey, originally surveyed the mountain in 1852 and dubbed it Blue Mountain. It was later renamed in his honor. Easter sunrise services have been held at the base of the cross since 1923. ♦ Off Portola Dr

13 West Portal Avenue In this shopping area that serves neighborhood residents, most of the small businesses are concentrated between Ulloa Street and 15th Avenue.

13 Cafe for All Seasons ★$$ The food at this trendy, attractive Forest Hill establishment is tasty, fresh, and au courant, with creative pastas always on the menu. Although it can be noisy, it's worth a visit if you're in the area. ♦ California ♦ M-F lunch and dinner; Sa-Su brunch and dinner. 150 West Portal Ave (at 14th Ave). 665.0900

14 St. Francis Wood Beautifully landscaped, this development of large, expensive homes has gates and a fountain designed by **John Galen Howard**, a noted Beaux Arts architect. It is rich in Spanish Revival structures. Although a well-established, affluent neighborhood, it is solidly bourgeois and located in the less-than-fashionable southern fog belt (the cream of San Francisco's society lives on the north side of the city). The entry gate—marked by gardens and a central fountain—is an impressive site. ♦ Portola Dr (at St. Francis Blvd)

15 Commodore Sloat School This renovation of an existing public grammar school, together with a new extension by **Marquis Associates**, has been designed as a series of courtyards. It is faced with stucco and sports a nautical look, with large portholes that have become a feature of the school's design. ♦ Ocean Ave (at Junipero Serra Blvd)

16 Sigmund Stern Memorial Grove A 63-acre grove of eucalyptus, redwood, and fir trees shelters a sunken natural amphitheater. This is a favorite spot among city dwellers for its free, Sunday-afternoon summer concerts, which showcase a variety of programs from opera to jazz to dance. Reserve a picnic table in advance (call 666.7027 the Monday morning preceding the concert) to make the most of the day. Most of the park's benches are reserved for senior citizens and people with disabilities, on a first-come, first-served basis. The yellow gingerbread **Trocadero Clubhouse** (pictured below) in the grove was once a gambling house and hideout for Abe Rueff, a political shyster. It was renovated by **Bernard Maybeck**, who left the two bullet holes in the door as souvenirs of the shoot-out that led to Rueff's capture, and was spruced up again in the late 1980s. ♦ Sloat Blvd (at 19th Ave). 252.6252

Trocadero Clubhouse

17 Stonestown Galleria California's first regional shopping center, and the third in the entire US, was built and owned by the Stoneson family in 1951, then sold to a Chicago realty firm in 1990. Shops are located beneath skylit vaulted ceilings in a Neo-Classical setting with bubbling fountains. It was originally conceived as a city-within-the-city, and although much of the merchandising has gone upscale, the original concept still remains. There is a medical building, a supermarket, a movie theater, a drugstore, two main department stores (**Nordstrom** and **Emporium**), and 120 other shops selling everything from specialty foods to music boxes. The free parking gives this mall an edge over downtown stores.
♦ Daily. 19th Ave (at Winston Dr). 564.8848

18 San Francisco State University This 100-acre campus, part of the California state university system, provides undergraduate and graduate programs for approximately 26,000 students. Celebrated graduates have included actor Danny Glover, singer Johnny Mathis, authors Anne Rice and Ernest Gaines, Congressman Ron Dellum, and California's legislative power, Willie Brown. The university's **McKenna Theatre** often has programs that are open to the public including a monthly chamber music series. ♦ 1600 Holloway Ave (at 19th Ave). 338.1111

19 San Francisco Zoo In recent years, the zoo (see the map below) has had its share of woes, including the 1989 earthquake, which damaged a few exhibits; scandals regarding some zookeepers' treatment of the elephants; and design flaws in the much-heralded primate center. Still, millions of dollars have been spent on innovative exhibitions, and management is dedicated to transforming this 65-year-old institution into a world-class zoo; it already attracts more than 1.2 million visitors annually. Natural habitats are gradually taking the place of cramped, fenced enclosures, with nearly a thousand exotic animals hanging from treetops, roaming through fields, and lounging on foggy islands. These settings enable visitors to see the animals behaving more naturally. The **Thelma and Henry Doelger Primate Discovery Center** highlights this philosophy. Here, from multilevel walkways, you can watch many species of monkeys and apes leap from tree to tree. The **Phoebe Hearst Discovery Hall** has 23 interactive exhibitions, including computer terminals where you can play "Construct a Primate." **Gorilla World** is

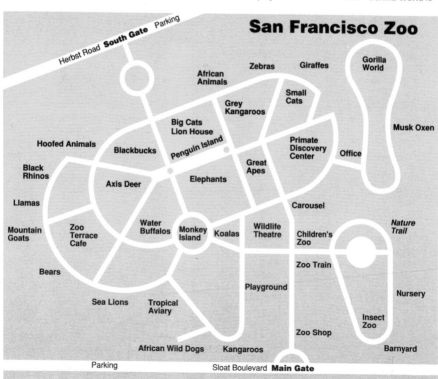

San Francisco Zoo

one of the planet's largest naturalistic gorilla exhibits, with two young and five adult gorillas.

This is also one of only a handful of zoos in the country that have koalas. The cuddly, eucalyptus-eating marsupials, native to Brisbane, Australia, live on a grassy knoll in **Koala Crossing.** When the weather is bad, they move to an indoor thicket of eucalyptus boughs. Black tie is always required on **Penguin Crossing,** where a colony of more than 60 Magellanic penguins with names such as Anne Arctica, Popsicle, and Oreo nestle in specially landscaped burrows. The **Lion House** is home to African lions and Siberian, Sumatran, and Bengal tigers. A crowd always shows up at 2PM (except on Monday) to watch the feeding of the big cats. The **Children's Zoo** features a **Barnyard** where you may pet and feed the assorted menagerie of domestic animals, as well as an **Insect Zoo,** featuring everything from a working beehive to the Costa Rican wood cockroach. The *Zebra Zephyr Train* takes you on an informative 20-minute safari tour, daily during the spring, summer, and fall, and on weekends in the winter.

The zoo opened in 1929, and now takes up 65 of its allocated 125 acres of land. The rest of the park is scheduled to be developed before the turn of the century under the Zoo 2000 Plan. At press time, the **Feline Conservation Center**—a new home for the resident cougars, jaguars, and leopards— was under construction. ♦ Admission. Daily. Tours weekends. Sloat Blvd (at 45th Ave). 753.7083

20 **Lake Merced** Once part of a ranchero, this large, tree-lined freshwater lake is one of San Francisco's standby reservoirs. It is also a trout-fishing hole, with good catches available year-round. Small craft for trips around the lake can be rented at a boathouse run by the Recreation and Parks Department. Rowboats, canoes, and paddleboats are available every day (weather permitting). **The Boathouse** bar and restaurant ($; 1 Harding Blvd. 681.2727) is nearby, and a barbecue area is across the road from the restaurant. ♦ Boat rentals: daily from an hour before sunrise to an hour after sunset. Off Harding Blvd (adjacent to the zoo). 753.1101

21 **Ingleside** One of the city's first racetracks opened here to a crowd of 8,000 people on Thanksgiving Day in 1885. Twenty years later the track was closed, and Ingleside Terrace was built in its place. Development was slow until the Twin Peaks Tunnel was completed in 1917 and large-scale residential construction began. The loop of the racetrack is now Urbano Drive. ♦ Bounded by Junipero Serra Blvd, Holloway Ave, Ashton Ave, Ocean Ave, and Cerritos Ave

The Yeast Also Rises

San Franciscans lay such possessive claim to sourdough bread that many visitors assume it originated here. But the truth is the ancient Egyptians actually whipped up the first batch of sourdough more than 4,000 years ago. Columbus supposedly carried a sour starter on his voyage to America, and the Pilgrims routinely used sour starters in bread making.

When commercially available yeasts and baking powders began to be produced in the 19th century, sour starter fell out of favor. (The starter, a combination of fermented flour, water, and sugar that makes the dough rise, had to be sustained from batch to batch, with the baker replenishing the ingredients on a weekly basis and storing it in a cool place.) Once cooks could readily purchase yeast and baking powder, the use of sour starters was largely limited to folks who lived far from settlements. During the Alaskan Gold Rush in the 1890s, for instance, prospectors used sour starters so extensively they earned the nickname "sourdoughs." And since many set sail for the Yukon goldfields from San Francisco, the bread became inexorably linked with the city.

Although it is, of course, possible to bake sourdough bread anywhere, San Franciscans maintain that the flavor of their loaves cannot be duplicated. Chef and cookbook author Bernard Clayton, determined to test this chauvinistic assertion, imported samples of San Francisco sourdough starter to his home in Bloomington, Indiana. Each time, however, no matter how carefully he tried to preserve the integrity of the starter, the batch metamorphosed into what he called "Bloomington sourdough bread," which had a distinctly different flavor. "I came to appreciate," he finally lamented, "that to bake San Francisco sourdough bread consistently I would probably have to live there."

Clayton and other aficionados claim that the unique flavor of the local bread can be attributed to the spores, fungi, and bacteria that waft through the San Francisco air. So popular is this theory, in fact, that one of the chefs at a top Nob Hill hostelry is rumored to have maintained the same batch of sourdough starter for years in a box on the hotel's roof so it may absorb all those San Francisco treats.

Golden Gate Park

By the middle of the 1800s, the relatively new city of San Francisco was determined to shape itself along the grandiose lines of the well-established East Coast and European metropolises. Civic pride, fueled by a desire to have a public park comparable to New York City's Central Park, was behind the development of **Golden Gate Park**, a 1,017-acre oasis of greenery, museums, and recreational facilities stretching from the **Haight** to the **Pacific Ocean**. The project's beginnings were tempestuous and mired in difficulties. Squatters, who claimed ownership by right of possession, slowed progress for years after the city originally petitioned the board of land commissioners for the property in 1852.

Renowned landscape architect **Frederick Law Olmsted,** who had designed New York City's Central Park, paid a visit to the proposed park site, laughingly called "the great sand bank," at the invitation of the board of supervisors. He took one look at the seemingly inhospitable tract of land, declared the project impossible, and advised that another location be chosen. But **William Hammond Hall** took up the gauntlet, and designed a layout for a park that respected the land's natural contours. By 1866 plans were under way to transform the barren, windswept, shifting sand dunes into a verdant oasis that would function as the lungs of the city.

Work began in 1871 with reclamation and development of the **Panhandle,** the block-wide strip of land between **Fell** and **Oak Streets** that leads into the park from **Baker** to **Stanyan Streets**. Public-spirited citizens donated funds for most of the buildings and statues in the park.

A dour and determined young Scot named John McLaren was the gardening wizard whose expertise and vision shaped the park that many naysayers had regarded as a white elephant. When he took on the formidable task in 1890 as superintendent of gardening, his formula was to plant grass to "tack down the sand," and then plant trees. Though many of his initial efforts were buried underneath mounds of sand, his crews persistently coaxed and coddled the struggling plants with manure and humus. Through perseverance that continued for more than half a century, until his death at age 96, McLaren lovingly tended his "white elephant"; trees grew and thrived, and the park evolved into a forest enhanced by lakes and meadows.

Affectionately known as "Uncle John," McLaren developed a correspondence with horticulturists all over the world that paid off with a rich bounty of

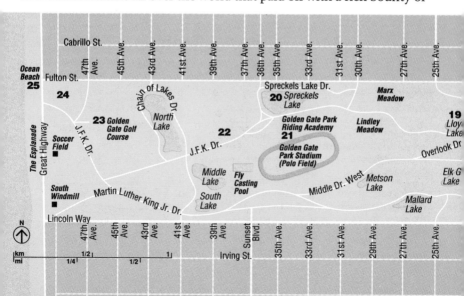

plants and trees. He planted about a million trees and introduced 700 new species of trees and shrubs to California in 1931 alone. His germinated seeds grew into gigantic trees up to 80 feet tall.

The feisty Scotsman battled regularly with City Hall to prevent the encroachment of non-park-related enterprises into *his* empire. One time, he thwarted construction of a streetcar line through the park by arguing that some of his precious trees would have to be uprooted to accommodate it. In turn, the engineers explained that they had planned the route through unplanted areas, but McLaren insisted they were wrong. When the supervisors arrived at the site the following morning to mediate the argument, they were greeted by shrubbery, small trees, and rhododendrons, which resulted in their veto of the streetcar proposal. What they didn't know was that 300 of Uncle John's employees had been busy planting all those shrubs only the night before. McLaren continued to shape the park until the end of his life, firmly rooted in his conviction that it was a place to be used and enjoyed, rather than a look-but-don't-touch showplace. He forbade "keep off the grass" signs, and tucked pompous-looking statues into corners where they would soon be hidden by rapidly growing shrubs. After the city's 1906 earthquake and fire McLaren had to rebuild many of the landscaped areas because thousands of displaced residents had set up camp in the park. At age 90, still superintendent of the park, he was asked what he wanted for a birthday gift; his response was "10,000 yards of good manure." When he died, Uncle John took one last ride through his beloved park on 14 January 1943 with 400 grieving gardeners and foremen standing at attention. His statue stands at the entrance of the **Rhododendron Dell**.

In the 1970s it was discovered that much of the park was dying, as trees planted when the park was first born had reached maturity. A reforestation program was instituted, and thousands of new trees were planted.

Golden Gate Park today is a countryside of flower beds, meadows, lakes, gardens, waterfalls, rolling hills, and forests. You could spend days in it and be unaware of the surrounding metropolis. The park offers something for everyone: recreational facilities for baseball, soccer, horseshoe pitching, fly casting, golf, horseback riding, tennis, and picnicking. And it has a huge network of walking paths and bicycle tracks, more than 6,000 varieties of flowers, dozens of species of trees, bowling greens, bocce courts, a football field, stables, and checker pavilions.

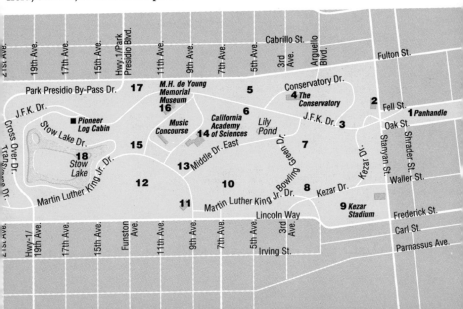

Over the years, the park has been the site of many special events, including the famous annual Bay to Breakers race, which features more than 100,000 runners, joggers, and walkers (many of them dressed in costumes—or wearing nothing at all) panting their way to the finish line at **Ocean Beach**; the summer Shakespeare in the Park festival; the free Opera in the Park concert in September; and Comedy Celebration Day in July.

Some park structures were damaged in the earthquake that struck on 17 October 1989. The bandshell in the **Music Concourse** sustained the most extensive devastation; at press time the structure was under renovation.

The park is well used by residents and visitors by day (especially on Sunday, when a large section of **JFK Drive**, which traverses the park, is closed), but city-sense is advised: Lone strollers and joggers should stick to populated areas. Neither parking (unless authorized for special events) nor sleeping is permitted in the park between 10PM and 6AM—though at dusk many of the city's homeless roll out their sleeping bags on the benches and in the thickets. Rain or shine, several free guided walking tours take place on the weekends from May through October. Lasting an hour and a half to two hours, these tours operate under the auspices of the Friends of Recreation and Parks. For information on meeting places and itineraries, call 221.1311. The Panhandle and **Golden Gate Park** also have beautiful—albeit unmarked and obscure—bicycle trails, including the seven-and-a-half-mile route from the Panhandle through the park out to **Lake Merced**. To find out more about bike, bus, or special-interest tours, call 750.5105.

Area code 415 unless otherwise noted.

1 Panhandle The trees here are the oldest in the park. Beginning with barley, then sand grass, then blue gum and live oak trees, park engineer **William Hammond Hall** gradually worked up the botanical chain as the hardier plants took root and more diversified shrubs could be planted. ◆ Bounded by Stanyan and Baker Sts, and Fell and Oak Sts

2 McLaren Lodge The home of John McLaren throughout his long term as superintendent of the park now serves as the headquarters of San Francisco's Recreation and Parks Department. Park information and maps are available in this Richardsonian Romanesque pile of sandstone. ◆ M-F. Fell St (at Stanyan St). 666.7200

3 JFK Drive On Sunday, this street is closed to auto traffic from Kezar to Transverse Drives, and open to roller skaters, in-line skaters, skateboarders, and joggers, many of them locomoting to private rhythms emanating from their headphones. Skate-rental facilities are located nearby on both Fulton and Haight Streets. ◆ Between Kezar and Transverse Drs

4 The Conservatory The oldest existing building in the park, the Conservatory was modeled after the Palm House at Kew Gardens in London and erected by **Lord and Burnham** in 1878 for eccentric millionaire James Lick. The structure was shipped from Dublin around Cape Horn and survived both the 1906 earthquake and a major fire.

The permanent displays of tropical plants and flowers are enriched by seasonal flower shows. Tours are given by prior arrangement. The valley surrounding the Conservatory is also worth exploring; it's received three national awards for landscape excellence. ◆ Nominal admission; reduced admission for seniors and children (6-12 years); free, children six and under; free daily 9AM-9:30AM and 4:30PM-5PM. Daily. Off JFK Dr. General information 641.7978, tours 928.0671

5 Shakespeare in the Park A temporary outdoor theater is erected annually in **Liberty Tree Meadow** for professional performances of the Bard's work. ◆ Free. Sa-Su Labor Day-30 Sept. Off JFK Dr (west of the Conservatory). 666.2222

6 Rhododendron Dell This memorial to John McLaren honors him with his favorite flower. There are more than 3,000 plants and 500 species here. ◆ Between JFK Dr and Middle Dr E, and the California Academy of Sciences

The 1,017-acre Golden Gate Park is the largest constructed park in the world.

Restaurants/Clubs: Red   Hotels: Blue
Shops/ Outdoors: Green   Sights/Culture: Black

7 Tennis Courts Some 21 courts, just north of the **Children's Playground,** draw players of all levels of expertise. ♦ Nominal fee. Reservations required. Off Bowling Green Dr (at Middle Dr E). Advance reservations 753.7101; same-day reservations 753.7001

8 Children's Playground One of the first public playgrounds to be built in an American park, this includes a gloriously restored carousel housed in a turn-of-the-century Greek temple. The animals and turning platform were made in New York by the Herschell-Spillman Company around 1912, and came to San Francisco sometime after the 1939 World's Fair on Treasure Island. The wooden menagerie consists of 62 animals, two chariots, one turning tub, and one rocker, all revolving to various show tunes, polkas, and mazurkas coming from the 55-year-old organ. The six-year restoration project involved cutting away rot and mildew, filling pitted surfaces, and sanding and applying brilliantly colored lacquers. Children under 39 inches ride free if accompanied by a paying adult. ♦ Carousel: nominal fee. Daily June-Sept; Th-Su Oct-May. Off Martin Luther King Jr. Dr (near Kezar Dr)

9 Kezar Stadium This 10,000-seat facility is used for community activities, high school sports, soccer, and track. ♦ Kezar Dr (at Martin Luther King Jr. Dr)

10 Baseball Diamonds You may play on the two baseball diamonds in the **Big Rec Ball Field** with advance reservations, or, if you prefer softball, there's a first-come, first-served softball diamond near the **Children's Playground.** ♦ Off Martin Luther King Jr. Dr (at Seventh Ave). 753.7024, 753.7025

11 S.F. County Fair Building Known as the **Hall of Flowers** to locals, this building is used for special events ranging from cat shows to floral exhibitions. ♦ Ninth Ave (off Lincoln Way)

12 Strybing Arboretum This arboretum is a quiet sylvan retreat, with many paths among the 6,000 or so species of trees, plants, and shrubs, both native and exotic. Be sure to visit the **Garden of Fragrance** for visually impaired nature lovers, watched over by a statue of St. Francis of Assisi. Labels are in Braille and plants are selected especially for their taste, touch, and smell. Maps are available at the **Strybing Bookstore** at Ninth Avenue and Lincoln Way, and tours are given daily. ♦ Free. Daily. Ninth Ave (off Lincoln Way). 661.1316

13 Shakespeare Garden Flowers and plants mentioned in Shakespeare's sonnets and plays are featured in this garden. ♦ South of the California Academy of Sciences on Martin Luther King Jr. Dr (at Middle Dr E)

14 California Academy of Sciences A special favorite of families, this nonprofit scientific institution (see the plan below) is located on the south side of the **Music Concourse,** facing the **M.H. de Young Museum.** The academy was founded in 1853 just following the Gold Rush, and is the West's oldest scientific institution. The facility incorporates museums, exhibit halls, a planetarium, and an aquarium. The various exhibition halls are often rented out for elegant private functions (guests don't seem to mind being watched by the immobile menagerie as they wine and dine).
♦ Admission; free the first Wednesday of every month; reduced admission for seniors

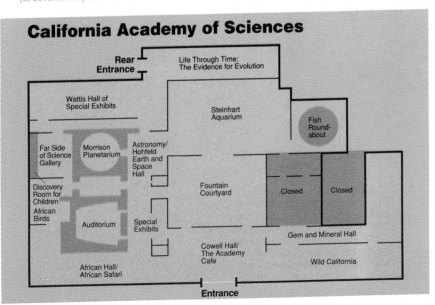

California Academy of Sciences

Rear Entrance

Life Through Time: The Evidence for Evolution

Wattis Hall of Special Exhibits

Steinhart Aquarium

Fish Round-about

Far Side of Science Gallery

Morrison Planetarium

Astronomy/ Hohfeld Earth and Space Hall

Discovery Room for Children

African Birds

Fountain Courtyard

Closed

Closed

Auditorium

Special Exhibits

Gem and Mineral Hall

Cowell Hall/ The Academy Cafe

Wild California

African Hall/ African Safari

Entrance

and children (6-17); free children five and under. Daily. South side of the Music Concourse (between JFK Dr and Middle Dr E). 750.7145

Within the California Academy of Sciences:

Steinhart Aquarium This classic European-style aquarium is a must-see—especially for children. It holds the most diverse collection of sea life in the world, with more than 14,000 species of fish, plus an array of reptiles, amphibians, marine mammals, and penguins. When you enter, there's invariably a crowd gathered around the rails overlooking the **Swamp,** a simulated native habitat for alligators, lizards, tortoises, and other reptiles. Check out the bird-eating spider, too. You can watch the beloved seals, dolphins, and penguins being fed. A particular favorite, though it makes some viewers dizzy, is the **Fish Roundabout,** where visitors find themselves surrounded by a doughnut-shaped 100,000-gallon tank in which an assortment of sea life, including sharks and bat rays, glides past. Don't miss the **Touch Tidepool**, where you may pick up and inspect live sea urchins, sea cucumbers, hermit crabs, and sea stars. The aquarium is also home to the largest living tropical-coral-reef exhibit in the US.

Morrison Planetarium Entertaining and educational sky shows are presented in northern California's largest indoor universe, beneath a 65-foot-high dome.

Also part of the planetarium is the **Laserium,** where, for an additional charge, viewers may gaze at intricate, multicolored light patterns drawn onto the planetarium dome by a one-watt krypton gas laser as a five-watt argon laser slices the air with searing blue beams. All this is done to the accompaniment of stereo music that holds particular appeal for young rockers—and for older folk, who may find it all very reminiscent of the light shows of the psychedelic 1960s and 1970s. The hour-long light-and-music show is choreographed in advance, but no two performances are exactly alike. Tickets are available in advance through **BASS** outlets or at the academy a half-hour before showtime. ♦ Admission; reduced fees for seniors and for children 17 and under. Planetarium 750.7141, Laserium 750.7138

Wild California Dazzling dioramas display California's grandeur—from a southern desert to wave-hammered islands—in this handsome hall, which allows viewers the thrill of exploration without the perils. One highlight is the exhibition of battling, life-size elephant seals set against a 14,000-gallon aquarium and seabird rookery display.

Wattis Hall of Special Exhibits Formerly the site of an anthropological display, this hall now features special exhibits that change about every four months. They range in theme from monarch butterflies to endangered species to the science behind the TV show "Star Trek."

African Safari African animals are portrayed in their natural habitat in a series of dioramas. The **African Waterhole** exhibition includes on-location animal recordings and a lighting cycle from dawn to dusk.

Far Side of Science Gallery Get a hilarious perspective on science with 159 original *Far Side* cartoons by well-known zany cartoonist Gary Larson.

Hohfeld Earth and Space Hall You'll get all shook up on the popular **Safe-Quake,** which simulates two of San Francisco's famous tremors. Also, under a neon solar system, you may learn about forces that shape the earth and the planets. Another favorite exhibit is the **Foucault Pendulum,** which swings continually as the earth rotates, knocking over a set of pins about every 20 minutes to demonstrate the progress of our revolving planet.

Gem and Mineral Hall More than 1,000 specimens, from gold to granite, may be found here, including a 1,350-pound quartz crystal from Arkansas. Bauble lovers leave wide-eyed.

Discovery Room for Children These hands-on nature exhibits are of interest to adults as well as children. They are also ideal for people with disabilities—there is a lot to touch and all exhibits are easy to reach. ♦ Tu-Su.

The Academy Store Located near the entrance hall, this is a fine place to find books, posters, toys, and gifts for naturalists of all ages. ♦ Daily. 750.7330

The Academy Cafe $ On the lower level of **Cowell Hall,** this cafeteria serves family fare—essentially hot dogs, sandwiches, and salads. ♦ American ♦ Daily lunch. 751.5002

Life through Time: The Evidence for Evolution Opened in 1990, this permanent exhibition housed in the **Peterson-McBean Hall** journeys through 3.5 billion years of evolution, using living specimens, fossils, and models. The trip begins with early life in the sea, where visitors encounter the radiation of single-celled organisms, and continues on through the millennia, with dinosaur exhibitions and displays chronicling the development of mammals.

15 Japanese Tea Garden This and the **Music Concourse**—both built for the California Midwinter International Exposition of 1894—are the only structures gardener McLaren did not have torn down after the fair ended. In 1895 the tea garden became the charge of the Hagiwara family, who tended it with loving devotion. Makato Hagiwara is credited with inventing the fortune cookie here. Ironically, the cookies have come to be called Chinese fortune cookies and are a favorite item of the tourist trade in Chinatown. The Hagiwara family maintained the garden until World War II, when they, along with 110,000 other Japanese-Americans, were sent to internment camps. This jewel of **Golden Gate Park** is so artfully designed that even the hordes of visitors cannot mar the tranquil experience.

Architecture, landscape, and humans blend subtly and beautifully in a harmonious pattern of bridges, footpaths, pools, flowers, trees, statuary, shrines, and gates. It is especially breathtaking in April when the cherry trees are in bloom. The *Bronze Buddha,* donated by the Gump brothers in 1949, was cast in Japan in 1790. The **Shinto Pagoda** is a five-tiered wooden shrine. The **Moon Bridge,** also called the **Wishing Bridge,** casts its semicircular reflection in the pool below, making a full circle.

The piles of old stones in a clearing behind the tea garden are the disassembled remains of a medieval Cistercian monastery from Spain. In 1932 William Randolph Hearst bought the monastery, had it dismantled and shipped over here, and later donated it to the **M.H. de Young Memorial Museum.** Except for the reconstruction of the chapel portal, which still stands in the **de Young**'s central court, and the unobtrusive incorporation of some of the ruins in retaining walls and rockeries around the park, the stones have never been reassembled, largely due to lack of funds. There is also a gift shop and a **Tea House,** serving tea, soft drinks, juices, and cookies. ♦ Admission; reduced admission for seniors and children (6-12); free children five and under; free daily 9AM-9:30AM Mar-Oct; 8:30AM-9AM, 5PM-6PM (or until sunset) Nov-Feb. Daily. Near the Asian Art Museum (between JFK and Martin Luther King Jr. Drs). 666.7024

M.H. de Young Memorial Museum

AMERICAN ART

To tour the galleries chronologically, follow the alphabetical course:

A	7.	17th and 18th Centuries. Colonial period arts
B	9.	18th Century. Silver by Paul Revere; paintings
C	8.	Late-18th and Early-19th Centuries. Paintings; Federal-period furniture
D	6.	Federal parlor from 1805 Massachusetts house
E	10A.	Dufour wallpaper; Samuel Gragg chairs
F	10.	Early-19th Century. Paintings; furniture; decorative arts
G	11.	19th Century. Sculpture
H	12.	19th Century. Shaker and Folk Art
I	13.	Mid-19th Century. Paintings; Belter furniture
J	13A.	The American Galleries
K	17.	Mid-19th Century. Paintings
L	19.	Late-19th Century. Paintings
M	16A.	Late-19th Century. Paintings
N	18.	Trompe l'oeil and Still-life Paintings
O	16.	Impressionists and Expatriates. Paintings
P	15.	Artists and the West. Paintings; sculpture
Q	14.	Late-19th and Early-20th Centuries. Sculpture
R	33.	Late-19th Century. California paintings
S	34.	Arts and Crafts Movement. Stickley furniture; ceramics; paintings
T	35.	Early-20th Century. Paintings
U	21.	20th-Century Realism. Paintings
V	28, 29.	20th Century. Mixed media

ANCIENT ART

1. Egypt, Greece, Rome, and the Near East

BRITISH ART

3. Regency Anteroom: Furniture, silver
4. George III Dining Room in the Adam style
5. Paintings, rococo-style furniture

TEXTILES

22., 27. Theme exhibitions from the permanent collection

GLASS GALLERY

25. Drinking vessels from the 16th century

AFRICAN ART

42. Works from sub-Saharan Africa

ART OF THE AMERICAS

43. Works from Mesoamerica, Central and South America, and the West Coast of North America

SPECIAL EXHIBITIONS

36., 37. Viewpoints
39. Works on paper
41., 44. Special and traveling exhibitions; inquire at the Information Desk

16 M.H. de Young Memorial Museum

The museum evolved from the California Midwinter International Exposition of 1894, held in the park, when civic leader and *San Francisco Chronicle* publisher Michael de Young initiated a building program to establish a permanent museum and expand its size and collections; the cornerstone was laid in 1917. The renovated galleries, which surround a central courtyard, feature American paintings, sculpture, and decorative arts from Colonial times to the 20th century,

including more than 100 paintings from the collection of Mr. and Mrs. John D. Rockefeller 3rd, and an extraordinary group of trompe l'oeil and still life paintings from the turn of the century, including the masterworks of William M. Harnett, John F. Peto, and Alexander Pope (see the floor plan above).

There is a strong showing of traditional arts of the Americas and Africa, and some British art from the 16th through 19th centuries. The collection of central Asian tribal rugs is one of the country's most comprehensive.

American artists represented in the museum include John Singleton Copley, Charles Willson Peale, James Peale, Rembrandt Peale, Paul Revere, Mary Cassatt, John Singer Sargent, and James McNeill Whistler. British artists such as Joshua Reynolds, Thomas Lawrence, Thomas Gainsborough, and George Romney are also represented, as well as such 20th-century American artists as Wayne Thiebaud, Georgia O'Keeffe, Grant Wood, and Reginald Marsh.

Hearst Court, which welcomes visitors as they enter the museum, features periodically changing exhibits. Surrounding the court is a survey of American silver and glass, from early free-blown objects to iridescent works by Louis Comfort Tiffany and later works by Frederick Carder for Steuben.

The well-stocked bookstore sells small artifacts and museum replicas, plus books, posters, cards, and slides. ♦ Admission; free the first Wednesday of every month; reduced admission for seniors and children (12-17); free children 11 and under. W-Su. North side of the Music Concourse (off JFK Dr). 863.3330

Within the M.H. de Young Memorial Museum:

Cafe de Young ★$$ You can reach this pleasant cafeteria through galleries 22 and 25 of the museum and get a decent snack or lunch at a reasonable price. Any salad or fish dish is bound to be good. You may take your repast outside in the adjacent small garden with its trellises and clipped hedges and pretend you're in France. ♦ American ♦ W-Su lunch. Ground level. 752.0116

Asian Art Museum of San Francisco
This museum opened in 1966 after Avery Brundage donated his world-famous collection of Asian art to San Francisco. Located in the **de Young**'s west wing, the collection (see the floor plan above) contains more than 10,000 paintings, sculptures, ceramics, decorative objects, bronzes, architectural elements, jades, and textiles gathered from all over Asia. The exhibitions are rotated periodically, as only about 15 percent of the extensive collection can be displayed at one time. (In 1998 the museum will relocate to the **Civic Center** building that now houses the **San Francisco Public Library,** where there will be 50 percent more exhibition space.)

The first floor shows objects from China and Korea. The second floor is devoted to the arts from the rest of Asia. ♦ Separate admission; reduced admission for seniors and children (12-17); free children 11 and under. W-Su. 668.8921

Asian Art Museum

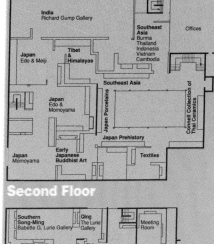

Second Floor

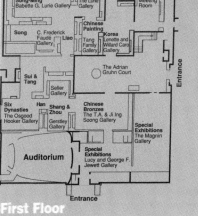

First Floor

17 Rose Garden Fifty-three beds of award-winning roses bloom here in great variety. ♦ South end of Park Presidio Blvd (between JFK Dr and Fulton St)

18 Stow Lake This is the largest lake in the park and the only place to rent bicycles, rowboats, paddleboats, and motorboats. Bring your own food to picnic by the shore, or pick up something at the small concession stand. ♦ Boathouse and snack bar: Tu-Su. Stow Lake Dr (between JFK Dr and Martin Luther King Jr. Dr). 752.0347

Within Stow Lake:

Strawberry Hill Located in the middle of **Stow Lake** is this artificial island, which once stored water for the park. The cascading **Huntington Falls** add to the picturesque setting. On its shores is the elaborate **Chinese Pavilion,** a gift from the government of Taiwan in 1984 and a popular spot for weddings, relaxation, and reflection. Footbridges connect from the shore, and a winding road leads to the island's 428-foot-high peak, from which there are good views of the city.

159

19 Portals of the Past These two columns once graced the porch of a Nob Hill home, and were all that remained after the 1906 earthquake. They suffered some damage in the quake of October 1989. ♦ North side of Lloyd Lake (off JFK Dr)

20 Spreckels Lake This small lake is the setting for operating and watching model motorboats and sailboats. It is also a way station for a variety of migratory birds. ♦ 36th Ave (off Fulton St)

21 Golden Gate Park Riding Academy A great way to see the park is on one of the guided trail rides offered here. The jaunts last about an hour (they're all walking, no cantering or trotting) and must be scheduled two or three days in advance. Riders must be at least eight years old. ♦ 36th Ave (at JFK Dr). 668.7360

22 Buffalo Paddock Strictly speaking, the shaggy creatures that roam this 35-acre enclosure are American bison. The park is home to 14 of them (one male and 13 females), many brought here in 1984 to replace descendants of the original herd, which was genetically weakened from years of inbreeding. ♦ West end of JFK Dr (east of Chain of Lakes Dr)

23 Golden Gate Golf Course This nine-hole course is open to the public. ♦ Daily. Off 47th Ave (between Fulton St and JFK Dr). 751.8987

24 North Dutch Windmill Built in 1902, this windmill was rededicated in 1981 after its restoration. Surrounding it is the **Queen Wilhelmina Tulip Garden,** a rainbow of color in the spring. ♦ Near 47th Ave and JFK Dr

25 Ocean Beach Near the celebrated **Cliff House** on the **Great Highway** and west of the park itself, this beach is easily accessible. Wading, jogging, stone collecting, and picnicking are popular, but swimming is not safe due to the strong undertow. ♦ Off the Great Highway

Historical Highlights of San Francisco

1579—Sir Francis Drake anchors on the northern California coast.

1595—Captain Sebastian Cermeno is shipwrecked north of the **Golden Gate,** claims the land for Spain, and names it *Puerto de San Francisco.*

1769—Spanish explorers, led by Don Gaspar de Portola, discover **San Francisco Bay.**

1776—Padre Junipero Serra founds the **Mission of St. Francis** on the shore of **Lake Dolores.** Captain Juan Bautista begins building the **Presidio.**

1792—George Vancouver anchors off **Yerba Buena Cove,** the spot from which San Francisco grew.

1806—California is declared a province of the Republic of Mexico.

1846—The American flag is raised in **Portsmouth Square** and Yerba Buena becomes San Francisco. Captain John C. Fremont coins the term "Golden Gate."

1848—The Gold Rush begins.

1854—The first lighthouse is built on **Alcatraz Island.**

1864—Young reporter Mark Twain begins writing about life in San Francisco for *Morning Call.*

1869—The transcontinental railroad is completed, providing new trade and travel routes to the West.

1871—The development of **Golden Gate Park** begins.

1872—The first Japanese ship arrives in San Francisco loaded with tea.

1873—The cable car comes to San Francisco.

1876—Electricity lights up San Francisco just in time for author Jack London's birth.

1904—Bank of Italy, later to become Bank of America, is created by Italian merchant A.P. Giannini.

1906—Earthquake and fire destroy much of the city.

1915—The Panama-Pacific International Exhibition, commemorating the opening of the Panama Canal, is held in San Francisco. More than 18 million people attend.

1927—**San Francisco International Airport** opens.

1934—5 July is "Bloody Thursday," when a head-on confrontation between the Industrial Association scabs, the International Longshoremen's Union, and the police takes place.

1936—The **Bay Bridge** is dedicated.

1937—The **Golden Gate Bridge** opens.

1945—The United Nations Charter is signed in San Francisco.

1960—**Candlestick Park** opens.

1963—**Alcatraz** is closed because of old age, while renovated **Ghirardelli Square** opens.

1967—The Summer of Love comes to San Francisco: hippies, the Free Speech Movement, drugs, and the sexual revolution.

1974—**Bay Area Rapid Transit (BART)** makes its first run through the Transbay tube.

1978—Mayor George Moscone and Supervisor Harvey Milk are shot to death in their offices. Dianne Feinstein is appointed mayor.

1982—The **San Francisco 49ers** win Superbowl XVI against Cincinnati. They repeat their victory two, seven, and eight years later.

1986—The Downtown Plan limits building in San Francisco.

1989—A 7.1 earthquake hits the city.

1993—**Yerba Buena Gardens,** the multimillion-dollar arts and cultural center, officially opens.

1994—Most of the 200-year-old **Presidio,** the nation's oldest continuously used military post, is transferred from the Army's jurisdiction to become part of the **Golden Gate National Recreation Area.**

Bests

Rand Castile
Director, Asian Art Museum of San Francisco

The best of the Asian Art Museum:

Seated Buddha (Gilt bronze; China; dated AD 338). The world's oldest dated Chinese Buddha sculpture—as beautiful as it is venerable.

Lacquer Incense Box with Gardenia Decoration (Carved cinnabar-red lacquer; China; inscribed "Made by Zhang Cheng," who was a famous Yuan-dynasty [13th-14th centuries] lacquer artist). We have one of the finest collections of Chinese 10th- to 14th-century lacquers. This piece is exceptional for its elegant, deeply carved design.

King of Hell (Scroll painting; Korea; Choson period, 15th-16th centuries). A very important acquisition; a rare old Buddhist painting to add to our growing collection of Korean art.

Dog (Earthenware burial pottery; China; Western Han period, circa 1st century BC). My favorite piece in the collection; he has an alertness that makes me smile.

Siva and Devi (Sandstone sculptures; Khmer; late 11th century). The understated royal elegance of Khmer (Cambodian) civilization at its best; the most elegant stone in the collection.

Rhinoceros Tsun (Ceremonial wine vessel; China; late Shang dynasty, 11th century BC). This rhino has attained world celebrity for its ample and unique form.

Umbrella-bearer (Schist stone sculpture; India; Gandhara, circa 3rd century). The sensuous curve of the umbrella as it envelops the figure is wonderful.

Nyoirin-Kannon (Wood/dry-lacquer sculpture; Japan; Hein period, AD 900-950). Radiates a calm, cool assurance and inner peace.

Vessel in the Shape of a Stag (Earthenware; Iran; circa 10th century BC). In its elegant simplicity, this piece is timeless in design.

Summer Mountains Misty Rain (Hand scroll by Wang Hui; China; dated 1668). It was a coup to find what I think is the best painting by the most innovative Orthodox School artist of the 17th century; works like this are rare.

Seated Ganesha, Elephant-Headed God (Stone sculpture; India [Hoysala]; 12th-13th centuries). A particularly appealing image of the rotund, humorous god.

Two Birds on a Blossoming Branch (Painted scroll by anonymous artist; China; Southern Song dynasty, 12th-13th centuries). The courtly grace of the paired birds is captured in the delicate, exquisite brushwork.

Tiger (Nephrite [jade]; tan with brown markings; China; late Eastern Zhou, 4th-3rd centuries BC). Among the most refined of objects, this jade is unusual for its color and form.

The first buffalo born in San Francisco was delivered in Golden Gate Park on 21 April 1892.

Joan Jeanrenaud
Cellist, Kronos Quartet

In the Morning

North Beach: Get up and head for **Cafe Puccini** on Columbus Avenue for cappuccino, orange juice, and pastries, then wander around, maybe going all the way up to **Coit Tower** for a great walk and vista of beautiful San Francisco.

In the Afternoon

Marin Headlands: Going north over the **Golden Gate Bridge** are the Marin Headlands. Take the Stinson Beach exit and make a left on Tennessee Valley Road. Make sure to stop at the fruit stand on the corner. Go as far as you can until you come to a parking lot. Get out and walk to the beach—even as far as Stinson Beach, or anywhere on the beautiful headlands. Coming here always reminds me of why we live in the Bay Area.

In the Evening

Chez Panisse: In Berkeley, world-renowned, and worth the trip across the bay or halfway around the world! Another choice would be dinner at the **Hayes Street Grill** and an evening at the **San Francisco Opera.**

Christopher Ford
Regional Director, Guardian Angels

Why do San Franciscans lead the country in developing innovative new approaches to difficult problems like street crime? Why, it's the coffee, of course. We love our coffee as much as we love our city, and that's why unarmed community patrols have taken to the streets alongside Guardian Angels to combat neighborhood crime. Two of my favorite places for the life's-blood brew are **Soma** at 12th and Howard and **The Royal Ground** on Polk and Pine. My morning coffee is usually followed by a killer workout at the **World Gym Showplace Square.** Next, a tour of the **Alcatraz "the Rock" Island,** followed by a cocktail (I suggest a martini, although I don't drink) at the **Cafe Majestic** on Sutter and Gough, which has an impressive butterfly collection and in the evening has an absolutely elegant piano player, Don Asher. **La Cumbre** on Valencia, a great burrito joint, is my suggestion for dinner; if it's still light out, check out the graffiti across the street. It's very artistic. Keep your eyes open over dinner for the likes of Robin Williams or Bobby McFarren, who frequent the place. Feel free to stop by the local Guardian Angels office or look for one of the many community patrols we've helped organize throughout the city. When meeting San Franciscans, always speak from your heart and you will be well received.

The city's skateboarders, bicyclists, in-line skaters, runners, and strollers know that the best days to visit Golden Gate Park are Sundays and holidays.

The Richmond/Presidio

Endless rows of stucco dwellings line the avenues of the staunchly middle-class and family-oriented Richmond district. The area contains more residential land than any other in San Francisco, and that's how the residents want it to stay. In fact, political donnybrooks have been aimed at developers who wanted to knock down single-family homes and replace them with multiple units.

In another era the Richmond was known as "the dunes," and it took all day to reach **Seal Rocks** by railroad and horse-drawn carriage from downtown. Before 1900 most of the San Franciscans in the windy, foggy Richmond were the deceased inhabitants of the **Municipal Cemetery** or the **Chinese Cemetery.** After a street was cut through the area in 1863, however, a few roadhouses opened, and the first of what would turn into a series of **Cliff Houses** was built by Sam Brannan, though it soon burned to the ground.

Then along came Adolph Sutro, an engineer who made his fortune in the Comstock Lode. As mayor of the city, he set about to open the Richmond for development and created a Victorian fantasy castle on the bluff to replace the **Cliff House** that had been destroyed. Then he erected a fabulous group of glass-enclosed, oceanside swimming pools called the **Sutro Baths;** planted **Sutro Forest;** and built his own house and elaborate gardens, which he opened to the public. After providing such incentive for people to visit the area, the "Father of the Richmond" built a steam railroad on **California Street** to ease their way. Now only ruins mark the place where the once spectacular baths were situated, and a few marble statues are all that remain of the mansion. But Sutro's project served its purpose—to attract potential residents to the district. Thousands of houses were built here between 1910 and 1930. While many are bland stucco homes of no distinction, one neighborhood offers exceptions: **Sea Cliff.** This long-established enclave of the well-to-do, tucked between **Lincoln Park** and the **Presidio,** contains many grand mansions, a number of them built on sheer rock cliffs overlooking the Pacific Ocean.

After World War I, hundreds of Russians and East European Jews moved into the Richmond district. Their religious centers still form the major landmarks: **Temple Emanu-El,** on Arguello Avenue at Lake Street, and the gold-domed **Cathedral of the Holy Virgin,** on Geary Boulevard at 26th Avenue. Russian restaurants and Jewish

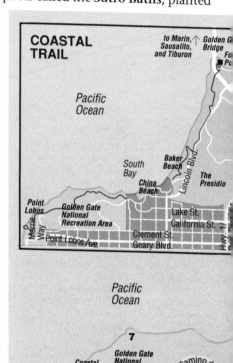

businesses continue to thrive alongside the enterprises of the Japanese who moved in after World War II. More Japanese live here than in any other neighborhood. And so many Chinese have bought houses along **Clement Street** that the stretch between **First** and **11th Avenues** is called "New Chinatown."

Clement Street mingles the traditions of Asia and Europe in a profusion of Chinese restaurants, Italian pizzerias, Irish bars and bookstores, Russian bakeries, Asian markets, and Middle Eastern and German delis. Austrians, Armenians, Hungarians, Ukrainians, Czechs, and Caucasian refugees from Shanghai and Singapore are all united into Clement's warmhearted community. The concentration of inexpensive restaurants is staggering, and given the keen competition, there's a lot of turnover.

The **Presidio**, on the other hand, is a district apart. This former military outpost is more than 200 years old and encompasses 68 square miles of land and water. A large portion of the area recently became part of the **Golden Gate National Recreation Area (GGNRA)**. In addition to verdant scenery and a variety of views, it has two great beaches (**Fort Point** and **Winfield Scott**), old-time fortifications, a golf course, a lake, and picnic sites everywhere.

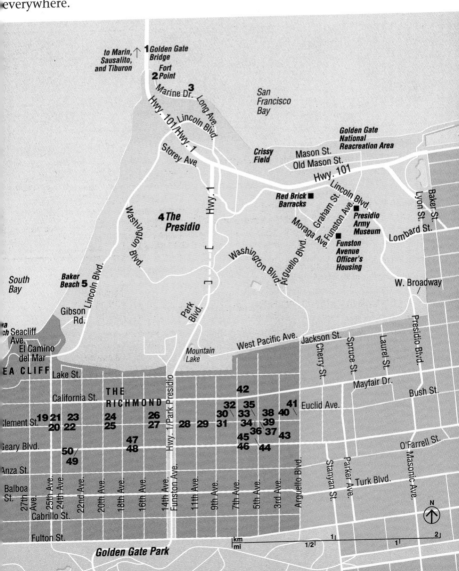

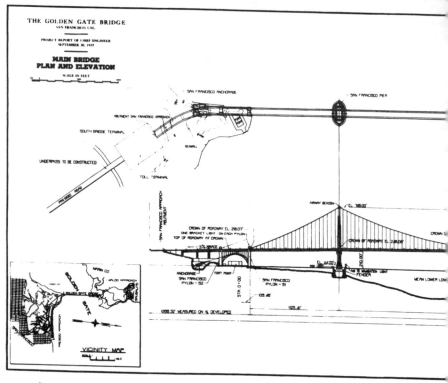

THE GOLDEN GATE BRIDGE
SAN FRANCISCO, CAL.

PROJECT REPORT OF CHIEF ENGINEER
SEPTEMBER 30, 1937

**MAIN BRIDGE
PLAN AND ELEVATION**

SCALE IN FEET

Area code 415 unless otherwise noted.

1 Golden Gate Bridge San Francisco's pride and joy (illustrated above) is undoubtedly one of the most beautiful bridges in the world, on account of its spectacular location, graceful lines, Moderne detailing, and emblematic color. The clear span of more than 4,200 feet was the longest in the world until 1959, when New York City's Verrazano-Narrows Bridge was built. Although there is some controversy about who actually designed the bridge— some scholars say an engineer named Charles Ellis should get the credit—**Joseph Strauss** was chief engineer of the project, which took four and a half years and $35 million to complete. It was finally and officially inaugurated on 28 May 1937, when President Roosevelt punched a telegraph key in the White House, giving the cue 3,000 miles away for a clamor of bells, sirens, and foghorns, squadrons of Navy planes, and the most enormous peacetime concentration of naval strength ever. Over 200,000 pedestrians had swarmed across the structure the day before, and an endless parade of politicos' vehicles traversed the bridge the day after its opening.

At mid-span, the roadway is 260 feet above the water, a height requested by the Navy to allow its battleships to pass beneath. One of the piers is located in the water and the other is on the Marin shore. The main cables are 36.5 inches in diameter. The bridge was designed to withstand winds of more than 100 miles per hour and to be able to swing at mid-span as much as 27 feet. The best views are from **Vista Point** on the Marin side and from **Fort Point** below on the San Francisco side.

On 24 May 1987, more than 200,000 pedestrians took over again to celebrate the bridge's 50th anniversary. Winners in a silly and hard-fought battle with local bureaucracies, they took advantage of the closure of the bridge for a few hours and walked across, their weight flattening the center span, causing the bridge to drop 10 feet, and their numbers, pouring onto the bridge from both sides, creating a bad case of pedestrian gridlock.

The celebration included marching bands, poster contests, steelworkers from Pottstown, Pennsylvania (where the bridge steel was made), brilliant fireworks displays, more politicos, and the pièce de résistance—the inauguration of the lighting of the 746-foot-tall towers.

Although the bridge was built for the automobile age, its designers wisely included sidewalks, doubtlessly recognizing the fact that it must be crossed on foot to be properly appreciated. The bridge is 1.2 miles across, and the walk, round-trip, takes about an hour. Pedestrians use the walk on the east side daily from 5AM to 9PM. Bicyclists share the path Monday through Friday, but must use the west side on the weekend. And don't forget to take an extra sweater—it's awfully windy up

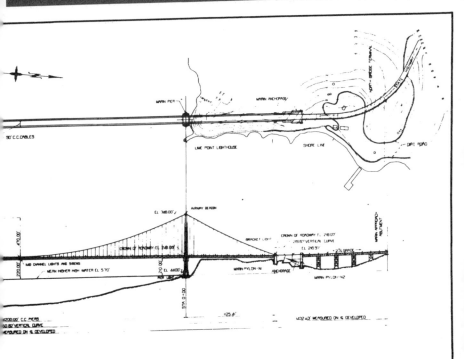

COURTESY OF THE GOLDEN GATE BRIDGE HIGHWAY AND TRANSPORTATION DISTRICT

there. You'll find a convenient parking area east of the **Toll Plaza,** and nearby, a glass roundhouse containing a **Visitor's Center.** One of the two surrounding gardens is a memorial to the bridge workers; the other is a friendship garden that pays tribute to Pacific Rim nations.

Since its opening, the bridge has become as symbolic of San Francisco as the Eiffel Tower is of Paris. On the darker side, both structures have an unenviable record for suicides. Few people survive the fall.

But the bridge itself is in good health and has aged well. With the additional network of girders installed in 1987 to strengthen the roadway and new suspender ropes, it is stronger than ever and just as beautiful—the most photographed structure built by humans in the world. ♦ Toll southbound Hwy 101

2 Fort Point The fort lies under the southern end of the Golden Gate Bridge and was built between 1853 and 1861 to guard San Francisco from sea attack. It houses a museum filled with old swords, guns, cannons, uniforms, and historic photographs of earlier days. There are guided tours (advance reservations required); Civil War cannon-loading and -firing demonstrations are held twice a day when the museum is open. ♦ Free. W-Su. Off Lincoln Blvd (at Long Ave; take Long Ave to Marine Dr). 556.1373

3 Golden Gate Promenade The promenade extends from **Fort Point** underneath the Golden Gate Bridge to **Aquatic Park** and provides three and a half miles of spectacular bay views. It's also popular for biking and fishing. ♦ Between Fort Point and Aquatic Park

4 The Presidio Located at the entrance to the Golden Gate on the northernmost point of the San Francisco peninsula, the **Presidio** was a military outpost for more than 200 years. In the 1770s, while American colonists were writing the Declaration of Independence, the Spanish rulers of Mexico established a series of missions and military posts on the West Coast. The farthest north of these posts was this spot. The original installation was a walled camp 100 yards square surrounded by a palisade-type wall.

When the Mexicans gained their independence in 1822, they took over the site until it was forcibly possessed in 1846 by the United States. Originally, the 1,400-acre area consisted of bare hills and rocks. In the 1880s it was planted with pine and eucalyptus trees that today form one of the most beautiful wooded areas in the city. Union regiments trained here during the Civil War. After the 1906 earthquake and fire, it became a refugee camp for the homeless and injured. During World War II it was the headquarters of the Fourth Army and Western Defense Command.

165

The site is no longer a military outpost, and most of it recently became part of the **Golden Gate National Recreation Area (GGNRA)**. Despite the change, the historic buildings will be retained, but 301 newer structures will be torn down to allow for the creation of open space or forest.

Established in 1972, the **GGNRA** encompasses 34,000 acres and is one and a half times larger in area than San Francisco. The park covers more than 68 square miles of land and water, including 28 miles of the Pacific Ocean, Tomales Bay in Marin, and the San Francisco coastline. Its diverse natural environment offers sandy beaches, rugged headlands, grasslands, forests, lakes, marshes, and streams. While the area around **Fort Mason** in San Francisco has been developed, the rest of the expansive preserve is maintained as closely as possible in its natural state by the National Park Service.

Places to visit include Baker Beach off Lincoln Boulevard and the gun emplacements **Battery Chamberlain, Battery Crosby,** and **Batteries Cranston, Marcus Miller,** and **Boutelle** near the Golden Gate Bridge. A *Historical Trail Guide* produced by the National Park Service features the many historic and scenic points; additional information is available by calling the **Visitor's Information Center** at 556.0865.
♦ Main entrances: Lombard St (at Lyon St), Presidio Blvd (at Broadway), Arguello Blvd (at Jackson St), Lincoln Blvd (at 25th Ave), and Golden Gate Bridge Toll Plaza. 561.2108

Within the Presidio:
Presidio Army Museum Formerly the **Old Station Hospital** and built in 1857, this is the oldest surviving building in the **Presidio.** On view are numerous uniforms, weapons, photographs, and other memorabilia pertaining to the Army's history in San Francisco. ♦ Free. W-Su. Lincoln Blvd (at Funston Ave). 556.0856

Funston Avenue Officers' Housing This group of houses along Funston Avenue constitutes some of the oldest and—depending on whom you ask—finest Victorian structures in San Francisco. Built in 1862, these elegant wood-frame structures housed Army officers for over a century.
♦ Off Lincoln Blvd

Red Brick Barracks Built in the Georgian style between 1895 and 1897, the stately brick barracks flanking the **Parade Ground** off Montgomery Avenue served as the enlisted men's first permanent barracks at the **Presidio.** ♦ Off Funston Ave (at Lincoln Blvd)

5 Baker Beach Although swimming is dangerous at this mile-long stretch of sandy shore, the fishing is fine, especially for striped bass. There are picnic and barbecue facilities, as well as drinking water and rest rooms, but no camping. Dogs on leashes are allowed.
♦ Daily sunrise-7PM. Main entrance at SW corner of Gibson Rd (off Lincoln Blvd)

At Baker Beach:
Baker Beach Bunkers These concrete bunkers were built to defend the Golden Gate Bridge from aerial attack during World War II. The guns have been removed, but the clear, functional shapes are still visible. ♦ Battery Chamberlain (next to Baker Beach)

6 China Beach Nuzzled into a cove is one of the few San Francisco beaches where swimming is permitted. Popular with locals, this small stretch of sand was named after the Chinese fishers who used to camp here. No dogs are allowed. There are public rest rooms and limited parking. ♦ Daily sunrise-7PM. At the end of Seacliff Ave (off El Camino del Mar)

7 Lands End The wonderful views from this promontory should be appreciated by the skilled hiker only. ♦ Park at Point Lobos Ave and Merrie Way and follow the marked trails, or go to the lot at El Camino del Mar and Point Lobos Ave adjacent to the *USS San Francisco Memorial* and follow the trail to Lands End

8 Coastal Trail On a sunny day, this trail, stretching from the Golden Gate Bridge to the **Cliff House,** is a must for bikers, joggers, and heavy-duty walkers. It's not the easiest trail to follow, with several splits, dead ends, and a detour through comedian Robin Williams's neighborhood in the China Beach area, but the tranquility and the spectacular scenery make it another of the many reasons for San Franciscans's love affair with their city. ♦ Starts at Fort Point and ends at Point Lobos

9 Point Lobos The beautiful westernmost tip of San Francisco was named by the Spanish after the sea lions, whom they called *lobos marinos* (sea wolves). ♦ Follow the trails from the parking lot at El Camino del Mar and Point Lobos Ave

10 Sutro Baths Opened in 1896 by Adolph Sutro, this three-acre spa resembled the baths of imperial Rome in scale and splendor. Six saltwater swimming pools heated to different temperatures sparkled beneath a colored glass roof. The building was destroyed in a spectacular fire in 1966. Today the remains look like classical ruins. An algae-covered puddle is all that is left of the baths, but the National Park Service is considering a laser-image reconstruction of the once majestic structure. ♦ Follow the trails from the parking lot at El Camino del Mar and Point Lobos Ave

11 Sutro Heights Park Its bluff-top site overlooking the **Cliff House** and ocean beyond makes this park an ideal spot for sunsets and

Restaurants/Clubs: Red
Shops/ ♠ Outdoors: Green
Hotels: Blue
Sights/Culture: Black

beach views. This was formerly the home and grounds of Adolph Sutro, a mining engineer, mayor, and one of the city's great benefactors. He bought much of the seafront property in the city and planted a forest of eucalyptus on Mount Sutro. The park has a haunting charm, with fragments of statuary lying half-hidden among the groves of fir, Monterey cypress, and Norfolk Island pine. Take a close look at the rock cliffs. Because of slides, the slope has been reinforced with concrete and finished to look just like the real rock. ♦ Point Lobos Ave (at 48th Ave)

12 Cliff House San Francisco families used to make day trips from the big city to sun at this resort spot, originally built in 1863. Later the house (pictured above) became associated with local powerbrokers, crime bosses, and their molls. When the schooner *Parallel,* loaded with dynamite, crashed on the rocks below, one whole wing of the building was lost in the explosion. Seven years later, on Christmas Day, the original building burned to the ground.

Adolph Sutro rebuilt it in 1895, and this one also burned within the year. Little remains of the fifth and last building on the site, which opened in 1909. Architecturally insensitive remodeling and repair work have obliterated the building's original character. It now houses the **Cliff House Restaurant,** a disappointing tourist lure ($$; 386.3330). Soon, though, the area may get a whole new look. The National Park Service is considering a $19.6-million renovation. If everything goes as planned, the existing structure will get a much-needed face-lift and a **Museum of Urban Amusements** will be built, along with a visitor's center and an elaborate stairway to the **Sutro Baths.** ♦ 1090 Point Lobos Ave (at the Great Hwy)

Within the Cliff House:

Musée Mécanique This large collection of antique mechanical amusement machines, a tawdry tribute to the days of the penny arcade, claims to be the world's largest collection of coin-operated automatic musical instruments. ♦ Free. Daily. 386.1170

Camera Obscura Children love this replica of Leonardo da Vinci's invention. The camera is trained on **Seal Rocks** and Ocean Beach and the image magnified on a giant parabolic screen. ♦ Nominal charge. Daily, weather permitting. 750.0415

13 Seal Rocks Four hundred feet offshore and below the **Cliff House,** the rocks swarm with sea lions and various seabirds. Watching them loll about is a favorite Sunday pastime for San Franciscans. ♦ Offshore from the Cliff House (off the Great Hwy)

14 Ocean Beach When San Franciscans say "the beach," they are referring to this one, which stretches the length of the Great Highway. The undertow is extremely dangerous, swimming is prohibited, and wading is inadvisable, but it's fun for sunning, strolling, and beach games. ♦ Anza St (at the Great Hwy, continuing south)

15 Lincoln Park Some 270 verdant acres on the Point Lobos Headlands provide striking views of the bay and Golden Gate Bridge. ♦ Main entrance Clement St (at 34th Ave)

Within Lincoln Park:

Lincoln Park Municipal Golf Course Tee off at this 18-hole public course that offers sweeping views of the Golden Gate Bridge. ♦ Daily, sunrise to sundown. 34th Ave (at Clement St). 221.9911

16 West Fort Miley's Gun Batteries This former military site is fun to explore. Picnic and barbecue facilities, drinking water, and rest rooms are available. ♦ Lincoln Park (next to the VA Hospital). Ranger station 556.8371

17 The California Palace of the Legion of Honor Built in 1916 by **George Applegarth**, this museum commands a broad view of the city and the bay from its hilltop site in the park. Applegarth's building, based on the Palais de la Légion d'Honneur in Paris, was given to the city in 1924 by Mr. and Mrs. Adolph Spreckels in memory of California's dead in World War I. The museum features paintings, sculpture, and decorative arts presented in a chronological sequence, illustrating the development of European art from the medieval period through the beginning of the 20th century. At press time, the museum was closed for renovation and seismic upgrading; call ahead for reopening date. ♦ Lincoln Park (off Legion of Honor Dr). 750.3600

18 El Mansour ★★$$ The big attraction here is the belly dancer who flutters and spins each night around 8PM, but the good Moroccan food shouldn't be overlooked. The fixed-price meal includes lentil soup, salad, and entrées of lamb, seafood, chicken, or rabbit. This is finger food at its best. ♦ Moroccan ♦ Daily dinner. 3123 Clement St (at 34th Ave). 751.2312

18 Tsing Tao ★★$$ This plain Chinese restaurant is distinguished by good food at remarkably low prices. The chili-pepper prawns are a favorite. Consider also the braised chicken legs, the hot-and-sour soup, and the shredded pork with garlic and eggplant in Szechuan sauce. The waiters are as helpful as can be, so don't hesitate to question them about dishes that sound good. ♦ Mandarin/Szechuan ♦ Daily lunch and dinner. 3107 Clement St (at 34th Ave). 387.2344

19 Greco-Romana ★$ If you can deal with the poor service, this informal restaurant is worth a visit for the good pizzas and fresh salads. ♦ Greek/Italian ♦ Daily lunch and dinner. 2448 Clement St (at 25th Ave). 387.0626

19 The Courtyard ★$$ This yuppified restaurant, with a brick-tile floor, blue-cushioned basket-weave chairs, and comfortable, upscale appeal, looks like a place that belongs in Marin County rather than in the Richmond district. It's particularly pleasant for brunch, and there is an agreeable bar for sociable drinkers. ♦ California ♦ M-Sa lunch and dinner; Su brunch, lunch, and dinner. 2436 Clement St (at 25th Ave). 387.7616

20 Shimo ★★$$ Chef Shimo-san expertly carves fish and seafood that is so fresh, it's nearly alive. Start your lunch or dinner off with the *ama ebi* (raw prawns), *saba* (mackerel), or *mirugai* (briny clams). The tempura treats have the lightest touch of sesame oil. This authentic sushi bar has a small tatami room in back. ♦ Japanese ♦ Tu-Su dinner. 2339 Clement St (at 24th Ave). 752.4422

20 Bill's Place ★$ One of the most popular hamburger joints in the neighborhood also makes old-fashioned milk shakes—a far cry from what's offered by fast-food chains. Eat on the back patio in good weather. ♦ American ♦ Daily lunch and dinner. 2315 Clement St (at 24th Ave). 221.5262

20 Silver Moon ★★$$ The chef at this Chinese vegetarian and seafood restaurant is a master of culinary illusion. Here you can order "shrimp" and "poultry" that look and taste like the real animal, but aren't. Also worth the indulgence are the "true" seafood pot stickers, scallops à la Hunan, and Szechuan eggplant. ♦ Chinese ♦ Daily lunch and dinner. 2301 Clement St (at 24th Ave). 386.7852

In 1987, the fireworks for the Golden Gate Bridge's 50th-birthday celebration cost nearly $500,000.

21 Family Sauna Shop Treat yourself to a dry-heat, Finnish-style sauna, whirlpool hydro-therapy, therapeutic massage, or herbal facial at this clean, well-run, legitimate place. It's a far cry from luxurious, but they do a fine job. ♦ Daily. 2308 Clement St (at 24th Ave). 221.2208

22 San Wang ★★$$ To add just a bit of confusion to the culinary landscape, this place also uses the name **San Wong.** But whatever you call it, the food is terrific, particularly the chewy, hand-pulled noodles. Also delicious are the San Wang clams and the dry-fried shrimp. ♦ Mandarin/Szechuan ♦ Daily lunch and dinner. 2239 Clement St (between 23rd and 24th Aves). 221.1870. Also at: 1682 Post St (at Laguna St). 921.1453

22 Narai ★★$$ This is one of the few places in San Francisco to offer Chou Chow cooking, a Cantonese offshoot that makes use of chili peppers, duck, goose, and citrus fruit. As the owners are Thai (but of Chou Chow extraction), the menu also includes Thai food. One of Clement Street's best Asian restaurants, it makes a noble, though not altogether successful, stab at looking more attractive than many with its bamboo-patterned gold wallpaper. Among the many outstanding dishes are deep-fried crab rolls, silver noodles with minced pork, and deep-fried quail. ♦ Chou Chow/Thai ♦ Tu-Su lunch and dinner. 2229 Clement St (between 23rd and 24th Aves). 751.6363

22 Mescolanza ★★$$ Decorated in an understated way with blue-gray walls and blue-and-white tablecloths, this always-packed place attracts a loyal and enthusiastic clientele who come for the excellent pizza and pasta dishes. ♦ Italian ♦ Daily dinner. Reservations recommended. 2221 Clement St (between 23rd and 24th Aves). 668.2221

22 Kum Moon ★$$ This spartan restaurant is always jammed. Lemon chicken, sweet-and-sour spareribs, and rainbow chicken (fried, with vegetables on top) are the house specialties. Daily specials are also offered. ♦ Cantonese ♦ Daily lunch and dinner. 2109 Clement St (between 22nd and 23rd Aves). 221.5656

23 Yet Wah ★$$ There's a more comfortable, Western-style atmosphere here than can be found in most Chinese restaurants along Clement Street, though the food has received mixed reviews of late. This is part of a family-owned empire that includes seven other branches around the Bay Area. ♦ Mandarin ♦ Daily lunch and dinner. 2140 Clement St (at 23rd Ave). 387.8040. Also at: Pier 39 (The Embarcadero, at Grant Ave). 434.4430; 5238 Diamond Heights Blvd (at Gold Mine Dr). 282.0788

Alejandro's

24 Alejandro's Sociedad Gastronomica ★★$$ An absolute madhouse, this dining spot serves huge portions of Spanish/ Mexican/Peruvian food in a pan-Latino setting. The paella is loaded with shellfish, sausage, chicken, pork, fresh vegetables, and saffron-coated rice. Try the rabbit, the boned trout, and the tapas, which are done to perfection. And don't miss the *conchitas parmesanas* (scallions with butter, wine, grated cheese, eggs, and jalapeños). There's also a whole menu page of Mexican entrées that are as good as the best in the Mission district. Be prepared to wait, even with a reservation. ♦ Spanish/Mexican/Peruvian ♦ Daily dinner. Reservations recommended. 1840 Clement St (at 20th Ave). 668.1184

25 Laghi ★★$$ This small storefront restaurant, named for chef/owner Gino Laghi, who once presided over **Modesto Lanzone**'s kitchen, features made-from-scratch food on a menu that changes daily. Offerings might include such dishes as braised radicchio, *cappallacci alla crema di parmagiano* (meat-filled dumplings in parmesan cream sauce), or braised quail, served in a setting heavy on knotty pine. ♦ Italian ♦ Tu-Su dinner. Reservations recommended. 1801 Clement St (at 20th Ave). 386.6266

26 Abbe's Very gently used clothing from the closets of the city's gentlewomen is this shop's stock in trade. It's a real designers' graveyard for those who want to resurrect high fashion on a budget. ♦ Tu-Sa. 1420 Clement St (at 15th Ave). 751.4567

27 Abbe's A continuation of the store across the street, this one also offers impressive labels on women's second-time-around clothing, cleared from some of the fanciest closets in town. ♦ Tu-Sa. 1431 Clement St (at 15th Ave). 751.0202

28 Red Crane ★★$$ The Szechuan clams and prawns in lobster sauce are particularly impressive at this seafood/vegetarian restaurant. Meatless dishes such as almond-pressed "duck" made from bean curd and "chicken" curry made from gluten are also winners. These dishes could fool the eye and the palate of the most die-hard carnivore. ♦ Chinese ♦ Daily lunch and dinner. 1115 Clement St (at 12th Ave). 751.7226

29 Royal Thai ★★★$$ This restaurant is renowned for such dishes as roast duck sautéed with spinach, ginger, and black-bean sauce, and a spicy squid salad. The ingredients are fresh and the service is friendly. ♦ Thai ♦ M-F lunch and dinner; Sa-Su dinner. Reservations recommended. 951 Clement St (at 11th Ave). 386.1795

29 King of China ★$ Although this huge second-floor restaurant usually looks as if it could use a thorough cleaning, it draws a crowd hungry for the wide selection of dim-sum delicacies, including quail egg *sui mai* and shrimp *har gow,* and rice noodles stuffed with peanuts, pork, and black mushrooms. Some of the better dinners are exquisitely prepared rockfish with ginger, coriander, and scallions, and spinach sautéed with ginger. ♦ Cantonese ♦ Daily lunch and dinner. 939 Clement St (at 11th Ave). 668.2618

30 Ocean ★★$$ This Cantonese restaurant specializes in seafood; the salt-and-pepper prawns and other fish dishes are remarkable, and are never served in the cornstarched sauces that characterize bad Cantonese cooking. There are two negatives: The wait can be long at peak hours and the service is rude. ♦ Cantonese ♦ Daily lunch and dinner. 726 Clement St (at Ninth Ave). 221.3351

30 Clement Street Bar and Grill ★★$$ The kitchen specializes in creative pastas, grilled meats, and fowl, all at reasonable prices. The dark wood paneling, plants, and linen tablecloths contribute to the pleasant, relaxed ambience. ♦ American ♦ Tu-F lunch and dinner; Sa-Su brunch and dinner. Reservations recommended. 700 Clement St (at Ninth Ave). 386.2200

31 Cafe Maisonnette ★★$$ Sophisticated food with a nouvelle accent is served at this intimate (just nine tables), side-street French restaurant. Prices and the quality of the fare are slightly more upscale than what is generally found in this neighborhood. The small menu, which seldom reaches beyond its grasp, might offer such choices as ravioli stuffed with spinach, goat cheese, and walnuts, or sautéed pork loin with apples and calvados. ♦ French ♦ Tu-Su dinner. Reservations recommended. 315 Eighth Ave (at Clement St). 387.7992

32 Haig's Delicacies In addition to coffees and teas, this long-established specialty shop carries a marvelous collection of olives, Middle Eastern baked goods, and other pantry foods from India, Europe, and the Middle East. ♦ M-Sa. 642 Clement St (at Eighth Ave). 752.6283

33 Green Apple Books One of the Richmond district's largest bookstores, this place has more than 50,000 used and new volumes on hand. Weekend insomniacs can always find a good read to pass the time. ♦ Daily; F-Sa until midnight. 506 Clement St (at Sixth Ave). 387.2272

34 Taiwan Restaurant ★★$ This airy, contemporary Deco restaurant serves Taiwanese food, not often seen in San Francisco. Taiwanese cuisine rejects the fire of Hunan and Szechuan in favor of subtle sweet/salty and garlicky flavors. Not to be missed are the spareribs and the Taiwan Country Favorite Chicken. ♦ Taiwanese ♦ Daily lunch and dinner. Reservations recommended. 445 Clement St (at Sixth Ave). 387.1789

35 Last Day Saloon Extremely popular with the post-college crowd, this bawdy but friendly bar books a variety of dance bands—from reggae to rock—Wednesday through Sunday. The bottom floor has pool tables and dart boards, while the top floor is for dancing. ♦ Cover. Daily until 2AM. 406 Clement St (at Fifth Ave). 387.6343

36 Toy Boat ★$ In addition to selling windup toys, this delightful little cafe makes delicious coffees, Italian sodas, and desserts. This is a perfect place to go for Double Rainbow ice cream after music at the **Last Day Saloon.** ♦ Cafe ♦ Daily breakfast, lunch, and dinner. 401 Clement St (at Fifth Ave). 751.7505

37 Golden Turtle ★★★$$ The proliferation of Vietnamese restaurants in the Bay Area has resulted in a real winner here (the name comes from the English translation of the name of the owner/chef, Kim Quy Tran). The food in this small, family-run dining spot looks as good as it tastes. Two Vietnamese staples—crispy imperial rolls and a juicy, aromatic five-spice chicken—are outstanding here, but also try some of the more unusual dishes, like sour fish soup. ♦ Vietnamese ♦ Daily lunch and dinner. 308 Fifth Ave (at Clement St). 221.5285. Also at: 2211 Van Ness Ave (between Broadway and Vallejo St). 441.4419

38 Mai's ★★$$ There are things on the menu here not to be missed by any Asian-food gourmet. The *la lot* beef (exotically seasoned charcoal-grilled ground beef wrapped in a leaf resembling that of a grape) is spectacular. Also try the imperial rolls and the chicken salad. ♦ Vietnamese ♦ Daily lunch and dinner. Reservations recommended. 316 Clement St (between Third and Fourth Aves). 221.3046

38 Blue Danube This popular 1960s-style coffeehouse usually plays classical music. When the weather is sunny, a wall of glass doors overlooking Clement Street is opened wide. ♦ Coffeehouse ♦ Daily. 306 Clement St (between Third and Fourth Aves). 221.9041

39 Kasra ★$ The menu is limited, but the selections are all quite tasty. Try the sautéed eggplant for starters and progress to the sensational kabobs. You can wash it all down with *doogh* (a yogurt seltzer). ♦ Persian ♦ Daily dinner; F-Su lunch. Reservations recommended. 349 Clement St (at Fourth Ave). 752.1101

40 Plough & Stars A real Irish bar with live Irish music every night, it's at its wildest, of course, on St. Patrick's Day. ♦ Daily until 2AM. 116 Clement St (at Third Ave). 751.1122

41 Eats ★$ This decidedly rustic-looking diner serves trenchermen's portions and does something wonderful for brunch called an omelette cake—fashioned of layers of egg, cheese, mushrooms, onions, spinach, tomatoes, and sour cream. ♦ American ♦ Daily breakfast and lunch. 50 Clement St (at Arguello Blvd). 752.8837

41 Satin Moon This shop provides a wide selection of designer fabrics for those who know how to sew a fine seam. ♦ Tu-Sa. 32 Clement St (at Arguello Blvd). 668.1623

42 Mandalay ★$$ The city's first Burmese restaurant is best suited to the gastronomically curious. Green-tea salad and *satay* dishes are among the interesting menu choices. ♦ Burmese ♦ Daily lunch and dinner. 4448 California St (at Seventh Ave). 386.3895

43 Pat O'Shea's Mad Hatter ★★$$ As well as being a friendly neighborhood sports bar, this place boasts a fine kitchen, which produces delicious and unusual specials at low prices. (Don't mind the awning that reads, "We cheat tourists and drunks.") After lunch, pub grub, such as nachos, burgers, and chicken wings, keeps the crowd happy as they watch televised games. ♦ American ♦ Daily lunch. Reservations required for large parties. 3848 Geary Blvd (at Third Ave). 752.3148

44 Cafe Riggio ★$$ Redolent of garlic, this popular trattoria uses local California products and emphasizes fresh ingredients. Appetizers and seafood entrées are best here. ♦ Italian ♦ M-Sa dinner. 4112 Geary Blvd (between Fifth and Sixth Aves). 221.2114

45 Kabuto ★★$ Although a bit dingy, this Richmond-district restaurant has garnered a great reputation for sushi. ♦ Japanese ♦ Daily dinner. 5116 Geary Blvd (at Sixth Ave). 752.5652

SHENSON'S

45 Shenson's Delicatessen ★★$ This kosher deli is as close as San Francisco gets to replicating a New York City deli experience. It serves homey salads, cold cuts, and soups. The smoked whitefish is to die for, as is the rich, flavorful borscht. Food can be eaten on the premises or taken home. ♦ Deli ♦ M-Sa. 5120 Geary Blvd (at Sixth Ave). 751.4699

46 Mike's Chinese Cuisine ★★$$ A favorite Cantonese restaurant, this place is known for its steamed fish and excellent egg rolls. It also crosses into a few other provinces and does a commendable Peking duck and Mongolian beef. ♦ Cantonese ♦ M, W-Su dinner. 5145 Geary Blvd (at Sixth Ave). 752.0120

47 Hong Kong Flower Lounge ★★★$$ This San Francisco branch of a well-patronized restaurant operation (also in Hong Kong and suburban Millbrae, California) was a hit the moment the doors opened. The noise level of the 180-seat dining room is intimidating, but the Cantonese dishes draw the crowds. Lobster, fish, and crab tanks are testimony to the freshness of the seafood. The roast chicken is outstanding, as is the lunchtime selection of dim-sum delicacies. ♦ Cantonese ♦ Daily lunch and dinner. Reservations recommended. 5322 Geary Blvd (between 17th and 18th Aves). 668.8998

48 Russian Renaissance ★$$$ Icons and live Russian music are featured at this dark, atmospheric restaurant. Though the food is good, the real attraction here is the ambience, which brings images of czarist Russia to mind. ♦ Russian ♦ Daily dinner. 5241 Geary Blvd (at 17th Ave). 752.8558

48 Joe's Here's where you'll find the best ice cream out on the avenues, particularly the Its—Joe's version of the famous Its It (vanilla ice cream sandwiched between two oatmeal cookies and dipped in chocolate). ♦ Ice Cream ♦ Daily. 5351 Geary Blvd (between 17th and 18th Aves). 751.1950

49 Ton Kiang ★★$$ Along with the new, improved decor is a new, improved Asian menu specializing in dim sum. The high-quality cuisine comes prepared with a variety of Chinese cooking techniques, including roasted, stir-fried, deep-fried, steamed, and barbecued—all in one presentation. Constantly busy, this is an ideal place for those who like to have a taste of everything and still fit through their front door. ♦ Hakka/Cantonese ♦ Daily lunch and dinner. 5827 Geary Blvd (at 22nd Ave). 387.8273. Also at: 3148 Geary Blvd (at Spruce St). 752.4440

50 Khan Toke Thai House ★★★$$ This is one of the best, longest established, and most elegant of San Francisco's growing crop of Thai restaurants. Even though some of the dishes are very spicy, there's always a memorable contrast of textures and flavors; you can taste far more than the chili peppers. The pork balls and squid are superb as appetizers. So are the stews with curry and coconut milk, the noodles, and the fish. You may sit on the floor at low tables if you want. ♦ Thai ♦ Daily dinner. 5937 Geary Blvd (at 24th Ave). 668.6654

Bests

Joshua Cohn
Architect

San Francisco is full of contrasts: The second-densest city in the United States, it is surrounded by water, and a bridge away from the bucolic splendor of the Marin Headlands. Yet it is a small city. Only seven miles square, it is compact and urban, filled with distinct neighborhoods.

Walking is essential to begin to appreciate the beauty of the city. The walk to **Aquatic Park** along Larkin Street is fantastic. Pause at Francisco Street for the spectacular view of **Alcatraz, Angel Island,** and the **Golden Gate Bridge** before descending the stairs to **Ghirardelli Square.** Either browse in the shops, have a coffee overlooking the bay, or continue to the beach at **Aquatic Park.** Stroll along the promenade, take a peek into the **National Maritime Museum** (a Streamline Moderne building with nautical overtones, it is filled with exquisite ship models, murals, and mosaics, a fine work of architecture). Continue walking out onto the spiral pier to have a wonderful on-the-water view of the **Golden Gate,** as well as a diorama-like view of the city behind you (sunset is best; the bridge glows and the city sparkles in the darkness behind you).

Have a hot dog with sauerkraut and a draft Anchor Steam beer at the bar (quite reasonable) of **Stars** restaurant before an evening out at the opera or symphony.

Walk or ride a bicycle across the **Golden Gate Bridge.** The bay is constantly in flux; tankers, aircraft carriers, and an occasional submarine glide below you (if you are lucky, you may find the fog hovering at the walkway level—the bridge seems to be floating on clouds).

The view of the entire bay area is best from **Coit Tower,** but resist driving: You may be stuck in your car waiting for your turn to glimpse the view. Instead, walk up the **Filbert Steps** off Sansome Street. Here you leave the noise of the city and stroll through pastoral gardens ascending wooden stairs and walks to **Coit Tower.**

Day Trips

Beyond San Francisco's immediate boundaries are the thriving, vital cities of the **East Bay**, where the weather is often warmer and sunnier than in fog-covered San Francisco. **Berkeley**, across the **Bay Bridge**, is home to the state's prestigious branch of the **University of California**. Oftentimes derisively called "Berserkley" by nonresidents and residents alike, it is a city with a political matrix that's frequently radical and either totally out of sync with the rest of the nation or on the cutting edge of political change. Also across the Bay Bridge is **Oakland**, a metropolis locked in a struggle to combat drugs and poverty—not to mention overcoming the ravages of 1991's devastating fire in the hills—and working hard to enlarge its position as a strong commercial and convention center.

In contrast, on the northern side of the **Golden Gate Bridge** are the softly undulating hills of mellow **Marin County**. Cross the bridge, and the first town you'll reach is **Sausalito**, a little gem of a place frequently compared to the hill towns on the Riviera. Once a fishing village, Sausalito is now an upscale community of suburbanites who enjoy their pretty hillside homes, abundant greenery, and quaint village atmosphere.

The prosperous **Peninsula** area to the south of San Francisco is home to **Stanford University**, one of California's finest private institutions of learning, and **Silicon Valley**, the center of the nation's computer industry. It is also home to many Bay Area millionaires, who have settled in such posh communities as **Hillsborough, Los Altos, Woodside**, and **Portola Valley**. One of the most magnificent mansions in the area, **Filoli**, with its superb gardens, is now a landmark open to the public.

About two and a half hours south of the city lies the magnificent **Monterey Peninsula**, home of the popular **Monterey Bay Aquarium**, the charming seaside village of **Carmel** (where Clint Eastwood was mayor not too long ago), and some of the most stunning coastal scenery in the world.

Finally, if you're a wine connoisseur, no trip to the Bay Area would be complete without a visit to **Napa/Sonoma Wine Country**. In addition to possessing some of the world's finest vineyards, the Napa and Sonoma areas are home to lovely inns, marvelous massage centers, idyllic scenery, and enough good restaurants to make a gourmet's heart go pitter-patter. For a complete guide to this beautiful region, consult *Northern California Wine Country Access,* also from ACCESS Press.

Area code 415 unless otherwise indicated.

Marin County

Blessed with a sense of whimsy and an affluent, educated, and creative populace, Sausalito doesn't march in lockstep with most suburban communities. In the 1970s the town's mayor was Sally Stanford, who had retired to the bayside community after years of running San Francisco's premier bordellos, lending new meaning to the term "Madam Mayor." Stanford died in 1982, but you can still see her influence at the **Chart House** restaurant (201 Bridgeway Blvd, at the corner of Second and Main Sts, 332.0804), which stands at the site of her old **Valhalla** restaurant and retains many of her decorating touches.

To really savor the day, take a ferry ride to Sausalito, starting at San Francisco's **Ferry Building** (located at the foot of Market St and The Embarcadero) or at Fisherman's Wharf (for scheduling information, call 332.6600). You can also get there in a half-hour via

Golden Gate Transit buses (332.6600) or by automobile across the Golden Gate Bridge. If you decide to drive, be aware that parking in Sausalito is usually difficult and the city's traffic cops are uncannily vigilant. Parking is likely to be easiest on the hilly streets.

When you've debarked from the ferry in Sausalito, walk left along the shoreline (called **Bridgeway Boulevard**), and drink in the bay views and glorious vistas of San Francisco. Right by the ferry pier, which is in the heart of downtown Sausalito, you'll see the small **Viña de Mar Park,** named for Sausalito's sister city in Chile. The park delights the eye with statues of elephants and a fountain that came from the Panama-Pacific Exposition of 1915. You may take a photo in front of the park, but you may not walk in. (It's been closed to the public for many years because it drew drug addicts and other unsavory characters.) Bridgeway Boulevard is still called **Old Town,** reflecting its status as a historic district where the first Portuguese fishers settled in the late 18th and early 19th centuries. Walk past **Scoma's** (588 Bridgeway Blvd, 332.9551), a popular seafood restaurant with a branch in San Francisco, and **Horizons,** right next door (331.3232), one of the best places in town to enjoy a drink on the deck. Stop if you're ravenous, but be forewarned that the view is often more satisfying than the meal. **Horizons** serves brunch all day, and it's one of their best efforts. Just beyond the waterside restaurants, look out onto the bay and see if the seal sculpture by Bay Area artist Benny Bufano is visible (it pops out at low tide). Walk back along the side of the street with all the shops, some of them charming, some just selling touristy whatnots and junk. Take a short detour to explore the shops along **Princess Street.** If you feel energetic, keep on walking—Princess leads to the back streets, which are lined with lovely homes. If you get lost, just keep walking downhill and you'll eventually be back on Bridgeway, where you should pop in at **Laurel Burch's Gallerié** at No. 539 (332.7764). The gallery, once a firehouse, is filled with Burch's work. (She's a local artist who is nationally known for her bright-colored jewelry and other accessories.)

You might want to stop at the convivial **Bar with No Name,** more popularly known as the No-Name, for the obvious reason; no sign identifies the place (757 Bridgeway Blvd, 332.1392). Sometimes there's live jazz, and invariably there's a local clientele swapping conversation around communal tables.

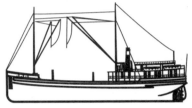

If you're feeling flush, have breakfast, lunch, or dinner at the **Casa Madrona** (801 Bridgeway Blvd, 331.5888), a delightful little hotel that meanders up the hillside and has a terrace for alfresco dining. The food is California/French.

Continue walking along Bridgeway Boulevard or hop aboard one of the buses that frequently makes its way along the street, checking first to see if it stops at **The Bay Model** (Marinship Way, off the east side of Bridgeway Blvd, 332.3871). Be sure to have plenty of change in your pocket—the buses require exact fare.

The Bay Model is a working model of the whole San Francisco Bay and the Delta region. It features interactive exhibits, self-guided tours, and a permanent exhibit of the World War II shipyard, "Marinship." It is open Tuesday through Sunday from Memorial Day to Labor Day; the rest of the year it's open Tuesday through Saturday. Arrangements for tours may be made for groups of 10 or more by calling in advance. Admission is free.

Docked near the **Bay Model** is the *Wapama* (pictured above), a steam-powered 1915 schooner that once hauled lumber and passengers. *Wapama* tours take place Saturday at 11AM; on Saturday at 12:30PM there's also a tour of the *Hercules,* a venerable old steam tub (free admission; children under 12 years of age are not permitted on the vessel tours).

Farther north along Bridgeway Boulevard is a community of floating homes (Sausalito doesn't like to call them houseboats). Turn onto Gate 6 Road. (If you end up on the freeway, you've gone too far.) The greatest concentration of homes can be seen at Gates 5, 6, and 6½. Some are spacious, some are funky, some are exquisite little waterborne jewels. One even has a helipad (you'll find it on **Issaquah Dock,** at the very end). Issaquah Dock, at Gate 6, also has more serious gardeners than any of the other piers. Arguments continue to rage between those charged with protecting the bay and the "anchor-outs," those who live freely anchored out in the water on what in some cases appear to be floating junkyards. (Anchor-outs prefer to drop anchor in the bay rather than tie their boats to the docks.) Those who anchor out are generally a breed apart from those who tie their homes up at piers and pay to have their waste pumped. For years, city leaders have tried to roust the bohemian anchor-outs, and for years, the rebellious anchor-outs have successfully blocked those moves.

Complete information on the Napa and Sonoma Valleys, including shops, hotels, restaurants, and an extensive description of wineries, can be found in the ACCESS Press guidebook Northern California Wine Country Access. To order a copy, call 800/331.3761, fill out the order form at the end of this book, or try your local bookstore.

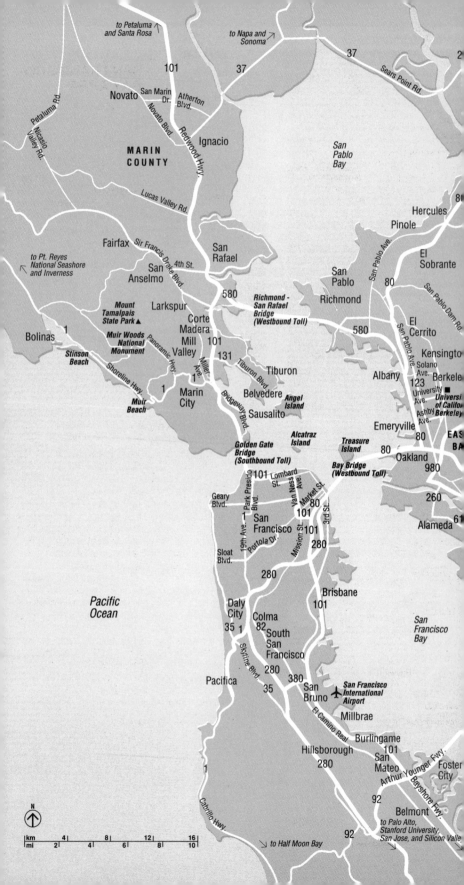

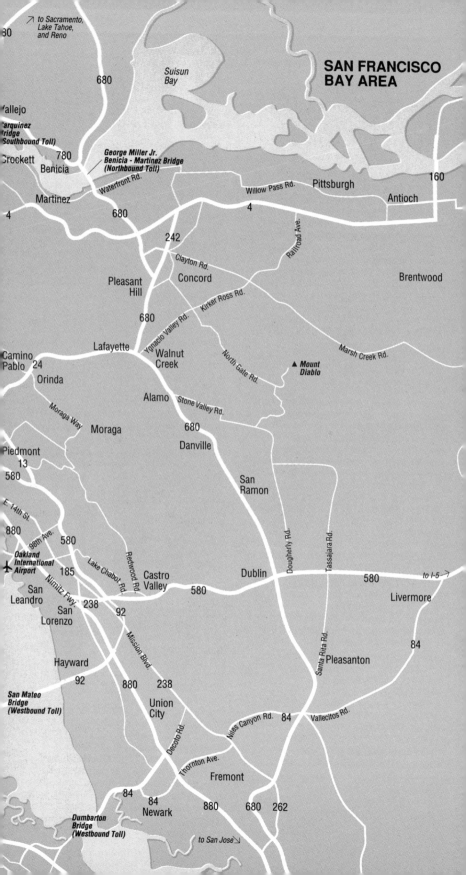

Muir Woods, Mount Tamalpais, and Point Reyes

Muir Woods, on Shoreline Drive in **Mill Valley,** is a national monument located in the middle of **Mount Tamalpais State Park.** Both are open daily until sunset (Park Ranger Station, Pan-Toll, is at 801 Panoramic Hwy, Mill Valley; Muir Woods information 388.2595, Mount Tamalpais and ranger station 388.2070). Within the approximately 559 acres of redwoods are many trails, some paved and wheelchair-accessible. Those who can stay for only a short time can see many of the highlights in one to two hours. Within **Muir Woods** are some of the tallest and oldest coast redwood trees in the state, and a stand of virgin redwoods. The oldest tree has been around for 1,100 years; the tallest is 257 feet high. This tranquil wonderland of proud, giant trees also includes **Redwood Creek,** where steelhead and salmon come to spawn and then die (there's no fishing). A **Visitors' Center,** built in the rustic 1930s style of cedar and stone, was deliberately designed to look inconspicuous. It's located at the park's main entrance, and includes a snack bar and gift shop.

Hardy types can hike from **Muir Woods** to the surrounding **Mount Tamalpais State Park.** "Mount Tam," as it's popularly known, rises majestically 2,221 feet above sea level. The park includes a variety of terrain, and is renowned for its sensational panoramic views on clear days and its abundance of colorful wildflowers during the springtime. There are many trails, suitable for hikers of all levels. The park is home to a variety of wildlife: herds of deer, many types of birds, some snakes (including the seldom-encountered rattlers), and the rarely seen bobcats and mountain lions. There is no public transportation going into the woods or park, but among the companies that offer private tours to the redwoods are **A Day in Nature** (673.0548) and **Great Pacific** (626.4499). If you are driving from San Francisco, take Highway 101 north across the Golden Gate Bridge and turn off at the Stinson Beach–Highway 1 exit. Follow the signs to the area's parking lots.

If hiking Mount Tam doesn't do you in, you might want to tackle some of the scenic trails a little farther north at the **Point Reyes National Seashore.** There's backcountry camping, stables, a lighthouse on a spit of land that affords great whale watching in season (approximately January through April), and miles and miles of stunning unspoiled seashore.

If all this touring has given you an appetite, Marin boasts at least two outstanding restaurants: **The Lark Creek Inn** (234 Magnolia Ave, Larkspur, 924.7766), where owner/chef Bradley Ogden turns out magnificent American regional cuisine in a sublime country setting; and the informal, exuberant **Buckeye Roadhouse** (15 Shoreline Hwy, near Hwys 101 and 1, Mill Valley, 331.2600), run by the same team that owns the very popular **Fog City Diner** in San Francisco and **Mustards Grill** in Yountville.

Downtown traffic in Oakland was so congested in 1890 that horse-drawn vehicles were restricted to a five-mile-per-hour speed limit.

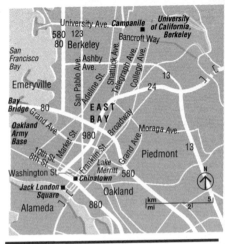

University of California, Berkeley

Across the Bay Bridge in the bustling East Bay lies Berkeley, which manages to combine an East Coast intellectual energy with a Californian New Age consciousness. A city of ideas, both worthy and wacky, Berkeley rates a visit because of its outstanding university, restaurants, and cultural programs, as well as its quirky lifestyle. This is also the site of some of the Bay Area's best bookstores, including **Cody's** (2454 Telegraph Ave, at Haste St, 510/845.7852) and **Black Oak Books** (1491 Shattuck Ave, at Vine St, 510/486.0698).

The easiest way to reach Berkeley from San Francisco is by **BART** (788.2278), a half-hour ride from downtown. Get off at the **Berkeley** station and walk east for three blocks on Bancroft Way to reach the southern end of the campus. The **Visitor Information Center** is located in University Hall, Room 101, at University Avenue and Oxford Street. Free student-led campus tours, lasting approximately one and three-quarters hours, include the interior of the main library, a typical classroom, the interiors of most of the sports facilities, the exterior of the **University Art Museum,** and a typical 500-seat lecture hall. The tours are on Monday, Wednesday, and Friday at 10AM and 1PM, and occasionally on Saturdays (510/642.5215). Reservations are not necessary, but it's a good idea to confirm scheduled tours, as the campus closes between semesters and on holidays. There is a modest charge for the ride to the top of the Campanile (pictured on page 176), the campus tower that provides an aerial view of the Bay Area. To fully appreciate the intellectual energy that swirls around this campus, visit when classes are in session.

After the tour, go on to explore some of the campus offerings in greater depth. The **University Art Museum,** just off campus in a 1970 building designed by **Mario Ciampi,** has a good collection emphasizing 20th-century painting and sculpture. The museum is open Wednesday through Sunday; admission, free on Thursday 11AM-noon (2626 Bancroft Way, 510/642.0808). Within the museum you'll find the Pacific Film Archive, a large movie library, and the **George Gund Theater,** which schedules a wide range of international films during the week (510/642.1124).

The university's **Phoebe Hearst Museum of Anthropology** is in **Kroeber Hall** (Bancroft Way and College Ave, 510/643.7648). Named after its principal benefactor, the museum focuses on cultural anthropology. A gift store sells ornaments, books, and ethnic arts and crafts. The museum also offers services to the public, including free specimen identification and, for a charge, fumigation of artifacts. It is open daily; nominal admission.

The **Lawrence Hall of Science** (Centennial Dr, near Grizzly Peak Blvd, 510/642.5132) is a memorial to Ernest O. Lawrence, the first University of California professor to win a Nobel Prize (he won for physics in 1939). A favorite destination for visitors, the hall contains an interactive science museum, traveling science exhibitions, and a planetarium. Opened in 1968, it was designed by the San Francisco firm **Anshen and Allen** in an octagonal shape to represent the eight branches of physical science: biology, astronomy, geology, physics, chemistry, nuclear science, mathematics, and space science. Two levels of the building offer splendid views. If you have time, there's a 50-minute show in the planetarium. (Children under six are not admitted.) The hall is open daily; nominal admission. The planetarium's shows are on Saturday and Sunday at 1PM, 2:15PM, and 3:30PM; additional nominal admission.

The University of California's **Botanical Garden** is located in **Strawberry Canyon,** just above the stadium (510/642.3343). There are wonderful views of the bay from this site. Free tours take place Saturday and Sunday at 1:30PM and last about an hour. The garden is arranged according to the plants' geographical origins, and includes a redwood grove, a large native-plants section, South African plants, Asian plants, and economic plants (those used for food, fiber, and medicine). Another area is dedicated to plants that eat insects, a desert and rain-forest house filled with orchids, cacti, and succulents, and a garden of rosebushes. There's a nice lawn for sun worshiping and tables for picnicking.

Just outside the university campus, on ever-popular **Telegraph Avenue,** the street scene is alive with street musicians, small shops, and food, jewelry, and clothing vendors (you can *still* buy top-quality tie-dyed T-shirts, pants, and undergarments here).

Seven blocks north of the campus is **Chez Panisse** (1517 Shattuck Ave, 510/548.5525), generally regarded as the birthplace of California cuisine and the training ground for many famous Bay Area chefs. Although some critics sniff that her place isn't what it used to be, celebrity owner/chef Alice Waters is determined to maintain her high standards and keep her menus fresh and original. Even if you don't care to splurge for the expensive prix-fixe meals downstairs, be sure to try the lighter meals—which include inventive pizzas and calzones—upstairs at the **Chez Panisse Cafe.** A few miles away is **Cafe Fanny** (Cedar and San Pablo Sts, 510/524.5447), another Alice Waters venture (it's named after her daughter), which offers breakfast only.

Oakland

Even though Gertrude Stein scathingly said of her hometown that "there is no there there," in fact, there is quite a bit here to see and enjoy. Oakland has a thriving port (it has taken substantial business away from the port of San Francisco), wonderful historic buildings, a restored **Old Town,** and charming residential neighborhoods.

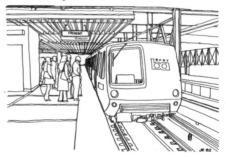

The easiest way to get to Oakland is by **BART** (illustrated above). The ride is a mere 12 minutes from San Francisco's **Powell Street** station to the city center, where you'll get off at **12th Street and Broadway.** The restored Old Oakland area is on the right of Broadway, and Oakland's **Chinatown** (still unspoiled by tourism) sits on the left. Chinatown is dotted with restaurants, herbalists, and shops catering to the needs of daily life. In addition to the Chinese, the neighborhood is home to many other Asian immigrants, including Filipinos, Japanese, Koreans, Vietnamese, Burmese, and Cambodians. The **Kum Hay Teahouse** (Eighth and Franklin Sts, 510/834.4478) looks as if it's been transplanted right from the streets of Asia.

Old Oakland, bounded by Washington Street and Broadway, Eighth, and 10th Streets, is a historic Victorian neighborhood of structures dating from 1868 to 1881. The buildings have been restored and developed by architects **Storek & Storek** as a retail and office complex. The **Pro Arts Gallery** (461 Ninth St, 510/763.4361) features the work of Bay Area artists, and mounts eight exhibitions plus two major art events annually, including the famous Open Studios in June.

If you're thirsty, head for the **Pacific Coast Brewing Co.** (906 Washington St, between Ninth and 10th Sts, 510/836.2739). The brewmasters will draw one of the specialty brews or any of the 19 other beers in stock while you relax, possibly over some pub grub or a game of darts. Another tempting possibility is the long-established **Gulf Coast Oyster Bar and Restaurant** (Eighth and Washington Sts, 510/836.3663), where you'll enjoy some of the tastiest Cajun meals to be found outside of Louisiana. If you like exotic foods, try **Fana Restaurant** (464 Eighth St, 510/271.0696), where authentic Ethiopian food is served family style or as entrées. The food is tasty and spicy, and all dishes are served with homemade *injera* bread for sopping up the flavors.

On Oakland's waterfront is **Jack London Square**, a rather contrived but pleasant waterfront development, and, nearby, the **Jack London Village**, another touristy oasis, featuring several shops and a Jack London museum. Between the village and the square is Jack London's transplanted sod-roofed log cabin, where he once passed a Yukon winter, another attraction open to the public. One of the most authentic watering holes in the area is **Heinold's First and Last Chance Saloon** (56 Jack London Sq, 510/839.6761), a favorite hangout of the celebrated writer. At the dock is **Scott's Seafood Grill & Bar** (73 Jack London Sq, 510/444.3456), one of the outstanding seafood restaurants in the area. For earthier waterfront ambience, try the produce warehouse district, covering about 24 blocks east of the square and south of Broadway. The **FDR Pier** (Clay St and The Embarcadero) gives good views of working port operations, as do **Port View Park**, next to the Seventh Street Terminal, and **Middle Harbor Park** (at Middle Harbor Rd).

Also worth a visit is the historic **Paramount Theater** (21st St and Broadway), a spectacular example of Art Deco architecture by **Timothy Pflueger.** Inside the movie palace, which has been converted to general entertainment use (conventions, symphonies, theater, ballet, classic movies, and such), there's a mind-blowing assemblage of gilt, silver railings, columns, and marble. Two-hour tours are offered the first and third Saturday of each month at 10AM, but not on holidays or when an activity is planned within the theater. No reservations are required. There is a small charge, and no children under age 10 are allowed. For more information, call 510/465.6400.

Definitely try to make room for a trip to **The Oakland Museum** (10th and Oak Sts, 510/834.2413), about a 15-minute walk from the **Paramount Theater.** Covering a four-block site, the multilevel building (see the plan above) with terraced gardens is designed by **Kevin Roche.** The structure incorporates galleries of ecology, history, and art, all of which emphasize California's diversity. The museum is open Wednesday through Sunday; donation.

Another point of interest is **Lake Merritt** (bordered by Lakeside Dr, Lakeshore Ave, and Grand Ave; information 510/562.7275, sailboat house 510/444.3807), which offers boat rentals, sailing lessons, a strolling/jogging path, a garden center,

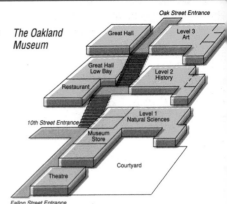

The Oakland Museum

Fallon Street Entrance

and a bird sanctuary. If you're ready to sit back and relax for a while, catch a movie at the grandiose **Grand Lake Theatre** (Grand Ave and Lake Park, 510/452.3556)—they don't make 'em like this anymore. And, finally, top off your day with a meal at the **Bay Wolf Cafe** (3853 Piedmont Ave, 510/655.6004), a lively, upscale restaurant serving California cuisine with French and Italian influences.

Palo Alto/Stanford University

Fueled by the intellectual fires at **Stanford University,** Palo Alto is an oasis of energy and culture in the suburban desert. (OK, it's a mixed metaphor and a trifle hyperbolic, but you get the idea.) Movie houses play foreign and art films, restaurants serve a variety of international cuisines to a casual-chic crowd, a bookstore and a cappuccino place mark every corner, and everything from child-care centers to exercise facilities reflects cutting-edge thinking. Furthermore, there's excellent shopping, from a lively downtown with trendy boutiques to the **Stanford Shopping Center,** a mall so magnificent that more than one local has asked that her ashes be scattered here.

Rail service on **Caltrain** will get you to the Peninsula. (Get off at **Palo Alto** and then walk downtown through the pocket park to the shopping center.) For rail schedule information, call 495.4546 or 800/660.4287 (in the Bay Area). If you plan on doing a lot of local exploration, the best way to approach this area is by automobile. Take Highway 280, heading south, exiting at Sand Hill Road. It's the turnoff right after Woodside Road. Take Sand Hill Road east for 10 traffic lights, and you'll find yourself at the **Stanford Shopping Center** (between Sand Hill and Quarry Rds, west of El Camino Real). The shopping center is also served by **SamTrans** bus *7F*. The ride takes about an hour from San Francisco. For scheduling information, call 508.6200 or 800/660.4287 (in the Bay Area).

The **Stanford Shopping Center** is a retailing paradise and one of the most attractive mercantile complexes to be found, incorporating 150 stores in an open mall. It is anchored by several of the leading department and specialty stores in the Bay Area, including **Emporium, Macy's, I. Magnin, Nordstrom, Neiman-Marcus,** and **Saks Fifth Avenue.** Travel services include **Thomas Cook Foreign Exchange** and **American Express.** In addition, you can choose from a variety of restaurants at various price levels. After you've shopped yourself into a state of hunger, there's the **Cafe Andrea**, which serves high tea and light sandwiches, and **Bravo Fono,** a lovely spot for lunch and memorable homemade ice cream. **Max's Opera Cafe** serves overstuffed deli sandwiches, **Ristorante Piatti** offers Italian fare, and **Gaylord's** provides upscale Indian food.

Although dedicated shoppers can easily spend the entire day at this mall-to-end-all-malls, Palo Alto's thriving downtown shouldn't be neglected. In addition to a host of interesting boutiques (mostly along University Avenue and its cross streets), Palo Alto is home to a number of fine restaurants, including the ever-popular **Il Fornaio** (Italian; 520 Cowper St, 853.3888), **Maddalena's** (French; 544 Emerson St, 326.6082), **MacArthur Park** (American; 27 University Ave, 321.9990), and **Cafe Pro Bono** (Italian; 2437 Birch St, 326.1626). And if you're an old-movie buff, be sure to take in a classic flick at the wonderfully restored **Stanford Theater** (221 University Ave, 324.3700), which warms up audiences with lively organ music on weekend nights.

One-hour tours of **Stanford University,** one of California's most prestigious private educational institutions, are given free of charge daily, from 11AM to 3:15PM. It's best to call ahead (723.2560) to be sure that tours are being offered, as the university closes to the public for holidays, semester breaks, and final exams. The tour begins at the information booth in front of the **Main Quad** (at the end of Palm Dr). Tours cover the central campus area, including administration buildings, classrooms, student union, bookstore, art gallery, chapel, **Hoover Tower,** and the main quadrangle area. The tower's observation platform (open daily from 10AM to 11AM and from 1PM to 4:30PM; nominal admission) offers panoramic views of the area, including the Santa Cruz Mountains. The **Stanford Memorial Chapel** and the **Leland Stanford Jr. Museum** both suffered structural damage during the 1989 earthquake. The museum is still closed, but the church reopened in 1992. Tasty, inexpensive food is offered at the **Tresidder Student Union** on campus, which includes a coffeehouse, cafeteria, and bakery counter.

Visitors can also tour the **Stanford Linear Accelerator Center (SLAC),** a world-class physics laboratory with a mind-blowing two-mile-long linear electron accelerator. Tours are available by appointment only (call 926.2204); not recommended for children under 11. You might also want to visit the **Stanford Medical Center** (advance reservations required; call 723.6389) or take the hospital's "Art in the Atrium" audio tour. For more information, call 510/723.7160.

Filoli Mansion

Located in the exclusive community of **Woodside,** this mansion was built between 1916 and 1919 by architect **Willis Polk** for prominent San Franciscans Mr. and Mrs. William B. Bourn II. The 16 acres of gardens were laid out by Bruce Porter, with the subsequent help of Isabella Worn. The homesite was chosen partly because it was near the Spring Valley Water Company, headed by Bourn, and partly because it reminded him of Ireland's Lakes of Killarney. The Bourns lived at the mansion until their deaths in 1936, whereupon the estate was acquired by Mr. and Mrs. William P. Roth, who kept it until 1975. Mrs. Roth then deeded it to the National Trust for Historic Preservation. The mansion is an important example of American country-house architecture, and is one of the few in the state intact in its original setting. The house and gardens are within the **Crystal Springs Watershed,** south of San Francisco. The now-mature gardens reflect the meticulous care during the nearly 40 years the Roths occupied the estate. The garden is a successful blend of the formal and the natural. A focal point is the Italian Renaissance **Tea House,** designed by **Arthur Brown Jr.,** who also designed the nearby **Carriage House,** dominated by a bell tower. The structure houses a collection of antique carriages.

Filoli is best reached by taking Highway 280 to the Edgewood Road exit, then turning right on Cañada Road. Follow Cañada Road and keep an eye peeled for the small, unobtrusive sign on the right side of the road. The gate on the left side is where you enter. The house and gardens are open for guided tours Tuesday through Saturday from mid-February to mid-November; advance reservations are required, and there is an admission charge. You may also take the self-guided tours every Friday and the first Saturday and second Sunday of every month from March through November; reservations are not required and there is an admission fee. Limited wheelchair access is available, but prior notification is requested to ensure that special entrance arrangements can be made. Guided hikes through the property are available by reservation from September through June. Children accompanied by an adult are welcome. For general information, call 366.4640. For tour or hiking reservations, call 364.2880.

The 1989 Earthquake's Epicenter

A relatively obscure state park on the Peninsula was thrust into prominence after the 17 October 1989 earthquake for the simple reason that the park contains the site of the temblor's epicenter. Plan on some rugged hiking if you go. To get here, follow Highway 1 south from Santa Cruz to the Seacliff Beach exit. Turn left to State Park Drive, and turn right at Soquel Drive. Proceed for just over half a mile. Look carefully on your left for signs marking the entrance to **Forest of Nisene Marks State Park**. Go left onto Aptos Creek Road, and follow the road for approximately three miles. It dead-ends at the trailhead parking lot at the Porter Family Picnic Area. The hike goes up Aptos Creek Fire Road for about a mile and a half. Right after crossing a bridge, turn right onto the **Aptos Creek Trail** and follow it through redwood forests and streams about another mile and a half to a sign that marks the epicenter. The great redwoods here were cracked and broken like matchsticks from the force of the quake.

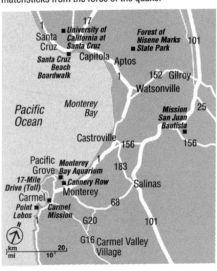

Santa Cruz

Ninety minutes south of San Francisco on the coast, Santa Cruz proper suffered a lot of damage in the 1989 earthquake, particularly in the downtown pedestrian mall, but much has survived intact. The laid-back, college-town feel of Santa Cruz has a lot to do with the **University of California at Santa Cruz** (408/459.0111). Its eight colleges form an impressive campus nestled among the redwoods. For more Californiana, check out the history of one of the area's central attractions at the **Surfing Museum** (Lighthouse Pt, off Westcliff Dr, 408/429.3429). But far and away, the one reason you should stop here is to ride on the Giant Dipper at the **Santa Cruz Beach Boardwalk** (408/426.7433), considered by most wooden-roller-coaster aficionados to be the best in the world. Also take a stroll on the carnival-and-cotton-candy boardwalk.

The best food in this town is not found at fancy French restaurants. **India Joze** (1001 Center St, between Union St and Chestnut St Extension, 408/427.3554) serves excellent Indian/Indonesian/Middle Eastern fare, and the calamari is widely acclaimed. For a casual meal on a rose-garden patio, stop in at **The Crêpe Place** (1134 Soquel Dr, at Seabright Dr, 408/429.6994). Choose from a variety of crepes, or create your own combination. The ultimate in Santa Cruz hippie-vegetarian fast food can be found at **Dharma's** (4250 Capitola Rd, between 42nd and 43rd Aves, 408/462.1717)—known as McDharma's until the litigious burger company sued over the "Mc."

Monterey Peninsula

The peninsula is two and a half to three hours from San Francisco, but the scenic drive makes getting there half the fun. Interstate 280 is rightfully known as America's most beautiful interstate, and it provides the quicker route south. Exit Interstate 280 at Highway 17 to Santa Cruz, then pick up Highway 1 south to **Monterey** and **Carmel**. It takes longer to follow Highway 1 all the way down the coast, but the quaint seaside towns and relaxed pace make the drive worthwhile.

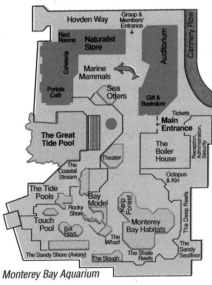

Monterey Bay Aquarium

The capital of Spanish and Mexican California, Monterey has preserved its heritage. Discover downtown's Spanish architecture on the **Path of History,** a three-mile walking tour. Maps are available from the Visitor Information Center (401 Camino el Estero, at Del Monte Ave). Monterey's sardine canneries inspired John Steinbeck's description, "a poem, a stink, a grating noise, a quality of light, a tone, a habit, a nostalgia, a dream." His **Cannery Row** (on the bay between David Ave and the Coastguard Pier, south to Lighthouse Ave), shut down by the depletion of the local sardine schools, has been renovated into a collection of shops, galleries, and restaurants, with much of the area's old character (but not the stench) preserved. A thoroughly modern but must-see attraction is the **Monterey Bay Aquarium** (886 Cannery Row on the bay, 408/648.4888), a renowned collection highlighting the local underwater ecology, including Monterey's giant kelp forests (see the floor plan on page 180).

Carmel, just south of Monterey, is the home of the **Carmel Mission** (3080 Río Rd, 408/624.3600), one of the most beautiful and well preserved of the California missions. It was founded in 1770 by Friar Junipero Serra and is his final resting place. Poets and painters later discovered the spectacular coast around Carmel that had attracted the Spanish settlers, and formed an artists' community that thrives to this day. Although undeniably touristy, Carmel has been preserved as a small Mediterranean-type village, with no street addresses on downtown buildings and no traffic signals (but *lots* of traffic, especially on weekends). Former mayor Clint Eastwood was an integral part of the fight to prevent development. Stop in at Clint's **Hog's Breath Inn** (San Carlos St between Fifth and Sixth Aves, 408/625.1044), though he probably won't be around. For a romantic and scenic stay-over, try the **Highlands Inn** (Highland Dr, off Hwy 101, 408/624.3801), where Sean Penn and Madonna honeymooned. The lounge at the stately old hotel is a wonderful place to enjoy a cocktail as the sun goes down.

The Monterey Peninsula you've seen on TV, and really shouldn't miss in person, can be found on the **17-Mile Drive.** The circular tour takes you past grand and pricey homes, past some of the world's most famous championship golf courses, and along California's stunning central coastline. If you can't bear to leave this area or pass up the great golfing, check in at the expensive **Lodge at Pebble Beach** along the 17-Mile Drive (408/624.3811).

If you're feeling a mite peckish, try one of the following stellar peninsula restaurants: **Fresh Cream** (French/California; Heritage Harbor complex at Pacific and Scott Sts, Monterey, 408/375.9798), **The Old Bath House** (Continental; 620 Ocean View Blvd, Pacific Grove, 408/375.5195), **Casanova (Northern** Italian/French; Fifth Ave between Mission and San Carlos Sts, Carmel, 408/625.0501), or **Central 159** (California; 15th St at Central Ave, Pacific Grove, 408/655.4280).

The Wine Institute, the California wine industry's trade organization, provides very helpful information on California wines, wineries, and referrals to classes on related subjects. For free information from this organization, send your request and a self-addressed, stamped envelope to: Wine Institute, 425 Market St, Suite 1000, San Francisco, CA 94105, or call 415/512.0151.

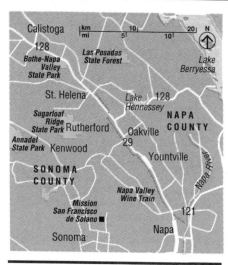

Wine Country

Any visit to the Bay Area should include a few relaxing days of wine tasting, bike riding, and even hot-air ballooning in the wine country. The valleys of this primarily northern California region stretch from the Pacific coast to the Sierra Nevada, carpeting the area with more than 400,000 acres of vineyards. Fabled **Napa and** Sonoma Counties, just one and a half to two hours north of San Francisco, are dotted with nearly 300 wineries producing such premium wines as Chardonnay, Cabernet Sauvignon, Zinfandel, and Pinot Noir, as well as charming bed-and-breakfast inns and excellent restaurants. September and October are the height of the grape harvest, and the aroma of fermenting wine is everywhere. This is also the most crowded time for touring, so make advance reservations; also, a car is a must to explore this vast region.

Another option is a hot-air balloon. This art of riding above the ground was discovered by the French aristocracy in 1783. (The first balloon flight was made by a sheep, a duck, and a rooster!) Today, the wine country's stunning scenery has turned ballooning in northern California into big business. It's a costly experience, but one you won't soon forget. There are numerous companies in the area that can provide this bird's-eye view of the vineyards, including: **Adventures Aloft** in Yountville (707/255.8688); **Balloon Aviation of Napa Valley** in Yountville (707/252.7076); **Napa Valley Balloons Inc.** in Yountville (707/253.2224); **Balloons above the Valley** in Napa (707/253.2222); **Napa's Great Balloon Escape** in Napa (707/253.0860); **Bonaventura Balloon Company** in Napa (707/944.2822); and **Once in a Lifetime Hot Air Balloon Co.** in Calistoga (707/942.6541).

Most wineries offer tastings and tours around the storage casks. Some take you through limestone caves carved out long ago by Chinese laborers. Though some of the wines can probably be purchased more cheaply at discount shops, one advantage to buying at the source is that you might discover one you like that's not easily found elsewhere. Most of the wineries now charge a small fee for tastings, but tours are usually free. As you make your way through the wine country, stop at one of the many roadside stands for first-rate apple cider, jam, nuts, and fresh vegetables and fruits.

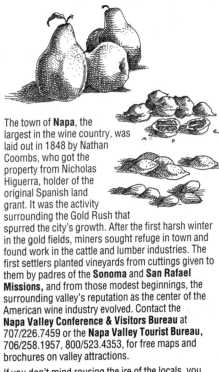

The town of **Napa**, the largest in the wine country, was laid out in 1848 by Nathan Coombs, who got the property from Nicholas Higuerra, holder of the original Spanish land grant. It was the activity surrounding the Gold Rush that spurred the city's growth. After the first harsh winter in the gold fields, miners sought refuge in town and found work in the cattle and lumber industries. The first settlers planted vineyards from cuttings given to them by padres of the **Sonoma** and **San Rafael Missions,** and from those modest beginnings, the surrounding valley's reputation as the center of the American wine industry evolved. Contact the **Napa Valley Conference & Visitors Bureau** at 707/226.7459 or the **Napa Valley Tourist Bureau,** 706/258.1957, 800/523.4353, for free maps and brochures on valley attractions.

If you don't mind rousing the ire of the locals, you might want to go for a ride on the **Napa Valley Wine Train**. This controversial enterprise, which involves three-hour dining, drinking, and sight-seeing excursions in Pullman lounge cars, was fought by many valley folk who feared it might change the serious nature of the wine industry. You won't see much of Napa while on the train—passengers don't disembark en route—but the food is delicious and the surroundings are quite luxurious. For more information, contact the train company (1275 McKinstry St, 707/253.2111, 800/427.4124). If you opt for a great meal without the choo-choo ride, **Bistro Don Giovanni** (4110 St. Helena Hwy, 707/224.3300) is a popular spot for gourmet dining in the city of Napa. Napa wineries include the family-run **Trefethen Vineyards** (1160 Oak Knoll Ave, 707/255.7700), **Stag's Leap Wine Cellars** (5766 Silverado Trail, 707/944.2020), and **The Hess Collection Winery** (4411 Redwood Rd, 707/255.1144), which offers a high-powered art collection as well as a number of popular wines.

Almost halfway into the valley as you drive from San Francisco, **Yountville** is where the wine country begins to stir the emotions. George Yount, who came here in search of new frontiers, was the first US citizen to be ceded a Mexican land grant—the 12,000 acres making up the heart of Napa Valley called **Rancho Caymus.**

While in Yountville, try an old-fashioned American breakfast at **The Diner** (6476 Washington St, 707/944.2626), Italian fare at popular **Piatti** (6480 Washington St, 707/944.2070), the exuberant California cuisine at **Mustards Grill** (7399 St. Helena Hwy, 707/944.2424), or the latest venture of famous chef Jeremiah Tower, **Stars Oakville Cafe,** in nearby Oakville (7848 St. Helena Hwy, 707/944.8905). The **Vintage Inn** (6541 Washington St, 800/351.1133 in CA, 800/982.5539) and the bed-and-breakfast-style **Magnolia Hotel** (6529 Yount St, 707/944.2056) are two good bets for lodging. Nearby wineries include **Domaine Chandon** (1 California Dr, 707/944.2280), which produces sparkling wine by the traditional *méthode champenoise* and also has a very highly regarded (and expensive) restaurant; the venerable **Robert Mondavi Winery** (7801 St. Helena Hwy, Oakville, 707/963.9611); and the **Beaulieu Vineyard** (1960 St. Helena Hwy, Rutherford, 707/963.2411).

St. Helena, a friendly small town in the heart of the vineyards, has come alive in the past few years with some exceptional restaurants and inns. And yet, walking down Main Street is like taking a step back in time—it's easy to imagine long white dresses and parasols emerging from the arched doorways of the stone buildings. Main Street is a portion of the valley's main highway, and has been a significant thoroughfare all the way back to the days of the horse and buggy. The stone bridges and buildings in the area were constructed by European stonemasons and Chinese laborers in the late 19th century. Outlaw Black Bart, who led a dual life as a schoolteacher and wrote poetry when he wasn't busy robbing stagecoaches, was one of the notorious characters who made his way through Main Street before his capture in 1883. Author **Robert Louis Stevenson** and his new bride also passed through the town. The newlyweds spent most of the summer of 1880 in nearby Calistoga.

St. Helena is heaven on earth for serious foodies. Some good—no, make that great—dining choices: **Terra** (French/Italian; 1345 Railroad Ave, 707/963.8931), **Ristorante Tra Vigne** (Italian; 1050 Charter Oak Ave, 707/963.4444), and **Trilogy** (French/California; 1234 Main St, 707/963.5507). The Rhineland-inspired **Beringer Vineyards** (2000 Main St, 707/963.7115) and, by appointment only, **Frog's Leap** (3358 St. Helena Hwy, 707/963.4704) are among the wineries worth a visit.

With its geysers, hot springs, and lava deposits, **Calistoga** is a clear-cut reminder of the valley's tempestuous geological beginnings. Some of the eruptions formed the gray stone with which the Italian and Chinese workers built bridges and wineries. The first spa at Calistoga was built by Sam Brannan, California's first millionaire. He designed a spectacular hotel, now known as **Indian Springs,** to attract wealthy San Franciscans. Brannan also brought the first railroad to the valley and donated a costly engine to the first fire department. He coined the name Calistoga by combining the names California and Saratoga (the famous New York resort). Set in the middle of the wine country, this small town, with its Western-style main street still intact, is known for its mineral water and mud baths.

Almost every motel or inn is equipped with at least a Jacuzzi. Contact the **Calistoga Chamber of Commerce** (1458 Lincoln Ave, 707/942.6333) for a list of spas.

Quaint Calistoga hotels include the **Larkmead Country Inn** (1103 Larkmead La, 707/942.5360) and the **Mount View Hotel** (1457 Lincoln Ave, 707/942.6877). There are also some very good restaurants here, including **All Seasons Café** (1400 Lincoln Ave, 707/942.9111) and the **Catahoula Restaurant & Saloon** (1457 Lincoln Ave, 707/942.BARK). Be sure to tour **Sterling Vineyards**, which is entered via a scenic tramway (1111 Dunaweal La, 707/942.5151); the **Clos Pegase** winery (1060 Dunaweal La, 707/942.4981; pictured above) and its art gallery, designed by **Michael Graves;** and the gracious **Château Montelena** (1429 Tubbs La, 707/942.5105).

In the nearby and less congested Sonoma Valley lies the historic town of **Sonoma** with its eight-acre plaza, the largest in California. The plaza, laid out by General Mariano Vallejo in 1835, is ringed by boutiques, restaurants, and galleries. The stone structure dominating the area is **City Hall,** built to look the same on all sides. Wonderful adobe structures from the Mexican era, Western-type edifices, and stone buildings surround the plaza. Vallejo's soldiers trained here, and this was the site of the 25-day Bear Flag Party revolution in 1846 (still celebrated each 14 June). Contact the **Sonoma Valley Visitors Bureau** (453 First St E, 707/996.1090), for maps and information about the valley.

When you get hungry from all this touring, try Sonoma's **Ristorante Piatti** (405 First St W, 707/996.2351), which serves regional Italian cuisine, and the **Feed Store Cafe & Bakery** (529 First St W, 707/938.2122). A little farther afield in Sonoma County is **John Ash & Co.** (4330 Barnes Rd, Santa Rosa, 707/527.7687), where both the food and the prices are breathtaking. This area is also rich in pleasant accommodations, including the **Victorian Garden Inn** (316 E Napa St, Sonoma, 707/996.5339), the luxurious **Sonoma Mission Inn & Spa** (18140 Sonoma Hwy, Boyes Hot Springs, 707/938.9000), the **Beltane Ranch B&B** (11775 Sonoma Hwy, Glen Ellen, 707/996.6501), and the **Kenwood Inn** (10400 Sonoma Hwy, Kenwood, 707/833.1293). **Gundlach-Bundschau** (2000 Denmark St, Sonoma, 707/938.5277), a historic and lovely winery, the **Buena Vista Winery** (1800 Old Winery Rd, Sonoma, 707/938.1266), the **Matanzas Creek Winery** (6097 Bennett Valley Rd, Santa Rosa, 707/528.6464), and **Kenwood Vineyards** (9592 Sonoma Hwy, Kenwood, 707/833.5891) are among the valley's noteworthy vintners.

Quentin L. Kopp
California State Senator

Nothing rivals a stroll through **Telegraph Hill** to furnish a sense of San Francisco's maritime history. The smell of the bay and the bellow of foghorns transform the city into a bygone era. Follow that with a walk through **North Beach,** stopping at **St. Peter's and St. Paul's Church,** originally built as a Roman Catholic church for San Francisco's Italian community.

Continue southward aboard a cable car at Mason and Columbus Streets to **Union Square** and the **Financial District** or travel north to **Fisherman's Wharf.** Stroll the wharf, then dine at one of the stellar restaurants in the area, such as **Scoma's.**

A trek along **Marina Boulevard** is a must, viewing the **Marina Green** and the **St. Francis** and the **Golden Gate Yacht Club.** Inspect **Aquatic Park** on the way to the **Marina,** traverse the **Presidio** and **Fort Point,** stop and enjoy a superb vegetarian meal at **Greens** in **Fort Mason** before journeying to **Sea Cliff, China Beach,** and the **Cliff House.** The **Civic Center** is indispensable, with an inspection of the magnificent **City Hall,** albeit tattered by the 1989 earthquake. **City Hall** can be rich with operatic themes of political tragedy, hope, and despair. But for real live opera, walk across the street and examine the beauty of the **Opera House** and a performance—if you can get a ticket! The **Main Library,** the **Museum of Modern Art,** and the **Davies Symphony Hall** complete your tour of the stately **Civic Center.** From there, it's a scintillating visit to **Golden Gate Park,** the **de Young Museum,** the **Academy of Sciences,** the **Conservatory,** the **Shakespeare Garden,** the **Polo Field** (perhaps a game of rugby, Gallic football, or hurling is in full swing), and the **Arboretum.** Continue to the **Legion of Honor** in the outer **Richmond** district and view the **Golden Gate Bridge** from **Land's End.** It's spectacular!

A convivial gathering over fish at **Sam's Grill** on Bush Street or **Jack's Restaurant** on Sacramento Street is indispensable to one's psychic health. Only the natives can inform joggers about the spiritual uplift of a morning jog around the six miles of **Lake Merced,** which is west of **Twin Peaks,** that part of San Francisco in which my most loyal voters live. For the spectator, **Candlestick Park** is a superb venue for football, notably the **San Francisco 49ers,** and, if the **Giants** are winning, fans seem oblivious to the reputed wind conditions and ghoulish temperatures.

For magnificent vistas, you must sit on top of **Twin Peaks** or the crest of **Portola Drive** as it becomes **Market Street.** For more culinary pleasures, try **Stars** in the alley between Golden Gate Avenue and McAllister Street at the **Civic Center** (de rigueur California cuisine and LA-style people watching) or the **Yank Sing** on Battery Street for dim sum. In sum, opportunities for pleasing, memorable moments in "The City That Knows How" are prolific, so let your energy be your guide—if I can't be with you!!

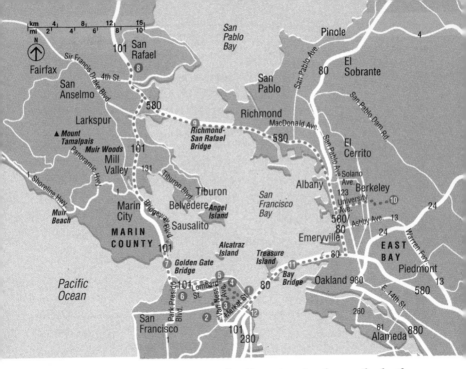

Architecture Tours

San Francisco is a haven for both Victorian architecture (including the "Painted Ladies"—Queen Anne houses with elaborate ornament highlighted in bright colors) and pioneering Modern and Post-Modern structures, built after the 1906 earthquake and fire devastated the city.

Bay Area Architectural Blitz

Before embarking on this driving tour of the Bay Area's architectural highlights, review a commercial road map of the area and familiarize yourself with the following directions. Plan on parking the car at some points so you can really admire the buildings.

This tour begins at the (1) **Ferry Building,** at the foot of Market Street, designed by architect **Arthur Page Brown** in 1894. Modeled after the Cathedral Tower in Seville, Spain, this building was for many years the tallest in San Francisco. Drive down Market past the (1) **Hyatt Regency Hotel,** a distinct component of the San Francisco skyline designed by **John Portman and Associates** in 1973, and the (1) **Crown Zellerbach Building,** a 1959 design by **Hertzka and Knowles** and **Skidmore, Owings & Merrill** set back from the street at Battery. Make a "soft" right onto Sutter Street to see the **Citicorp Building,** a 1984 **William Pereira and Associates** design, with its lovely atrium. At 1 Sutter (on your left) is the **Crocker Galleria,** a three-level, glass-barrel-vaulted shopping arcade modeled after Milan's vast Galleria Vittorio Emanuele, and on your right is the **Hallidie Building,** designed by **Willis Polk and Company** in 1917, which purports to have the world's first curtain-wall glass facade. Take a left at Stockton Street, and turn right on Market. Continue to McAllister Street and bear right to the (2) **Civic Center,** acclaimed as the most magnificent

assortment of Beaux Arts buildings in the US. There you will see **City Hall,** the main part of the complex, designed in 1915 by **Bakewell and Brown; Louise M. Davies Symphony Hall,** designed by **Skidmore, Owings & Merrill,** which first opened in September 1980 and was remodeled in 1992; the glorious and opulent **Opera House,** which opened on 15 October 1932; and the **Veteran's Building,** former home of the San Francisco Museum of Modern Art, also by **Bakewell and Brown.** Turn right on Franklin Street and left on Geary until you reach (2) **St. Mary's Cathedral** at Gough Street. Continue to Laguna Street, make a right, then right again on California Street. Continue across Van Ness and up Nob Hill to Jones Street, where **Lewis P. Hobbart's** (3) **Grace Cathedral** is located. This lovely Neo-Gothic church was modeled after Notre Dame in Paris. Head on to Mason Street to see the city's most illustrious hotels: the (3) **Mark Hopkins** (familiarly known as "The Mark"), best known for **Timothy Pflueger's Top of the Mark** cocktail lounge with its panoramic vista of the bay and the city's hills, and the **Fairmont,** which opened in 1907 in celebration of the city's renaissance one year after the earthquake. Continue downhill on California to the Financial District. At Kearny Street view the (3) **Bank of America World Headquarters,** a 1969 structure by **Wurster, Bernardi, and Emmons Inc.** and **Skidmore, Owings & Merrill,** with **Pietro Belluschi** as design consultant, with its dark-red marble facade that changes colors with the time of day. Turn left on Sansome Street and left on Washington past the **(3) Transamerica Pyramid,** designed in 1972 by **William Pereira and Associates,** which has become a landmark because of its singular form and position at the end of Columbus Avenue. Take Columbus Avenue toward North Beach—en route notice the Art Deco–ish **(4) Coit Tower** on top of Telegraph Hill, and turn left on North Point Street until you reach **(5) Ghirardelli Square,** the converted chocolate factory that is now a shopping complex. The transformation was done by **Wurster, Bernardi & Emmons Inc.** and **Lawrence Halprin & Associates** from 1962 to 1967. Turn left on Van Ness, right on Bay, and head westward through the Marina district to Marina Boulevard. At Lyon and Baker Streets is **Bernard Maybeck's (6) Palace of Fine Arts,** with its characteristic Roman rotunda with two curvilinear columns. Next, head north on Highway 101, across the **(7) Golden Gate Bridge** into Marin County. Take the Alexander Avenue exit, veer right, and drive through downtown **Sausalito** (note the private homes clinging to the steep hillside). At the end of town, get back on Highway 101 north. You may want to make a side trip to **Tiburon** and **Belvedere,** where you'll see some of the most expensive housing in the country. Continue north on Highway 101 for 15 miles, past San Rafael, to the North San Pedro Road exit, to take a look at the **(8) Marin County Civic Center** by **Frank Lloyd Wright,** begun in 1957 (Wright died in 1959). Built atop the crests of three low hills, this was one of the American master's last efforts. Note the prevalence of the circle motif in the building's design, including the decorative grilles, pavements, and custom-designed furniture; be sure to walk up to the viewing deck next to the library. Then return south on Highway 101 through San Rafael and take the I-580 exit. Drive across the **(9) Richmond–San Rafael Bridge;** look to the right and see **San Quentin** prison. Follow signs for Oakland through the industrial area along Cutting and Hoffman Boulevards, and join I-80 at Albany. Exit at University Avenue and travel 1½ miles east until you reach the **(10) University of California, Berkeley,** at Oxford Street. Turn right on Oxford and left on Durant. Park at the garage on Durant and Telegraph Avenue or on the street. On campus see the **(10) Campanile** (there's a great view of the Bay Area from the top) and the handsome granite-clad **(10) Mining and Metallurgy Building** of 1907 by **John G. Howard,** who designed many buildings and other structures on campus. Afterward, drive up Durant to Piedmont and take a look at the **(10) Sigma Phi** frat house, designed by famed Arts and Crafts architects, the brothers **Greene & Greene.** Most of the old mansions on this strip are fraternity or sorority houses. Turn left on Piedmont, left on Bancroft Way, and continue down University Avenue. Follow University to I-80/I-580 southbound for San Francisco. Return to the city via I-80 across the **(11) Bay Bridge** (toll). Then exit on Fremont Street, take a left onto Howard Street, and go past **(12) Yerba Buena Gardens,** which include the mostly underground **Moscone Convention Center** by **Hellmuth, Obata & Kassabaum,** and the recent **Center for the Arts Galleries and Forum** by **Fumihiko Maki** and Center for the Arts Theater by **James Stewart Polshek,** which opened in 1993.

Sights for Sore Eyes

The hilly Bay Area, especially San Francisco, is renowned for its sweeping views. Here are a few of the very best:

Golden Gate Bridge Vista Point From the south end of the bridge at the toll plaza, you can see the islands in the bay, the bridge, and the north waterfront.

Telegraph Hill Look down on the bay, the bridge, and the north waterfront.

Twin Peaks From the top of Market Street you can scan the best of the Bay Area in every direction—the city, the bay and its islands, the bridges, and the mountains to the north and south.

Strawberry Point Catch a glimpse of San Francisco's skyline from the point just off Highway 101 at the end of Seminary Drive.

Mount Tamalpais On a very clear day, the summit views extend to the Farallon Islands, east to Mount Diablo and the East Bay, and sometimes as far as the Sierra Nevada, 200 miles away.

House Calls: San Francisco's Premier Estates

For a tour of some of the city's most notable residences, start at the top of **(1) Telegraph Hill,** and walk down the **Filbert Steps** on the east side. Some of the oldest houses in San Francisco are perched precariously on these steep slopes— notice the Carpenter Gothic style of many. Access to these homes is only by footpath and steps. Turn right on **(2) Powell Street,** where you will see a particularly fine row of Post-Modern houses on the west side of **(3) Vandewater Street,** a short alley between Powell and Mason Streets, half a block south of Bay Street. Note the condominiums by **Esherick Homsey Dodge and Davis,** at **No. 22;** **Donald MacDonald, No. 33;** and **Daniel Solomon, No. 55.** All three structures were built in 1981. Turn left onto Mason Street, right onto Francisco Street, and continue across Columbus Avenue up **Russian Hill** to Leavenworth Street. Turn left here and cross Union Street to the corner of **(4) Green Street,** where you can see one of the best examples of 1930s-style apartment towers.

Continue on Leavenworth Street until California Street, turn right, and follow the cable-car tracks to Van Ness Avenue; cross Van Ness and continue to Franklin Street. Turn right and look for the superb Queen Anne–style **(5) Haas-Lilienthal House** at 2007 Franklin Street (tours are available) in affluent **Pacific Heights,** with many substantial dwellings on its slopes. From Franklin Street, turn left on Broadway. You will pass a series of apartment towers and mansions as you approach the **Presidio,** and many fine Victorian houses on the surrounding streets. Take a left on Fillmore Street, then a right on **(6) Clay Street** to see the row of false-fronted Italianate houses between Fillmore and Divisadero Streets opposite **Alta Plaza Park.**

Now turn right on Divisadero Street, continue to the summit of the hill, and take a left at Pacific Avenue. The famous **(7) 3200 Pacific** block

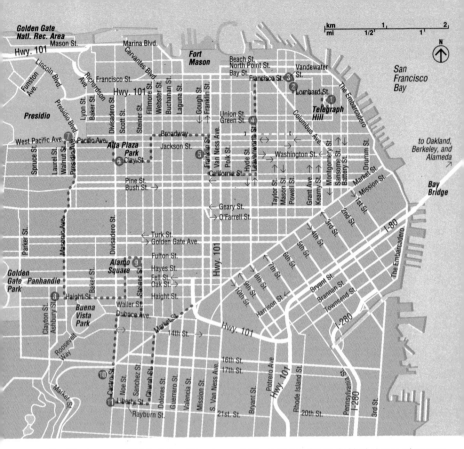

between Presidio Avenue and Walnut Street boasts houses by **Bernard Maybeck, Ernest Coxhead, Willis Polk**, and others. Turn left on Walnut Street, left on Jackson Street, and right on Presidio Avenue, which zigzags and becomes Masonic Avenue (veer right when the road divides, or, if you miss the split, turn right onto Geary Boulevard and left onto Masonic Avenue). Cross the **Panhandle** of **Golden Gate Park** to **Haight Street,** which runs through the **(8) Haight-Ashbury** district, with its many ornate late-Victorian houses, some painted in bright colors that emphasize their elaborate facades. Turn left onto Haight Street to Scott Street, turn left, and then

right onto Fulton Street six blocks away, where you can see the group of identical 19th-century houses on the east side of **(9) Alamo Square.** Turn right onto **Steiner Street.** Head south to **Duboce Avenue** and take a right. Proceed to **Castro Street,** turn left, and then continue to **Market Street.** At Market and Castro is **(10) Castro Commons,** a condominium complex completed in 1982, designed by **Daniel Solomon and Associates.** A gridded wall separates the triangular courtyard from busy Market Street. Four blocks farther south along Castro Street at **(11) Liberty Street** is a good cross section of older San Francisco dwellings of various styles.

Bests

William Stout
Architect and Owner/William Stout Architectural Books

Vesuvio Cafe after work. They have wonderful bartenders, and the second floor offers a great view of Broadway/Columbus Avenue and **City Lights Books.** Across the street is **Tosca Cafe.**

The mud baths in **Calistoga** are a great treat. We stay at the **Calistoga Inn**—a small hotel that has a bar and restaurants.

Favorite restaurants: **Buca Giovanni** (wonderful northern Italian cuisine) and **Caffè Macaroni** on Columbus Avenue.

Freda Scott
Freda Scott, Inc./Marketing and sales of fine commercial art

Britex Fabrics on Geary Street is the best fabric store in the US. I love to buy gorgeous silks and mohairs—and then decide how to use them.

Crate & Barrel on Grant Avenue has inexpensive gifts and goodies for the home.

The street artists on **Grant Avenue** are fabulous.

Lunch at **Splendido's,** looking out at the San Francisco Bay and the **Ferry Building.** Unusual atmosphere, *great* homemade breads and desserts—everything is yummy.

Spend the afternoon shopping on **Haight Street** for wonderful vintage clothing and 1960s memorabilia. Afterward, visit the **de Young Museum** and then go to the beach.

Shirley Fong-Torres

Owner/President, Wok Wiz Chinatown Tours & Cooking Company

I dine out four to five nights a week, not because I like to eat (ha ha) but in order to give the best eating tips to my friends and visitors. I have made it my lifetime project to seek out the best hotels, restaurants, and entertainment in our city.

Parking spaces, whenever I can find one, *anywhere*.

Breakfast or brunch is a "must" at **Campton Place** before a day of shopping at **Union Square**.

A cable-car ride up **California Street**. Check into the prestigious **Huntington Hotel** on Nob Hill. Have small talk and a drink in their piano bar, then adjourn to dinner in the **Big Four Restaurant**—fabulous abalone when it is in season. Go across the street for a dazzling view of the city at the **Top of the Mark** in the **Mark Hopkins Hotel,** or the **Crown Room** of the **Fairmont.**

Take a walk to **Chinatown**—do not miss the open markets along **Stockton Street**. Take a short walk to **Yank Sing** to dim sum to your heart's content.

Stroll along Columbus into **North Beach.** Laugh, laugh, laugh at the **Club Fugazi**'s *Beach Blanket Babylon,* followed by a late supper at **Moose's** or **Buca Giovanni** (homemade pasta with porcini mushrooms), or see my pal Mario at his funky **Cafe Macaroni** (eat anything he suggests!).

Teenagers head for the **Hard Rock Cafe** on Van Ness, while their parents yearn for the tastiest steaks nearby at the famous **Harris' Steak House.**

Romantics get away to the **White Swan Inn,** are pampered at dinner at the **Ritz-Carlton's Dining Room** by top maître d' Nick Peyton, and escape to the **Four Seasons Clift** for cheek-to-cheek dancing on weekends.

Twice a month, minimum, I "do sushi and sake" at **Sanppo's** in Japantown.

Seafood lovers alert—roast crab at **Crustacean**; the freshest oysters on the half shell are at **Scott's** at The Embarcadero, and **Swan's Oyster Depot**; out-of-this-world lobster tails at **Bentley's,** the liveliest steamed fish Chinese style or swimming prawns at **Harbor Village.**

See a movie at **Gateway Theatre,** stick around for dinner at **Square One** (amazing desserts) or a short walk to the **Cypress Club** (simply amazing).

Go for a cruise on the bay, or walk across the **Golden Gate Bridge.**

Bathe yourself in chocolate at **Ghirardelli Square.** Indulge in an exceptional dinner at the **Mandarin,** beginning with Mushu seafood and California wine.

Afternoon tea at the **Ritz-Carlton, Four Seasons Clift,** or **St. Francis' Compass Room.**

Have a shot of Chinese whiskey and hang out with bartender Jimmy, before feasting on **Tommy Toy's Cuisine Chinoise.**

For the adventurous, soar to the skies in a **San Francisco Helicopter** tour.

A day at **Golden Gate Park,** the **Japanese Tea Garden, Asian Art Museum.**

Watch the sunset from the **Cliff House.**

The "second Chinatown" on **Clement Street,** a neighborhood sprinkled with Asian and Occidental restaurants and businesses.

Spend a night at the **Mandarin Oriental** for one of the best views of the city from your bathtub, with a glass of champagne, naturally. Good night!

Amy Rennert

Editor in Chief, *San Francisco Focus* Magazine

I came to San Francisco after college, eager to experience a place I had read about and dreamed about from 3,000 miles away. I was immediately inspired by the physical beauty of northern California, the diversity and open-mindedness of its residents, and the "work hard but have a life" mentality. I never left.

Some of my favorite places:

Zuni Cafe—for chef Judy Roger's Mediterranean cooking, for the Caesar salad, for the classical music they play during the quiet breakfast hours, for the arts and media crowd—a good portion of my paycheck has gone here over the years.

Candlestick Park—for SF Giants day games—it's too cold at night.

Palace of Fine Arts—for walks and picnics and the **Exploratorium.** This **Maybeck** relic of the Panama-Pacific Exhibition is part poetry and part ancient ruin.

Kyo-Ya—for an authentic Japanese experience, for the stunning setting, for the freshest raw fish and selection of grilled foods, for a sake list that is as extensive as the better wine lists, and for the friendly, knowledgeable service. In the **Sheraton Palace Hotel,** at the corner of New Montgomery and Jesse Streets.

Peet's—for low-fat *doppio alto latte machiattos,* even though it's a mouthful to say, and for the best coffee in America. Several locations in the Bay Area.

A Clean Well-Lighted Place for Books—for browsing, buying, and listening to authors who read from their new works. In Opera Plaza in San Francisco.

Britex Fabrics—for four floors of the world's most exotic fabrics and notions and for the knowledgeable owners and staff.

Meadowood Resort in St. Helena, **Timberhill Ranch** in Cazadero, **Ventana Inn** in Big Sur, and the **Sonoma Mission Inn** in Boyes Hot Springs—for great weekend getaways.

Alcatraz Island—for the ride on the **Red and White Fleet** ferry that takes you there, for the audio tour complete with the voices of former prisoners and guards, and for the views, inside and out.

Index

*Bold page numbers indicate
main references.*

A

A.A. Cantin Architects **25**

The Abandoned Planet
Bookstore **132**

Abbe's **169**

Abigail Hotel $ **19**

Abiquiu ★★$$ **41**

The Academy Cafe $ **156**

The Academy Store **156**

Ace Cafe ★★$$ **30**

Acorn Books **12**

Acorn Tea and Griddle ★★$$ **30**

Acquerello ★★★$$$ **72**

Act IV ★★$$$ **16**

Adobe Bookstore **132**

Adriano, Cafe **104**

Adriatic ★★$$ **72**

African-American Historical
and Cultural Society **103**

African Safari **156**

AHC Apparel **28**

Aioli ★$$ **76**

Airports **5**

Albion **131**

Albona ★★$$ **89**

Alcatraz Island **98**

Alejandro's Sociedad
Gastronomica ★★$$ **169**

Alfred Dunhill of London **38**

Allegro Ristorante Italiano
★★$$ **75**

Alliance Française **71**

Allrich Gallery **37**

All Seasons Café **183**

Allure **142**

Alta Plaza Park **112**

Amelio's ★★$$$$ **91**

American Pie **117**

American Rag **71**

ANA Hotel $$$$ **26**

The Anchorage **86**

Anchor Brewing Co. **134**

Anchor Oyster Bar & Seafood
Market ★★$$ **141**

Anderson, John 141

Andrea, Cafe **179**

The Andrews Hotel $ **49**

Angel Island **98**

Anshen and Allen 177

Anthony Shoe Service **35**

Antonio's Antiques **29**

Apartment Towers **111**

Applegarth, George 61, 112,
167

Aqua ★★$$$ **55**

Aquarius Records **144**

Aquatic Park **84**

Arch **96**

The Archbishop's Mansion Inn
$$$ **124**

Architecture Tours **184** (chapter
and map), 186 (map)

Artaud, Theatre **133**

Art Center Bed & Breakfast $$
107

Artery **126**

Arts Commission Gallery **15**

Asakichi **121**

Asian Art Museum of San
Francisco **159**

Asimakopoulos ★★$$ **134**

Aston Pickwick Hotel $ **26**

The Atrium ★★$$$ **54**

Audiffred Building **24**

Audium **123**

B

Babylon ★★$$$ **74**

Backen, Arrigoni & Ross 89,
111

Bad Man Jose's ★★$ **140**

Bahia ★★$$ **18**

Bahia Tropical **18**

Baja Cantina ★$$ **106**

Baker Beach **166**

Baker Beach Bunkers **166**

Bakewell, John Jr. 11

Bakewell and Brown 11, 14 184

Balboa Cafe ★$$ **106**

Balclutha **84**

Bally of Switzerland **37**

Banana Republic **33**

Bank of America World
Headquarters **57**

Bank of California **56**

Bank of Canton of California **56**

Bare Necessities **138**

Barney's Gourmet Hamburgers
★$ **105**

Bar with No Name **173**

Baseball Diamonds **155**

Basic Brown Bears **134**

Bastille, Cafe **58**

Bath Sense **116**

Bay Area Architectural Blitz **184**

Bay Area Overview **174** (map)

Bay Area Rapid Transit (BART)
7

Bay Bridge **22**

Bayfront Theater **103**

The Bay Model **173**

The Bayview Opera House **135**

Bay Wolf Cafe **178**

Bazaar Cada Dia **44**

The Bead Store **138**

Beale St. Grill ★$ **25**

Beaulieu Vineyard **182**

Beaver Bros. Antiques **17**

Bechelli's Coffee Shop ★★$
105

Bed and Breakfast Inn $$ **107**

Bedford, Hotel **76**

Belden Park Tacquería ★$ **58**

Belden Place **58**

Bella Voce Ristorante & Bar $$
79

Bell'occhio **31**

The Bell Tower ★★$ **73**

Belluschi, Pietro 57, 123, 184

Beltane Ranch B&B **183**

Benkyodo Confectioners ★$
122

Bentley's ★★$$$ **59**

Beresford, Hotel **48**

Beresford Arms, Hotel **76**

Beringer Vineyards **182**

Best Comics and Rock Art
Gallery **86**

Best Western Miyako Inn $$
122

Beyond Expectations ★★★$
116

The Big Four ★$$$ **79**

Bill's Place ★$ **168**

Birkenstock **72**

Index

Restaurants

Only restaurants with star ratings are listed below. All restaurants are listed alphabetically in the main (preceding) index. The restaurant price ratings are based on the average cost of an entrée for one person, excluding tax and tip.

★★★★ An Extraordinary Experience

★★★ Excellent

★★ Very Good

★ Good

$$$$ Big Bucks ($25 and up)

$$$ Expensive ($15-$25)

$$ Reasonable ($10-$15)

$ The Price Is Right (less than $10)

Index

Hotels

The hotels listed below are grouped according to their price ratings; they are also listed alphabetically in the main (preceding) index. The hotel price ratings reflect the price of a standard room for two people for one night during the peak season.

$$$$ Big Bucks   ($180 and up)

$$$ Expensive   ($120-$180)

$$ Reasonable   ($80-$120)

$ The Price Is Right (less than $80)

Credits

Writers and Researchers
Rebecca Poole Forée
Matthew Richard Poole

Writers (Previous Edition)
Mona Behan
Bea Pixa

ACCESS®PRESS

Editorial Director
Lois Spritzer

Managing Editor
Laura L. Brengelman

Senior Editor
Beth Schlau

Associate Editors
Kathryn Clark
Kathleen Kent

Contributing Editors
Susan Cutter Snyder
Joanna Wissinger

Map Editor
Karen Decker

Assistant Map Editor
Susan Charles

*Manager of Design
and Production*
Cherylonda Fitzgerald

Senior Designer
Claudia Goulette

Designers
Barbara J. Bahning Chin
Carrē Furukawa

Map Designers
Michael Blum
Teresa Cunniff
Patti Keelin

*Manager, Electronic
Publishing*
John Day

Printing and Otabind
WEBCOM Limited

*Acknowledgments
(Special Thanks)*
Jim Andrews
**Joshua S. Cohn,
Architect**
Erika Lenkert
Janean Marie Selkirk
Jerry Stanton
Ron Warren

Palace of Fine Arts

RIK OLSON

Printed in Canada

ACCESS® Guides

Name _____ Phone _____

Address _____

City _____ State _____ Zip _____

Please send me the following ACCESS® Guides:

☐ **BARCELONA** ACCESS® $17.00
0-06-277000-4

☐ **BOSTON** ACCESS® $18.50
0-06-277143-4

☐ **BUDGET EUROPE** ACCESS® $18.00
0-06-277120-5

☐ **CAPE COD** ACCESS® $18.00
0-06-277123-X

☐ **CARIBBEAN** ACCESS® $18.50
0-06-277128-0

☐ **CHICAGO** ACCESS® $18.50
0-06-277144-2

☐ **FLORENCE/VENICE/MILAN** ACCESS® $18.50
0-06-277081-0

☐ **HAWAII** ACCESS® $18.50
0-06-277142-6

☐ **LAS VEGAS** ACCESS® $18.50
0-06-277177-9

☐ **LONDON** ACCESS® $18.50
0-06-277129-9

☐ **LOS ANGELES** ACCESS® $18.00
0-06-277131-0

☐ **MEXICO** ACCESS® $18.00
0-06-277127-2

☐ **MIAMI & SOUTH FLORIDA** ACCESS® $18.50
0-06-277178-7

☐ **MONTREAL & QUEBEC** ACCESS® $18.00
0-06-277079-9

☐ **NEW ORLEANS** ACCESS® $18.50
0-06-277176-0

☐ **NEW YORK CITY** ACCESS® $18.00
0-06-277124-8

☐ **NEW YORK CITY RESTAURANT** ACCESS®
$12.00
0-06-277130-2

☐ **ORLANDO & CENTRAL FLORIDA** ACCESS®
$18.50
0-06-277175-2

☐ **PARIS** ACCESS® $18.00
0-06-277132-9

☐ **PHILADELPHIA** ACCESS® $18.00
0-06-277065-9

☐ **ROME** ACCESS® $18.50
0-06-277150-7

☐ **SAN FRANCISCO** ACCESS® $18.00
0-06-277121-3

☐ **SAN FRANCISCO RESTAURANT** ACCESS®
$12.00
0-06-277126-4

☐ **SANTA FE/TAOS/ALBUQUERQUE** ACCESS®
$18.00
0-06-277148-5

☐ **SEATTLE** ACCESS® $18.00
0-06-277149-3

☐ **SKI COUNTRY** ACCESS®
Eastern United States $18.00
0-06-277125-6

☐ **SKI COUNTRY** ACCESS®
Western United States $18.50
0-06-277174-4

☐ **WASHINGTON DC** ACCESS® $18.00
0-06-277077-2

☐ **WINE COUNTRY** ACCESS®
France $18.50
0-06-277151-5

☐ **WINE COUNTRY** ACCESS®
Northern California $18.00
0-06-277122-1

Prices subject to change without notice.

Total for **ACCESS®** Guides:	$
Please add applicable sales tax:	
Add $4.00 for first book S&H, $1.00 per additional book:	
Total payment:	$

☐ Check or Money Order enclosed. Offer valid in the United States only.
Please make payable to HarperCollins*Publishers*.

☐ Charge my credit card ☐ American Express ☐ Visa ☐ MasterCard

Card no. _____ Exp. date _____

Signature _____

Send orders to: HarperCollins*Publishers*
P.O. Box 588
Dunmore, PA 18512-0588